American Slavery and Russian Serfdom in the Post-Emancipation Imagination

AMANDA BRICKELL BELLOWS

American Slavery and Russian Serfdom in the Post-Emancipation Imagination

The University of North Carolina Press *Chapel Hill*

*This book was published with the assistance of the
Authors Fund of the University of North Carolina Press.*

© 2020 The University of North Carolina Press
All rights reserved
Set in Arno by Westchester Publishing Services
Manufactured in the United States of America

The University of North Carolina Press has been a member of the
Green Press Initiative since 2003.

Library of Congress Cataloging-in-Publication Data
Names: Bellows, Amanda Brickell, author.
Title: American slavery and Russian serfdom in the post-emancipation
   imagination / Amanda Brickell Bellows.
Description: Chapel Hill : University of North Carolina Press, [2020] |
   Includes bibliographical references and index.
Identifiers: LCCN 2019046673 | ISBN 9781469655536 (cloth ; alk. paper) |
   ISBN 9781469655543 (paperback ; alk. paper) | ISBN 9781469655550 (ebook)
Subjects: LCSH: Freedmen—United States—In mass media—History—
   19th century. | Peasants—Russia—In mass media—History—19th century. |
   Collective memory—United States—Cross-cultural studies. | Collective
   memory—Russia—Cross-cultural studies. | Slaves—Emancipation—
   United States. | Serfs—Emancipation—Russia.
Classification: LCC E185.61 .B423 2020 | DDC 973.7/14—dc23
LC record available at https://lccn.loc.gov/2019046673

Cover illustrations: Top, G. G. Miasoedov, *Busy Time for the Mowers*, 1887
(© State Russian Museum, St. Petersburg); bottom, Winslow Homer,
The Cotton Pickers, 1876 (courtesy of the Los Angeles County Museum of Art).

A previous version of chapter 4 was published in Russian as "Post-Emancipation
Representations of Serfs, Peasants, Slaves, and Freedpeople in Russian and American
National Art, 1861–1905," *Novoe literaturnoe obozrenie* (New Literary Observer) 6 (2016):
7–25. A version of chapter 5 appeared as "Selling Servitude, Captivating Consumers:
Images of Bondsmen in American and Russian Advertisements, 1880–1915," *Journal of
Global Slavery* 1, no. 1 (2016): 72–112.

To My Children

May you grow to love the pursuit of knowledge

To My Husband

Thank you for encouraging me to become a historian

Contents

Illustrations

Acknowledgments

It has been a fascinating experience to study American slavery and Russian serfdom over the past decade. I would like to express my sincere gratitude to the people and institutions who offered guidance and support as I researched and wrote this book. The New-York Historical Society and the Eugene Lang College of Liberal Arts at the New School provided me with a Bernard and Irene Schwartz Postdoctoral Fellowship in 2016. American Councils funded my Russian archival research in St. Petersburg and Moscow through its generous Title VIII Research Scholar Program. The members of the History Department of the European University at St. Petersburg facilitated my access to Russian archives and welcomed me into their community. My Russian language training was made possible by the U.S. Department of Education through its Foreign Language Area Studies Academic Year and Summer Fellowships, granted by Duke University and the University of North Carolina at Chapel Hill. Additional archival research in the United States was supported by a one-month research fellowship at the Gilder Lehrman Center for the Study of Slavery, Resistance, and Abolition at Yale University; a seminar hosted by the National Endowment for the Humanities and the City University of New York Graduate Center; and a research trip supported by the Robert Bosch Foundation in conjunction with the German Historical Institute, the University of Chicago's Department of History, and the Heidelberg Center for American Studies.

The staff members of Russian and American archives and libraries were extremely helpful in finding and granting access to materials. At the New-York Historical Society, I would like to thank Michael Ryan, Jill Reichenbach, Nina Nazionale, and Ted O'Reilly for their assistance in locating unusual and interesting primary sources. I would also like to thank Alexander Tarasov of the Russian National Library for allowing me to view the Poster Collection, for discussing notable advertisements with me, and for directing me to the Russian National Library's rich Ephemera Collection. I am very grateful to Lisa Egorova for her assistance in obtaining images and locating pertinent documents at the State Tret'iakov Gallery. At Yale's Gilder Lehrman Center, David Blight, Michelle Zacks, Tom Thurston, and Melissa McGrath were incredibly welcoming. I thank them for their friendship and for providing access to the center's remarkable collection of books on global slavery. I would also like to thank Nicholle Young of the Charles W. Chesnutt Library Archives and Special Collections at Fayetteville State University and Jerrold Brantley of Emory University, for his aid in viewing the Joel Chandler Harris collection holdings. The librarians and archivists at Yale's Beinecke Rare Book and Manuscript Library, Duke University's David M. Rubenstein Rare Book and Manuscript Library, the Russian State Archive of Literature and Art, the Russian State Historical Museum, the Metropolitan Museum of Art, the Schomburg Center for Research in Black Culture, the American Antiquarian Society, the Frick Art Reference Library, Harvard University's Houghton Library, and the New York Society Library were also very helpful in providing access to their outstanding collections. The University of North Carolina at Chapel Hill's librarians Nadia Zilper and Kirill Tolpygo and the University of Illinois at Urbana-Champaign's librarian Helen Sullivan provided expert research guidance as well. Finally, I would like to thank Olga Malkina and Lucya Koroleva, who welcomed me to Russia in 2013 and gave me outstanding editorial advice over the years.

I am very thankful to Fitz Brundage and Louise McReynolds for their invaluable support and insightful editorial instruction. I admire them tremendously as renowned researchers. I am also very appreciative of the intellectual guidance of Bill Barney, Peter Kolchin, and Heather Williams. Peter Kolchin has been an inspiration to me ever since I first read his groundbreaking book *Unfree Labor: American Slavery and Russian Serfdom*. I am grateful for his thoughtful advice throughout the development of this book. In addition, I would like to thank Bill Ferris for his kindness and support. Bill's passion for his research and his generous spirit have always inspired me.

I am indebted to the many scholars who critiqued versions of my book's chapters at national and international conferences. In addition, I would like to thank my New School colleagues Elaine Abelson, Oz Frankel, Federico Finchelstein, Aaron Jakes, Natalia Mehlman-Petrzela, Julia Ott, Laura Palermo, Emma Park, Claire Potter, Jeremy Varon, and Eli Zaretsky for their insightful comments. At Yale, David Blight provided helpful advice during my research fellowship summer of 2018. This book also benefited from scholarly conversations and e-mail exchanges with Joshua Brown, Don Doyle, Dominque Jean Louis, Nick Juravich, David Silkenat, and Natalie Joy.

It was been an absolute pleasure to work with Chuck Grench and Dylan White at the University of North Carolina Press. I sincerely thank them for their thoughtful guidance and advice throughout the publication process.

In closing, I would like to express my gratitude to Sarah McNamara, Liz Ellis, Stephen Riegg, Adam Domby, Catherine Bateson, Holly Pinheiro, Cathal Smith, and Hilary Green for their friendship. I would also like to thank Sam Olden, who celebrated his hundredth birthday in March 2019, for deepening my interest in history. I am so grateful for the love and support of my grandparents, Mary and Henry, my parents, Anita and Mark, my sister, Missye, and my brother, Matt. I am also thankful for the encouragement of family members Deb and Charlie Bellows, Maureen Bellows, Gary Demele, Charles Bellows, Erica Smith, Briana Brickell, and Brian Knapp. I dedicate this book to my husband, Marcus, who has given me unwavering support throughout every step of this journey, and to my children, whose love of learning about the world around them is wonderful to behold.

All translations are my own. I completed the Russian transliteration in accordance with the romanization table outlined by the Library of Congress. Russian dates follow the Julian calendar, which was approximately twelve days behind the Gregorian calendar during the nineteenth century.

Introduction

This book is the first monograph-length comparison of the ways in which the people of two disparate countries, Russia and the United States, reacted to the nearly simultaneous abolition of serfdom and slavery during the mid-nineteenth century. Emancipation freed millions of Russian serfs and enslaved African Americans who subsequently strove for absorption into the national polities as subjects and citizens. In both nations, the post-emancipation era was characterized by territorial expansion, population growth, immigration, industrialization, and modernization, phenomena that further complicated notions of Russian and American national identity.

During the fifty years that followed the abolition of serfdom in 1861 and slavery in 1865, Russians and Americans of all backgrounds responded to societal transformation through cultural production. Authors, artists, and businessmen produced mass-oriented images of serfs, peasants, enslaved African Americans, and freedpeople in literature, periodicals, illustrations, paintings, and advertisements, sources that circulated widely in the public sphere. As acts of imagination and remembrances, these portrayals were a lexicon of representation that creators and audiences endowed with significance and interpreted in competing ways. Elite Russians and Americans, or those who wielded the greatest political, economic, or social power, typically portrayed serfs and enslaved people as victims on the eve of abolition, as contented rural laborers whose simple way of life attracted nostalgic audiences during an industrial, expansionist age, and, at the turn of the twentieth century, as disruptive rural-to-urban migrants. Russian peasants and African American freedpeople countered these depictions by producing dignified self-representations that illuminated their traditions, communities, and accomplishments. Ultimately, these diverse textual and visual images shaped collective memories of two systems of bondage, affected the development of national consciousness, and influenced public opinion as peasants and freedpeople strove to exercise their newfound rights.

Navigating the seas of change after emancipation was no easy task for nineteenth-century Russians and Americans. In Russia, Tsar Alexander II's issuance of the Emancipation Manifesto on February 19, 1861, liberated 40 percent of the nation's people from bondage and was the first of several modernizing policies that produced substantial change.[1] The former serfs, now *poddannye* (subjects), strove to manage their villages' communal land, establish schools, and participate in national initiatives by serving alongside their former owners on local governing bodies like the *zemstva* (provincial assemblies). However, Russia's autocratic government extended few political rights to the former serfs, who, like landowners, lacked elected representation at the national level. Racism did not influence the dynamics of assimilation in Russia, because peasants and landowners largely shared the same ethnicity, language, and Russian Orthodox religion.[2] But neither emancipation nor subsequent government-initiated reforms eliminated the barriers created by an estate system from the era of Tsar Peter the Great that divided the population into different social groups.[3] Indeed, the Russian nobility and the peasantry remained culturally distant from one another through the early twentieth century.[4] Although the peasantry and proreform intellectuals harbored great hopes about the potential for individual uplift, political representation, and national progress after 1861, the newspaper *Nedelia* (The Week) lamented in 1871 that while "much had changed, many dreams were not realized, [and] much did not turn out as expected."[5]

In the United States, *Harper's Weekly* issued a buoyant pronouncement of national peace in July 1865, shortly after the Civil War ended, by declaring that "every question within the nation [would soon] be wisely settled."[6] Ultimately, the popular periodical's assertion proved premature. The war's conclusion brought the challenge of integrating four million formerly enslaved African Americans into a total population of about thirty-six million people in 1865.[7] One essential factor that shaped the dynamics of assimilation was race: African Americans composed a demographic minority in a nation of approximately thirty-two million white citizens.[8] In their post-emancipation efforts to exercise their right to vote, gain literacy, acquire property, or establish businesses, freedpeople met strong resistance from Americans who viewed the color of their skin as a sign of racial inferiority that precluded them from equal treatment under law. During the post-emancipation period of rebuilding known as Reconstruction (1865–1877), the states' ratification of the Fourteenth and Fifteenth Amendments secured for African Americans citizenship and, for African American men, the franchise. But these early guarantees of African Americans' civil rights crumbled during the 1870s, 1880s, and 1890s due to legal challenges to Reconstruction-era laws, the passage of new "Jim Crow" legislation that severely curtailed black liberties, and a significant rise in acts of violence against African Americans intended to enforce racial subjugation.

Why contrast the reconstruction of two disparate societies that were thoroughly transformed by emancipation?[9] Comparative history enables the identification of the individual or shared aspects of a historical case.[10] While some elements of a particular situation are unique, others transcend geographic or temporal boundaries and appear in starkly different contexts. *American Slavery and Russian Serfdom in the Post-Emancipation Imagination* draws inspiration from an approach described by Theda Skocpol and Margaret Somers as "comparative history as the contrast of contexts."[11] They argue that this technique is useful because it enables scholars "to bring out the unique features of each particular case . . . and to show how these unique features affect the working-out of putatively general social processes."[12] In its comparison of two post-emancipation countries, this book juxtaposes the contrasting ways in which Russians and Americans remembered the analogous institutions of serfdom and slavery through the production of images and identifies the conditions that contributed to their creation. Ultimately, by placing the post-emancipation eras of these two nations in comparative perspective, we glean useful information not apparent from the separate study of each country.

Comparative historians have long noted the intriguing parallels between Russia and the United States, two dynamic nations with legacies of bonded labor, expansive geographic ambitions, and rich literary and artistic traditions. Their primary avenue of exploration, however, has been the history of serfdom and slavery.[13] While the earliest comparative studies of human captivity focused on the Atlantic world, Peter Kolchin's pioneering work *Unfree Labor: American Slavery and Russian Serfdom* (1987) was the first to draw attention to the parallels between slavery and serfdom, two institutions of bondage established in the first half of the seventeenth century and abolished just four years apart.[14] Subsequent comparisons of Russian serfdom and American slavery have assessed the similarities and differences between the political, economic, demographic, and social aspects of the two systems, providing a critical historical foundation for twenty-first-century scholars seeking to analyze cultural, aesthetic, or intellectual elements of servitude.[15]

Indeed, most historical research comparing Russian serfdom and U.S. slavery covers each institution's origins, practice, and abolition rather than the turmoil of the post-emancipation era. A growing number of American scholars, however, have begun to transform the field of Reconstruction studies by expanding its geographic reach and its traditional periodization (1865–1877) to acknowledge what W. Fitzhugh Brundage calls the "longue durée of reconstruction."[16] In addition, other historians have recently used or advocated the application of comparative history's methodological approach to the study of societies seeking to integrate formerly bonded populations.[17] In articles or chapters, they assess class divisions, free labor conditions, the role of gender in policy making, and racial tensions in postslavery societies, all important aspects of reconstruction in different countries. Nevertheless, little comparative or transnational work has been done to date that investigates the ways in which cultural sources influenced the absorption of formerly bonded populations through analogous processes of mass communication.[18]

Scholars of Russian and American history have separately examined depictions of serfs, peasants, enslaved African Americans, or freedpeople in various publications during recent decades. In the case of Russia, Cathy Frierson's *Peasant Icons: Representations of Rural People in Late Nineteenth-Century Russia* (1993) focuses primarily on firsthand accounts or descriptions of peasants by imperial Russia's educated elites, while Jeffrey Brooks's article "The Russian Nation Imagined" (2010) surveys images of Russia's diverse peoples (including the peasantry) from popular illustrated journals and *lubki* (popular prints) that targeted and reached a broader audience.[19] Andrew Donskov is one of the few Russian scholars to have assessed representations of the Russian peasant in nineteenth-century plays, whereas numerous researchers interested in commercial images of the peasantry have examined the wealth of surviving advertisements, ephemera, and *plakaty* (posters).[20] Finally, academics evaluating Russia's itinerant painters, the Peredvizhniki (Wanderers), have also paid close attention to their depictions of serfs and peasants in the style of Russian Realism during the late nineteenth century.[21]

By contrast, U.S. historians who have examined textual or visual representations of enslaved African Americans and freedpeople have been influenced by a cohort of scholars whose research concentrates on the broader field of memory studies. Many academics have produced important works that explore the multitude of ways in which Americans remembered and commemorated the U.S. Civil War or the abolition of slavery through ceremonies, monuments, and rituals during the nineteenth and twentieth centuries.[22] Other scholars engaging in memory studies have chosen to focus on particular elements of the antebellum, Civil War, or postwar experience; for instance, scholars have assessed representations of the "Old South," slavery, planters, freedpeople, soldiers, and much more in photography, art, advertisements, literature, illustrated journals, and ephemera from the late nineteenth and early twentieth centuries.[23] Their research helps explain the influence of various forms of imagery at a time when more Americans than ever before subscribed to printed periodicals, attended art exhibitions, and purchased a wide range of consumer goods.

American Slavery and Russian Serfdom in the Post-Emancipation Imagination breaks new ground as the first comparison of textual and visual mass-oriented depictions of former serfs and enslaved African Americans from the post-emancipation era in Russia and the United States. This juxtaposition identifies the ways in which the subjects and citizens of two disparate societies responded to emancipation by constructing collective memories through cultural production. In both the United States and Russia, textual and visual post-emancipation imagery composed what Alon Confino calls "shared cultural knowledge" that was passed down from one generation to the next through "vehicles of memory."[24] By studying this heterogeneous body of remembrances, it is possible to detect important correspondences between the ways in which Russians and Americans of diverse backgrounds imagined their pasts and futures through the creation of archetypes that served analogous societal purposes.[25]

This book also pinpoints the parallel and divergent ways in which Russians and Americans received images through the study of the manufacture, dissemination, and consumption of the aforementioned representations. It not only catalogs the most influential representations but also places these images within their proper historical contexts in order to evaluate their forms, functions, and evolutions. Furthermore, this book views representation as more than *l'art pour l'art;*[26] instead, it considers the motivations of painters, writers, and businessmen, the messages embedded within depictions, and the ways audiences processed images at different moments in time.

Indeed, cultural production served as an essential tool in the fight to influence popular opinion about explosive post-emancipation issues. After the abolition of serfdom and slavery, peasants and freedpeople sought to acquire jobs, establish businesses, and participate in political or civic affairs. In many cases, nonpeasant Russians and white Americans opposed their efforts to achieve these goals. Landowners and businessmen refused to pay their laborers adequate wages, urban workers pushed back against rural-to-urban migrants who sought jobs, and in the United States, white citizens prevented African Americans from voting for representatives whom whites feared would institute policies that threatened their privileged status.

While some Russians and Americans responded to the sweeping societal changes that followed emancipation through acts of violence like rioting or lynching, others turned to literature, art, and other forms of mass media. Ardent advocates of emancipation, for instance, urged readers in radical short stories, fictional autobiographical narratives, drama, and poetry during the 1860s to act compassionately toward peasants and African Americans. An alternate response, however, was that exhibited by authors from Russian and American landowning families. During the 1870s, 1880s, and 1890s, they produced mass-oriented works of historical fiction that sought to uphold the ideology of civilization through portrayals of peasants and freedpeople who preferred bondage to freedom. The popularity of these revisionist stories attests to middle-class readers' opposition to change and to the authors' shared method of responding to the challenges to the way of life they sought to preserve. Meanwhile, the visual culture of the late nineteenth century reflected similar divisions among artists. In oil paintings, illustrated periodicals, cartoons, and advertisements that reached both literate and nonliterate audiences, Russians and Americans of diverse backgrounds debated the consequences of abolition, the rights of citizenship and subjecthood, urban migration, and the decline of traditional folk culture. At the turn of the twentieth century, African Americans and Russian peasants increasingly challenged through important counternarratives representations produced by men and women who had never experienced bondage. Using fiction and other forms of visual culture, they depicted the experiences of former serfs and enslaved people in complex, humanizing ways.

By placing portrayals of peasants and African Americans in comparative perspective, *American Slavery and Russian Serfdom in the Post-Emancipation Imagination* identifies striking representational similarities and illuminating differences that better explain the individual histories of the abolition of serfdom and slavery. First, I argue that it was primarily Russian and American elites' twin desire to maintain power in the face of change that resulted in their parallel portrayals after emancipation. For instance, white and nonpeasant authors' and artists' depictions of peasants and freedpeople contentedly continuing to serve their former owners reveal their resistance to the transformation of the historical power dynamics governing owner-laborer relationships. Meanwhile, images of freedpeople and peasants as perpetrators of urban disorder serve as additional evidence of their anxieties about the activities of liberated bonded laborers. These corresponding representations emerged from starkly different contexts; while racism played a central role in shaping post-emancipation social dynamics in America, conceptions of racial difference between landowners and serfs were largely absent in Russia. Peasants and freedpeople also produced similar self-representations of ambitious, dignified men and women that contradicted existing stereotypes of former serfs and enslaved African Americans as naive, lazy, or violent. They shared the goal of giving voice to their experiences and countering caricatures created by whites and nonpeasants after emancipation.

Second, I contend that Americans' and Russians' divergent depictions of peasants and freedpeople stem from differing conceptions of race and ethnicity, the varying degrees of political power exercised by peasants and freedpeople, and their distinct cultural backgrounds. White Americans saw African Americans as racially inferior; racism drove their actions and infused many of their representations of enslaved African Americans and freedpeople. In a situation unique to the United States, whites also felt threatened by the Reconstruction Amendments, which gave African Americans citizenship and the right to vote. In response, whites enacted black codes and terrorized African Americans to retain their political power. These dynamics contributed to white Americans' production of demeaning representations of freedpeople; whites used these images to justify their suppression of African Americans. Ultimately, whites' commitment to racial supremacy and fear of losing power served as a major barrier to the acquisition of freedom and the securing of civil rights for African Americans during the century that followed the abolition of slavery.

By contrast, Russia's former serfs appeared in a broader range of portrayals that included the peasantry as representatives of Slavic culture and as egalitarian urban denizens. While racism constrained the imagination of many white Americans, the lack thereof in the Russian context enabled the cultivation of a more expansive post-emancipation imagination. Political dynamics also played a crucial role. After emancipation, peasants did not receive political rights that seriously challenged the authority of Russian aristocrats; instead, nobles and peasants alike remained the subjects of an autocratic tsar. Violence plagued the post-emancipation South, but relations between the Russian peasantry and aristocracy were less fraught with tension during the late nineteenth century. Nonetheless, factors including poverty, war, a universal lack of civil liberties, and class antagonisms ultimately led to total social upheaval during the Russian revolutions of 1905 and 1917.

American Slavery and Russian Serfdom in the Post-Emancipation Imagination is organized chronologically and thematically. Each of its six chapters evaluates depictions of serfs, enslaved African Americans, peasants, and freedpeople in a particular medium that played an essential role in influencing popular opinion. Chapter 1, "Radical Literature on the Eve of Emancipations," discusses the parallel work of antiserfdom and antislavery literary authors in Russia and the United States during the late 1850s and the 1860s. Poet Nikolai Nekrasov, playwright Aleksei Pisemskii, and authors Louisa May Alcott and

Martha Griffith Browne each crafted profoundly sympathetic images of Russian serfs and enslaved African Americans in literature or drama.[27] These writers sought to evoke empathy in ambivalent or unreceptive readers by emphasizing the suffering formerly bonded people endured under oppressive systems that restricted their freedom of choice and kept them in poverty. Browne's fictional *Autobiography of a Female Slave* (1857) and Alcott's complex portrayals of enslaved African Americans and freedpeople in the short stories "M.L." (1863) and "My Contraband" (1863) inspired antislavery sentiments in some readers and challenged others to conceive of a post-emancipation nation defined by wholly new relationships between whites and blacks. Their fictional stories circulated alongside freedpeople's autobiographical narratives that gained significant attention during the decades preceding emancipation. Meanwhile, Pisemskii and Nekrasov persuaded many ambivalent, educated, and, often, urban Russians to consider the plight of the rural population in the play *A Bitter Fate* (1859) and in poems published during the 1860s. Serf narratives were rare in Russia due in large part to censorship laws, so fiction, drama, and poetry served as essential sources of information about serfdom for Russian readers.

During the decades that followed emancipation, textual and visual representations of peasants and freedpeople shaped the public conversation about what it meant to be Russian or American in a new, modern age. After the abolition of serfdom and slavery, Russia and the United States underwent political, economic, and social transformations.[28] During the postbellum era, the United States continued its westward push as pioneers established farms and towns in territories in the middle, southwestern, and western regions of the continent.[29] The federal government forced numerous Indian tribes onto reservations and introduced compulsory policies to assimilate Native Americans.[30] Meanwhile, Russia simultaneously expanded westward, southward, and eastward during the second half of the nineteenth century and annexed parts of the Caucasus, modern-day Kazakhstan, Uzbekistan, Alaska, and the Amur region.[31] The empire's expansion was primarily driven by a desire for land and power, by the ruling class rather than the peasantry.[32] Like the United States, Russia sought to incorporate not only former serfs but also new ethnic groups into the populace. For the imperial government, however, territorial control had historically come second to the control over and assimilation of the diverse peoples living across the empire.[33] The Russian Empire's expansion necessitated the redefinition of its traditionally Slavic and pro-European national character.[34] In both countries, the growth of empire reshaped preexisting conceptions of Russian and American national identity.

Although some Americans and Russians managed to keep pace with the rapid changes of the post-emancipation era, others hoped to restore elements of the old order.[35] Chapter 2, "Popular Historical Fiction," describes how writers from landowning families addressed audiences' latent apprehensions through the creation of fictional representations that idealized rural agricultural work and the relations between owners and bonded laborers during the 1870s and 1880s. The faithful former serfs in the stories of Grigorii Danilevskii, Vsevolod Solov'ev, Evgenii Opochinin, Evgenii Salias, and authors published in *Moskovskii listok* (Moscow Sheet) and the loyal African Americans in the tales of white, Southern authors Thomas Nelson Page and Joel Chandler Harris appealed to a broad swath of Russians and Americans who viewed the pre-emancipation era with growing wistfulness.[36] Through historical fiction, readers reflected on the supposed simplicity of a period when the social positions of owners and their so-called servants were clearly defined within a distinct hierarchical system. Furthermore, audiences confronting increasingly diverse national populations were drawn to literature that depicted binary social relationships as an escape from the demographic complexities of the post-emancipation age.

While some Americans and Russians easily adjusted to the dramatic social changes of the post-emancipation era, others resisted developments that challenged their preferred way of life. In fin de siècle Russia, nobles and peasants alike remained frustrated with the nation's transformation. After the assassination of Tsar Alexander II in 1881 by a member of the revolutionary organization the People's Will, his successor, Tsar Alexander III, rolled back the nation's liberal reforms and cracked down on what he saw as destabilizing radical activity. During this reactionary period, landownership among members of the nobility declined and the number of peasant farmers increased, but aristocrats ensured that they could monitor peasant activity during the 1890s.[37] Many former serfs who continued to live in rural villages were dissatisfied with the quality or size of their allotted land and the burden of the redemption payments that were a condition of their emancipation; they expressed their disapproval through periodic protests.[38] During the late nineteenth century, however, industrialization and urban expansion weakened the traditional borders between imperial Russia's rural villages and bustling cities. Manufacturers built new factories that promoted urban growth and offered rural peasants salaried jobs that provided an escape from the hardships of agricultural labor. In cities, many urban peasants earned consistent wages but endured difficult working conditions and long hours. Some struggled with alcoholism and engaged in petty crimes that urban elites characterized as "hooliganism," an early twentieth-century phenomenon that Joan Neuberger calls "part of the process of class self-identification and self-assertion ... in connection with rapid urbanization, industrialization, and the spread of education."[39] Factors including poverty, labor strife, and strained relations between members of different estates produced an uneasy populace and contributed to the outbreak of protests and violence during the revolutions of 1905 and 1917.

In the U.S. South, many whites responded to black progress by establishing discriminatory "Jim Crow" laws that disfranchised African Americans and necessitated racial segregation in public places ranging from waiting rooms to conveyances.[40] Opportunities for economic advancement were also limited in the countryside because a widespread system of sharecropping kept many formerly enslaved people in poverty. After emancipation, Southern states also passed laws that criminalized conditions such as vagrancy, legislation that led to the conviction and imprisonment of thousands of freedpeople.[41] Prisons began leasing imprisoned laborers to privately owned institutions or companies in what became known as the convict-lease system.[42] To enforce post-emancipation Jim Crow laws, whites employed forms of violence to subjugate African Americans, creating an atmosphere of terror that many people hoped to escape. In response to the oppressiveness of life in the Jim Crow South during the late nineteenth century and in pursuit of greater economic opportunity, thousands of freedpeople began migrating to growing metropolises where they hoped to find a chance for a better life. American industrialization and urbanization generated better career prospects for African Americans, but these phenomena also created new sets of challenges. Violence against African Americans also plagued cities where racism and heightened interracial economic competition fueled conflicts between urban workers.[43]

Mass-oriented periodicals of the late nineteenth century acknowledged these political and demographic changes in the illustrations of serfs, enslaved African Americans, peasants, and freedpeople that filled their pages. Thanks to advancements in printing and distribution technologies, these publications circulated widely in both Russia and the United States among educated and nonliterate audiences. Chapter 3, "Illustrated Periodicals and Lithographs," reveals the competing ways in which illustrators, typically young, white, male artists, portrayed post-emancipation agricultural labor conditions, black and peasant folk culture, rural-to-urban migration, and more in mass-oriented engravings and cartoons. Some images contained historically revisionist themes that mirrored or expanded on those of the era's sentimental historical fiction. For example, illustrators portrayed rural African Americans and peasants as contentedly working on their former owners' estates or engaging in rituals and holiday celebrations, images that reflected both countries' growing interest in folk culture and national identity. Building on popular apprehensions about peasants' and freedpeople's departure from traditional agricultural roles, artists also depicted rural-to-urban migrants from both groups as unmoored, disorderly individuals who engaged in uncivil activities and threatened city dwellers' ways of life. Furthermore, illustrators continued to represent both rural and urban African Americans and peasants as lacking intelligence in simplistic, one-dimensional illustrations that show how late nineteenth-century perceptions of intrinsic difference existed in both the presence and absence of actual ethnic differences between different social groups. By contrast, periodicals targeting black and peasant readerships depicted African Americans and peasants as hardworking, upstanding members of urban communities, representations that served as vital counterpoints to those circulating in periodicals with predominantly white or nonpeasant audiences.

Oil paintings also played a crucial role in shaping the parameters of discourse about former serfs and enslaved African Americans during the late nineteenth century thanks to growing support for the concept of national art. Chapter 4, "Oil Paintings," explores the works of prominent Russian and American nineteenth-century artists. While some hailed from landowning or abolitionist families, others were descended from enslaved or enserfed individuals. Many of these painters participated in leading organizations like Russia's Society of Traveling Art Exhibitions and New York's National Academy of Design. Russian and American artists depicted African American and peasant experiences of captivity, the processes of their liberation, their postemancipation civic roles as soldiers and students, and their experiences as rural-to-urban migrants. Their representations circulated more widely than ever before thanks to traveling exhibitions and the visual reproduction of their works in journals and magazines.

The late nineteenth-century phenomena of industrialization and urbanization also led to the invention of new forms of art. Businesses increasingly employed illustrators to create captivating advertisements that would attract potential consumers. Chapter 5, "Advertisements and Ephemera," focuses on representations of former serfs and enslaved African Americans in the colorful posters, trade cards, and ephemera that inundated the public sphere. In both Russia and the United States, many businesses created nostalgic images of servile peasants and African Americans that mirrored archetypes found in periodicals and popular historical fiction. Notably, however, some Russian companies sought to capitalize on the demographic changes transforming the nation by creating radically egalitarian ads that targeted urban peasants, who possessed growing purchasing power and constituted a majority of the total population. By contrast, U.S. businesses, many of which were white-owned, largely ignored African Americans as a potential consumer group. They focused instead on attracting white buyers, who composed the demographic majority in the United States, through disparaging, racialized imagery that mocked African Americans. Thus, while most American commercial materials reinforced representational stereotypes of the era, many Russian advertisements challenged existing ideas about the former serfs' inferior social position through unique visual portrayals of an integrated peasantry.

At the turn of the twentieth century, slavery and serfdom seemed increasingly distant to the generation of Russians and Americans born after emancipation. Instead of yearning for a return to an idealized past, a new cadre of authors and artists, some of whom were African American or from the peasant estate, focused on representing the achievements of and obstacles facing contemporary peasants and African Americans. Chapter 6, "Literature and Visual Culture at the Turn of the Twentieth Century," examines the pioneering literature, illustrations, and photography of men and women from diverse backgrounds who challenged the nostalgic representations of the previous decades by depicting the complexities of the post-emancipation era. In Russia, the playwright Anton Chekhov, the son of a serf, shocked audiences with his realistic portrayal of rural poverty in the short story "The Peasants" (1897).[44] Russian readers also learned about the distinct hardships urban peasants endured in short stories like "Thoughts" and "Other People's Money."[45] In the United States, authors Kate Chopin and Charles Waddell Chesnutt confronted audiences with the thorny issues of racial identity, interracial relationships, and violence in *Bayou Folk* (1894) and *The Wife of His Youth, and Other Stories of the Color Line* (1899).[46] Their tales drew from personal experience and firmly acknowledged the realities of late nineteenth- and early twentieth-century Russian and American life by portraying the transformation of the pre-emancipation order, the trials of migration, rural and urban poverty, and the formerly bonded laborers' experience of social integration. Visual culture like photography and Russian *lubki* (popular prints) added to the growing diversity of representations of African Americans and peasants. Sociologist W. E. B. Du Bois's photographs of upper- and middle-class black families, African Americans' cartes de visite, and popular illustrations targeting peasant audiences served as critical counterpoints to representations historically generated by whites and nonpeasants. Together, these thought-provoking portrayals confronted earlier depictions of freedpeople and emancipated serfs who preferred bondage to liberty and defied depictions of violent freedpeople in turn-of-the-century stories by authors like Thomas Dixon Jr.

The variety of mass-oriented cultural representations of serfs, enslaved African Americans, peasants, and freedpeople within each country shows a range of perspectives about bondage and emancipation. Intriguingly, however, depictions whose correspondences crossed national boundaries reveal that Russians and Americans from different backgrounds responded in parallel ways to abolition and the social transformation that followed. Representational differences also necessitate further reflection about the unique ways in which ethnic and class-based distinctions between owners and former serfs or enslaved people shaped the dynamics of the post-emancipation era. Ultimately, these depictions serve as important evidence of how two societies remembered, imagined, and challenged the legacies of the abolition of serfdom and slavery.

CHAPTER ONE

Radical Literature on the Eve of Emancipations

In the spring of 1861, the United States teetered on the brink of war. Americans anxiously wondered if tensions between the North and the South could be resolved after the recent secession of seven states, but there would be no peace. The Confederate bombardment of Fort Sumter on April 12 marked the formal commencement of hostilities that would last until General Robert E. Lee's surrender to General Ulysses S. Grant at Appomattox Court House, Virginia, in April 1865. When Massachusetts author and abolitionist Lucy Larcom learned of the outbreak of war in Charleston in 1861, she recorded in her diary: "This day broke upon our country in gloom; for the sounds of war came up to us from the South,—war between brethren; civil war."[1] Although the conflict between the North and the South centered on the right to own slaves and to expand slavery westward, Larcom did not believe that emancipation was certain. Instead, she contemplated the events unfolding before her, wondering, "What ruin [the rebels] are pulling down on their heads may be guessed, though not yet fully foretold."[2]

Four million African Americans remained enslaved when the Civil War began. They resided in fifteen states where slavery was legal, eleven of which ultimately seceded from the Union. The outbreak of war occurred after what John Stauffer describes as "the fragmentation of America," a phenomenon that largely occurred between the 1830s and South Carolina's attack on Fort Sumter.[3] This period was characterized by sectional arguments about whether slavery ought to be legally permitted in new territories and states as the nation expanded westward.[4] The fear of disunion, or what Elizabeth Varon calls "the dissolution of the republic," haunted Northerners and Southerners during the antebellum era.[5] Events including the Nullification Crisis of 1832–1833, the passage of the Fugitive Slave Law in 1850, and the Kansas-Nebraska Act of 1854 produced significant sectional turmoil and debate among advocates and opponents of slavery.[6] Throughout these crises, many white Americans opposed war and the breakdown of the Union, but they maintained a plurality of opinions about slavery's future.

Slave owners may have been the most vociferous defenders of bonded labor, but citizens involved in the trade of enslaved Africans or goods produced by slaves also feared that slavery's demise would harm their economic interests. For instance, New York City's cotton merchants, whose wealth was largely derived from the purchase and sale of cotton grown by enslaved men and women, likely worried that abolition would upend their business model.[7] Furthermore, trading centers like New York City held what Calvin Schermerhorn argues were "the strongest financial links in the chain of credits and debts responsible for slavery's vitality," a fact that challenged abolitionists' notion of a "free North" and "a slave South."[8] In April 1861, *Harper's Weekly* lampooned Northern businessmen opposed to abolition with a caricature of a New Yorker named "Cotton Pork," a "patriot" described as "dead against civil war." Pork implores the reader: "'Carry the sword and torch into happy plantations—and write off our outstanding Southern claims? Stain the national flag with American blood—and hand over the Southern market to foreigners? Never, never, never!'"[9]

By contrast, a group of predominantly Northern activists that included Larcom, ex-slave Frederick Douglass, William Lloyd Garrison, Wendell Phillips, and others staunchly opposed slavery. They supported abolition, a crusade that historian Manisha Sinha calls "a radical, democratic movement that questioned the enslavement of labor" and employed a range of approaches to convince the American population that slavery had no place in the republic.[10] Many prominent antislavery leaders of the 1840s and 1850s favored immediate abolition over gradual emancipation or colonization schemes that sent African Americans abroad. Some abolitionists encouraged enslaved men and women to escape or rebel against their owners in the years leading up to the Civil War.[11] John Brown, a passionate opponent of slavery who led a raid on the federal armory at Harper's Ferry in 1859, espoused and preached a kind of militant abolitionism that appealed to some but seemed too radical to others.[12] Brian Holden Reid argues that Brown's actions highlighted the divisions among abolitionists of the era: while some "saw slavery as an unutterable evil that could be destroyed only by force," others hoped the federal government would step in to prevent the Southern states from leaving the Union and restore peace before violence "disrupt [ed] the existing pattern of race relations in the South."[13]

The abolitionist movement grew in strength during the tumultuous years that preceded the outbreak of war, but many white Americans, even those who disliked slavery, found the abolitionists' views too extreme. Historian Adam I. P. Smith characterizes most mid-nineteenth-century Northerners as nonabolitionists or nonradicals who composed a "conservative majority."[14] They shared what he calls "a commitment to defend a free labor society in which white men could govern themselves, build communities, and make their way in the world," but viewed slavery as "an institution that was not inherently antagonistic to the survival of the Union."[15] Some white Northerners only opposed the expansion of slavery into new territories or states, while others supported gradual emancipation or colonization.[16] Thus, when Northern and Southern Unionists enlisted in the army in 1861, Gary Gallagher notes, "the loyal citizenry initially gave little thought to emancipation in their quest to save the Union" and abolition did not appear to be a certain consequence of victory.[17] Confederate soldiers, by contrast, even those who did not own slaves, fought to preserve the institution of slavery in the South. Many viewed their struggle as a battle for freedom from Northern oppression, not recognizing the incongruity of what historian James McPherson describes as the paradoxical "pairing of slavery and liberty as . . . twin goals."[18] By the war's end, however, the abolition of slavery had become a central goal of the Union army.

The experience of war also prompted discussion about the abolition of serfdom in Russia, where twenty-three million peasants were enserfed. Tsar Alexander II issued the Emancipation Manifesto on February 19, 1861, but he began considering the process of liberation shortly after Russia's defeat in the Crimean War (1853–1856).[19] Aware of his country's need to modernize, the tsar established a committee to advise him about emancipation, instead of making a formal announcement about the possibility of abolition that would have caused widespread peasant unrest.[20] Next, the tsar's government established provincial committees comprising two elected and two governor-appointed nobles that would ostensibly help craft the terms of emancipation in 1858.[21] Two years after the committees' deliberations began, the final manifesto was published.

During the years preceding abolition in Russia, as in the United States, public opinion about the prospect of emancipation was mixed. There was no abolitionist movement in Russia that paralleled that of the United States due to strict censorship laws and policing that prohibited the formation and expansion of such a program.[22] For the most part, the peasantry remained unaware of the ongoing negotiations at the state level regarding the potential plans for emancipation. Historian Hugh Seton-Watson has observed that while "the reforming minority of landowners" and other liberal, public voices from the urban intelligentsia were "most articulate" in supporting the tsar's push for emancipation, most landowners opposed abolition but were "ineffective in expressing their views."[23] The nobility were essentially unified in spirit, but they did not form a cohesive movement to challenge the tsar's government. Instead, planters on provincial committees sought to craft emancipatory terms that would minimize their losses, with desired outcomes that varied by region. While aristocrats possessing fertile land hoped to keep ownership of their territorial property, those with less productive acreage preferred monetary remuneration in the form of redemption payments.[24] Despite the nobility's disapproval of emancipation and the potential for upheaval among the peasantry, expectations of civil unrest upon the issuance of the manifesto were largely unrealized. According to an officer who was on duty the evening before the tsar's announcement, "There were no disturbances; the morning of Russia's great day passed as peacefully as the preceding night."[25] Even A. I. Levshin, a statesman who took part in the reform process, reflected with wonder: "For a long time I could not understand how the bureaucrats tackled such a great and terrible business with such ease."[26]

Despite the staunch opposition of different groups of people within both countries, autocratic Russia and the republican United States would successfully free millions of serfs and enslaved African Americans just four years apart. Nonetheless, emancipation was hardly an inevitable by-product of the Crimean War and the Civil War that resulted in territorial destruction and the deaths of hundreds of thousands of soldiers. Political, military, and economic forces markedly shaped the course of these events, but social and cultural forces also played an influential role. Indeed, the fight to end serfdom and slavery occurred not only in the corridors of power but also in the world of letters that shaped popular attitudes about the future of serfdom and slavery.

Chapter 1 considers the efforts of four writers who, with varying degrees of success, employed strikingly similar strategies to transform public opinion toward Russian serfs and enslaved African Americans on the eve of abolition. Russian poet Nikolai Nekrasov and playwright Aleksei Pisemskii and American authors Martha Griffith Browne and Louisa May Alcott produced original works of fiction, poetry, and drama that humanized the experience of bondage in distinct ways.[27] Their literary depictions of serfs and enslaved people are worthy of study for two reasons. First, they provide insight into the emancipatory imagination of four writers from privileged backgrounds who had never personally experienced enslavement or enserfment. Aristocrat Nekrasov and slaveholder Browne used sentimental language and imagery to encourage audiences to sympathize with oppressed serfs and slaves, whereas nobleman Pisemskii and Northern abolitionist Alcott helped audiences imagine bonded laborers as integrated citizens through radical portrayals that depicted loving interracial or inter-estate relationships.

Second, literary scholars and historians have not adequately examined the ways in which these authors sought to inspire abolitionist emotions in readers. For example, Alcott is best known for her internationally acclaimed children's literature, such as the novel *Little Women* (1868), while her progressive short stories have been given scant scholarly treatment.[28] Although American scholars are much more familiar with writers like Fedor Dostoevskii and Lev Tolstoi than with Pisemskii or Nekrasov, perhaps because the most recent English-language biographies of Nekrasov and Pisemskii were published in the 1960s, Russianists consider the playwright and poet to have significantly contributed to the nation's literary canon.[29] Even less is known about the ways in which they produced profoundly new depictions of Russian serfs and peasants. Lastly, Browne's fictional slave narrative warrants analysis because of its uniqueness as the work of an elite, white Southern woman who co-opts the voice of the oppressed to serve the abolitionist cause. While important scholarship has focused on the rhetorical strategies employed by the authors of autobiographical slave narratives, far less work has been done on assessing the tactics of the writers of fictional slave narratives.[30] Ultimately, by comparing the works of these four authors, we find surprising consonances between their singular, daring representations of enslaved African Americans and Russian serfs at a moment when the future of slavery and serfdom remained uncertain.

Antislavery and Antiserfdom Literature in the United States and Russia during the 1840s and 1850s

The printed word became an increasingly important means of transmitting information and ideas to a wide audience during the mid- to late nineteenth century.[31] The reading revolution occurred in both Europe and the United States as a result of technological advances in the papermaking and printing processes that made possible the mass production of books.[32] Industrialization facilitated the distribution of literature; for instance, expanding railway systems helped deliver newspapers, magazines, and books to curious readers across the two countries' vast territories.[33] Together, these innovations enabled publishers to meet growing demand for reading materials at a time when more people could read than ever before. Literacy rates rose in both the United States and Russia during the nineteenth century, although numbers varied by region, ethnicity, class or estate, and gender. In 1850, just 1 out of every 156 Americans was illiterate except in the U.S. South, where 1 in 16 people could not read.[34] As a group, white Americans of European descent possessed the lowest rate of illiteracy, with men and women reading in equal numbers.[35] In Russia, the first national census was taken in 1897 and recorded that 21 percent of the total population was literate, with lower literacy rates among the rural peasantry and women and higher rates in urban areas.[36]

During the years immediately preceding the abolition of serfdom and slavery, both Russians and Americans consumed varying amounts of literature pertaining to the topics of enslaved African Americans, serfs, and emancipation. In the United States, the earliest antislavery literature appeared during the late seventeenth century, and men and women of all backgrounds continued to decry the slave trade and slavery over the course of the next 150 years.[37]

Autobiographical slave narratives, often penned by men and women who escaped from slavery with the help of their editors, were one of the most popular types of writing among American readers. Scholars estimate that one hundred such accounts were published by American and European presses before the Civil War, including *Narrative of the Life of Frederick Douglass* (1845) and *Narrative of William W. Brown, a Fugitive Slave* (1847), which together sold tens of thousands of copies.[38] By contrast, Russia's autocratic government prohibited the publication of potentially inflammatory works and employed literary censors who excised sensitive material from texts or banned entire books. Indeed, there are fewer than twenty known serf narratives in existence, none of which was published prior to the abolition of serfdom.[39]

Russian and American readers removed from estate and plantation life also learned about slavery and serfdom through fiction during the 1850s. Harriet Beecher Stowe's antislavery novel *Uncle Tom's Cabin; or Life among the Lowly* (1852) was well known in both countries. Born in 1811 and raised in Litchfield, Connecticut, Stowe was inspired by the passage of the Fugitive Slave Law in 1850 to write a book condemning slavery.[40] Appalled by stories of reenslaved African Americans that appeared in the news with growing frequency, Stowe felt compelled to "speak a word for freedom and humanity."[41] She began to draft *Uncle Tom's Cabin*, explaining to her editor, Gamaliel Bailey: "Such peril and shame as now hangs over this country is worse than Roman slavery, and I hope that every woman who can write will not be silent."[42] Stowe's dramatic, sympathetic depiction of suffering enslaved African Americans instantly captivated national and international readers. In America, the novel was first printed in installments in the *National Era* and subsequently sold three hundred thousand copies during the first year of its publication in book form.[43] Stowe's antislavery text immediately roused passions and spurred debate in both the South and the North. In 1852, the *Southern Literary Messenger* excoriated the "inflammatory publication" whose "representations of Southern slavery" were "calculated not merely to wound and outrage the feelings of Southerners . . . but to . . . disseminate throughout the Union dissensions and hostilities."[44] By contrast, Northern reviews were overwhelmingly positive; for example, New York's *Christian Inquirer* called *Uncle Tom's Cabin* "the book for the times" that showed "the system of slavery . . . with singular truthfulness and remarkable wisdom."[45] These opposing appraisals indicate the extent to which some nineteenth-century Americans believed that fictional representations of slavery could influence public perceptions of it. Slavery's opponents and supporters feared that literature reinforcing the other side's cause would shift the debate over slavery's future.

Uncle Tom's Cabin made a powerful impression on educated Russians as well after its initial publication in three different literary journals between 1857 and 1858.[46] Author Ivan Turgenev and poet Nikolai Nekrasov were particularly moved by the story and noticed parallels between American slavery and Russian serfdom. Nekrasov, editor of the *Contemporary*, which published the text in its entirety, wrote in a letter to Turgenev: "It is noteworthy that this has been most opportune: the [emancipation] question has been very much in the public eye with respect to our own Negroes."[47] Turgenev received his copy of the book from abolitionist Maria Weston Chapman and remarked in his correspondence to her that he was "more than once sadly struck by the applicability of Mrs. Stowe's accounts to what [he knew] about similar horrors. . . . Many of the scenes described in the book seem like an exact depiction of equally frightful scenes in Russia."[48]

Ivan Turgenev related to Stowe's descriptions of American slavery through his own experience growing up as the son of a serf-owning landowner.[49] A member of the nobility, Turgenev was born in 1818 and spent his childhood at the expansive Spasskoye estate surrounded by his family and their two thousands serfs.[50] His memories of serfdom likely contributed to his decision to help foster antiserfdom sentiment among Russian readers through the publication of fictional literature akin to that of Stowe that sympathetically portrayed serfs as individual human beings with distinct desires and emotions.[51] Only a handful of works critiquing serfdom made it past the Russian censors, who, Hannah Goldman argues, "immeasurably distorted and impoverished the literature against serfdom."[52] One such text is Turgenev's *Notes of a Hunter* (1852), which was published the same year as Stowe's *Uncle Tom's Cabin*. This collection of twenty-one short stories is told from the perspective of a landowner living in the Orel Province. The nobleman describes to the reader his encounters with a range of serfs in differing circumstances and expresses his desire on more than one occasion that their conditions should be improved or that they should live as free men. Although scholars have debated whether Turgenev intended his collection to serve as an antiserfdom tract, Michael Hanne has persuasively argued that the primary "feature of the work which seems to have so radically shifted the attitudes to serfdom of many of [Turgenev's] readers . . . is simply the degree of attention which it accords to the serfs and the closeness and detail with which the serfs are observed," a technique that contradicted mid-nineteenth-century "Russian *literary* convention, in which serfs were traditionally treated as mere background figures, or stock comic characters."[53] As one critic of the late nineteenth century observed of Turgenev, he "dared to show not only his pity but his affection for the Russian peasant, often narrow-minded, ignorant, or brutal, but good at heart. He undertook to reveal to the Russians this being which they scarcely knew."[54] Thus, although Turgenev was considerably more restrained in his criticism of serfdom than Stowe was in her depiction of slavery, their fictional works served the comparable purpose of bringing the issue of abolition to the forefront of public consciousness in their respective countries during the early 1850s. Due to the scarcity of serf narratives in Russia, Turgenev's sketches played an especially important role in humanizing the peasantry.

Nikolai Nekrasov's Sympathetic Poetry

Turgenev's peer, Nikolai Nekrasov, built on his predecessor's success in evoking empathy for serfs on the eve of abolition. Nekrasov created numerous expressive poems over many years that detailed the hardships of rural life for peasant men, women, and children. Reflecting on Nekrasov's life in an obituary published shortly after his death, *Vsemirnaia illiustratsiia* (Worldwide Illustration) declared that the poet's central achievement was instigating an "awakening of public consciousness" in 1856, a year of uncertainty in which "questions were being raised" about the potential "emancipation of the peasantry."[55] With Russia recently defeated by the British, the French, and the Ottoman Empire during the Crimean War (1853–1856), Russian society sought to comprehend "the reasons for [the country's] military loss."[56] The direction of literature of that period "had become predominantly accusatory," and Nekrasov's sharply critical, unsentimental, and realistic poems about the *narod* (folk) "could not have been more in line with public sentiment and were met by the public with rapture."[57] Readers who felt apathetic about the future of serfdom or uninterested in the peasants' fate could not help being moved by poems like "A Forgotten Village" (1855) or "On the Volga" (1860), which detailed the trials of serfdom and forced labor in their variations.

Indeed, biographer Sigmund S. Birkenmayer has claimed that Nekrasov, "more than any other Russian poet, made his contemporaries aware of the existence of the *muzhik* [peasant] and his problems" during the years that preceded and followed the abolition of serfdom.[58]

Nekrasov's compassion for the peasantry was born of experience; he grew up in the rural town of Greshnevo in the Yaroslavl Province, near the Volga River, on his family's estate.[59] As a child, he witnessed his father's ill treatment of the serfs who resided there and subsequently formed a deeply unfavorable impression of the system.[60] Although Nekrasov was generally reserved in public as an adult, the topic of serfdom always invigorated him. His nephew, Aleksandr Fedorovich Nekrasov, recollected that, when the subject of a conversation turned to serfdom, his uncle "became excited and agitated and spoke [about it] strongly and angrily."[61] Aleksandr Fedorovich also recalled Nekrasov's respectful attitude toward the peasantry, recounting a memorable occasion in the countryside when he witnessed "peasants from neighboring villages approaching [Nekrasov], the majority of whom were hunters, but who had different conversations [with him], many asking his advice about their own peasant affairs."[62] Indeed, it was Nekrasov's unique understanding of the peasants' way of life and his comprehension of their "sufferings of the people," as he described it, that brought their experiences to life through poetry for readers far removed from Russia's rural villages.[63]

Nekrasov turned to literature at a critical moment in the history of Russia's intellectual development. His future as a poet and an editor of one of the nation's most important literary journals, however, was far from certain when he arrived in St. Petersburg in 1838. Although his father wanted him to go into the military, Nekrasov decided to enroll in the university where a childhood friend attended.[64] His father refused to support his academic endeavors, however, and for a period of time Nekrasov lived in abject poverty in St. Petersburg.[65] Despite his precarious situation, the young Nekrasov published his first collection of poems, *Dreams and Sounds*, in 1840. It was received with mixed reviews, but Nekrasov's first foray into the literary world brought him into contact with Vissarion Belinskii, an important critic whom biographer Murray Peppard deemed the decade's "czar of letters."[66] Belinskii was a "man of the forties" who condemned what he saw as Russia's intellectual and developmental backwardness and advocated truthful depictions of historical realities in art and literature in order to inform readers' views and effect liberal change.[67] His views influenced many of his peers, including Nekrasov, who applied his ideas to the craft of poetry and to his selection of works as the new editor of the journal the *Contemporary*.[68] After meeting Belinskii, Nekrasov began to produce verses in the style of Realism that addressed or even criticized the social conditions of mid-nineteenth-century Russia.[69]

During the late 1840s and 1850s, Nekrasov produced three poems that deliberately drew attention to the adversities that Russia's serfs faced in urban centers like St. Petersburg or on isolated rural estates. Through verse, Nekrasov condemned the actions of landlords by criticizing their absenteeism, their lack of compassion, or their decision to physically abuse their serfs. One early untitled and unpublished poem (1848) may reflect an event that transpired during Nekrasov's early years in St. Petersburg. Written from the perspective of a resident of the nation's capital, the poem recounts its narrator's visit to Haymarket Square. Stopping by the trading center one evening, he comes across a young female peasant being whipped with a knout. Nekrasov focuses not on the unidentified perpetrator of the brutal deed but on the serf's stoicism: "Not a sound from her breast, / only the whip was whistling, playing . . . / and to the Muse I said: 'Look! / Your blood sister!'"[70] Here, the reader imagines the crowd that surrounded the woman and hears the deafening silence, broken only by the swish of the scourge as it swings through the air. Nekrasov's poem is effective because of its simplicity; his sensory descriptions provoke a visceral response to the depicted scene of brutality and oppression. Although the poem was not published until after serfdom's demise, these verses demonstrate what one of Nekrasov's readers described as the poet's ability to "create discordant music and monstrous paintings" that teach audiences to remember that "here, at this very moment, while we are breathing, there are people who are suffocating."[71]

The poet was also inclined toward self-examination, unafraid of publicly critiquing the landowning class of which he was a part for the ways in which the nobility neglected their serfs. His poem "A Forgotten Village" (1855) tells the story of an estate where chaos and uncertainty reign. There, an elderly serf named Nenila begs the landlord's bailiff for fresh wood with which to repair her hut, but he rejects her request. Nenila tells herself that "master will come," to aid her in her hour of need, but he does not appear.[72] Next, a neighboring usurer claims a substantial slice of the serfs' land. The peasants protest his unjust actions, but to no avail, and again decide that they must wait for their owner to send a surveyor to rectify the situation. Even the social structure of the estate is collapsing; the third stanza explains that although the serf Natasha has "fallen in love with a free grain farmer," the powers that be opposed her romance. Once again "repeats the choir, 'The master will come!'"[73] But the *barin* (nobleman) does not arrive in time to correct the inefficiencies and rectify the injustices plaguing his estate. In his absence, "Nenila dies . . .

the usurer reaps an enormous harvest . . . and Natasha no longer talks deliriously about a wedding."[74] When the longed-for landlord finally returns to his estate, he is but a corpse lying "in an oaken casket." His son is now the estate's "new master," a man whom the peasants hope will improve their situation. The elderly peasants mourn their former landlord by singing funereal songs, while the new owner "wiped away his tears," but instead of staying, he "sat down in his carriage—and permanently departed for St. Petersburg."[75]

The peasants of the "forgotten village" represented the thousands of serfs who resided on Russia's estates in a sort of purgatory where they were forced to wait indefinitely for the resolution of problems that required landlord intercession. Absenteeism was an exceedingly common phenomenon among wealthy landowners.[76] For example, in an analysis of three districts in the province of Saratov, historian Peter Kolchin discovered that almost 70 percent of estate owners with fewer than twenty serfs did not live on their rural property.[77] According to Priscilla R. Roosevelt, many estates were like "isolated islands in a rural vastness," where few landlords would have wished to spend a long, monotonous winter.[78] In St. Petersburg, Nekrasov's readers may have been members of the absentee landowning families he critiqued.

"A Forgotten Village" exposed many of serfdom's hardships and injustices to nineteenth-century audiences and placed blame squarely on neglectful landlords. But Nekrasov most forcefully condemned bonded labor in the poem "On the Volga" (1860), which described Russia's *burlaki* (barge haulers). Drawing from memories of his childhood home in Greshnevo, a village located just seven kilometers from the Volga River, where he watched the *burlaki* at work, Nekrasov painted a vivid portrait that both presaged and rivaled Il'ia Repin's famous painting *Barge Haulers on the Volga* (1870–1873).[79] The poem's narrator recalls: "Suddenly, I heard groans, / and my gaze fell upon the shore / . . . / [where] along the river / a crowd of barge haulers crawled."[80] Their lamentations pierce the stillness of the countryside; the narrator hears "their unbearably wild / and terribly clear . . . rhythmic funereal cry / and [his] heart trembled within."[81] Here, Nekrasov refers to the work chants of the Volga *burlaki* that they sang as they performed the loathsome task of hauling barges upriver while harnessed together in a unit called an *artel'*.[82] In unison, these peasants, forced into gang labor by their abject poverty, performed a fearsome, backbreaking task that sapped their strength and will to live. Later in the poem, the narrator approaches the workers and converses with them, an event that permanently impresses on him the reality of their absolute misery. He recalls the image of one dejected man wearing rags, in "wretched poverty / bleary face / and, expressing reproach, / a quiet, hopeless gaze."[83] Ultimately, the narrator is transformed by his encounter, describing in the poem's conclusion how "bitterly, bitterly, [he] wept / when in the morning [he] stood / on the shore of his native river / and for the first time called her / River of Slavery and Anguish."[84] Nekrasov's observation of the Volga barge haulers left a lasting impression on his psyche, one that compelled him to transform images into words that would haunt Russian readers.

Nineteenth-century critics generally praised the ways in which Nekrasov, known in his day as the "poet of revenge and sorrow," represented the peasantry in verse.[85] One biographer commented that Nekrasov's poetry "exhibited a love for the folk with genuine power" and compared him to Turgenev, who also "knew the peasantry and loved them."[86] But, he claimed, there were important differences between writers like Turgenev and Nekrasov who portrayed the peasantry in fiction or verse and others who applied a more ethnographic or experiential approach. The critic contended that, while Turgenev "watched the peasantry from the position of a landowner-hunter" and Nekrasov's poetry was also the "*notes of a hunter*," for the latter author much about the peasantry remained "unknown and unrevealed, and therefore he rarely saw in them falseness."[87] The reviewer concluded that this distinction accounted for the inherently literary quality of Nekrasov's peasant representations.[88] But Nekrasov's apparent disregard for the peasantry's flaws did not diminish the widespread appeal of his poetry; rather, audiences appreciated his sentient representations of the serfs who were hitherto largely depicted as the mere property of the nobility. Indeed, as an early twentieth-century critic later reflected, Nekrasov's most important literary contribution during the 1840s and 1850s was his ability "to tear away the cloak of idealization relating to landlord-estate life."[89]

On his deathbed, Nekrasov was deemed Russia's "favorite contemporary poet," a title he earned after producing myriad verses that lamented the social conditions that peasants endured as a result of serfdom and its vestiges.[90] Masses of people joined his funeral procession on December 30, 1878, when his coffin was transported from his St. Petersburg apartment to the Novodevich'e cemetery.[91] *Vsemirnaia illiustratsiia* reported the impressive event, recounting how "representatives of the sciences, literature, journalism, many young people, pupils from not only institutions of higher education but also gymnasiums, civilian and military schools" attended.[92] Those who led the procession sang plaintive melodies, while followers carried "enormous laurel wreaths" bearing inscriptions like "Singer of the people's suffering," "Immortal voice of the *narod*," and "Glory to the sympathizer of the people's misery."[93] After the coffin arrived at the church, university professor

M. P. Gorchakov delivered a eulogy that characterized Nekrasov as the "poet of the folk" who voiced "the feelings of anguish and the thoughts of the Russian *narod,* connected by his strong hope and robust faith in veracity, goodness, and truth."[94] Judging by the public response to his death, Gorchakov's words captured the prevailing spirit of the day among Nekrasov's mourners. Through his stirring poetry, Nekrasov evoked in readers both pity for the downtrodden serfs during the years leading to emancipation and pride in the peasantry's folk culture that would later begin to represent Russia's national heritage.

Martha Griffith Browne's *Autobiography of a Female Slave* (1857)

The United States possessed no national poet of slavery comparable to Nikolai Nekrasov, but Northern citizens learned about enslaved African Americans' experiences on Southern farms and plantations during the years preceding the Civil War from newspapers, autobiographical slave narratives, and fictional literature. Abolitionists like Frederick Douglass, William Lloyd Garrison, and Maria Weston Chapman founded newspapers and annuals containing articles, essays, and literature about slavery and emancipation that reached thousands of readers.[95] Kimberley Lystar has argued, however, that slave narratives targeting white, middle-class Northern readers were "the most important factor in the growth of the abolition movement."[96] Formerly enslaved African Americans often worked with abolitionist editors, who transcribed their statements and helped create gripping stories that partially reflected slaves' historical experiences.[97] Sold as pamphlets for twenty-five cents apiece or in bound form for approximately one dollar, thousands of narratives flooded the market in response to steadily increasing consumer demand during the 1840s and 1850s.[98] Fictional literature, particularly works that employed sentimental rhetoric to appeal to readers' emotions, also played an important role in eliciting sympathy in audiences and encouraging them to join the fight to abolish slavery.[99] According to the *National Anti-Slavery Standard,* the category of abolitionist literature exploded in the early 1850s; the newspaper enthusiastically proclaimed, "A few years ago there was no antislavery literature. . . . Now, every publisher and every press pours out antislavery books of every form and description, lectures, novels, tracts, and biographies."[100] As the volume of abolitionist literature grew, however, slavery's advocates fought back in an impassioned battle to shape popular opinion.

Proslavery Southerners expressly feared the potential impact of Northern antislavery literature. At the Commercial Convention of the Southern States, held in Memphis in 1853, a resolution was adopted that championed "the encouragement of a home press" and "the publication of books adapted to the educational wants and social conditions of the States," particularly those that supported what the *New Englander* called a new "slave literature."[101] According to the New Haven–based journal, Southerners hoped to counter Northern abolitionists through the promotion of writing in which "the praises not of Freedom, but of Slavery, are to be sung; the heroic deeds, not of the valiant liberator of nations, but of the successful slave master of a Negro plantation, to be celebrated; the triumphs . . . of him who has most bravely defended the cause of Slavery before the tribunal of the world, to be recorded."[102] Although the proponents of this resolution did not succeed in their task of creating a slave literature that surpassed that of the North in popularity during the pre-emancipation era, their words indicate that they recognized literature's power to influence popular attitudes about the possibility of national emancipation.

Fictional slave narratives competed with autobiographical slave narratives as sources of information for readers who knew little about slavery. These unique publications have been largely ignored by scholars of fictional antislavery literature who typically have focused on best-selling novels like Stowe's *Uncle Tom's Cabin*. Nonetheless, these stories are worthy of attention because they reveal the ways in which nonslave authors envisaged the experience of slavery or chose to portray it to audiences whom they hoped would support the abolitionist cause. A handful of authors, primarily those who despised slavery, crafted imaginary accounts of life in bondage during the pre-emancipation era.[103] Some writers even attempted to pass off their narratives as authentic to avoid being accused of distorting the facts by defenders of slavery.[104]

Examples of antebellum fictional slave narratives include Richard Hildreth's *The Slave, or Memoirs of Archy Moore*, two volumes (1836); Jabez Delano Hammond's *Life and Opinion of Julius Melbourn* (1847); Peter Neilson's *Life and Adventures of Zamba, an African Negro King* (1847); Emily Catharine Pierson's *Jamie Parker, the Fugitive* (1851); and Martha Griffith Browne's *Autobiography of a Female Slave* (1857). Browne serves as an example of an author who sought to promote the abolitionist cause through a fictional narrative disguised as a truthful account of a woman's enslavement. Although Browne's initial effort to fool reviewers was short-lived, readers continued to be deeply affected by her realistic story after her identity was disclosed. Even twentieth- and twenty-first-century scholars have mistakenly assumed that Browne's realistic work is an authentic slave narrative.[105]

Like the Russian poet Nekrasov, Browne was the child of a planter and an opponent of bonded labor. A native of Kentucky, she inherited six enslaved African Americans from her father after his death.[106] Desiring to liberate her human property in the 1850s but lacking the funds to support them in freedom, she decided to write her fictional narrative.[107] According to a biographical newspaper article written by the prominent abolitionist Lydia Maria Child in 1862, Browne was a "generous young soul [who] was filled with such deep abhorrence of slavery."[108] In a letter to Child, Browne described the joy she felt on the day she liberated her enslaved laborers, recounting that "it was a blissful moment" for her when she "placed the deeds of manumission in their hands" and that she did not "expect to experience such a thrill of happiness again."[109] As a white Southerner, Browne appears to have held progressive views for her day regarding emancipation and racial equality. For instance, Child reported that, in their correspondence, Browne "marvel[ed] at Northern apathy concerning an institution [slavery] whose baneful effects extend[ed] to everybody and everything connected to it."[110] Furthermore, Browne thought it absurd that a free African American "should be robbed of his wages on account of a black skin," as unjust an action as if it had been "on account of black eyes or black hair," and lamented that "Northern minds [were] generally so slow to recognize this principle."[111] Such perspectives were highly unusual for a Southern slaveholder, but Child was quick to point out that Browne's compassion for African Americans was born from experience. Browne's "moral sense received no aid from abolitionists," Child avowed, and she "manifested sympathy with the slaves from her very childhood."[112]

Browne's concern for enslaved African Americans is evident in her sensitive portrayal of a female slave named Ann, the heroine of *Autobiography of a Female Slave*.[113] While most nineteenth-century slave narratives were composed by men during the first half of the nineteenth century, *Autobiography* illuminated particular aspects of bondage that were unique to enslaved women.[114] Browne writes from the perspective of Ann, a woman who claims that her story is "the truthful autobiography of one who has suffered long, long, the pains and trials of slavery."[115] She introduces herself to readers as the daughter of a white man and "a very bright mulatto woman" from one of Kentucky's southern counties.[116] As a child, Ann is sold to Mr. Peterkin, a vicious slave owner who uses violence as his preferred means of coercion. While living on his estate, she endures a beating that brings her to the point of death, narrowly avoids being raped by a white slave trader, and witnesses the separation of families through the sale of an enslaved female wrongly accused of theft. Ann's fortunes take a turn for the worse when she moves to Louisville with one of her white mistresses. There, she is imprisoned and sentenced to receive two hundred lashes after defending herself from the sexual advances of a white man. After Ann is sold again to a new owner, she experiences additional tragedies including the suicide of her fiancé and the death of her enslaved mother from physical abuse. Although Ann is ultimately liberated by her new mistress, she concludes her tale by lamenting that she "had out-lived all for which money and freedom were valuable, and . . . cared not how the remainder of [her] days were spent."[117]

Browne's *Autobiography* purported to be an authentic tale in several respects: its title, its first-person narrative style, the tracing of the author's lineage, and the narrator's decision to geographically ground the story. Like many contemporaneous antebellum slave narratives, *Autobiography of a Female Slave* also contained a plot structure, language, and imagery that were familiar to nineteenth-century readers. Scholar Laura Browder argues that abolitionists helped create a "formula for slave autobiographies" evidenced by "styles that typically make up" such accounts, including "the documentary, the sentimental novel, the account of pornographic violence, and the testimony of Christian redemption."[118] Browne followed many of these conventions through her use of emotional language, descriptions of abuse inflicted by slave owners, and the narrator's pronouncements of faith.[119]

Her style was so persuasive that several publications did not immediately identify it as a fictional work. In November 1856, the *Liberator* published the first newspaper review of *Autobiography*, stating that it could not "even surmise the name of its author," while the *New York Evangelist* speculated in December 1856, "Though this book bears the title of an Autobiography, it has evidently been put into shape by a more skillful hand than that of the African bondwoman, whose sorrows and sufferings it records."[120] By January 1857, however, Browne's true identity as a Southern slave owner from Kentucky was revealed to readers through a new review published by the *Liberator*.[121]

Although *Autobiography* was a work of fiction, readers still found themselves captivated by the novel's compassionate depiction of the life of an enslaved African American woman. Browne employed several literary strategies to achieve this goal. First, she constructed and dismantled stereotypes about African Americans through her humanization of enslaved characters in order to challenge readers' negative perceptions. For instance, the slave owner Mr. Peterkin voices the argument, familiar to many during the mid-nineteenth century, that African Americans were inherently inferior to white Americans. When discussing the topic with his son and a doctor, Mr. Peterkin asserts, "Niggers was made to be slaves, and yer kan't change their Creator's design. . . . [A] nigger's mind is never half as good as a white man's."[122] Mr. Peterkin's claims echoed those of Richard Colfax, an early nineteenth-century author whose pamphlet *Evidence against the Views of Abolitionists, Consisting of Physical and Moral Proofs of the Natural Inferiority of the Negroes* (1833) articulated the notion that whites constituted a superior race.[123] Believing that racial characteristics were fixed, many nineteenth-century Americans reasoned that it was unnecessary to abolish slavery and acceptable to deny free African Americans opportunities. Browne, however, through the voice of Ann, criticized Americans in positions of power for adhering to this viewpoint. Reflecting on African Americans' position in society, she declares to the reader: "How unjust it is for the proud statesman . . . prouder of his snowy complexion than of his stores of knowledge . . . to assert, in the halls of legislation, that the colored race are to the white far inferior in native mind!"[124]

To further advance this argument, Browne created African American characters whose efforts to receive an education and whose desire to live as free citizens countered nineteenth-century stereotypes about African Americans' intellectual abilities. For instance, Ann read textbooks and novels in secret as a young enslaved girl, and when she traveled to Boston for the first time as a free woman, she recounted meeting African Americans who were "finely educated, in the possession of princely talents, occupying good positions, wielding a powerful political influence, and illustrating, in their lives, the oft-disputed fact, that the African intellect is equal to the Caucasian."[125] Moreover, while in bondage, Ann constantly expresses her hope of being freed from slavery, describing the prospect of liberty as "a star shining through the clouds" and remarking how liberty enabled one to have the "power and privilege to go whithersoever [one] choose[s], with no cowardly fear . . . not shrink and cower before the white man's look, as we poor slaves must do."[126]

Browne also sought to humanize African Americans by showing their emotional responses to difficult situations. Some advocates of slavery sought to justify enslavement by positing that enslaved African Americans were unfeeling creatures no different from chattel, a view Ann articulates and rejects when she challenges the reader: "Why are we not all coarse and hard, mere human beasts of burden, with no higher mental or moral conception, than obedience to the will or caprice of our owners?"[127] Browne demonstrates enslaved people's capacity to feel pain by depicting several instances when families are torn asunder by traders. As a child, Ann witnesses her mother's grief when she herself is sold, recounting how the poor woman "gave full vent to her feelings in a long, loud, piteous wail . . . [giving a] cry of grief, that knell of a breaking heart, [that] rang in [her] ears for many long and painful days."[128] In addition, Browne depicts Ann as experiencing pain from physical abuse in a scene akin to that in Nekrasov's untitled poem about the female serf in Haymarket Square. As a young girl, Ann is beaten by Mr. Peterkin until her brain "burned and ached" and "tears and blood bathed [her] face and blinded [her] sight."[129] As an adult, she receives two hundred lashes "upon [her] bare back, each lacerating it to the bone," for resisting the sexual advances of a white man.[130] Browne's vivid descriptions of Ann's whippings and her anguished reaction to these abuses showed readers that enslaved people felt deeply the brutalities often inflicted by white men.

Finally, Browne urged readers to view African Americans through "colorblind" eyes, a radical rhetorical request in an era dominated by discussions about the science of racial difference.[131] According to historian Mark Smith, white Southerners of the mid-nineteenth century perceived race as an inherent trait identifiable not only through sight but also through a variety of senses. He argues that slaveholders in particular believed "blacks could always be spotted . . . in terms of smell, sound, taste, and touch."[132] Surprisingly, Browne uses the characters' dialogue to introduce to readers what is now thought of as a postmodern idea: that race is a social construction.[133] For instance, the enslaved woman Polly remarks to Ann, "If dey would cut my finger and cut a white woman's, dey would find de blood ob de very same color," a statement to which Ann responds, "There is a God above, who disregards color."[134] Although proponents of slavery historically referenced the Old Testament of the Bible to justify bondage, Ann drew from Christianity's egalitarian elements to encourage readers to view African Americans anew.[135]

Through her fictional narrative, Martha Griffith Browne inspired in readers both empathy and a desire to alleviate enslaved people's suffering. Adopting the persona of a female slave, she sought to convey to readers the privations and adversities enslaved African American women endured, providing graphic, vivid descriptions that added new meaning to the style of literary realism similarly employed by Nekrasov in his poetry. But her fiction was not merely informative; it also served as a public call to action, for, as the *National Era* pronounced in its review of her work, "while sympathy at a distance may be well, self-denying devotion and love, in relieving the wretched, in the midst of the darkness and the danger, is still better."[136]

Aleksei Pisemskii's *A Bitter Fate* (1859)

Two years after the publication of *Autobiography of a Female Slave*, tensions grew in Russia as a handful of nobles and bureaucrats quietly negotiated the details of a manifesto that would liberate 40 percent of the Russian Empire's population. Although educated Russians were unable to debate publicly the merits or disadvantages of serfdom with complete freedom, literature served as a venue for veiled discussion of the most pressing political questions of the day. During the 1840s, liberal members of the Russian intelligentsia, sometimes called "Westernizers," advocated for the abolition of serfdom and Russia's modernization in "thick journals." These "men of the forties" sparred with the Slavophiles, intellectuals who, by contrast, encouraged reform that adapted Russia's historical institutions for use in the modern era. Men including Vissarion Belinskii promoted authors like Turgenev and Nekrasov, whose *Notes of a Hunter* and realistic poetry shaped Russians' views of serfdom through their moderate depictions of serfs as a reasoning, emotional people with whom the nobility ought to sympathize. But nonpeasant audiences were unprepared for Pisemskii's groundbreaking play *A Bitter Fate* (1859), which portrayed a landowner who treated his serf as his equal in a loving relationship that transcended the class boundaries of the era.

A Bitter Fate is the sole example of realistic Russian drama published during the nineteenth century that focused on the enserfed peasantry.[137] A dark composition that offers insight into the difficult choices confronted by serfs beholden to their landowners, *A Bitter Fate* boldly addresses subjects like infidelity, love between members of separate estates, personal honor, power, jealousy, and murder. Like Browne's *Autobiography of a Female Slave*, Pisemskii's work challenged readers to consider the deleterious effects of serfdom on peasant families and inspired them to empathize with serfs through his portrayal of the uniquely trying circumstances of bonded labor.

Born in 1821 to a serf-owning noble family living on an estate in the Kostroma Province of central Russia, Aleksei Pisemskii maintained throughout his life what biographer Charles Moser calls "an elemental coarseness of thought typical of the Russian *muzhik*, but quite unexpected in a literary figure of standing."[138] Although this trait was off-putting to many of his aristocratic peers, it indicates that he may have possessed the ability to comprehend the mentalities of the rural people among whom he lived in childhood. Pisemskii displayed great interest in literature from an early age while studying at the Kostroma gymnasium and later at Moscow University, where he read Russian works as well as French, German, and British books in translation.[139]

He also enjoyed the theater and acting.[140] After graduating, Pisemskii gained literary fame by publishing a number of short stories and articles between 1854 and 1856 in journals such as Nekrasov's *Contemporary* and *Notes from the Fatherland*.[141]

One of Pisemskii's most significant works, *A Bitter Fate* was completed over the course of 1859. The drama was initially rejected by censors due to Pisemskii's depiction of peasant violence against a landowner in its original conclusion, but he altered the ending to improve its chances of publication before resubmission.[142] Published in the *Library of Reading*, the play created an immediate sensation. In 1860, *Notes from the Fatherland* commented in its joint review of *A Bitter Fate* and Aleksandr Ostrovskii's *The Storm* (1859) that, in the previous year, "people had been compelled to discuss [these plays] at great length, and they even managed to divert the pragmatic attention of the Russian reader of current affairs."[143] Three years later, when *A Bitter Fate* appeared onstage in St. Petersburg, *Notes from the Fatherland* praised its originality, declaring that it was a "phenomenon not entirely ordinary in our stage literature."[144]

Pisemskii's new drama attracted attention and generated discussion because of its surprising plot and radical representation of the peasantry on the eve of serfdom's abolition. *A Bitter Fate* tells the story of a tragic love triangle between the serf Ananii, his wife, Lizaveta, and their owner, the landlord Cheglov-Sokovin.[145] Pisemsky was one of the first authors to use peasant dialect, a decision that contributed to the perceived authenticity of his characters.[146] Shortly after the play begins, the moralistic, hardworking Ananii returns to his village from business in St. Petersburg and learns of his wife's infidelity through her sexual relationship with their owner. To make matters worse, he discovers that Lizaveta recently gave birth to an illegitimate son. At first, she defends herself by referencing Russian landowners' tradition of asserting their right to rape female serfs, declaring, "It was not of my own will: there and then they too began to make dictates and commands, how was I to disobey?"[147] But Ananii soon realizes that the truth is more complicated: Lizaveta and Cheglov-Sokovin are in love with each other.

Over the course of the play, Lizaveta reveals that she has been unhappy during her marriage to Ananii, whom she was forced to marry at a young age. She boldly expresses her desire to leave her husband, declaring to Cheglov-Sokovin: "Let him cut me with a knife or drown me in a river, but I will either live near you or leave God's earth forever—do as you wish!"[148] In a startling move, however, Cheglov-Sokovin does not exercise his power as a landowner to separate Lizaveta from Ananii. Instead, he invites Ananii to his home to negotiate. Unable to come to an agreement with Cheglov-Sokovin or to convince Lizaveta to stay with him, Ananii does the unthinkable. In a fit of rage, he murders the innocent baby and flees the scene of the crime. According to a diary entry written by the Russian censor and former serf Aleksandr Nikitenko, *A Bitter Fate* originally concluded with Ananii's murder of his owner. But in Pisemskii's second ending, the version that was ultimately published, Ananii turns himself in to the authorities after his murder of the child, confesses his deed, and repents before God. In the play's final scene, before he is sent to prison, Ananii implores his peers: "Once again I bow to the earth: Although I am accursed, do not think badly of me and pray for my sinful soul!"[149]

Journalistic and authorial reviews attest to Russian readers' differing responses to the way in which Pisemskii represented the peasantry in *A Bitter Fate*. Several critics praised Pisemskii for what they believed were his accurate representations of serf life; for example, journalist Ivan Vasil'evich Pavlov, whom Pisemskii deemed "one of our first connoisseurs of our peasantry," reportedly gave a "complimentary review of *A Bitter Fate*" to Turgenev, for which Pisemskii was very grateful.[150] In addition, the journal *Notes from the Fatherland* described *A Bitter Fate* as a play that "deserved full attention" not only for its artistic merits but also, "most importantly, for its content."[151] The reviewer approved of the plot's historical nature, set during the era of serfdom, and applauded Pisemskii for "taking and displaying with strength . . . all that is tragic in this way of life, which attests to the talent of the author."[152]

Through its portrayal of the complex relationship between landowners and serfs, Pisemskii's gripping play made three significant literary contributions. First, Pisemskii revealed to readers the unique challenges that female serfs endured within the framework of a restrictive patriarchal system in which they were required to obey their husbands and their landlords.[153] Lizaveta is a powerless character whose fate is determined by the men around her. As an impoverished orphan with no security, Lizaveta recounts how she was coerced into marrying Ananii, describing how she was "carried away in some kind of bridal sleigh as if enchained," an event that made her feel as if she was being "buried into the ground alive."[154] In mid-nineteenth-century Russia, forced marriages were not uncommon for female serfs; frequently, landowners compelled them to wed at a young age or even selected their marriage partners.[155] Historian Christine Worobec contends in her study of post-emancipation Russia that infidelity was considered less acceptable for women than for men, particularly those who spent long periods of time away from their villages.[156] Although male peasants like Ananii could be expected to have extramarital trysts while away on business, women like Lizaveta were required to remain faithful to their husbands during their absence.

After facing the sexual advances of her owner, Lizaveta alone suffered the consequences of their liaison by giving birth to his child. The physical presence of a baby exposed her clandestine actions to those around her, provoking scorn from her neighbors and outraging Ananii upon his return. At the mercy of her husband, she fully submits to him, confessing, "My head . . . lies on the block: If you want to, chop it off, or, if you wish, have mercy upon me."[157] Ananii warns her that she "hasn't yet been beaten or tortured, though [she] deserves it," the milder of several threats that Ananii does not act on but which reminded nineteenth-century readers of the fact that wife-beating was a regular occurrence in pre-emancipation rural Russia.[158] Tired of living under Ananii's rule and afraid of his temper, Lizaveta decides to run away with her child. But her bold moment of courage pushes Ananii to his breaking point, and he consequently murders the child in a fit of rage. Lizaveta loses her mind with grief, her life ruined because she sought to break free from marital captivity. Like Browne's depiction of an enslaved woman who faced challenges including attempted sexual abuse, Pisemskii's representation of a subjugated peasant woman represented the many female serfs whose choices were similarly constrained by powerful landlords, oppressive husbands, and strict village standards regarding female behavior.

Second, through his portrayal of the troubled Ananii, Pisemskii showed readers that male serfs also encountered great difficulties and could display admirable characteristics in the face of adversity. Ananii's personal qualities of reliability, honesty, and faithfulness set him apart from what readers considered to be the stereotypical serf, whom Cheglov-Sokovin's bailiff describes as "some kind of peasant, a scoundrel, a drunkard, [who] has come from Peter without his cross."[159] By contrast, Ananii is a faithful Russian Orthodox believer who refuses to drink and works for months on end in St. Petersburg, returning home with luxurious goods for Lizaveta that are impossible to find in his rural village. Upon learning of his wife's unfaithfulness, Ananii laments that he often thought about Lizaveta during his time in the city, where he, too, might have engaged in unsavory activities. Instead, he explains to his wife, "I didn't want to pay attention to such business, remembering that I am a family man and a Christian."[160] Ananii's sense of honor and affection for his wife prevented him from breaking his marital vows.

The reader might also have been able to sympathize with Ananii's position as a serf who was largely powerless to prevent his owner from seducing his wife. A landlord's rape of his female peasants was not an uncommon occurrence in nineteenth-century Russia, but such actions were neither openly discussed nor portrayed in a negative light in nineteenth-century literature. Thus, it is especially notable that Pisemskii subtly condemns such behavior on the part of the nobility in his play. For instance, he portrays sexual relations between landowners and their female serfs as perennial in a conversation between an old peasant and Cheglov-Sokovin's bailiff, who reminds his compatriot: "We are now serving our third master; we, too, have seen a great deal in our era: think of the deceased . . . Aleksei Grigor'ich, [who], if only concerning the female sex, was the very same in all that occurred. . . . And in your family there were many of these happenings . . . you haven't yet forgotten that, I suppose."[161] Furthermore, Ananii responds in a remarkable way to his owner's attempts to rectify his behavior by paying him off. The serf rejects Cheglov-Sokovin's proposal, replying, "Sir, although I am a simple peasant . . . I have never sold my honor for any sum of money, great or small."[162]

Throughout the play, Ananii appears to be a self-respecting man whose sense of morality and personal honor surpass that of his owner, a radical representation of a male serf in 1859. Even after Ananii murders Lizaveta's child, when the reader is inclined to view his character with condemnation, Ananii quickly admits his deed to the police, begs his peers for forgiveness, and goes to jail without resisting arrest. As a result, Pisemskii's protagonist appears as a morally complicated serf for whom the reader feels a degree of pity despite the horrendous crime he commits. But while Pisemskii's portrayal may have evoked compassion for serfs in some critics, those inclined to idealize the peasantry could not forgive Pisemskii for depicting Ananii in such a negative light. For instance, Slavophile Konstantin Aksakov could not stomach a plot in which a peasant murdered a child, declaring in his review that "it was difficult to imagine a more unpleasant and even offensive impression than what [he felt] while reading this play."[163] He perceived Pisemskii's portrayal of Ananii's crime and subsequent repentance as implausible and unnatural, contending that the author did not possess the abilities required to "portray any moral person, and least of all, the Russian peasant."[164] Writing for the *Contemporary*, author Mikhail Saltykov-Shchedrin similarly disagreed with Pisemskii's attempt to portray "folk types," declaring that his representation of the Russian peasant brought to mind the following words: "A boor, a braggart, an idiot, and a drunkard."[165] Like Aksakov, a man with whom he diverged politically, he felt deeply offended reading the play, explaining that his "sense of decency [was] trampled to such a point, that it is even possible to think that the author himself is somewhat sorry."[166] These negative reviews demonstrate that Pisemskii undertook an exceedingly difficult task by portraying the Russian peasant as a figure possessing deep moral flaws. Although these two critics seem to have been repulsed by Ananii's actions and personal traits, Ananii's character possessed admirable qualities as well, making him one of the most developed representations of the Russian peasant at the time. Ultimately, Saltykov-Shchedrin's and Aksakov's censures reveal the extent to which proponents and opponents of serfdom alike recognized fictional representations' ability to shape public opinion of the peasantry.

Pisemskii's third and most important literary contribution to the debate about the morality and viability of serfdom was his subtle denunciation of several prevailing stereotypes of the peasantry, a strategy that Browne also employed to combat contemporaneous perceptions of enslaved African Americans. Like Browne, Pisemskii confronted planters' perspectives that Russian serfs were akin to animals through the dehumanizing dialogue that occurred between the landlord Cheglov-Sokovin, his bailiff, and his brother-in-law, a member of the landed gentry. The coldhearted bailiff asserts, "Our people are crude and backward," laughing at how "they are imagined as bears," as "they walk to work, but run home afterward."[167] In a separate scene, Cheglov-Sokovin's brother-in-law, Zolotilov, describes female serfs in unflattering terms that reveal his disdain for inter-estate sexual relations. He claims that a peasant woman is "a woodblock": "Even if you behave passionately toward her, she will calmly pick at a mossy wall the entire time. . . . Isn't it like falling in love with a half-animal?"[168] The viewpoints of these gentlemen do not reflect those of Pisemskii, who created emotionally complex female characters that defied such rudimentary characterizations. Instead, the author encouraged readers to view the peasantry through Cheglov-Sokovin's eyes rather than through the eyes of his odious bailiff and brother-in-law.

Pisemskii's challenge to readers was a radical one, because Cheglov-Sokovin may be the first landowner in Russian literature who purports to be "estate-blind" in his treatment of the peasantry. In a remarkable conversation reminiscent of the white planter John's speech to Ann, Cheglov-Sokovin explains to Lizaveta that it matters not to him "whether [she is] a noble lady, a serf, a merchant woman, or a duchess" and that these categories are equivalent to him in terms of how he loves her.[169] The landlord even treats Lizaveta's powerless husband, his own serf Ananii, with great respect. While negotiating Lizaveta's fate, Cheglov-Sokovin tells Ananii, "Forget that I am your master, and be completely honest with me."[170] These events demonstrate Cheglov-Sokovin's remarkably progressive attitude toward owner-serf relations and likely shocked proponents of serfdom and an estate system that strictly enforced a social hierarchy in which the peasantry existed on a level far beneath that of the gentry. Cheglov-Sokovin's liberal nature even unnerved the satirist Saltykov-Shchedrin, who bestowed on him the title of a "weak-foolish-liberal-drunk landlord," but who speculated that, had Cheglov-Sokovin "lived to see the abolition of serfdom, then perhaps he would have been a mediator and surprised Russia with his humanity."[171] Ultimately, *A Bitter Fate* exposed educated elites like Saltykov-Shchedrin to a radically new way of thinking about the peasantry and their relationships with the landowning nobility on the eve of serfdom's abolition.

Louisa May Alcott's Short Stories

In the United States, slavery's future could not be resolved through the war of words between Northern abolitionists and proslavery Southerners. Fighting broke out between the Union and the newly formed Confederacy in April 1861, but the first concrete step in the process of liberation was President Abraham Lincoln's issuance of the preliminary Emancipation Proclamation on September 22, 1862.[172] Part "act of justice," part "military necessity," this sweeping document declared that enslaved men and women living in Confederate territory were free.[173] Furthermore, Lincoln promised those who escaped from slavery the protection of the Union army, which he commanded to "recognize and maintain the freedom of such persons."[174]

During the Civil War, Northern authors and artists produced new images of African Americans that ranged from escaped slaves who reached Union army camps to soldiers who enlisted in the Union army. Prior to the issuance of the Emancipation Proclamation, enslaved African Americans who entered federal camps were popularly known as "contraband," or former enemy property that now legally belonged to the U.S. government.[175] Caught halfway between bondage and freedom in a sort of wartime limbo, these runaway enslaved people were the subject of numerous paintings, articles, and short stories between 1861 and 1865. Representations of African American soldiers wearing Union blue also generated significant public interest. These depictions of dignified black soldiers fighting to defend the United States and to secure the freedom of their brethren who remained in the Confederate South contrasted sharply with those of oppressed, enslaved African Americans that commonly appeared in autobiographical narratives and the fictional literature of Stowe, Browne, and others just years before.

Louisa May Alcott was one of the first writers to portray African Americans as soldiers and as wartime "contraband" in literature. Once called America's "Hans Christian Andersen," Alcott is best known for broadly appealing children's books like *Little Women* and *Little Men*.[176] Her significant literary contributions to the abolitionist cause, however, are less well known. A fervent abolitionist, Alcott not only advocated emancipation in her fiction but also depicted romantic, loving relationships between black and white characters in stories that Sarah Elbert calls "Alcott's boldest statements for human rights."[177]

Born to a progressive family in Germantown, Pennsylvania, in 1832, Alcott became an author who, according to one late nineteenth-century biographer, "scattered among a million of readers . . . the nearly one hundred and fifty thousand volumes of her writings" during her lifetime.[178] She received fan mail from as far away as St. Petersburg, Russia, and Honolulu, Hawai'i, a testament to the reach of her accessible, appealing writing style.[179] Alcott and her family lived through a tumultuous era of American history and witnessed, one newspaper recounted, the "assassination of Lincoln [and] the emancipation of slaves and serfs in America, Russia, and Brazil," events that "marked the period indelibly on the memory of mankind."[180] But Alcott was no bystander to history; rather, she participated in the Civil War by serving as a nurse in Washington, D.C., and sought to shape public opinion toward enslaved African Americans and freedpeople through short stories like "M.L." and "My Contraband."

Alcott's compassion for African Americans and desire to improve the world around her largely stemmed from her upbringing in Concord, Massachusetts, a town frequented by antislavery advocates including John Brown and Harriet Tubman. The Alcott family participated in abolitionist activities during the 1850s; her father, Bronson, a founder of the Transcendentalist movement, fought against the Fugitive Slave Law by attempting to free imprisoned runaway slaves, and the family sought to fund Brown's attack on Harper's Ferry.[181] As an adult, Alcott recalled that she "became an Abolitionist at an early age" and that her "greatest pride" was "in the fact that [she] lived to know the brave men and women who did so much for the cause, and that [she] had a very small share in the war which put an end to a great wrong."[182] Not content to merely observe the deeds of others, Alcott contributed to the antislavery movement through the publication of groundbreaking short stories featuring African Americans and to the Union war effort as a nurse.[183]

One of Alcott's most radical short stories is "M.L." (1863), a fictional account of an interracial romance between Paul, a formerly enslaved man, and Claudia, a white woman from New Orleans.[184] Written in 1860, just one year after Pisemskii published *A Bitter Fate*, "M.L." shares with the Russian drama a plot that centers on forbidden love between two people from separate worlds. But while Pisemskii saw no future for the serf Lizaveta and her owner Cheglov-Sokovin, Alcott depicts a couple determined to overcome the social condemnation of their interracial marriage, a prejudice that she calls "a sterner autocrat than the Czar of all the Russias."[185] When Claudia first meets Paul, she does not realize that he was once enslaved in Cuba. In fact, Alcott depicts Paul as displaying all the characteristics of a "pale-faced gentleman" who was "devoted to his books and art," made "experience his tutor," and was, in sum, "a man to command respect and confidence and love."[186] Little distinguishes Paul from the other men in Southern society, and Claudia, admiring his many positive traits, falls in love.

Halfway through the short story, however, Paul's identity as a formerly enslaved man is suddenly exposed by one of his enemies. In his revelation to Claudia about his past, Paul explains that although he "tried to become a chattel and be content," his father "had given [him] his own free instincts, aspirations, and desires," and he was unable to "change [his] nature though [he was] to be a slave forever."[187] In this scene, Alcott emphasizes Paul's sentience during the five-year period of his life in slavery in order to disprove the nineteenth-century belief that enslaved people were akin to animals, a strategy similarly employed by Browne in *Autobiography of a Female Slave*. But Alcott's representation of slavery contrasts with that of her predecessor in a critical way. While abolitionists like Browne highlighted the misery of slavery through descriptions of physical abuse, Alcott stresses that the experience of enslavement positively shaped Paul's character. For example, Paul refuses to see himself as a victim; instead, he explains to Claudia, "God knows they were bitter things to bear, but I am stronger for them now."[188] When finally emancipated, Paul claims, "I took the rights and duties of a man upon me, feeling their weight and worth, looking proudly on them as a sacred trust won by much suffering, to be used worthily and restored to their bestower richer for my stewardship."[189] Thus, Paul is a figure who focuses on future opportunities rather than on past hardships. His strength of character deeply impresses Claudia, who agrees to marry the formerly enslaved man and to stand by him forever.

Alcott's taboo romance was rejected by the *Atlantic* in 1860, perhaps because of her endorsement of interracial marriage, but it was ultimately published in the antislavery weekly the *Commonwealth* in early 1863.[190] About two years after Alcott drafted "M.L.," she decided to support the Union cause by serving as a nurse at the Union Hotel Hospital in Georgetown. When Alcott arrived in Washington, D.C., in December 1862, she was surprised by the intensity of her new position, recording the following January that she "never began the year in a stranger place . . . alone among strangers, doing painful duties all day long" and "surrounded by 3 or 4 hundred men in all stages of suffering, disease, and death."[191] Nonetheless, she threw herself into her work by dressing wounds, distributing food, cleaning, and writing letters on behalf of the injured soldiers.[192] In fact, she worked so hard that she took ill; as one late nineteenth-century biographer recorded, Alcott was "a veritable Florence Nightingale for courage, tenderness, and helpfulness . . . blessing scores of dying beds with her presence, and laboring until she herself was stricken down with fever."[193]

Severely ill with typhoid fever, Alcott was forced to return to her family's home in Concord, where she recovered over the course of several months. Her wartime experiences remained fresh in her mind, however, and she turned them into a short story called "Hospital Sketches," for which she earned $200.[194] Written from the perspective of "Tribulation Periwinkle," the realistic, albeit sentimental tale was largely based on the time Alcott spent working at the Union Hotel Hospital. After completing "Hospital Sketches," Alcott was told that she had finally discovered her "natural style, 'the blending of the comic & pathetic, & happy description of common things with the under current of sentiment which lends romance.'"[195] Americans were eager to read literature that depicted Civil War soldiers, battles, and other events and they devoured her work. In fact, the public response to "Hospital Sketches" was so great that publisher James Redpath decided to reprint the story in book form in August 1863.[196] Of the new book's critical reviews, Louisa's sister May recorded: "The notices so far have been very flattering and without doubt there will be a good sale for it. Her prospects were never better . . . for she has been so long unknown and yet having so much more talent, than a good many of the popular Atlantic contributors."[197] A little over a decade later, the publications *Hearth and Home* and *St. Nicholas Magazine* confirmed May's prediction, recounting that "Hospital Sketches" "became at once very popular" and "made [Alcott's] name known all over the North."[198]

Buoyed by the successful fictionalization of her nursing experiences, Alcott continued to write about topics pertaining to the Civil War in subsequent short stories and articles.[199] However, while the majority of Northern and Southern wartime literature focused on the experiences of white soldiers, Alcott countered the prevailing trend by turning her attention once again to enslaved African Americans and freedpeople.[200] Scholar Sarah Elbert contends that although Alcott's wartime correspondences do not discuss issues of race, she almost certainly met "contraband orderlies" at the Union Hotel

Hospital and mingled with people from all walks of life in the city.[201] These encounters likely inspired Alcott to produce another radical short story, an interracial romance between a formerly enslaved African American man and a white woman, titled "My Contraband."[202]

Alcott drew inspiration for "My Contraband" from her experiences in Washington, D.C., and from contemporaneous phenomena such as the increasing enlistment of African American soldiers and the growing number of enslaved people who fled to Union camps.[203] Her story describes the relationship between Robert, a black contraband, and Faith, a white nurse, but, unlike "M.L.," their attraction is a tangential event in a dark plot that revolves around the jealous relationship between two brothers of different races that recalls the fratricidal story of Cain and Abel. Serving as an orderly in Faith's hospital, Robert meets Ned, his white half-brother and former owner whose father raped Robert's mother. Ned appears to have inherited his father's proclivity for cruelty; years earlier he raped Robert's wife, an inhumane deed that motivates Robert to contemplate murdering him in retaliation. Nurse Faith convinces Robert to show mercy and chart a new path by enlisting in the Union army. While fighting bravely at Fort Wagner in the Fifty-Fourth Massachusetts, an all-black regiment, Robert is struck down by his nemesis, Ned. The former slaveholder does not remain victorious, however, because an African American soldier from Boston takes Robert's place in battle and kills him. Alcott's concluding twist, the death of a planter at the hands of a free African American man, may have unnerved white readers, particularly those from planter families who feared the prospect of a revolt by enslaved African Americans or the consequences of military defeat.

"My Contraband" shares important thematic elements with "M.L"; for instance, like Paul, Robert has not been weakened by his enslavement. Instead, Alcott describes him as a "strong-limbed and manly" person who "had the look of one who had never been cowed by abuse or worn with oppressive labor."[204] Robert also prizes his freedom highly; he explains to Faith that he refuses to take his owner's surname as his own, with a "look and gesture . . . [that] were a more effective declaration of independence than any Fourth-of-July orator could have prepared."[205] Alcott's representation of Robert as a contraband, however, is wholly unique. Comparing him to a bat in one of Aesop's fables, she writes that Robert "belonged to neither race; and the pride of one and the helplessness of the other, kept him hovering alone in the twilight."[206] Here, Alcott alludes to the slow process of integration, infrequently discussed in the fictional literature of the day, that left men like Robert in a tenuous, ambiguous position due to persistent racial prejudice. She unequivocally expressed her support for black liberation and assimilation, however, through her representations of formerly enslaved African Americans like Robert whom she depicts as serving the Union by "fighting valiantly 'for God and Governor Andrew.'"[207] As a result of such heroism, Alcott reminds readers, "the manhood of the colored race shines before many eyes that would not see, rings in many ears that would not hear, wins many hearts that would not hitherto believe."[208]

Alcott's most revolutionary appeal to readers is not merely for them to sympathize with former slaves, but to empathize with them in moments of anger. For instance, Robert is a flawed, human character who considers killing his former owner, but Alcott prompts readers to put themselves in his position and to consider his rage, asking them through Faith's internal monologue: "Why should he deny himself that sweet, yet bitter morsel called revenge? How many white men, with all New England's freedom, culture, Christianity, would not have felt as he felt then?"[209] Like Pisemskii, who invites audiences to forgive the murderous serf Ananii, Alcott urges readers to put themselves in the position of a formerly enslaved man seeking revenge and to resist condemning him for his sentiments. Her request was one of the boldest in nineteenth-century American antislavery literature.

Through their radical literary representations, Alcott, Browne, Nekrasov, and Pisemskii sought to change the ways in which their readers perceived Russian serfs and enslaved African Americans on the eve of abolition. While Nekrasov and Browne depicted bonded laborers as sentient beings in literature that inspired pro-emancipation sentiment, Pisemskii and Alcott challenged audiences to imagine the coexistence of serfs and enslaved people after abolition by portraying African Americans and peasants in sincere and loving interracial and inter-estate relationships. Through their depictions of vengeful serfs and enslaved African Americans, these authors brought even the most open-minded readers to their emotional limits by asking them to empathize with flawed characters. Ultimately, their works helped audiences envision a post-emancipation era in which the former dynamics between owners and bonded laborers were but a distant memory.

CHAPTER TWO

Popular Historical Fiction

The abolition of serfdom and slavery resulted in the liberation of Russian serfs and enslaved African Americans, but neither peasants nor freedpeople immediately acquired the full benefits of subjecthood or citizenship. After Tsar Alexander II's issuance of the Emancipation Manifesto in 1861, the peasantry reveled in their new status as emancipated subjects and expressed hopes about the rights to which they would be entitled. In a rare autobiographical account of his memories of the abolition of serfdom, the former serf E. P. Klimenov recorded in 1863 that, on hearing news of their emancipation, "brothers of the underclass shouted 'Hooray!' 'Hooray!' [while] others said, 'See here, now we will be able to run our own household,' 'Now we ourselves can marry and give away our daughters,' 'At last I will be able to conduct trade on my own!'"[1] His narrative attests to the enserfed peasants' desire to gain control of different aspects of their lives that ranged from the ability to determine their economic fate to the right to marry women of their choosing. Klimenov joyfully expressed his belief that "to everyone a lesson of mercy was given, now to every man personal rights and property rights were secured," positing that some of the peasants' most precious civil liberties related to their newfound legal status.[2] He delineated the changes he expected to see, predicting that "peasants in the midst of legal battles in courts will deal with one another judicially" and that the freed serf would be treated as "a subject of his Sovereign like all others."[3]

Some of Klimenov's predictions were realized during the postemancipation era, when additional state-initiated changes known as the Great Reforms further transformed the relationships between the different social groups that made up Russia's *soslovie* (estate system).[4] After emancipation, the tsarist government replaced the two legal systems that had governed serfs and peasants tied to state-owned land with one overarching legal code, *The Regulation of the Rural Estate*, which categorized both groups as belonging to *sel'skoe obshchestvo* (rural society).[5] The system granted the peasantry increased control over their affairs by giving additional authority to regional village communes and townships, historic peasant institutions that the authors of the manifesto hoped to preserve and adapt for the modern era.[6] When these organizations began managing to a greater extent the distribution of land and exercising their newfound ability to collect taxes, landowners likely resented their loss of power.[7] Peasants also gained new rights within the judicial system through reforms that enabled emancipated serfs to testify in court or serve as judges.[8]

At the same time, other aspects of the institutional framework of serfdom remained intact.[9] Many former serfs remained on their landlords' estates even after they legally became subjects of the Russian nation. Burdened by what one late nineteenth-century historian called "crippling" redemption payments for their liberation, the peasants found themselves "in clear ruin," unable to leave their landlords' property or to pay the state the required annual amounts.[10] By one estimate, former serfs overpaid by 40 percent the value of their land between 1861 and 1905, when the redemption payments were abolished.[11] More than a decade after emancipation, in 1873, ex-serf Aleksandr Nikitenko recorded in his diary that although "the condition of the peasants has generally been improving since emancipation . . . their mode of life is still very unsatisfactory almost everywhere in the empire," due in part to "the meagre land allotments in many provinces and the excessive, disproportionate compensation demanded for them" and to "very high taxes."[12] With peasants mired in debt and continuing to work on their former landowners' estates, it appeared to some as though serfdom persisted during the years following the tsar's issuance of the Emancipation Manifesto. Furthermore, as the former serf E. P. Klimenov acknowledged in 1863, although his fellow peasants, "with inexpressible anticipation, counted the months, days, hours until the emergence of the Manifesto of the Most Merciful," their new status as liberated peasants could not erase their shared history or the collective memory of their oppression.[13]

Like the former serfs, Russian *pomeshchiki* (landowners) also found it difficult to forget the pre-emancipation era, albeit for different reasons. The abolition of serfdom reduced their power and social stature as they slowly lost control over the peasantry and much of their land between 1861 and 1905. On the eve of emancipation, members of the nobility expressed a subdued reaction to the issuance of the Emancipation Manifesto for two reasons. First, they recognized that it was futile to resist the will of a tsar who purportedly declared to his State Council members in January 1861, "Autocracy established serfdom firmly in Russia, and it is autocracy that must end it."[14] Second, they played a role in crafting the terms of the document in order to minimize their losses. During the decades that followed emancipation, however, the nobility found themselves in an increasingly weakened position. Scholar Abraham Ascher claims that "the most striking manifestation of the nobility's decline was its loss of land," citing statistics that reveal landlords sold one-third of their arable property to merchants and peasants between 1861 and 1905.[15] Those who held on to their land faced a substantial reduction in market prices for crops during the late nineteenth century and did not adopt the modern technologies that could have increased productivity.[16] In a competitive global economy, the nobility were ineffective stewards and investors.[17] Resentful of their economic losses and reduced social status, they began producing and consuming sentimental literature that promoted a revisionist history of serfdom.

Meanwhile, in the United States, the Civil War's end brought similarly transformative changes. The ratification of the Thirteenth Amendment in 1865 nullified slave owners' claims to their human property, but freedpeople across the country remained in a precarious position because its text did not provide adequate protection of their civil rights.[18] In 1865, the federal government established the Freedmen's Bureau to help formerly enslaved African Americans navigate liberty. Chandra Manning argues that the creation of the bureau "marked a breathtaking departure" from the past as "the first U.S. government agency ever dedicated to humanitarian purposes ... [and] predicated explicitly on the assumption that a direct relationship existed between the national government and African Americans."[19] The Freedmen's Bureau provided freedpeople with material aid and sought to help African Americans negotiate new labor contracts, acquire pensions, and gain an education. But this radical institution could not fully protect them from the racism and violence that plagued the postwar South.[20]

Under Democratic president Andrew Johnson's administration, Southern states were quickly readmitted to the Union under lenient terms.[21] Upon rejoining the United States, many Southern state legislatures began to issue "black codes" that restricted freedpeople's abilities to live freely. *Harper's Weekly* described these laws as effectively "establish[ing] all of slavery but the name."[22] For example, white Southern planters "refused to sell land, so that no freedman could acquire a farm, and became of necessity a vagrant; and then the master class made vagrancy a crime, for which a man could be sold to labor," and also "denied the freedmen arms and the right of sitting upon juries."[23] The states' passage of black codes prompted the ratification of the hotly debated Fourteenth Amendment, a constitutional article that used broad, expansive language to guarantee the rights of citizenship to freedpeople through its declaration that "all persons born or naturalized in the United States, and subject to the jurisdiction thereof, are citizens of the United States and of the state wherein they reside."[24] But while the Fourteenth Amendment was intended to protect African American citizens from state-enacted injustices, it did so with limited success in subsequent decades because of Supreme Court decisions that narrowly interpreted its application.[25]

Like the Russian serfs, formerly enslaved African Americans exhibited a common yearning that Eric Foner describes as "a desire for independence from white control, for autonomy as individuals and as newly created communities, themselves being transformed by the process of emancipation."[26] As new citizens of a war-weary nation, African Americans acted on this deep-rooted impulse in profound ways. While millions of freedpeople remained on farms where they received paltry compensation as part of a new wage plantation system, thousands of others moved to rapidly growing metropolitan areas across the South.[27] One freedman, Irving E. Lowery, recalled that, on the day of his liberation in South Carolina, his white owner called together all the enslaved people to tell them of their new situation and that "their joy was unspeakable."[28] Most freedpeople remained on the plantation until January 1866, when, he recorded, "there was a breaking up, and a separation of the old plantation. Nearly all the slaves left and went out and made contracts with other landlords. A few remained for one year, and then the last one of them pulled out and made their homes elsewhere."[29] During the forty years that followed, Lowery wrote in an article titled "Current Incidents of Negro Industrial Achievements," freedpeople who had "left the old plantation with nothing—absolutely nothing" had made great strides, particularly in the acquisition of property. Lowery recorded that "the figures are almost incredible, but they are said to be based on government authority. . . . [Freedpeople] own 137,000 farms and homes, which consist of 40,000,000 acres."[30] After emancipation, African American freedpeople not only acquired farmland and other forms of private property but also formed families, established and attended schools, and ran businesses. After the ratification of the Fifteenth Amendment, which expanded the franchise to black men, African Americans ran for office and voted for political representatives. During Reconstruction, more than fifteen hundred black officeholders served as congressmen, peace officers, and sheriffs.[31] In fact, Foner argues that "black participation in Southern public life after 1867 was the most radical development of the Reconstruction years," a phenomenon that reshaped Southern politics and prompted white backlash.[32]

White Americans, particularly those residing in former Confederate states, resisted the presence of African Americans as free men and women in spheres previously restricted to whites. The freedman Henry Clay Bruce recorded that, in some instances, tensions between white and black citizens resulted from exaggerated fears about an increasingly competitive labor market. In his autobiographical narrative, he describes how "the freeing of the American slaves and their partial migration to these states, seeking employment, excited the enmity of the white laborers, particularly the Irish, because at that time they constituted fully seventy-five per cent of the laboring class, and who imagined that the influx of Negro laborers from the South, would divide the labor monopoly which they held."[33] The planter class vigorously resisted the integration of their formerly enslaved laborers in different ways. James L. Roark presents a persuasive analysis of elite white Southerners' attitudes toward freedpeople after abolition, arguing that the "master-slave relationship, with its enormous social distance and legally defined stations, allowed close contact, even intimacy, without threatening white status," but emancipation "drastically reduced the social distance between whites and blacks, prompting whites to . . . seek physical separation as a buttress to their own status."[34]

White Southerners, particularly Democrats, also opposed African Americans' efforts to exercise their right to vote. Seeking to reconsolidate their political, economic, and social power, many white Southerners supported the passage of black codes and other discriminatory laws. Some joined groups like the Ku Klux Klan, founded in 1865, which used terror and violence to intimidate or harm those who backed Republicans.[35] Congress passed the Enforcement Acts of 1870 and 1871 in an effort to weaken the Klan, but white supremacist violence continued to rage in other forms across the South during the late nineteenth century.[36]

After the Panic of 1873 and the subsequent depression, Northern whites increasingly hesitated to protect blacks' rights and prevent racial violence against them. The infamous Compromise of 1877 following the presidential election of 1876 secured for Republican candidate Rutherford B. Hayes the office of the presidency in exchange for his promise to turn a blind eye to the rise of Jim Crow in the South.[37] As president, Hayes called for the withdrawal of federal troops from Louisiana and South Carolina, two remaining Southern states where the Republican Party clung to power, which led to the Democratic Party's capture of the states houses there.[38] After Reconstruction ended in 1877, Southern states passed additional laws that further disenfranchised and segregated African Americans as part of a gradual but concerted effort that reached its zenith at century's end with the Supreme Court's endorsement of the "separate but equal" doctrine in *Plessy v. Ferguson* (1896). The outcome of this case pointed to the South's unwillingness—and the nation's—to protect freedpeople's civil rights.

These examples suggest that the post-emancipation dynamics between freedpeople and white Southerners were fraught as whites forcefully resisted African Americans' attempts to exercise their political voices and build new lives for themselves. In the North and West, many whites also felt threatened by black progress and unconfident of their position in the new post-emancipation order, a sentiment exacerbated by the arrival of millions of immigrants and the coerced assimilation of Native Americans during the late nineteenth century. Scholar Susan L. Mizruchi characterizes the postbellum era as one in which the United States realized its potential as "the first multicultural modern capitalist society," a paradoxical place in which diversity was alternately hailed and feared, because while some Americans and businesses welcomed new workers, others "aggressively manipulated racial hostility, fanning the flames of nativism, devaluing and excluding through various means blacks and ethnic others, and defending the social Darwinism that legitimated claims of Anglo-Saxon purity."[39] As in Russia, white Americans turned to literature that offered a romanticized history of slavery that seemed to justify their resistance to the assimilation of freedpeople.

Nostalgic Historical Fiction in the United States and Russia

Reflecting on the emergence of a "new Southern literature" in the *Evening Post* in 1887, journalist Walter Hines Page urged young writers to comprehend "the unique, the unsurpassably rich, [and] the infinitely adaptable materials which it is their peculiar heritage to use."[40] He argued that the South's newest generation of authors should capitalize on their unique inheritance: the experience of the Confederacy's defeat in the Civil War, its pre-emancipation "groupings of figures and races ... scenes of caste, wealth, indolence, and pride," which, with other attributes, constitute "a whole world apart—that social world of the old South—unlike all that ever went before or can ever come again!"[41] During the late nineteenth century, Thomas Nelson Page and Joel Chandler Harris fulfilled Page's request by drawing on the South's history to produce romantic stories that described idyllic antebellum plantations where white slaveholders and enslaved African Americans lived harmoniously. Together, these authors contributed to a new literary genre that celebrated what Page perceived to be the South's exceptional past.

But to what extent were the South's history and idealistic postwar literature truly unique? Historian K. Stephen Prince supports the idea of a distinctive South, arguing that it was a "social construct" that "served as a cornerstone of southern (and American) identity."[42] The idea of Southern exceptionalism was what Prince calls "a lived reality for late nineteenth- and early twentieth-century Americans," or a way of thinking that shaped Northerners' views of the South and Southerners' self-conceptions.[43] The notion of the South as a place with a distinct history and culture permeates late nineteenth-century literature and contemporary scholars' assessments of its defining characteristics. For example, historian Alan T. Nolan argues that the Lost Cause myth that pervaded the works of Page and Harris was an especially "American legend."[44] Scholar David McWhirter sees Southern literature itself as playing "a prominent role" in the promotion of the idea of Southern exceptionalism; he contends that it has shaped "successive constructions and reconstructions of 'the South,' both as a unique regional culture, and as a privileged locus . . . for understanding the broader modern U.S. culture to which it stands in tense relation."[45] Historian Laura F. Edwards similarly considers the South's position within the broader nation, concluding that "what made the South distinctive was always its comparison to somewhere else."[46]

The South's history as a region comprising slaveholding states that seceded from the Union and resisted reunification following their defeat during the Civil War is certainly rooted in time and place. Its tradition, however, of idealizing the pre-emancipation era in literature is not entirely unique because Russian landowners concurrently mourned in fiction their loss of wealth and power after the abolition of serfdom. The *pomeshchiki* differed from Southern planters as *dvorianstvo* (members of the aristocratic estate), but they shared with these Southerners the sense that they were representatives of a privileged, civilized group whose status had been diminished through emancipation. Like Harris and Page, Russian noblemen Grigorii Danilevskii, Vsevolod Solov'ev, Evgenii Opochinin, and Evgenii Salias crafted romantic tales about Russia's pre-emancipation era in which paternalistic landlords provided their cherished serfs with a high standard of living. Their nostalgic stories particularly appealed to educated, middle-class readers who had never experienced serfdom or slavery. Young Russians and Americans of the 1880s and 1890s composed a new generation of citizens too young to have witnessed firsthand the past relationships between bonded laborers and landed elites, but they were acutely aware of the new social hierarchies and identities developing around them. As a way of confronting the painful aspects of their inherited national histories, many Americans and Russians embraced the narratives embedded in fictional tales that eulogized serfdom and slavery.

An examination of a Russian nobleman's memoir illuminates the *pomeshchiki's* collective mentality during the post-emancipation era. In *Recollections:*

From Serfdom to Bolshevism (1924), Nikolai Vrangel' describes his life growing up on a rural estate in the Iamburgskii District. In many ways, Vrangel''s memoir parallels that of a white Southerner reminiscing about his childhood on his antebellum plantation. For instance, when Vrangel' describes his peasant caregiver, he employs words that recall those of a planter speaking about his African American mammy.[47] On the family property, Vrangel' remembers fondly, he "suckled at the breast of a serf nurse [and] grew up in the hands of a serf nanny [who] took the place of [his] deceased mother."[48] Although he acknowledges some of serfdom's negative attributes, Vrangel' espouses a paternalistic view of the institution, claiming that his father's serfs "lived richly" and "prospered" and that "the house servants were well dressed, well shod, and well nourished."[49] Furthermore, he laments the fact that many of his contemporaries do not know what he deems to be the truth about serfdom, condemning those who "judge it completely inaccurately, drawing conclusions not from the aggregate, but from the most extreme events about which they have learned."[50] Ultimately, Vrangel' concludes, "Life under serfdom was not sweet, but it was not as terrible as it is usually written about today."[51]

The reasons for his nostalgia for the pre-emancipation era become clearer when he describes the impact of the abolition of serfdom on his family's estate and the relations between the freed serfs and their former owners. After his graduation from college abroad, Vrangel' returned to Russia and found that his home had changed greatly. After their liberation, the youngest generation of the family's serfs "permanently departed and worked in different places," but they were supposedly unable to successfully acclimate to their new circumstances.[52] Furthermore, Vrangel' was shocked to find his family's estate in disrepair; buildings had collapsed, logs were rotting in the pond, and paths were overgrown with brush.[53] Vrangel' quizzed his father about the condition of the property, and he responded by explaining that it was "simply impossible to employ the local [peasant] laborers" because they refused to use the new mowing machine he had purchased in an effort to modernize the farm.[54] Vrangel''s description of the estate and retelling of his conversation with his father indicate that some landowners and their former serfs sustained uneasy relationships after emancipation. Vrangel' contends that, while peasants celebrated their newfound freedom, some landlords seeking to maintain productive estates, like Vrangel''s father, chafed at the peasantry's rejection of their terms of service.

Although Vrangel''s father generally supported the liberation of the peasantry, even working alongside former serfs on the district council, he shared with Vrangel' several anecdotes that further attest to the challenges of the post-emancipation era and the negative reactions of landlords following the abolition of serfdom. Vrangel''s father recounted a story about a "rich and influential landlord who was sentenced to house arrest for beating his servant," a right permitted under serfdom but forbidden during the post-emancipation era.[55] Members of the nobility resented their reduced power and a post-emancipation social order in which, as nobleman and anarchist Petr Kropotkin recorded in his memoirs, peasants had lost "all traces of servility" and "talked to their masters as equals talk to equals, as if they had never stood in different relations."[56] Some landlords, like Vrangel''s elderly neighbor who declared in a written complaint that the new order effectively "equated the serf with the nobleman," refused to accept their new social rank.[57] These aristocratic men found it difficult to cope with the new order and their diminished statuses, sentiments that help explain why many found appealing the revisionist literary accounts of the pre-emancipation era that romanticized the prior relationships between landowners and serfs.

A comparison of these cultural phenomena contributes to the fields of American and Russian history and literature in several ways. First, it illuminates hitherto unknown parallels between the strategies of authors who sought to shape national memories of slavery and serfdom through the production of popular literature. Belletrists Danilevskii, Solov'ev, Opochinin, and Salias, several of the most widely read writers in late nineteenth-century Russia, are largely unknown to Western scholars of Russian history, their biographies appearing primarily in English-language encyclopedias or surveys of Russian literature.[58] Even less is understood about the content of their short stories and the important role they played in shaping collective memories of serfdom. Second, although the post-emancipation eras in Russia and the United States differed in important ways, the evaluation of their two literary traditions identifies striking correspondences between the ways in which writers from landowning Russian and American families responded to the abolition of serfdom and slavery. Third, this comparison highlights the notable contrast between the emergences of two similar literary traditions from different historical contexts: while racist presumptions defined the late nineteenth-century United States, racial considerations were largely absent in late imperial Russia.

An analysis of Russian post-emancipation historical fiction also broadens Western scholars' understanding of the environment in which better-known fictional works were produced and received in Russia. For instance, historians are familiar with aristocrat Lev Tolstoi, the internationally acclaimed iconoclast whose idealization and personal imitation of the peasantry captivated and shocked nineteenth-century Russian readers and critics. According to biographer Rosamund Bartlett, Tolstoi was a "repentant nobleman, ashamed at his complicity in the immoral institution of serfdom," who saw "the peasants as Russia's best class, and her future."[59] He became "a member of the intelligentsia, the peculiarly Russian class of people united by their education and usually critical stance toward their government" whose views were much more extreme than those of the overall Russian population.[60] In this way, Tolstoi grew to be a politicized figure whose outlook mirrored that of the Populists of the 1870s more than the attitudes of his peers. In his historical epic *War and Peace* (1869) and novel *Anna Karenina* (1877), Tolstoi depicted the peasantry as a noble people whom aristocrats ought to emulate, a representation that did not widely resonate among the broader population. For instance, scholar A. V. Knowles describes the public's befuddled response to *War and Peace,* arguing that, among other factors, "the idealization of the peasantry . . . proved rather too much . . . for the critics to cope with."[61] Thus, while scholars of prominent Russian literary figures like Tolstoi have written about the public's general discomfort with his portrayal of the peasantry, few have discussed the less celebrated but extraordinarily popular representations of serfs in historical fiction that challenged Tolstoi's narrative. Ultimately, an analysis of the range of works that presented revisionist, idealized accounts of serfdom provides a more complete picture of the late nineteenth-century literary field in Russia.

Origins of Historical Fiction about Serfdom and Slavery

Russian authors Grigorii Danilevskii, Vsevolod Solov'ev, Evgenii Salias, and Evgenii Opochinin and Southern writers Thomas Nelson Page and Joel Chandler Harris succeeded in capturing the public's imagination through historical fiction that built on and reinterpreted older literary traditions. In Russia, the earliest works of historical fiction include Nikolai Gogol's *Taras Bulba* (1835) and Aleksandr Pushkin's *The Captain's Daughter* (1836).[62] Gogol (1809–1852), a member of the gentry born in present-day Ukraine, produced additional works that significantly influenced the development of Russian literature. His novel *Dead Souls* (1842) was one of the first satirical representations of Russian landowners and serfs. Although few notable novels appeared during the 1850s and early 1860s, the publication in 1869 of Tolstoi's groundbreaking epic *War and Peace,* set during the War of 1812, ushered in a new era in which historical fiction became increasingly popular.[63] Considered by some commentators to be second-rate writers whose works fell far short of

Tolstoi, authors like Danilevskii, Solov'ev, and Salias produced novels and short stories during the second half of the nineteenth century that attracted thousands of Russian readers who expressed renewed interested in their nation's past and culture.

The resurgence in nationalist enthusiasm was fueled by Russia's rout in the Crimean War (1853–1856) and by the upheaval produced by Tsar Alexander II's numerous legislative initiatives during the era of Great Reforms.[64] Scholar Olga Maiorova argues that Russia stood at the threshold of a new age, a moment when "the crescendo of self-criticism and the search for developmental models" came together and "began to evolve into full-fledged attempts to redefine the nation."[65] The efforts of statesmen, intellectuals, and artists to articulate what it meant to be "Russian," however, were complicated by the empire's expansion to encompass territory in the Caucasus and Central Asia between 1860 and 1890.[66] Now "operating in a composite imperial terrain," historian Laura Engelstein posits, Russian men and women strove to understand how they could best "construct a sense of national pride in relation to a state that included a mix of cultures, languages, and traditions."[67] Evidence of the public's growing interest in Russia's diverse peoples can be seen in magazine articles like *Niva*'s "Narody Rossii" (Peoples of Russia) series and in the popularity of events such as the Moscow Ethnographic Exhibition of 1867, attended by eighty-six thousand people, which depicted different ethnographic groups through a series of displays featuring costumed mannequins.[68] Through these initiatives and others, organizers emphasized the dominance of the "Great Russian" people over the empire's newest minority groups.[69]

Nationalism also emerged as a central theme in the art, music, and literature of the era. Scholar Dan Ungurianu points to the contributions of composers Modest Musorgskii and Nikolai Rimskii-Korsakov, artists Il'ia Repin and Grigorii Miasoedov, and Russian revivalist architects as additional evidence of the creative class's fascination with Russia's cultural heritage.[70] Literature proved to be one of the most fruitful areas for historical reflection. Ungurianu has found that, between 1870 and 1890, 160 new books of historical fiction were published, an occurrence that sociologist Nikolai Mikhailovskii described as akin to "blini churned out in massive quantities during Shrovetide."[71] The explosion of fictional works that idealized and glorified Russia's history appalled many literary critics who deplored their simplistic, frivolous nature, but the public enjoyed reading dramatized interpretations of their country's past. For instance, readers devoured Salias's fictional tales of heroic princes and princesses, tsars and the nobility, and, in the words of an early twentieth-century Russian encyclopedia essay about Salias, stories that included representations of serfs as "'faithful servants,' the slaves of their masters."[72] His contemporaries, Danilevskii, Solov'ev, and Opochinin, pursued a similar literary strategy by penning stories that romanticized life for the peasantry under serfdom. They depicted fond, brotherly relations between landowners and their loyal retainers or portrayed the serfs as a dedicated group of people who received ample support from their landlords. Like the African Americans of Page's and Harris's tales, Russia's peasants of late nineteenth-century historical fiction preferred life under serfdom to liberty.

In the United States, the sentimental short stories of Page and Harris functioned as a subset of the broader category of Southern plantation literature, which grew in popularity during the early nineteenth century following John Pendleton Kennedy's publication of *The Swallow Barn, or A Sojourn in the Old Dominion* (1832).[73] A native of Maryland who summered in present-day West Virginia, Kennedy depicted in his novel a peaceful plantation where enslaved African Americans faithfully served the paternalistic white owners on whom they relied.[74] The success of Kennedy's novel encouraged other authors who similarly set their tales in Southern locales. Although the works of James Kirke Paulding, William Alexander Caruthers, and Nathaniel Beverley Tucker did not gain the degree of national recognition that those of Page and Harris would achieve, they established the conventions of the genre.[75] In subsequent nineteenth-century Southern plantation literature, Kenneth M. Stampp observes, white authors began to consistently depict enslaved African Americans using the archetype of the "Sambo," the "perpetually dependent, irresponsible child," a representation that differed from eighteenth-century depictions of the dangerous, potentially rebellious slave who threatened to overthrow the established order.[76] Stampp persuasively contends that a direct link existed between "the appearance of Sambo and the growing moral attack on slavery" in antebellum America; the notion of the helpless, dependent enslaved African American "was always one of the proslavery writers' major arguments for keeping the Negro in bondage."[77] Stampp's argument can be similarly applied to post-emancipation plantation literature; indeed, the reemergence of the Sambo figure in the short stories of Page and Harris coincided with African Americans' growing independence and success in the fields of politics, business, and education during the 1880s and 1890s. Post-emancipation literature depicting African Americans as inferior bolstered white Southerners' arguments favoring Jim Crow laws that would restore their political, economic, and societal power.

Alexander McClurg's 1892 review of Harris's *On the Plantation* in the *Dial* expresses the prevailing mood among many white Americans during the late nineteenth century.[78] McClurg, a captain of the Eighty-Eighth Regiment, Illinois Volunteer Infantry, during the Civil War, praises the author's representations of "the old plantation negro and the old negro house servant," calling them "very interesting and attractive people" who exhibited "quaint good sense . . . and natural courtesy," but he asks the reader, "Why has the negro of to-day so completely lost the best traits that marked his race at that time?"[79] In answering his own query, he blames the abolition of slavery, which "smit[ed] . . . the victims as well as the oppressors," African American freed-people's acquisition of the right to vote, and, finally, the freedperson's "effort to seem the peer of the whites," which made him lose "some characteristics of his own which once made his race attractive and lovable."[80] The only solution to the problems of this post-emancipation "period of transition," McClurg concludes, is to hold out hope that "another hundred years may develop the negro of to-day into something much better than now seems probable."[81] Thus, American readers like McClurg found themselves drawn to the literature of Page and Harris because these authors created appealing representations of African Americans as servile, contented, enslaved men and women. By writing in dialect and incorporating elements of African American folklore and culture, Page and Harris sought to add verisimilitude to their portrayals of enslaved people that helped convince readers of the veracity of their underlying message about white superiority. Readers who had never experienced slavery firsthand but who resented black progress during the post-emancipation era preferred the depictions put forth by Page and Harris and empathized with the white slave owners of the antebellum South.

Biographical Connections

The most popular late nineteenth-century authors of historical fiction share several important biographical features. Each of the six aforementioned authors came from the landowning class, a fact that may partly account for his interest in portraying positive relations between slaveholders and bonded laborers during the pre-emancipation era. In the United States, Thomas Nelson Page was born in 1853 on a plantation constructed by enslaved African Americans in Hanover County, Virginia, where he witnessed the Union and Confederate armies trudging up and down the path leading to Richmond.[82] Both Thomas and his younger brother, Rosewell, fondly recalled the family's relationship with their slaves.[83] In an autobiographical account of his childhood written for Thomas's daughter Evelyn, Rosewell recorded that he and his siblings frequently visited four enslaved children in "the backyard where they lived" and with whom he "liked very much to play."[84]

As an adult, Thomas Nelson Page similarly portrayed the family's relationship with their enslaved laborers as one of affection and mutual respect. In his essay "The Old-Time Negro," Page asserted that the "relation between masters and servants was one of close personal acquaintance and friendliness, beginning at the cradle and scarcely ending at the grave."[85] Of all the enslaved people on a given plantation, Page declared, the mammy figure was "the closest intimate of the family," a maternal woman understood only by those "who were rocked on her generous bosom, slept on her bed, fed at her table, were directed and controlled by her, watched by her unsleeping eye, and led by her precept in the way of truth, justice, and humanity."[86] However, Page's insistence that mammies and their young charges always maintained affectionate ties was more than sentimental musing; as Micki McElya points out, white Southerners who "shared memories of mammy or claimed some affinity with a mammy figure were necessarily claiming a part of that class legacy and status."[87] By describing his family's membership in the slave-owning class, he sought to establish his authority as an elite, white Southerner whose account of black-white relations could be trusted by Northern middle-class readers lacking firsthand experience with slavery.

Page also wrote in dialect as he attempted to create the authentic voices of his literary subjects. This aspect of his work thrilled audiences, particularly during public gatherings when Page read aloud to his enthusiastic fans. After Page narrated the short story "Unc' Edinburgh's Drowndin'" to audiences in Macon, Georgia, one reporter claimed that "Mr. Page's dialect was as it should have been from a native Virginian, simply perfect."[88] The journalist recounted that, when Page told of an African American freedman's "devotion to his dashing young master in a strain that touched every heart," he revealed to listeners "the amusing weakness of the negro with that fidelity to nature which distinguishes the genuine artist."[89] By positioning himself as a Southern gentleman and reliable raconteur through his ostensible familiarity with African American speech, Page gained the trust of his readers. Indeed, as another critic noted, Page's works, "while intensely Southern, are broad in their view and national in their feeling," winning him friends and fans in the North and South alike.[90] Having successfully cultivated a reputation as a dependable storyteller, Page effectively promoted fictional stories that idealized pre-emancipation race relations and helped achieve the goal of white reconciliation during the 1880s and 1890s.

Like Page, Harris came from an elite, white Southern family. Born in 1845 in Eatonton, Georgia, Harris was raised by his mother, Mary Harris, after his father, an Irish day laborer, left shortly after his birth.[91] Abandoned by her lover, Mary was aided by friends and members of her family, which Julia Collier Harris describes as "a prominent one in middle Georgia," with "well-known connections in that part of the State."[92] Her son, Joel, received a private school education and grew up in relative comfort with his devoted mother.[93] In 1862, Harris, who took his mother's last name, responded to a job advertisement for a printing apprenticeship at a local paper called the *Countryman*.[94] In a biographical article for *Lippincott's Monthly Magazine*, Harris recounted his experiences working at the *Countryman*, which was housed at one of several plantations scattered across the countryside. There, Harris recalled, he listened to the stories of local enslaved African Americans and "absorbed the stories, songs, and myths" without knowledge of their future "literary value."[95] "Uncle" George Terrell, an enslaved African American who later served as the model for Harris's black storyteller, "Uncle Remus," was one of several men and women who imparted to the teenage boy many of the tales that would later bring him worldwide acclaim.[96]

Like Page, a lawyer who wrote historical fiction, Harris later maintained dual careers as a journalist and an author. After creating the popular character Uncle Remus for a newspaper column in the *Atlanta Constitution*, where he served as an associate editor, Harris began writing fiction on a part-time basis.[97] His first volume of stories, told from the perspective of a freedman named "Uncle Remus" to a white boy, brought him immediate renown and set him up for a lengthy career as an author of repackaged African American folktales written in dialect.[98] Harris also shared with readers idealistic memories of black-white relations from the antebellum era that mirrored those of Page, a testament to their common vision of the past. In his fictionalized memoir *On the Plantation* (1909), he recorded that, as an apprentice living on the estate, "the negro women looked after him with almost motherly care, and pursued him with kindness, while the men were always ready to contribute to his pleasure."[99] After the abolition of slavery, Harris remembered that the youngest generation of laborers abandoned the estate, while older workers stayed on "in their accustomed places."[100]

Harris's nostalgic depictions of the pre-emancipation South, presented to readers in *On the Plantation* and in more than 185 "Uncle Remus" folktales, resonated with white Northern and Southern readers. Page, who wrote to Harris that, upon first reading *Uncle Remus*, he felt "every nerve and sense tingling and delighted as [he] used to do when [he] was a little boy," later argued in an article for *Lippincott's Monthly Magazine* that above all else its "masterly setting and narration" appealed most to readers.[101] Page believed that audiences were "translated bodily to the old man's fireside in his cabin," a testament to Harris's skill in "preserv[ing] the folk-lore . . . in its verisimilitude of coloring, tone, and substance" and genius in "reproduc[ing] the Southern civilization" as "the 'setting'" for his characters.[102] But Harris gave the acquaintances of his youth primary credit for his fictional material, explaining to author Ambrose Bierce in 1896, "Even the Remus business is not my own, but is composed of stories originally told to me by negroes."[103] Like Page, Harris created an idealized version of the antebellum South for readers, but he did so by retelling African American folktales through the voice of a docile character whom Andrew Carnegie called "the Slave in his most attractive form, the storyteller of his Master's children."[104] Through his representation of a harmless, submissive freedman, Uncle Remus, Harris captured the imagination of white readers, stimulated public interest in African American culture at a time when racial tensions remained high, and tacitly reinforced whites' belief that freedpeople ought not to challenge their societal position.

Russian authors Salias, Danilevskii, Solov'ev, and Opochinin similarly came from the Russian landowning estate. Salias, the most popular writer of the group, was born in 1841 to a French count and his Russian wife, who was a member of the aristocratic Sukhovo-Kobylin family.[105] Like Harris, Salias was primarily raised by his mother, a writer who published under the nom de plume Evgeniia Tur, after his wayward father spent the family's money and left Russia after taking part in a duel.[106] In addition, Salias also came to producing historical fiction through journalism after working for the *Sankt-Peterburgskie vedomosti* (St. Petersburg News) during the 1870s.[107] A prolific writer, Salias produced countless short stories and novels published in journals like *Niva* (The Grainfield), *Ogonek* (Little Flame), *Russkii vestnik* (Russian Messenger), and *Istoricheskii vestnik* (Historical Messenger) during the late 1870s and 1880s.[108] In novels like *Na Moskve* (In Moscow), *Arakcheevskii synok* (Arakcheev's Son), and *Peterburgskoe deistvo* (Petersburg Action), Salias described the relations between serfs and the owners they faithfully served.[109]

Danilevskii, Solov'ev, and Opochinin similarly descended from elite Slavic families and created literature that appealed to a mass readership. Danilevskii (1829–1890) was born to a Ukrainian landowner, while Solov'ev (1849–1903) came from an old Ukrainian-Polish family of famous intellectuals and writers.[110] Opochinin (1858–1928) was a member of an ancient but impoverished noble family from the province of Yaroslavl who, after completing his studies in Kiev, moved to St. Petersburg in 1879, where he helped run the Museum of Antiquities from 1879 to 1883.[111] All three men were involved in journalism during their literary careers; Danilevskii and Opochinin edited the newspaper *Pravitel'stvennyi vestnik* (Governmental Messenger) during the 1870s–1890s, while Solov'ev edited the journal *Sever* (The North) from 1888 to 1891.[112] Danilevskii's most famous works included *Mirovich* and *Kniazhna Tarakanova* (Princess Tarakanova), while Solov'ev's most popular stories and novels included his chronicle of the Gorbatov family: *Sergei Gorbatov*, *Volter'ianets* (The Voltairean), *Staryi dom* (Old House), *Izgnannik* (Outcast), and *Poslednie Gorbatovy* (The Last Gorbatovs).[113] A prolific writer, Opochinin wrote numerous short stories, essays, and books in which he attempted, like Harris, to re-create the domestic atmosphere of bygone days or to disseminate to mass audiences the folk traditions of the Russian peasantry.[114] Some of his most famous works included *Ocherki starorusskogo byta* (Sketches of Old Russian Everyday Life), his collection of short stories titled *Russkii okhotnichii rasskaz* (Russian Hunting Story), and the countless tales of historical fiction he published biweekly in the journal *Moskovskii listok* (Moscow Sheet) during the early twentieth century.[115]

The historical fiction of Salias, Danilevskii, Solov'ev, and Opochinin constituted what scholar V. A. Viktorovich called a "second wave" of retrospective works that captivated the public imagination.[116] Fans of Russian historical fiction, a genre that grew rapidly in popularity during the late nineteenth century, were not limited to a particular class.[117] Speaking of Solov'ev, Viktorovich argued that readers were drawn to the author's use of engaging plots and dramatic elements, features of his writing that were representative of the broader genre of historical fiction.[118] According to S. F. Gorianskaia's study of the reading habits of the workers, employees, and students who visited two public libraries in St. Petersburg, Solov'ev ranked in the top-ten most widely read authors.[119] However, Salias surpassed Solov'ev and Danilevskii in popularity; his works were checked out from the library of St. Petersburg with even greater frequency.[120] Russian readers even preferred Salias to playwrights Aleksei Pisemskii and Aleksandr Ostrovskii, author Fedor Dostoevskii, and British novelist Charles Dickens.[121] For the most part, literary critics did not equate mass-oriented historical fiction with serious literature; some even contended that Salias was merely a "slavish imitator" of Russian intellectual giant Lev Tolstoi.[122] Nonetheless, the public devoured the dramatic tales about Russia's past that flooded popular journals each year.[123]

Like Harris and Page, Salias, Danilevskii, Solov'ev, and Opochinin achieved literary success by establishing their reputations as reliable chroniclers of a pre-emancipation era. Solov'ev recorded that one of his central goals at the beginning of his literary career was to "acquaint the widest possible readership with the different interesting epochs of bygone Russian life, depicting them as they appeared to [him] through the free, unbiased study of historical materials."[124] In spite of this professed goal, however, critics were generally aware of the liberties that belletrists took in order to craft the most engaging stories. For instance, P. P. Sokal'skii, a nineteenth-century folklorist considering the place of Danilevskii's *Mirovich* among similar works, commented that readers of historical fiction typically grappled with a controversial question: "Is it necessary for a novelist to strictly adhere to historical facts, or is he free to use his own imagination when crafting historical dramas and novels?"[125] Although nineteenth-century literary critics would have answered Sokal'skii's query in different ways, most readers accepted the belletrists' decision to combine history and fiction to produce entertaining literature.

As in the United States, personal experience burnished an author's reputation and gave his historical fiction an additional layer of authenticity. As one biographer wrote in 1890 of Salias, "It goes without saying that the author had the opportunity to closely observe serfdom and . . . its foundational relations," knowledge that "gave him the opportunity to create extraordinarily lively, energetic, vivid pictures of life during the era of serfdom."[126] As descendants of noble families or children who grew up on rural estates, Salias, Danilevskii, and Solov'ev appeared to possess special knowledge about the conditions of serfdom and the dynamics between landowners and their peasants. Romanticized as they were, representations of faithful serfs and benevolent *pomeshchiki* appealed to readers who were attracted to idealized visions of the pre-emancipation era. Like the American readers who looked to the antebellum South for an escape from the complicated racial tensions of the late nineteenth century, Russians turned toward historical fiction that provided a welcome diversion from the post-emancipation realities of a new generation of peasants who demanded to be paid for their labor, asserted themselves in local political councils or judicial courts, or abandoned the estates of their former owners to compete for factory jobs in growing urban centers.

Representations of Serfdom and Slavery in Historical Fiction

Page, Harris, Salias, Danilevskii, Solov'ev, and Opochinin employed three similar literary strategies in their representations of serfdom and slavery. First, these authors created African American and peasant characters who described the abundant resources they enjoyed during the pre-emancipation era to convince readers that serfdom and slavery were paternalistic institutions essential to their survival. Page, Harris, and Opochinin subtly politicized these accounts by contrasting the supposed plenty of serfdom and slavery with the material scarcity of liberty for freedpeople and peasants. Second, in their literature, fictional serfs and enslaved men and women express their gratitude for the imagined benefits of bonded labor, while freedpeople yearn to return to the pre-emancipation era by fondly recalling their days of enslavement. Third, these six authors portrayed pre-emancipation relationships between owners and enserfed or enslaved people as intimate, comfortable, and trusting. In their stories, landowners, serfs, and enslaved African Americans form maternal or fraternal bonds in youth; black and peasant mammies nurse their young charges; and enserfed or enslaved children play alongside their owners' children. Together, Russian and American authors effectively crafted nostalgic images of serfdom and slavery that convinced late nineteenth-century readers of the merits of pre-emancipation systems of servitude and the social relationships that defined them.

Solov'ev, Danilevskii, and Page correspondingly created noble, peasant, or African American characters who describe serfdom and slavery as materially beneficial institutions that supported those who were enslaved or enserfed. In *Staryi dom* (Old House) (1883), the third novel in a five-part series about the aristocratic Gorbatov family, Solov'ev describes the institution of serfdom from the perspective of nobleman Boris Gorbatov. While visiting his parents' vast estate during the early 1820s, Boris gazes admiringly at his surroundings and praises the work of his mother, Tat'iana, as its manager. He observes how the *barynia* (landowner's wife) "continued by herself, as always, to take the lead in managing all aspects of the enormous property."[127] Promoting a paternalistic view of serfdom, Boris declares that his mother is "the benefactress of the thousands of peasant souls that belonged to her and her husband," calling Tat'iana "a true tsarina of her little state."[128] Instead of treating her human property cruelly, Boris's mother makes herself "accessible to all, rather than exciting fear in others," and, as a consequence, "all [the serfs] came to her, unafraid, with their needs, illnesses and sorrows, for a long time knowing that the mistress Tat'iana would help everyone who approached her."[129] Like Tat'iana, the landlord of the estate was also held in high esteem by serfs, who "never spoke an evil word against him"; instead, "all exclaimed, 'Without a doubt, he is a kind, good master who couldn't even scare a goose!'"[130] Boris's description of his parents' magnanimity gave nineteenth-century readers the impression that serfs were well cared for by compassionate landowners. Serfdom appeared to provide the peasantry with homes, a communities, and owners who provided them with support in times of want.

Like Solov'ev, Danilevskii similarly characterizes serfdom as a protective, stabilizing institution that benefited Russia's peasantry. In his novel *Kniazhna Tarakanova* (1883), Danilevskii recounts the intriguing story of Elizaveta Alekseevna Tarakanova's attempts to win the Russian throne by pretending to be the daughter of Empress Elizabeth and her lover, Count Alexei Razumovskii. In a noteworthy passage, Count Alexei Grigor'evich Orlov, one of Elizabeth's aides, speaks with his serf, Terent'ich Kabanov, about conditions near the imperial capital of St. Petersburg during the 1770s. Danilevskii depicts Terent'ich as an elegant man who wears clothing "in the latest fashion" and speaks eloquently thanks to his privileged upbringing. He writes that Terent'ich, a literate serf, wears a "kaftan . . . [and] slippers with pewter buckles" and pulls his hair back into a powdered plait.[131] Conversing with his owner over a glass of expensive wine, Terent'ich reminds Orlov that he resides on a beautiful estate characterized by "cheerful places, abundant fields . . . forests, and dark groves, [where] the serfs are *khlebopashtsy* [ploughmen], not impoverished peasants, thanks to [his] grace."[132] Dressed in luxurious clothing, well fed, and highly educated, Terent'ich appears as a servant whose needs have been met throughout his life. His description of Orlov's estate also gives readers the impression that the other serfs reside there happily and are appreciative of their owner's beneficence over the years. Finally, Danilevskii portrays Terent'ich as Orlov's peer and confidante, a testament to the ostensibly close relations that existed between landlords and serfs prior to abolition. Together, these details create a scene that seeks to reassure readers by presenting serfdom as a balanced system that ensured the peasantry's well-being thanks to paternalistic *pomeshchiki*.

Page similarly represented slavery in favorable terms through the voice of a formerly enslaved African American man. In his story, "Marse Chan: A Tale of Old Virginia," published in the *Century* in 1884, Page relates an encounter between the narrator, a white Southerner, and a freedman, named Sam, in 1872. Sam resides near the "once splendid mansions, now fast falling to decay," of pre-emancipation Virginia, where he attended his master, "Marse Chan."[133] The faithful formerly enslaved man regales the narrator with a bit of personal history, recounting his days as the "body-servant" to Marse Chan.[134] Like Terent'ich, Sam maintains a close relationship with his owner throughout their lives, even carrying Marse Chan's body from a Civil War battlefield after he suffers a mortal wound.[135] Page's protagonist plays a literary role comparable to that of Danilevskii's friendly serf Terent'ich: he serves as a reliable source who assures readers that enslaved African Americans thrived on plantations during the pre-emancipation era.

According to Sam, all the enslaved people on the plantation "loved ole marster . . . aldo' dey did step aroun' right peart when ole marster was lookin' at 'em."[136] Page's African American characters both adored and feared the man who cared for their needs, submitting to him like children to a father. Sam warmly recollects that "dem wuz good ole times," when "niggers didn' hed nothin' 't all to do—jes' hed to 'ten' to de feedin' an' cleanin' de hosses, an' doin' what de marster tell 'em to do; an' when dey wuz sick, dey had things sont 'em out de house, an' de same doctor come to see 'em whar 'ten' to de white folks when dey wuz po'ly."[137] With few responsibilities, light chores, and good medical care, the enslaved men and women of Page's historical fiction were satisfied with their lot. Perhaps most important, Page notes through the voice of Sam, "dyar warn' no trouble nor nothin'," a veiled reference to the tumultuous post-emancipation racial tensions that characterized the world in which his readers lived.[138] Indeed, Page's favorable representation of slavery even convinced several Northern critics that the antebellum system of slavery had positive attributes. A reviewer from *Lippincott's Monthly Magazine* observed that, "oddly enough, the celebrant" of Page's stories about "the glories of the old régime in Virginia just before and during the war, which is now receding far enough into history to bring out all its romantic, tender, and chivalrous side[s] . . . is in most cases the negro slave whose emancipation was effected by the war," while a critic for Delaware's *Wilmington News* praised *Marse Chan, and Other Stories* as "simple and direct in composition, genuine and accurate in narration," sympathetically presenting "the domestic life of the old slave period in its most attractive and alluring aspects."[139] Thus, Page's promotion of the idea that life for African Americans had diminished in quality following their emancipation gained traction among Northern critics and furthered the white reconciliationist cause by ignoring concerns about black rights in the post-emancipation era.

Page, Harris, and Opochinin also promoted romanticized histories of slavery and serfdom by creating characters who experienced servitude, tasted freedom, and either longed to return to their former condition or failed to support themselves after emancipation. For instance, Harris portrayed slavery as a protective system that provided African Americans with safety and comfort in his story "Free Joe and the Rest of the World" (1887).[140] In the short story, Harris contrasts the experiences of a freedman, Joe, with those of his enslaved peers living in the town of Hillsborough, Georgia, in 1850. While the enslaved people on neighboring plantations "laughed loudly day by day . . . Free Joe rarely laughed," and while his peers "sang at their work and danced at their frolics . . . no one ever heard Free Joe sing or saw him dance."[141]

Instead of living a carefree life within the confines of an ostensibly paternalistic system that met African Americans' needs and provided them with the work that became their life's purpose, Harris describes Joe as "a black atom, drifting hither and thither without an owner, blown about by all the winds of circumstance, and given over to shiftlessness."[142] To ensure that nineteenth-century readers harbored no doubts about the disadvantages of the formerly enslaved man's status, Harris emphasized that Joe "realized the fact that though he was free he was more helpless than any slave," because "having no owner, every man was his master."[143] Harris's representation of the destitute freed African American deeply moved readers including President Theodore Roosevelt, who told Harris in a letter that he doubted there was "a more genuinely pathetic tale in all our literature than 'Free Joe.'"[144] Indeed, the reader is meant to pity the freed man, agreeing with the enslaved Georgians who, rather than "envy[ing] him his freedom," viewed him as "an exile."[145] But, as Roosevelt aptly noted, stories like "Free Joe" were more than art; rather, they served an important political purpose as well. Harris's work was, in Roosevelt's words, "an addition to the forces that tell for decency, and above all for the blotting out of sectional antagonism."[146] By whitewashing slavery's negative characteristics, Harris sought to promote reconciliation between white Southerners who defended the institution and those who helped bring about its demise during the Civil War.

Like Harris, Page similarly created African American characters who struggled to survive outside of slavery. In his short story "Ole 'Stracted," published in *In Ole Virginia*, the reader meets a family of freedpeople living in a rundown cabin on an uncultivated field. The mother sang "a dirge-like hymn" while she daydreamed about "what they would do when the big crop on their land should be all in, and the last payment made on the house . . . , not reflecting that the sum they had paid on the property had never . . . amounted in any one year to more than a few dollars over the rent charged for the place."[147] Here, Page references the oppressive system of sharecropping that kept freedpeople in poverty for decades following emancipation to bolster his claim that African Americans were economically better-off enslaved. As the story continues, Page introduces readers to Ole 'Stracted, a freedperson who gives voice to Page's perspective through the articulation of his desire to be reenslaved.

Ole 'Stracted is a mysterious, aged African American who lives in a "ruinous little hut which had been the old man's abode since his sudden appearance in the neighborhood a few years after the war."[148] His neighbors, including the aforementioned family of sharecroppers, know little about him except for the story he constantly repeats, that "he had been sold by some one other than his master from that plantation . . . and that his master was coming in the summer to buy him back and take him home, and would bring him his wife and child when he came."[149] On his deathbed, Ole 'Stracted reveals that he grew up on a plantation alongside his white owner, whom he loved dearly. After running into hard times, Ole 'Stracted's master had to give up his human "property," but he promised to buy Ole 'Stracted back. During the forty years that ensued, a length of time possessing biblical significance as a period of personal trial, Ole 'Stracted "wucked night an' day . . . to save dat money [$1,200] for marster."[150] Living in poverty, he patiently awaits his former owner's return until the day of his death in the miserable cabin, when "his Master had at last come for him . . . [and] Ole 'Stracted had indeed gone home."[151] "Ole 'Stracted" is one of Page's most politicized short stories because it criticizes postwar conditions in order to support the notion that African Americans were better suited to slavery than to liberty. Without the protection of slave owners, Page's fictional literature suggests, freedpeople would fight to survive. Some, like Ole 'Stracted, would lament their liberty until the day they died.

Russian readers of the late nineteenth and early twentieth centuries were also familiar with the concept of the faithful emancipated serf. Evgenii Opochinin created a memorable character that is strikingly similar to Ole 'Stracted in his short story "Posledniaia 'dusha'" (The Last "Soul") in 1905.[152] The title of this remarkable story is a play on words, because serfs were called "souls," a term denoting the unit of measurement used by tax assessors. "The Last 'Soul'" describes the life of Tikhon, an emancipated peasant who waits patiently for his former owner to visit him every autumn. As the weather turns cold each year, Tikhon looks expectantly for the "prematurely bent figure" of Il'ia Vasil'evich Trubitsyn, and for Tikhon, "once [his] serf, [Trubitsyn] was still his *barin* [master]."[153] Impoverished and landless, like the "marster" of Page's story "Ole 'Stracted," Il'ia Trubitsyn "lived here and there among former acquaintances" but went on his way when he began "running low on halfpenny earnings and offerings of goodwill."[154] Tikhon always looked forward to the arrival of his former owner, who would stay with him until spring came. In preparation, he "slaughtered his young lamb, [and] sifted oat flour for *blini* [pancakes] . . . while his wife, Dar'ia, . . . well aware of the customs of the nobility, decocted a bite of mushrooms for the *barin* and boiled raspberry jam."[155] Tikhon did not consider these acts to be a form of charity, and his former owner likewise "found it to be perfectly natural on the part of the serf."[156] Indeed, when neighboring peasants asked him why he "knowingly fed a stranger," Tikhon always replied, "After all, he is our *gospodin* [lord], our *pomeshchik!*"[157]

During the landlord's penultimate visit, he and Tikhon sit in the peasant's *izba* (hut), and as they recalled "the old days vanished images from long ago were resurrected before their eyes and their former lives, forgotten and buried, rose as if awakened."[158] As the men speak, they look up at the gilded portraits of Trubitsyn's parents and grandfather that hang on the walls, pictures that Tikhon had procured from the estate sale of his owner's property.[159] In one striking passage, when Trubitsyn asks Tikhon why he does not complain or seek revenge against his family for the trials he endured as a serf, he responds by explaining that time had passed, and all had been forgotten.[160] Their dialogue recalls the reconciliationist language of American writers for whom the goal of white reunion took precedence over the acknowledgment of slavery's harsh realities.[161] In this scene, Opochinin correspondingly glosses over the animosities and estate barriers that persisted between the aristocracy and the peasantry during the decades that followed the abolition of serfdom in Russia. Nonetheless, Tikhon's story ends on a poignant note akin to that of Ole 'Stracted. Il'ia Trubitsyn departs as usual when spring arrives, taking as a gift the banknote that Tikhon had saved, much like the hardworking freedman who stored away his money in anticipation of his owner's return. During Trubitsyn's next visit the following winter, however, Tikhon takes ill after chopping wood in the forest on a cold day and, like Christ, dies on the third day of his illness. The former serf's landlord weeps over his grave, waving away Dar'ia and the other peasants who tried to comfort him, exclaiming, "Ah! You do not understand. After all, he was my last soul!"[162]

The striking parallels between Opochinin's "The Last 'Soul'" and Page's "Ole 'Stracted" show that Russian and American writers from the landowning classes portrayed former serfs and enslaved people in comparable ways. Both Tikhon and Ole 'Stracted loyally serve their owners throughout their lives, refusing to let the abolition of serfdom and slavery diminish their devotion. Each character also makes meaningful material sacrifices to support his former owner even in his own poverty. Finally, both Page and Opochinin depict the relationships between owners, peasants, and freedpeople as intimate, a calculated decision that moderated perceptions of forced labor by shifting the focus from state-enforced coercion to interpersonal ties.

Like Page and Opochinin, Harris and Salias produced novels and short stories that emphasized the familial connections between bonded laborers and their owners during the pre-emancipation era. One way in which these Russian and American writers achieved their goal of underscoring relational closeness was by employing the rhetorical strategy of substituting the words "serf" and "slave" with "servant." For instance, in Salias's *Peterburgskoe deistvo* (Petersburg Action) (1880) and *Arakcheevskii synok* (Arakcheev's Son) (1889), the author uses variations of the word "servant" to describe enserfed peasants, including "sluga," "sluzhitel'," and "dvornia." Meanwhile, Harris describes the character "Free Joe" as the former "body-servant" of a white Southerner named Major Frampton, and Page repeatedly refers to enslaved people as "servants" or "body-servants" in "Marse Chan," "Ole 'Stracted," and "Polly: A Christmas Recollection." By doing so, these Russian and American writers sought to create a more compassionate picture of slavery and serfdom for post-emancipation readers.

Page and Salias also characterized specific types of relationships between owners, serfs, and enslaved people as warm and affectionate; these included the brotherly relations between those who played together as children and the maternal ties between mammies and the children of their owners. For example, in Page's short story "Unc' Edinburg's Drowndin': A Plantation Echo," the freedman "Unc' Edinburg" of eastern Virginia recounts to a white narrator the history of his service to his former owner, "Marse George."[163] The two grew up together on the same property, where Unc' Edinburg was "born on a Sat'day in de Christmas, an [Marse George] wuz born in de new year on a Chuesday."[164] Like twin brothers, Unc' Edinburg and Marse George even shared the same mammy, who "nussed [both boys] . . . at one breast."[165] Throughout the remainder of their lives, both men remain faithful to each other. Unc' Edinburg follows Marse George to college and Marse George repays his enduring loyalty by rescuing him from a raging river.

Solov'ev described a similar relationship between the nobleman Boris Gorbatov and the serf dwarf Stepan in *Staryi dom*.[166] When Boris visits his family's estate during the early 1820s, he is greeted by his devoted "body-servant," whom he has known throughout his life.[167] During their impassioned conversation about events that have transpired in Boris's absence, Boris thanks Stepan for knowing his habits and preferences so well, reminding him, "We have been together since childhood—we were even born on the same day."[168] Reflecting further on Stepan's role in his life, Boris thinks to himself about how the dwarf "was neither servant nor lowly person, but a respected, beloved friend in their household" with whom Boris shared "the best memories of his childhood."[169] During the remainder of the scene, Stepan expresses his mutual affection to Boris, pledging to "forever inseparably serve" his "one and only *gospodin*," the man for whom he would "lay down his life."[170] Their dialogue concludes with a moment of familial affection when the two distinctive figures, "the rich and well-known *barin* . . . and the serf slave, in a shared burst of passion, hugged each other like brothers."[171] Despite the gulf that separated the nobility from the peasantry, Solov'ev characterized Boris and Stepan's relationship as one that transcended social boundaries. Like Page, Solov'ev represented the relationship between owners and their male serfs as defined by mutual affection and fidelity.

By comparison, Salias emphasizes not brotherly ties but the maternal association between female serf nurses and their white charges. He idealizes the connection between the *mamka*, the Russian equivalent of the African American mammy, and her infant owner by portraying the relationship as that which exists between a mother and her own child. In a passage from *Arakcheevskii synok*, Salias recounts the changing dynamics between Shumskii, an aristocrat, and the nurse of his childhood, the serf Avdot'ia. Salias describes her as "a woman of about fifty years of age, dressed as a simple *dvorovaia* [yard/servant] woman in a colorful cotton dress and with a kerchief tied around her head."[172] As time passed, Avdot'ia, "a very intelligent woman . . . observed and realized that the master was weary of her 'foolish love,' and reluctantly tried to be more reserved by not annoying him with fawning words and nicknames, as she had done before."[173] With each passing year, however, the "coldness in relations between the former nurse and her nursling grew" and Avdot'ia "grieved and sometimes wept, seeing that her nursling had completely stopped loving her."[174] Her owner now "no longer made any distinction between his former *mamka* and his father's other serfs," a fact that caused Avdot'ia great sadness, although she tells herself that "all of the people of the 'noble estate' shun their nurses when they become adults and 'go out into the wild.'"[175] Salias's sentimental description of Avdot'ia's grief and internal thoughts reveal to the reader the depth of her devotion to Shumskii. Although her former owner no longer cares for her, she maintains maternal affection for him that is no less powerful than that of the devoted Tikhon, Ole 'Stracted, or Unc' Edinburg.

Harris also depicts the loyal mammy figure in his short story "Mom Bi: Her Friends and Her Enemies," published in the collection *Balaam and His Master* (1891).[176] The tale takes place in the "aristocratic" town of Fairleigh, South Carolina, where a white gentleman, Judge Waynecroft, maintains "a most charming household, in which simplicity lent grace to dignity."[177] One of his enslaved laborers is a middle-aged African American woman known as "Mom Bi," who fascinates Judge Waynecroft's neighbors because of her unusual appearance and outspokenness. Harris describes her as a powerful "black Amazon" with a unique affliction: her "left arm was bent and withered, and she carried it in front of her and across her body, as one would hold an infant."[178] This inherently maternal feature serves to soften Harris's overall description of an enslaved woman whose "whole appearance was aggressive" and who gave viewers the impression that she was "a queer combination of tyrant and servant, of virago and mammy."[179]

Mom Bi's character is sterner than the emotional mammy who appears in Salias's *Arakcheevskii synok*, but she is no less loyal to her owner and his family. Harris characterizes Mom Bi as "an old family servant," using a term that denies her position as an enslaved woman, who was "ready enough to quarrel with each and every member of her master's family" about household affairs, but who also remained "ready to defend the entire household against any and all comers."[180] Indeed, the entire family relied on her; Harris writes that "her master and mistress appreciated and respected her, and the children loved her."[181] The author whitewashes the nature of slavery, however, by assuring readers that Mom Bi was more akin to a family member than a slave, declaring that "whatever effect slavery may have had on other negroes, or negroes in general, it is certain that Mom Bi's spirit remained unbroken."[182] Here, by deliberately emphasizing the fact that Mom Bi exerts her authority in confrontations against white and black people alike, Harris makes an effort to obscure the true nature of the mammy figure's historical societal position. Even a woman like Mom Bi who verbally rebelled nonetheless did so within the confines of the domestic sphere where she remained an enslaved woman.

Generated by authors from Southern and Russian landowning families, these literary examples compose two bodies of historical fiction that reveal the unusually similar ways in which aristocratic Russian noblemen and white Southerners from planter families depicted serfs and enslaved African Americans. In both the United States and Russia, stories that misrepresented the histories of slavery and serfdom gained popularity during a post-emancipation era characterized by the shifting power dynamics that saw formerly bonded laborers acquiring new rights and elites losing land and power. By whitewashing the legacies of two widespread systems of servitude, six Russian and American men presented mass-oriented historical narratives that primarily appealed to those who had never been enslaved or enserfed. Ultimately, a comparison of these works reveals that the romanticization of the pre-emancipation era in Southern literature was not a phenomenon unique to the post-emancipation United States.

Illustrated Periodicals and Lithographs

Nineteenth-century Americans and Russians read more literature than any previous generation thanks to increased leisure time and growing access to a variety of printed materials.[1] Capturing the attention of both countries' literate populations during a post-emancipation era of national self-reflection, illustrated periodicals played a vital role in shaping popular perceptions of newly emancipated Russian peasants and African American freedpeople during the late nineteenth century.[2] Periodicals reached a wide readership during this period due in part to their expansive content, engaging engravings, and incisive cartoons that commented on contemporary social topics. Mass-oriented representations of the peasantry and African Americans appeared not only in illustrated periodicals but also in lithographs. Currier and Ives, the printmaking firm based in New York City, created more than seven thousand unique lithographs depicting a range of subjects, including African Americans, during the nineteenth century.

Through these wide-ranging illustrations, artists from diverse backgrounds portrayed peasants and freedpeople in distinct ways. They painted rosy portraits of rural life; idealized historic relationships between owners, serfs, and enslaved people; critiqued emancipated laborers' decisions to migrate to urban areas; and dramatized traditional folk practices. While some artists disparaged former serfs and freedpeople by attributing to them negative physical and psychological characteristics, others created respectful representations of independent African Americans and peasants. Together, these images not only influenced public opinion but also reflected the changing relationships and power dynamics among different social groups in Russia and the United States.

The Growth of Periodical Publications and Printmaking

One of the most popular types of reading materials, illustrated periodicals could be found in almost any nineteenth-century middle- or upper-class household owing to their low cost and widespread availability. Filled with evocative illustrations and gripping fiction, poetry, or cartoons, these publications captured the minds of countless readers. Nineteenth-century readers enjoyed periodicals independently and at family gatherings, where they read them aloud as a form of entertainment. In an article about the art of reading, a columnist writing in the *Cultivator and Country Gentleman* described a household he knew in which the father "read to his children night after night, often for three or four hours at a time . . . chapters of Dickens or Thackeray, or a story from *The Atlantic*."[3] Reading was also a group activity in Russian households; the poet Boris Sadovskii recalled how, in his late nineteenth-century home, "the entire family gathered at the dining room table for evening tea, viewing the inventive headlines, drawings, and vignettes" of the journal *Sever* (The North).[4]

By reading periodicals, Americans and Russians grew increasingly aware of and connected to their nations and the wider world. *Harper's Weekly* and *Frank Leslie's Illustrated Newspaper*, later called *Frank Leslie's Weekly*, were two of the most popular American periodicals during the second half of the nineteenth century. With circulations that collectively reached over two hundred thousand, these publications targeted white middle- and upper-class readers who could afford their prices of between five and six cents per issue in 1860.[5] *Harper's Weekly* supported the Republican Party after the Civil War, while *Frank Leslie's* expressed pro-Democrat opinions in editorials during the 1870s.[6] Periodicals often specialized in specific subjects or targeted audiences such as women, children, or those of a particular religious or ethnic background. As African Americans migrated to cities, the number of black newspapers grew rapidly.[7] The first illustrated periodicals directed toward an African American audience were the *Indianapolis Freeman*, published from 1888 to 1927, and the *Colored American Magazine*, which ran from 1900 to 1909. Other specialized publications included *Godey's Lady's Book*, *Peterson's Magazine*, and *Frank Leslie's Ladies' Gazette of Fashion and Fancy Needlework*, which contained fashion plates, craft projects, and literature; agricultural journals such as the *American Farmer*, the *New England Farmer*, and the *Country Gentleman*; and religious magazines such as the *Boston Recorder*, the *Ladies' Repository*, and the *Christian Union*.

In Russia, subscription journals also experienced dramatic growth. Some of the most popular magazines, including *Vsemirnaia illiustratsiia* (Worldwide Illustration) and *Ogonek* (Little Flame), were slim, illustrated journals containing elaborate images.[8] During the late nineteenth century, each journal published fifty-two issues per year for between four and thirteen rubles each.[9] Russia's most popular journal, *Niva* (The Grainfield), reached more than 235,000 readers after circulation doubled between 1891 and 1900.[10] In the aforementioned publications, readers learned about domestic and international events, read fiction or poetry, and admired advertisements for soap, furniture, perfume, musical instruments, agricultural equipment, sewing machines, gramophones, clothing, and bicycles. Satirical periodicals like *Budil'nik* (Alarm Clock) and *Strekoza* (The Dragonfly) also appealed to mass audiences thanks to their humorous illustrations and cartoons that poked fun at contemporary Russian life.

The images that filled the pages of popular magazines became increasingly sophisticated and affordable during the second half of the nineteenth century. Inventions like the high-speed rotary press, which supplanted platen hand-presses that used laborious techniques from the era of the Gutenberg press, led to increased printing efficiency.[11] Scientific advancements in the realm of electrical science, such as electrotyping, transformed the woodcut production process through the use of electricity to create metallic molds, while photomechanical engraving led to image enhancements.[12] In 1894, *Current Literature* remarked on the rapid reduction in printing costs, noting, "Prints that five years ago sold readily for from $75 to $100 may be had now for $3, and prints of fairly good plates are to be had at every dry goods store and back-street picture shop for 40 cents, 50 cents and $1."[13] For the editors of illustrated periodicals, lower printing costs improved the bottom line and enabled them to include more images in each issue.

Readers were consequently able to appraise a broad range of inexpensive and wholly engaging publications. Some late nineteenth-century observers, however, like the author of the article "Reading Trash," feared that Americans' sampling of mass-produced publications would lead to mental decline. In *Littell's Living Age*, the anxious critic inveighed against the type of man he described as "the confirmed news reader . . . [who] gets through large portions of one or two other morning papers" and then undertakes "excursions into the prolific regions of the weekly, the monthly, the comic, and the illustrated periodicals." Such a reader, he warned, would discover that "all the time he can spare for reading is fully occupied in the pursuit of this fugitive literature" and is "destroying his brain power as surely as the man who smokes a short pipe at every spare hour is destroying his digestion."[14] Irrespective of the author's argument, his words reveal that the explosion of periodicals during the late nineteenth century led to a transformation of popular reading habits and routines.

Lithographs also constituted an important category of mass-oriented visual culture. Printmaking firm Currier and Ives, located in the nation's publishing center of New York City, led the way in producing commercialized art for a mass audience. During the postbellum era, Americans became increasingly interested in purchasing colorized lithographs. Calling themselves "the

Grand Central Depot for Cheap and Popular Pictures," Currier and Ives produced images of pastoral scenes, animals, maps, and historical events that tens of thousands of middle-class consumers collected and displayed in their homes.[15] Although the printmaking firm supported the Union cause during the Civil War, Currier and Ives created racist cartoons during the postemancipation era as part of its best-selling "Darktown" series between approximately 1875 and 1890.[16] New York City artist Thomas Worth and Scottish artist James Cameron produced highly offensive illustrations that mocked African American freedpeople in their efforts to exercise their rights as citizens and likely targeted white, middle-class consumers who may have perceived the lithographs as comedic.[17] With 95 percent of the market share of circulating lithographs, Currier and Ives played an outsize role in shaping popular perceptions of nineteenth-century American life, even when its representations were infused with racist ideology.

Ultimately, mass-oriented illustrations in both lithographs and periodicals helped create a popular national consciousness by uniting readers through exposure to shared information. Scholar Joshua Brown has found that the illustrated press used deliberate "visual strategies" to "depict news in postbellum America."[18] By implementing "visual codes and narrative approaches derived from the antebellum era," illustrated periodicals "concocted an elaborate normative diagram for their readers that helped make sense of the changing society surrounding them."[19] Images in periodicals shaped readers' perceptions of events they did not personally experience and influenced the ways in which they visualized peoples with whom they were unfamiliar. Furthermore, illustrations in periodicals did not always reflect the political viewpoints expressed in the papers' editorials; rather, periodicals permitted the publication of images that offered a range of perspectives.[20] With a wider circulation than paintings and a broader audience than literature, these influential illustrations reached large segments of the Russian and American populations.

Visual Representations of Serfs, Slaves, Peasants, and Freedpeople

A range of representations of serfs, slaves, peasants, and freedpeople appeared in illustrated periodicals and lithographs between 1865 and 1905. The most prevalent types of depictions can be seen in the most popular, widely read publications in Russia and the United States. These include engravings and cartoons in the Russian periodicals *Ogonek*, *Niva*, *Vsemirnaia illiustratsiia*, and *Strekoza* and the American periodicals *Harper's Weekly*, *Frank Leslie's*

Illustrated Newspaper, and *Scribner's Monthly.* They also include individually printed lithographs by American printmaking giant Currier and Ives, *lubochnaia literatura* and *lubki,* illustrated materials written for the peasantry, and illustrations of African Americans published in two of the earliest illustrated periodicals for a predominantly black readership, the *Indianapolis Freeman* and the *Colored American Magazine.*

In illustrated periodicals and lithographs targeting white and nonpeasant audiences, African Americans and Russian peasants were most commonly represented in several distinct ways. To begin with, illustrators frequently created sentimental portraits of rural black and peasant life that appealed to city dwellers in an age of modernization, industrialization, and labor conflict. Working on plantations under the watch of overseers, serfs, peasants, enslaved African Americans, and freedpeople appear content and docile. Other romanticized images focus on the social or cultural activities of peasants and African Americans through depictions of family gatherings, pastoral activities, and scenes involving the natural world. In these representations, rural peasants and African Americans do not threaten those outside their own social groups.

Another type of representation addresses the ways in which peasants and African Americans negotiated the transition from captivity to freedom. Some images depict impoverished, naive former serfs and freedpeople struggling to find work in gritty cities after challenging journeys from rural estates to urban centers. Other portrayals show peasants and freedpeople as unable to successfully assimilate or self-govern or as threatening to nonpeasant or white citizens. While rural illustrations typically feature harmonious relations between social groups, urban scenes portray disorder and chaos.

Additional depictions sought to display African American and peasant culture through ethnographic illustrations of men and women engaging in rituals and celebrations. For Russian readers, these representations helped foster a sense of nationalism, or what Boyd Shafer describes as "a shared belief in . . . a common ethnic origin" and "a common pride . . . in past and present achievements" that included "the cultural and the social."[21] Members of the nobility and intelligentsia who historically saw themselves as European grew increasingly interested in comprehending and celebrating the culture of Russia's *narod* (folk) during the second half of the nineteenth century.[22] By contrast, white Americans perceived African American traditions and customs as a source of fascination rather than as symbolic of what they believed fully represented "American" culture.

Periodicals and lithographs also contained disparaging portrayals of peasants and freedpeople that attributed to them negative characteristics or depicted them engaging in unsavory behaviors. Such images often appeared as caricatures or cartoons that provided a format in which nonpeasant Russians and white Americans voiced their fears about the post-emancipation absorption of former serfs and freedpeople. Offensive representations of African Americans portrayed exaggerated facial features, body parts, or speech. African Americans frequently appeared as helpless, stupid, and ignorant, traits that were similarly attributed to peasants in comparable Russian illustrations, which, in contrast, usually lacked racial undertones because of a shared ethnicity between peasants and aristocrats.

Rarely, periodicals and lithographs depicted African Americans and peasants as the victims of injustices or crimes inflicted by Americans and Russians with greater political, economic, or social power. Such images criticized planters' abuse of power, white violence, the sexual exploitation of enserfed and enslaved women, and wealthy elites' lack of concern for those in poverty. Depictions of peasants and freedpeople as respected members of society who appeared as social equals to those who had never experienced serfdom or slavery were also featured infrequently in engravings, lithographs, and cartoons.

Lastly, illustrated materials targeting black and peasant readerships enlarged the range of representations in white- or nonpeasant-owned mass-oriented periodicals. In engravings and photographs, African Americans and peasants appeared as urban professionals, working-class laborers, politicians, or respected members of their communities. These portrayals helped readers visualize the new experiences of the late nineteenth-century peasants and African Americans who moved beyond the boundaries of rural life to pursue opportunity and growth.

Rural Illustrations of African Americans and Russian Peasants

The sentimental images of rural life that frequently appeared in illustrated periodicals and lithographs belie the historical realities of servitude and the upheaval of the post-emancipation era. Serfs and enslaved African Americans were overjoyed at the prospect of their liberation from circumstances characterized by intense agricultural labor and severe restrictions in nearly every area of their lives, but conditions in rural post-emancipation Russia and the United States remained fraught with economic hardship and tension. In the American South, intimidation and violence were regular occurrences in

African Americans' daily lives. The artists and illustrators of numerous Russian and American periodicals and lithographs, however, chose to gloss over these conditions through portrayals of contented, peaceful peasants and African Americans.

One commonly featured subject was that of peasants and African Americans working in the fields to harvest various crops. *Vsemirnaia illiustratsiia*'s "Tabachnye plantatsii na iuge Rossii" (Tobacco Plantations in the South of Russia) shows two images depicting peasants gathering and preparing tobacco plants for curing. An accompanying article praises the crop for holding a "place of honor" among the "economic industries of southern Russia" thanks to the region's "good climate and virgin soil."[23] Dressed in traditional clothing, peasants collect tobacco in a field and strip the leaves from the stalks under the watch of a *nachal'nik* (boss), whose Western dress contrasts sharply with that of the peasantry. Indeed, the illustrator may have drawn inspiration from earlier representations of overseers from the American South; the peasants' *nachal'nik* sports a knee-length overcoat, vest, bow tie, and jaunty wide-brimmed hat. While the overseer instructs his laborers with an outstretched hand, the peasants obediently follow his commands without protest. These representations parallel those that appeared in *Harper's Weekly* in a series of images by Civil War artist-correspondent Alfred R. Waud, titled "Scenes on a Cotton Plantation."[24] As in the Russian images, the laborers' status as enslaved African Americans or freedpeople is somewhat ambiguous due to the correspondences between their conditions and those of the pre-emancipation era. Like their Russian counterparts, the African American men and women dutifully work in groups to complete their diverse responsibilities under the observation of an overseer. They plant and harvest cotton, remove seeds with the help of the cotton gin, and even find time to engage in leisure activities, including a commitment dance and a prayer meeting. In Waud's representation of the rural South, black laborers remain satisfied to continue working the land for white owners.

Late nineteenth-century Russians' and Americans' idealization of the relationships between owners, serfs, and enslaved people during the pre-emancipation era grew stronger with increased temporal distance from the abolition of serfdom and slavery. As chapter 2 covers in detail, men from landowning families produced popular historical fiction about rural estate life designed to appeal to mass audiences during the 1880s and 1890s. Their stories were published in the same periodicals that also printed nostalgic, sentimental illustrations of faithful Russian serfs and enslaved African Americans. Consider the image titled "Staryi barin" (Old Master), which was published in 1889 in Russia's

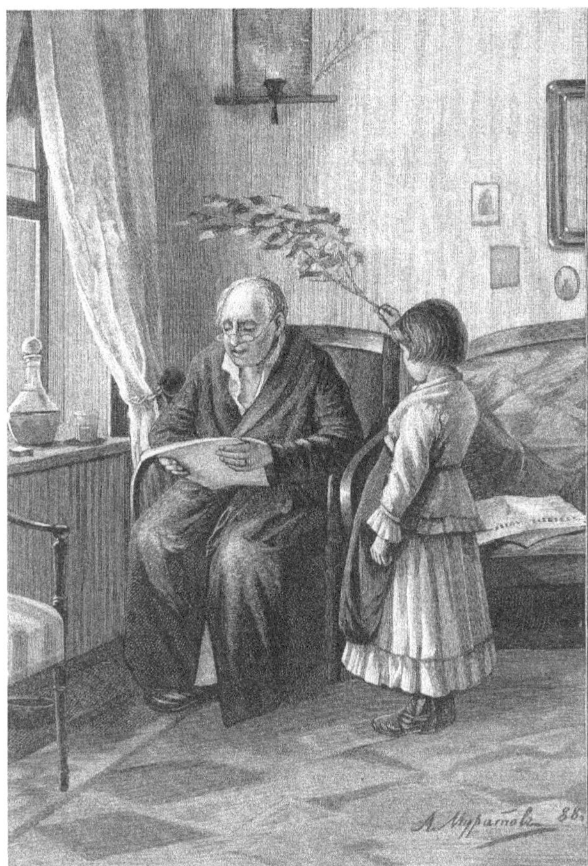

A. Muratov, "Old Master," *Niva*, no. 36 (1889): 892.

widely read journal *Niva*.[25] According to the accompanying text, the artist has "faithfully reproduced the type of the old *barin*," whose former serf fans him with a long, green branch while he reads his newspaper on a hot summer day. The artist's sympathies lie with the landowner, whose "*kazachki* [child-servant] . . . drives away the flies . . . [while he] complacently slumbers over his newspaper," a luxury to which he was accustomed and "could not part with . . . after the peasant reforms" of 1861. The text's claim that "there is nothing more difficult in later years than to abandon the habits developed by one's entire life" delicately encourages the viewer to adopt a sympathetic view of the elderly landowner.[26] Indeed, *Niva*'s upper-class readers may have found it hard to criticize an image that depicted such peaceful relations between a nobleman and his loyal former serf.

Other images subtly promoted the benefits of post-emancipation socio-economic systems that separated landowners and laborers by class, cultural

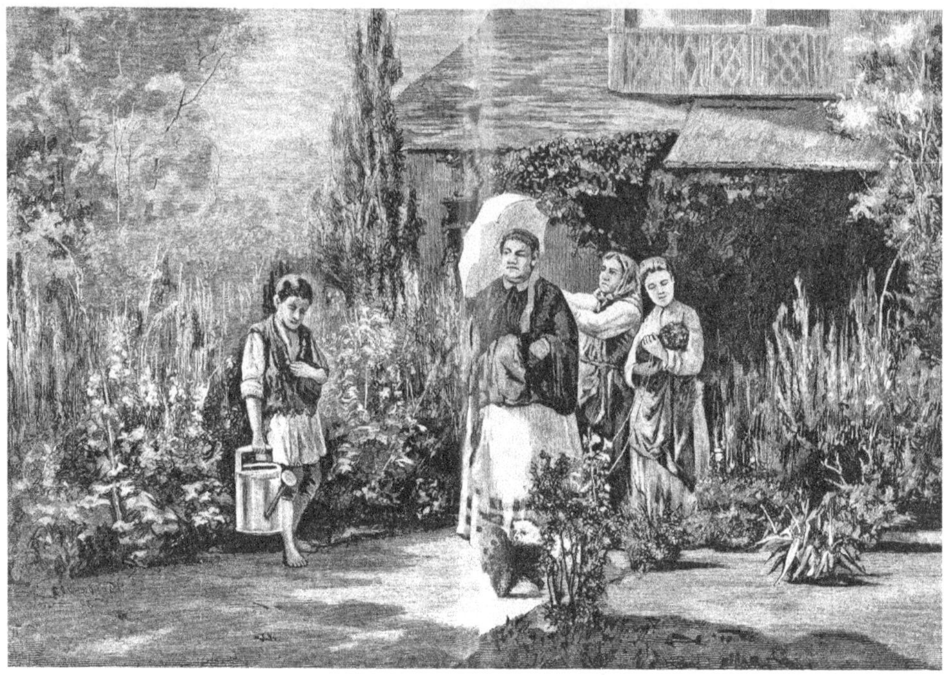

"In Their Own Domains," *Ogonek*, no. 18 (1882): 356–357.

background, or race. "V svoikh vladeniiakh" (In Their Own Domains), published in *Ogonek* in 1882, portrays an aristocratic landowner strolling through her lush garden on a sunny day.[27] Three peasant servants trail behind; one shades her face with an umbrella, another holds her dog, and a third carries a large watering can. Here, the mistress remains in total control of her former serfs, who, with heads bowed, quietly perform their respective tasks. Ultimately, the illustration depicts an estate unaffected by the abolition of serfdom; it is a place where the strict pre-emancipation power dynamics governing social relations continue unabated.

Freedpeople were similarly depicted as the devoted servants of their former owners in illustrations from the 1880s and 1890s. One of the most common representations was that of the loving "mammy," a black nurse who devoted her entire life to her owner's children. An idealistic article published in *Frank Leslie's Weekly* in 1893 describes the "mammy" as a "nursery chief" and "assistant housekeeper" on Southern plantations who was an "important member of the household, held in high esteem by all and especially regarded by the children, to whom she was something like a second mother." Her appellation was, in the male author's view, "a title of high nobility . . . when applied to a negro woman by white children." According to the author, the mammy's central role in the family extended beyond the children's youth; indeed, even after her owner's children had left home, the mammy always remained close to her female charges. On any occasion, the author claimed, "whether it be a picnic in the woods, a ball at a neighboring manor-house, a wedding, a christening, a sick bed, or a funeral, the '*mammy*' is there, full of sympathy, interest, and attention."[28] Mammies played a familial role akin to that of the *niania* (nanny/nurse) in wealthy Russian households. Like the black mammy, the peasant nanny helped manage domestic affairs and looked after the children. Russian actress Alisa Koonen (1889–1974) nostalgically recorded in her memoirs that her own nurse, the daughter of a serf, was "considered by all a member of the family, she ran the household, and for us [she] was like a second mother." A masterful chef, a seamstress, and an entertaining storyteller, she "was the center of our entire childhood," Koonen wrote.[29]

The African American mammy figure appeared in numerous engravings during the second half of the nineteenth century. An untitled engraving published in 1874 features a black mammy gently holding a white baby while an older child caresses her shoulder.[30] A bucolic scene, the mammy appears as a nurturing, maternal personage to the young white children for whom she cares. Late nineteenth-century illustrations typically depicted mammies as maintaining their elevated status within white families long after the children had grown up. For instance, Ohio-native Howard Helmick's drawing "Christmas in the South: Old Mammy's Christmas Cake" portrays an intimate scene inside a Southern kitchen.[31] A young white woman, presumably the former charge of "Old Mammy," admires a magnificent frosted cake while her mother looks on. The mammy stands with hands on hips, proud of her creation, while an elderly husband and a child bow to the white visitors.

Why was the image of the loyal servant so central to the construction of idealized representations of African Americans and Russian peasants during the post-emancipation era? The sentimental portrait of the mammy in *Frank Leslie's Weekly* offers an important clue. The author concludes his essay with the claim that the mammy figure is no mere historical relic; rather, he contends that she has survived the abolition of slavery and "will remain and flourish in the South so long as the whites and blacks live there together in natural amity."[32] If, as the author asserted, faithful freedpeople and peasants, like mammies and *nianias*, continued to contentedly serve their former owners on rural estates after emancipation, opponents of abolition could argue against the use of federal legislation or monarchical decrees to disrupt the supposedly harmonious, yet unequal, power dynamics that defined relations

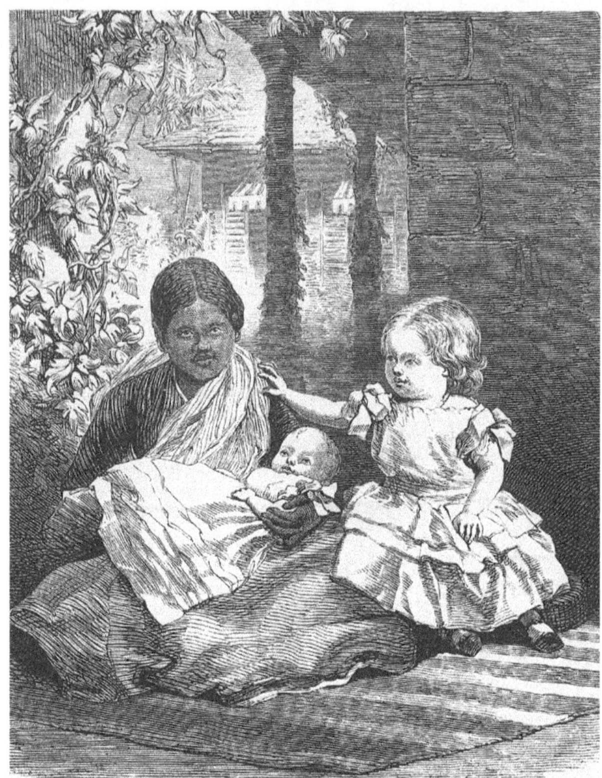

Drawing no. 8, untitled, unknown publication, 1874. Box 1, folder 7, "Children" (pp. 1–90), PR 17, Leslie Dorsey Collection, New-York Historical Society.

between owners and their formerly bonded laborers in the late nineteenth century. Ultimately, these artists' idealized representations of devoted peasants and freedpeople deliberately glossed over the tensions that characterized late nineteenth-century social relations, evidenced most dramatically in the U.S. South by rising lynching rates and other forms of violence.

Peasants and Freedpeople as Perpetrators of Urban Disorder

During the late nineteenth century, freedpeople and peasants were increasingly able to escape from the cycle of sharecropping and tenant farming that kept many people in rural poverty after emancipation. Rapid industrialization produced a growing number of job opportunities that attracted rural-to-urban migrants. In the United States, nearly four million positions for wage earners were added between 1889 and 1919 at manufacturing establishments having products valued at $500 or more.[33] Urban areas expanded dramatically due to the influx of immigrants from abroad and the in-country migration of rural residents. Between 1880 and 1920, the total U.S. urban population grew by 283 percent, from about fourteen million to fifty-four million people.[34] Both the quantity and the scale of cities grew dramatically between 1880 and 1920 as well; the total number of urban areas grew from 939 to 2,722, while the number of places comprising one hundred thousand inhabitants more than tripled.[35] Russian cities also expanded rapidly at the turn of the twentieth century. In-country migration increased sharply between 1880 and 1910, when the percentage of the population in European Russia holding passports doubled.[36] Just 7.8 percent of the Russian population resided in urban areas in 1851, but between the 1850s and 1913, the number of urban residents increased by almost 300 percent.[37] In Moscow, where 75 percent of the city's residents were born elsewhere, the urban population grew by 50 percent between 1882 and 1902.[38] Overall, these changing migration patterns significantly boosted Russia's total urban residency population.

In Russia, industrialization and urban expansion weakened the traditional borders between rural villages and bustling cities. Manufacturers built new factories that offered peasants salaried jobs, which provided an escape from the hardships of agricultural labor. Although author Lev Tolstoi famously depicted Russia's peasants as pure folk who lived simply without surrendering to earthly desires for wealth, many peasants migrated to cities, particularly after Petr Stolypin's reforms following the Revolution of 1905, which abolished peasants' redemption payments and permitted families to privatize and sell portions of communally held land, an act that gave peasants capital liquidity and increased freedom of movement.[39] Peasant migration from the central-industrial regions fueled this growth; statistics show that 75 percent of Moscow's migrants were from the peasant estate and that the vast majority of Moscow's factory workers were peasants.[40] By 1897, peasants made up approximately 50 percent of Russia's total urban population and approximately 75 percent of the total population.[41]

In the United States, approximately two hundred thousand African Americans migrated northward and westward between 1890 and 1900, but they remained a minority group in cities filled with Americans from diverse backgrounds as well as newly arrived immigrants.[42] In 1900, 77 percent of African Americans still lived in rural areas, while approximately 57 percent of whites resided in the countryside. African Americans constituted a comparatively small portion of metropolitan populations, but their presence fueled racial tensions among laborers competing against one another for jobs in densely populated cities.[43]

In Russia, nonpeasant elites responded to urban demographic changes through accusations and expressions of anxiety about urban violence. The term "hooliganism" came into usage at the turn of the twentieth century, a word that connoted everything from disorderly public behavior to offenses like theft and murder.[44] Through an analysis of St. Petersburg newspapers, Joan Neuberger found that members of the upper classes believed hooliganism was on the rise between 1900 and 1905; they "perceived an increase in rowdy public drunkenness," particularly on holidays or other days of rest, and worried that hooliganism "had become a sign of urban social disintegration and a symbol of the 'degeneracy' and 'danger' of the urban lower classes."[45] According to Neuberger, Russian elites believed that one of the defining characteristics of the hooligan was his "display of insolence or defiance . . . behavior previously circumscribed by noble authority [that] was now openly flaunted."[46] A 1913 governmental commission studying the problem of hooliganism declared that these criminals' victims were usually "cultured and propertied people," a claim that may have confirmed some elites' belief that urban peasants were particularly unruly.[47]

Images of disorderly urban peasants that gave voice to these concerns circulated widely in illustrated periodicals at the turn of the twentieth century. Russia's foremost satirical journal, *Strekoza*, published some of the nation's most critical representations of the peasantry. Founded in 1875, *Strekoza* published weekly and targeted a mass urban readership through its stories and cartoons. As a publication that purported to focus on humorous topics, *Strekoza* had the unique ability to address controversial issues of contemporary relevance through satire. In fin de siècle Russia, José Alaniz argues, cartoonists "learned how to make their points more subtly and evade the censor" under the guise of comedy.[48] On *Strekoza*'s pages, illustrators unceasingly disparaged the peasants through their depictions of drunk or violent men and women who were unable to effectively assimilate into urban life. Such representations reflected genuine urban problems including alcoholism and poverty; however, they served to elicit readers' contempt rather than to evoke sympathy.

Strekoza's illustrators primarily depicted the peasantry's abuse of alcohol in modern cities. For instance, a series of silhouettes called "Topical Terms" depicts different urban groups engaging in activities that illustrated phrases like "Shorter Working Hours," "Improving the [Quality of] Life," "Strike," and "Increase of Contentment."[49] Here, *Strekoza* pokes fun at new vocabulary expressing the labor concerns of the working classes that were increasingly used in public discourse following the Revolution of 1905. Under the phrase

"Holiday Break," an urban peasant lies unconscious on a park bench while his friend drinks alcohol from a flask, *Strekoza's* interpretation of how peasants might use their newfound leisure time. In an additional scene, "Shorter Working Hours," two peasants bring home a friend who lies unconscious in their wagon.

Images of brawling male peasants were also exceedingly common in *Strekoza's* pages during the late nineteenth and early twentieth centuries. Cartoons published during subsequent decades played on similar themes by suggesting that peasants were constantly engaged in senseless violent activity. For instance, an illustration published in March 1890, "Lunch Menu," depicts the visage of a disorderly male urban peasant, a "meatball" with a black eye. One month later, *Strekoza* followed up with a cartoon titled "Methods of Treatment," which showed three urban male peasants punching and kicking one another under the heading "Electricity."[50] Finally, "Comparatively," an illustrated dialogue between two friends, suggested that peasants frequently engaged in pointless quarreling. When the male urban peasant asks the female peasant if she is getting along with her husband, she replies, "Oh yes, I think that we get along very well: typically others fight every day, but we only brawl three times a week, no more."[51] Ultimately, illustrations depicting violent confrontations between urban peasants served as visual evidence that corroborated elites' anxieties. To members of the upper classes living in cities, rural-to-urban migrant peasants seemed to disrupt metropolitan life.

Urban elites perceived peasants as threatening in another important way that related to their antimodern proclivities. At the turn of the twentieth century, a period when mass epidemics swept through cities, the peasantry's instinctive resistance to change appeared to endanger public safety. Russia, a nation stricken by cholera more frequently than any other European country, experienced several notable outbreaks that affected both rural and urban areas in 1892, 1904, and 1907.[52] Nancy Mandelker Frieden has found that the epidemic of 1892 in particular "radicalized the medical profession," because the government, unable to cope with the scale of the disease on its own, cooperated with *zemstva*, regional medical groups, and doctors to provide care to the people.[53] Together, these organizations and individuals sought to educate the public about the ways in which they could reduce the likelihood of contracting cholera.

The illustrators of *Strekoza*, however, presented modern advice as going unheeded in a cartoon that depicts urban peasants stubbornly refusing to follow good health practices. Titled "Anti-Cholera Measures," the cartoon features images and text portraying foolish men, women, and children engaging in deceptive behavior that ignored the advice of the Sanitary Commission.[54] For instance, the text beneath a picture of an urban peasant selling fish with monstrous skulls to a middle-class urban denizen reads, "All measures taken for live fish cages on the [river] Fontanka ensure that the fish sold to consumers have been of the highest quality." Behind the urban peasant stands a woman in a kerchief, possibly his wife, who fills with tap water a jug labeled "fresh milk." Beneath her, the text advises, "It is very healthful and especially recommended to drink a glass of pure, undiluted, untouched milk as an anti-cholera measure."[55]

A related image depicts a peasant boy similarly striving to deceive consumers through cost-cutting actions that had the potential to spread disease. The child dips his cup into the river in front of a factory in order to fill up a pitcher of "raspberry kvass"; he will dye the water fuchsia and sell it to customers seeking to follow the anti-cholera advice that drinking the juice is a healthy way to quench their thirst.[56] This cartoon suggests that *Strekoza's* illustrators viewed the peasantry as an uncivilized group of people who put the health of their customers at risk. Refusing to adhere to modern recommendations about sanitary practices, men, women, and children appear to lie to consumers about the quality of the goods they sell. A final scene takes viewers inside an apartment where three disheveled peasants live in squalor. The father eats soup at a filthy table, a mother sleeps on a fly-covered bed, and a child squats on the floor amid rats and trash, smoking a pipe. The textual description emphasizes the importance of keeping urban apartments clean so that the cholera virus will have nowhere to thrive.[57] Ultimately, *Strekoza's* representations of the peasantry as simpleminded and untrustworthy likely confirmed some readers' anxieties about the peasantry's inability to serve as cooperative urban citizens.

In American periodicals and widely distributed lithographs, urban African Americans similarly appeared as unassimilated individuals who engaged in distasteful activities and instigated violence. A set of two images created by Currier and Ives, the New York City–based lithographic firm, features African American men engaging in dogfighting. In "It's a Sure Thing," a gang of African American men smoke cigars as they brag to one another about their canine participant in an upcoming dogfight.[58] A subsequent lithograph, "All Broke Up," reveals the aftermath of the gruesome event: the gang's ringleader sports a black eye and tattered clothing and has lost an ear. He pushes a wheelbarrow carrying the bloodied corpse of the dog, who has apparently lost the fight. The other members of the group similarly appear bruised and beaten as they lug the body of a man who may even have lost his life.[59]

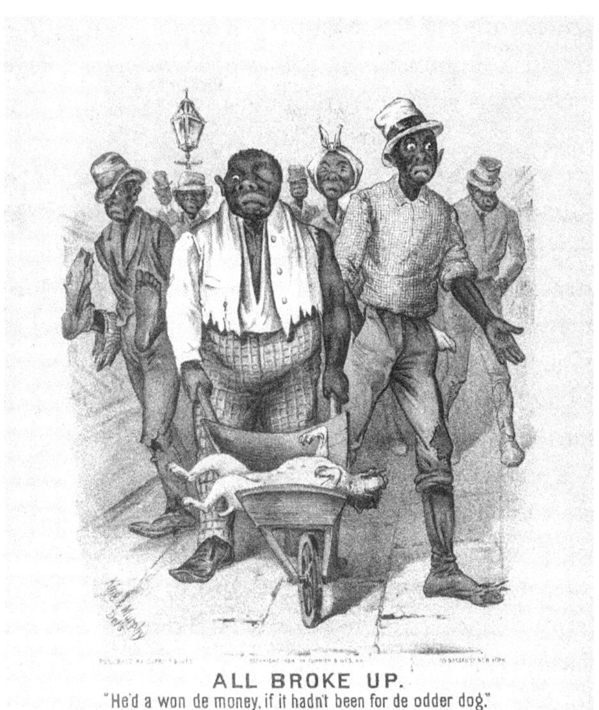

"All Broke Up," Currier and Ives, 1884. Flat file D, folder "Caricatures 1884," PR10-1, Caricature and Cartoon Collection, New-York Historical Society.

Such an illustration helped substantiate the stereotype of African American men as violent criminals, a concept promoted in articles and essays of the era. For instance, former New York police commissioner William McAdoo wrote in *Harper's Weekly* in 1906 that "one of the most troublesome and dangerous characters with which the police have to deal is the Tenderloin type of negro," an "overdressed, flashy, bejeweled loafer, gambler, and, in many instances, general criminal." McAdoo generalized about such individuals' proclivities, describing them as sloths who "never work," who could "be seen sunning themselves in front of their favorite saloons and gambling-houses," and who lurked about "heavily armed, generally carrying, in addition to the indispensable revolver, a razor," weapons they used "with deadly effect."[60] His description likely confirmed the views of whites who saw black urban residents as objectionable newcomers with criminal tendencies. Southerners like the popular novelist Thomas Nelson Page offered further support to this notion by arguing that African Americans possessed uniquely troublesome traits. In his essay "The Great American Question," Page described African Americans as prone to excitability by outside influences and claimed that when "in power [they] are, for the most part, arrogant, swaggering, dangerous, and intolerable."[61] Arguments like those of McAdoo and Page ultimately boosted popular conceptions of African Americans as violent and aggressive.

Additional illustrations portrayed African Americans as an undisciplined group of people who abused alcohol. For instance, Currier and Ives's "De Lime Kiln Club: A Temperance Racket" portrays an African American man named "Brother Gardner" addressing a group of black men in a private, club-like setting. Although they appear to listen raptly to their speaker's "celebrated lecture on temperance," almost all the audience members covertly drink alcohol from bottles tucked under their hats or hidden behind their backs. The speaker remains ignorant to the fact that his words have gone unheeded.[62] Representations like this one reflected the widespread view that alcoholism and other unhealthy lifestyles plagued urban African American communities. Late nineteenth-century scientific journals connected criminal behavior with alcoholism in articles that analyzed the factors causing psychological disturbances in African Americans. Social reformer Frances Kellor argued in her article "The Criminal Negro: Childhood Influences" that the parents of juvenile African American criminals engaged in drinking, smoking, and gambling, while an anonymous article comparing the mental health of different ethnic groups claimed that factors including "alcohol, vices, excesses in vicious habits, burden of support, overcrowded and unhealthy apartments, violations of rules of health and hygiene, idleness and general privation, political and religious excitement, etc." played central roles in causing insanity among African Americans.[63]

Strikingly, the author of the latter article categorizes the aforementioned activities as ones that concerned African Americans' "*abuse of freedom*," a statement that alludes to their condition as formerly enslaved people and to white Americans' disapproval of their ability to exercise their newfound liberty.[64] Such attitudes were also evident in a series of lithographs that ridiculed all-black towns by depicting African Americans as unable to properly self-govern. Currier and Ives's "The Darktown Fire Brigade—Slightly Demoralized" depicts the wreckage of the all-black firefighters' mule-drawn wagon, which has fallen off a bridge into a river before its drivers could reach the fire. Instead of working together to salvage its parts, however, the firefighters beat and wrestle one another in frustration.[65] A comparable lithograph, "The Darktown Fire Brigade—Under Full Steam," further humiliates its African American subjects.[66] In this illustration, the inept firefighters attempt to rescue hapless, oversexualized women in various states of undress; one woman's breasts are exposed as she runs from the burning house, and another climbs down a ladder while a firefighter sprays water at her bottom from his hose.

Other images from the series mocked freedpeople's capacity for overseeing their own justice system; for instance, "A Darktown Law Suit—Part Second" portrayed an attorney's attempt to resolve a legal dispute. During a meeting of four African American men on a farm, a bull runs roughshod through the group, knocking over the attorney and causing a pail of water to fall on his prostrate body.[67] The lawyer, drawn with cartoonish, racist facial features, appears both impotent and incompetent. Representations like these deliberately denigrated African Americans' attempts to exercise their newfound civil rights and to form their own communities, efforts that white Americans perceived as threatening to the existing racial hierarchy. While their emphasis on racial differences was unique to the dynamics of American life, their anxieties about societal changes were not. Indeed, both nonpeasant Russian and white Americans clearly expressed their discomfort with the demographic and emigrational changes in their urban landscapes through images of black- and peasant-inflicted disorder in illustrated periodicals and lithographs.

Visual Representations of Russian and African American Culture

The phenomenon of urbanization raised concerns among Russians and Americans about the loss of black and peasant cultural traditions. Between 1870 and 1890, a period of rapid industrialization that led to rural-to-urban migration and the disruption of village life, Russian authors, musicians, artists, ethnographers, and architects turned their attention to the historic traditions of the *narod* (folk). For many, the former serfs' collective identity as members of a historically rural population that composed a demographic majority was a matter of national heritage. Educated elites argued that Russian *narodnost'*, or national identity, could be found in the values and practices of the peasantry.[68] But elites increasingly recognized that peasants were not a monolithic group and sought to make sense of Russia's vast and expanding population by creating categories of people. Scholar Marina Mogilner contends that the concept of *narodnost'* "coexisted and, in a way, competed for academic prominence with such anthropologic categories as *tribe* (*plemia*), *race*, and a more politicized category, *people* (*narod*).[69] These ethnographic and scientific terms increasingly shaped the ways in which artists represented the peasantry during the late nineteenth century.[70]

After emancipation, educated Russian elites strove to preserve and reinterpret Russia's past through the preservation of knowledge about peasant practices through documentation and artistic creation. Researchers transcribed folk songs, architects constructed buildings in neo-Muscovite style, and musicians composed operas, symphonies, and ballets that retold events relating to the country's founding or brought traditional folktales to life onstage. One of the most influential movements was that of the Peredvizhniki (Wanderers), a group of artists who orchestrated a shift in the production of art that imitated European traditions to one that celebrated a uniquely Russian style.

Illustrated periodicals also presented to curious readers visual representations of different peasant groups accompanied by articles written in an ethnographic style that explained their folk traditions or heritage. For instance, the journal *Niva* published under the heading "Peoples of Russia" a series of articles about ethnic groups residing near the metropolitan centers of the empire, St. Petersburg and Moscow. *Niva's* "Russkie tipy: Zhenshchina Saratovskoi gubernii" (Russian Types: Woman from the Saratov Province) explored the lives of the peasants of the Saratov Province, located 521 miles southeast of Moscow. The article contains an illustration depicting a female peasant in a festive costume from her native region. With hands crossed gently at her waist, she looks calmly into the distance. The associated text seeks to disabuse the reader of the "generally accepted" notion that "peasant women possess almost no voice and no value in rural village societies"; indeed, its ethnographic study of the Saratov peasants reveals that these *devitsy-starchiki* (maiden spiritual-elders) played a central role both in their families and in the broader Saratov society.[71]

A similar illustration for the article "Pskovitianki" (Maids of Pskov) portrays a group of women in folk costume from the province of Pskov, located 180 miles to the southwest of St. Petersburg. The accompanying text presents an ethnographic account of the province and its peasantry by detailing the region's topography and the demographic trends that shaped rural life. A large portion of the essay is devoted to the intriguing rituals that governed the peasantry's social and religious lives. For instance, traditional wedding ceremonies lasted over the course of several days and were often separated into three distinct parts: the arrangement of the marriage, the preparations for the ceremony and the wedding itself, and the postnuptial celebrations.[72] The bride-to-be typically displayed continuous opposition to the impending prospect of marriage through wailing, lamentations, and rituals.[73] In *Niva*, the author describes in detail the Pskov peasantry's rituals that included "ne-

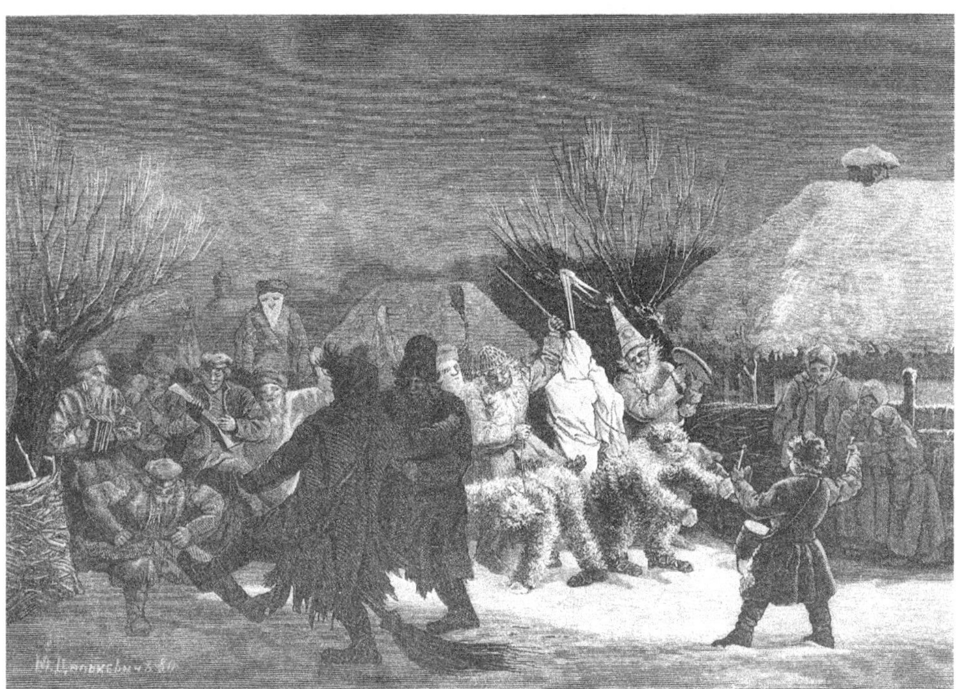

M. Dal'kevich, "Christmastime in the Village," *Vsemirnaia illiustratsiia*, no. 625
(January 1, 1881): 12.

vesta bezhit s zhenykhom," a bride's dramatic display of running away from
her groom, and her parents' ceremonial visit with the young fiancé and his
parting gift of vodka.[74] Other periodicals such as *Vsemirnaia illiustratsiia* and
Ogonek contained stand-alone, sentimental images alluding to rituals relating
to particular holidays or the changing of the seasons. "Gadan'e na suzhenogo"
(Divination of the Betrothed) depicts peasants girls in a snowy wood with
sheets covering their heads as they seek to predict who their future husbands
might be, while "Sviatki v derevne" (Christmastime in the Village) and "Russkaia maslenitsa—Maslenitsa obriady v XVII veke" (Russian Maslenitsa—
Maslenitsa Rituals during the Seventeenth Century) portray masked or
costumed peasants celebrating holidays that blended pre-Christian and Russian Orthodox traditions.[75]

Periodicals also frequently featured images that scholar Jeffrey Brooks describes as "representations of peoples of the empire," or depictions of the
peasantry that were at times a source of "autocratic pride."[76] As the government expanded the borders of the Russian Empire via military forays into the
south and east, Russia's rural subjects became increasingly multiethnic.[77]

Articles like "Narody Rossii—Tatary" (Peoples of Russia—Tatars), and its accompanying image depicting the shadowed silhouettes of two men driving a cart, recounted the centuries of history that shaped the Tatars' tribal life.[78] The author characterized contemporary Tatars, a historically nomadic people, as "farmers, living quietly, not engaging in different or special activities, and not prosperous."[79] But his pronouncements about their ethnic character contained a suspicious undertone that may have reflected the decades of warfare between the Russian Empire and the Tatars that occurred in the fifteenth and sixteenth centuries. Indeed, the author's assertion that the Tatars "often engaged in horse stealing, [possessed] a moody and secretive character, and were proud and evil by nature" suggests that he viewed them as outsiders yet to be fully accepted as fellow subjects.[80] Thus, as Russia's borders expanded, some representations of Russia's diversifying peasant estate became increasingly complicated.

As in Russia, American readers were similarly captivated by the folk traditions of the formerly enslaved. Some Americans shared their Russian counterparts' concerns that urbanization would cause the disappearance of African American culture, chief among them the freedpeoples' rich musical traditions. In an effort to preserve their heritage, historian and Northerner William Francis Allen published the first full-length collection of songs of enslaved African Americans in 1867. In its introduction, Allen declared that "the partial collections in the possession of the editors . . . should not be forgotten and lost, but that these relics of a state of society which has passed away should be preserved while it is still possible."[81] Unlike his Russian counterparts, however, Allen did not believe that African American songs and culture represented America's soul. He and many other late nineteenth-century white Americans saw their heritage and race as separate from that of formerly enslaved people. Nonetheless, they were fascinated by African American culture and the musical traditions that developed in the United States. Allen expressed this perspective when he wrote, "[Songs of enslaved people] are imbued with the mode and spirit of European music, often, nevertheless, retaining a tinge of their native Africa."[82] Like literate, urban Russians, white Americans felt connected to African Americans through elements of a shared musical tradition and the dark history of slavery that inevitably bound them.

After slavery was abolished, some freedpeople wanted to forget the melodies born from their oppression. But a group of African American men and women at Fisk University, a school for freedpeople in Nashville, Tennessee, organized a traveling choir that became known as the Fisk Jubilee Singers.[83] During the 1870s, they toured around the world, bringing spirituals and other songs of the enslaved to enthusiastic audiences. They even performed the abolitionist paean "John Brown's Body" for Russia's Grand Duchess Mariia Fedorovna just decades after her father-in-law, Tsar Alexander II, freed the serfs.[84] Ultimately, the choir's efforts sparked international interest in preserving the songs of enslaved African Americans, which were thereafter transcribed with growing vigor.

Illustrations in popular periodicals serve as evidence of the growing interest in African Americans' musical traditions during the late nineteenth century. Artists produced nostalgic engravings of enslaved African Americans and freedpeople in predominantly rural settings as they sang, danced, or played instruments. For example, *Scribner's Monthly*'s "Terpsichore in the Flat Creek Quarters" depicts a post-emancipation plantation dance where African American freedpeople joyfully jump in response to the caller's commands and the fiddler's tunes.[85] The caller even pokes fun at the absent white landowners in his declaration to the crowd, written in dialect and containing offensive language: "De white folks come it mighty handy, waltzin' 'roun' so nice an' fine; / But when you come to reg'lar *dancin', niggers leabes 'em way behin'!*"[86]

On other occasions, white spectators directly observed African Americans' musical traditions with the interest of an outsider peering into the world of another. Fiction writer Richard B. Kimball provided the reader with what appeared to be an authentic glimpse of antebellum plantation life in the sentimental tale "Story of an Old Traveler." During his extensive tour of Louisiana, the narrator describes the countryside of the 1830s as a place where he could "perceive the mansions of the wealthy planter and the cabins of his 'force.'" Alone in an unknown land where the narrator "encountered scarcely any white people" but passed "negroes . . . frequently," he was delighted to observe that "nearly every one of them was whistling or singing a plantation air, which made the aspect of things appear cheerful as [he] rode on."[87] The spirit of this textual description mirrors that of a contemporaneous image like "In Ole Virginny," an illustration in which a white couple exploring the grounds of a plantation discovers an enslaved family in the midst of a celebration. The patriarch sits on a chair in the garden, playing his banjo while children dance and clap around him. The well-dressed white spectators watch quietly from behind a fence, captivated by what may have appeared to them a curious spectacle.[88] Such images of rural, enslaved African Americans and freedpeople singing and dancing promoted an idealized vision of slavery that ignored the oppressive realities of their enslavement. These sentimental, retrospective images appealed to urban, middle-class readers in part because they offered an alternative to post-emancipation urban conditions defined by labor

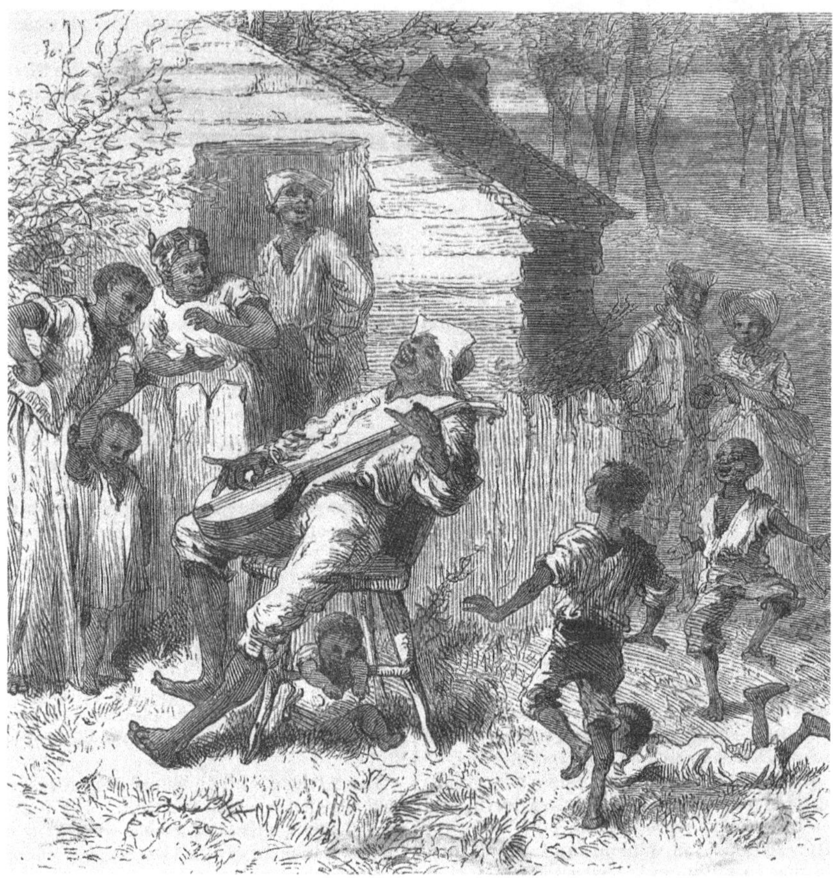

"In Ole Virginny," *Harper's Weekly*, 1876. Box 1, folder 8, "Children," PR 17, Leslie Dorsey Collection, New-York Historical Society.

competition, political strife, tense racial relations between black and white workers, and violence.

As in Russia, industrialization and urbanization ushered in a new, modern era that not only swept away past traditions but also upended the historically unequal power dynamics. Periodicals connected these two phenomena and suggested that the abolition of slavery and urban migration intensified the loss of African American cultural practices. For instance, a sketch titled "Market-Day in a Southern City" laments the ways in which abolition led to the decline of musical traditions. In the author's description of what he calls "the Tallahassee Negro," he characterizes African American freedpeople as possessing unique musical propensities. He wistfully predicts, however, that modernization, or "the tide of improvement [that] is setting steadily in this direction . . . will sweep away . . . the lazy, almost worthless, but light-hearted negro, perfectly happy while sitting in the sun and twanging a Jew's-harp, and regarding with profound respect a market-day or any other holiday that furnishes him with a valid excuse for idleness."[89] Significantly, the author tacitly signals his discomfort with the loss of more than musical heritage; his words contain seeds of apprehension about the type of African American that would *replace* the "lazy . . . light-hearted" freedman whom he perceived as "perfectly happy" spending his days playing his instrument for the public. To some readers, educated, entrepreneurial, and politically active African Americans represented a group poised to overturn the social order that characterized pre-emancipation power relations between blacks and whites. For them, the abolition of slavery and the loss of elements of the enslaved African Americans' cultural heritage undeniably heralded additional transformative societal changes.

Critical Representations in Illustrated Periodicals

Another category of visual representation in periodicals includes satirical imagery that belittled the character and intelligence of the depicted figures. In both Russian and American publications, such biting illustrations depicted peasants and African Americans with far greater frequency than those who owned serfs or slaves. On occasion, however, artists produced unique representations critiquing landowners or slaveholders by portraying them as morally flawed proponents of systems of oppression.

Russian peasants and African American freedpeople occasionally appeared as ignorant and foolish individuals, qualities that some white Americans and Russian elites perceived as justifications for the existence of pre-emancipation systems of servitude and the post-emancipation perpetuation of unequal power relations between former owners and liberated serfs or freedpeople. The Russian satirical journal *Strekoza* contained the most unflattering images of the peasantry, which were often produced as cartoons accompanied by textual dialogue between different characters. The 1885 sketch "Opytnaia niania" (Experienced Nurse), for instance, ridiculed a female peasant for her ineptitude and lack of self-awareness. During an interview with her potential employer and the mother's young son, the peasant woman reveals that her former charges were all deceased: "One drowned . . . the other fell out the window, and the third fell under a streetcar—and was crushed."[90] She speaks the truth forthrightly, unconcerned about what these facts might suggest to her employer about her abilities as a caregiver.

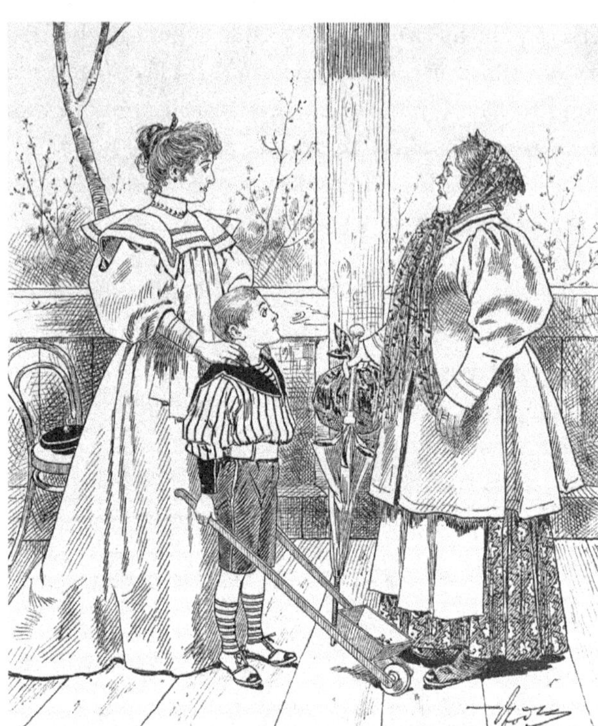

"Experienced Nurse,"
Strekoza, no. 22
(May 21, 1895): 1.

A similar cartoon produced during the same year also mocked the intelligence of a peasant servant during a discussion with her aristocratic mistress. In "Poniala" (Understood), the servant converses with her *barynia* (mistress), a loaded term that was used by serfs when they addressed their owners. After the peasant servant asks what she should do with a letter for her mistress, the imperious woman responds, "Why, I thought I told you to put it in the mug?" "Yes," replies the servant ingenuously, "but it's already been there three days, soaking. Should I throw it away or not? From the brew, there is nothing to drink."[91] Instead of storing the letter for safekeeping, the peasant woman has misinterpreted her mistress's instructions by attempting to steep the letter in hot water as if it were a tea bag. Such a caricature confirmed some readers' stereotypical views about the peasantry's innate lack of intelligence as well as incapacity for self-governance. Paternalistic illustrations such as these tacitly implied that the unequal power dynamics between members of the nobility and their servants in the post-emancipation era were justified on the basis of the peasantry's need for guidance and oversight.

American periodicals similarly caricatured freedpeople as unable to manage their own lives after emancipation. The *Harper's Weekly* cartoon

"Stumped," for example, portrays an African American freedman attempting to prepare a horse for a harness race on his humble plot of farmland. Sitting in his sulky, a two-wheeled lightweight cart, he urges the horse forward with his whip. Despite his best efforts, however, the unruly horse bucks and disobeys his commands, much to the delight of a group of African American children watching from a nearby fence post.[92] White readers may have interpreted such a representation as visual confirmation that freedpeople did not possess the skills required to manage their own livestock or, by extension, to live disciplined lives as a liberated group of people.

Other images simply served the purpose of mocking African Americans' intelligence. A turn-of-the-century cartoon, "Putting It Clearly," features a conversation between an African American man dressed in garish clothes and a black woman wearing a kerchief on her head. Both figures display cartoonish, racist features including large, protruding lips and wide, bewildered expressions. The man asks the woman in broken English, "What am an alibi?" She responds, "Dat's provin' dat yoh was at a prayer meetin' whar yoh wasn't in order to show dat yoh wasn't at de crap game whar yoh was."[93] Such a representation not only ridiculed the African American man's understanding of the law but also insinuated that he was undisciplined and hypocritical for skipping church to gamble with friends.

Demeaning images of African Americans and Russian peasants helped perpetuate the notion that these formerly enserfed or enslaved groups of people and their descendants were physically and mentally inferior to nonpeasants and whites. Artists created these images at historical moments when African Americans and peasants demanded the protection and expansion of their acquired rights. After emancipation, freedpeople and peasants exercised their political voices through participation in local, state, or federal political positions or elections. Throughout the Jim Crow era, they sought to attain the kinds of education that would provide access to new job opportunities and increasingly abandoned agricultural labor for factory work in urban centers. Thus, it is evident that the late nineteenth-century proliferation of critical cartoons speaks to the fearful or racist attitudes of artists and publishers, not to the true characteristics or behaviors of African Americans and peasants.

By contrast, periodical illustrations critiquing pre- or post-emancipation relationships between serfs, enslaved African Americans, and their owners were rare. Censorious images that did appear, however, typically condemned the treatment of bonded laborers. Although these representations seldom depicted violence, they occasionally alluded to the taboo subjects of interracial and inter-estate relationships between powerful men and subjugated women.

An undated cartoon from an unknown American publication, for instance, portrays a barefoot, enslaved African American carrying a white man, woman, and two children on his shoulders. The man, wearing a "C.S." (Confederate States) crown, admonishes the enslaved African American, "You ungrateful wretch, don't you know that you couldn't stand alone without us here to hold you up?" The man replies, "Couldn't I walk just as well without this load, Massa?"[94] The image clearly invites the reader's sympathy for the enslaved African American, whose journey is burdened by the heavy cargo he is forced to carry. Ultimately, the illustration begs the reader to consider the strength of whites' tenuous, paternalistic arguments that slavery benefited the enslaved.

American cartoonist Thomas Nast also produced illustrations of African Americans that criticized their treatment by whites and by the federal government during the post-emancipation era. One of the most prominent political cartoonists of the late nineteenth century, the German-born artist learned his craft at the National Academy of Design in New York City. After the Civil War, Nast primarily drew illustrations for *Harper's Weekly* that focused on contemporary issues, especially those of a political nature.[95] *Harper's Weekly* supported the Republican Party from the Civil War era until 1884, and Nast's cartoons often championed black rights during this period.[96] Two of his most famous illustrations were "The Union as It Was" (1874) and "Is *This* a Republican Form of Government? Is *This* Protecting Life, Liberty, or Property? Is *This* the Equal Protection of the Laws?" (1876). Both illustrations decried white violence against African Americans during Reconstruction through sympathetic representations of freedpeople. In "The Union as It Was," a white male member of the terrorist organization the "White League" shakes hands with a hooded Klansman. They agree to work together to oppress African Americans in the South, who are represented on a shield by a family huddling in fear under the heading "Worse than Slavery." Behind them, a schoolhouse burns and the body of a lynched African American hangs from a tree.[97] Two years later, Nast created a similarly heart-wrenching image depicting an African American man kneeling before the slain bodies of an African American man, woman, and infant as he turns his eyes to the heavens. In the background, a sign reads, "The White Liners Were Here," a grim reminder of the violence against freedpeople enacted by white terrorist organizations like the White Liners across the South during the Reconstruction era.[98] In both illustrations, Nast effectively confronted *Harper's Weekly's* readers with the reality of race relations in the post-emancipation South. Despite the passage of the Reconstruction amendments that were intended to

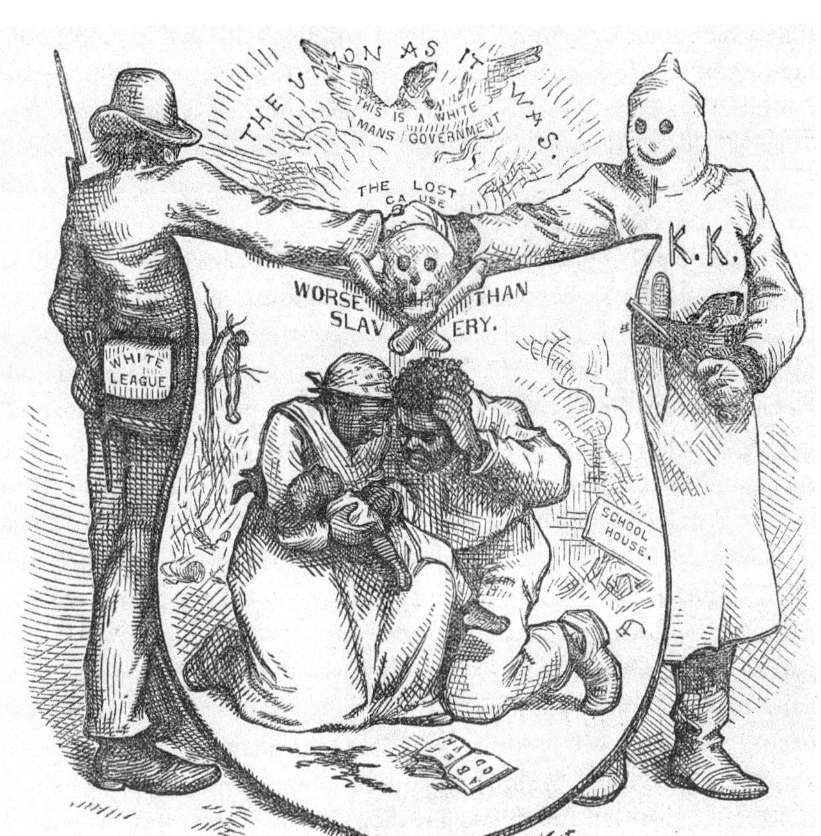

Thomas Nast, "The Union as It Was / The Lost Cause, Worse than Slavery," *Harper's Weekly* 18 (October 24, 1874): 878. New-York Historical Society.

abolish slavery and secure for freedpeople citizenship and the franchise, these laws were unable to fully protect African Americans.

In Russia, artists similarly criticized elites who mistreated the peasantry and abused their power during the post-emancipation era. A pair of identical illustrations printed in *Ogonek* and *Vsemirnaia illiustratsiia* subtly condemned aristocratic landowners for their greed and lack of empathy for their former serfs. In *Vsemirnaia illiustratsiia*'s "Oblomki prezhnego velichie: Matushka barynia" (Fragments of Former Greatness: Mother Mistress), an obese, unkempt landowner sits on the dilapidated porch of her manor, ordering about her female peasant servants with an extended hand. The former serfs do not make eye contact with her; instead, they obediently do her bidding.[99] Thanks to Russian censorship laws, the artist's criticism of the noblewoman is necessarily subtle; however, both his illustration's title and his unflattering drawing of the landowner reveal his sensibilities. Three years later, *Ogonek* reprinted the same illustration under a different title, "Ostatki proshlogo velichiia" (Remnants of Past Greatness). The replication of the image in a different publication suggests both the rarity of comparable portrayals and readers' interest in such a controversial topic.[100]

Another type of critical representation was that which alluded to the sexual exploitation of female bonded laborers. In both Russia and the United States, this taboo topic was rarely discussed in literature or art during the late nineteenth century. Isolated, notable examples included Thomas Satterwhite Noble's painting *The Price of Blood* (1868), which depicted a slave owner selling his mixed-race son; the radical short stories of abolitionist Louisa May Alcott; and Aleksei Pisemskii's play *A Bitter Fate* (1859), which described an ill-fated romance between a landowner and his female serf.[101] Sexual relations between enslaved or enserfed women and their owners, however, were not infrequent in Russia and the United States. As human property, enslaved African Americans were assaulted or even raped, wrongdoings evidenced in part by the testimonies of the formerly enslaved in their autobiographical narratives and by descriptions and photographs of enslaved, mixed-race people. Studies show that while the enslaved population grew by 20 percent between 1850 and 1860, the mixed-race population increased by 67 percent.[102] In Russia, censorship and different market dynamics prevented the publication of serf narratives, but scholars Priscilla R. Roosevelt and Peter Kolchin have found that some members of the nobility even housed serf harems in buildings on their extensive estates.[103]

Illustrated periodicals treaded carefully when addressing the subject of the sexual exploitation of enserfed or enslaved women. "Sblizhenie soslovii" (The Intimacy of the Estates), published in *Vsemirnaia illiustratsiia* in 1877, portrays a beautiful young female serf sweeping the ground with a broom. Her owner stands behind her with a lascivious grin on his face; he grasps her shoulder in one hand and holds a similarly phallic object, a long pipe, in the other. Together, the visual representation and the text clearly allude to his unwanted attention and its consequences.[104]

In the American context, the unusual illustration "Emancipated Slaves: White and Colored" appeared in *Harper's Weekly* in 1864 after the Union's capture of territory in Louisiana.[105] An illustration of a photograph, the drawing depicts emancipated freedpeople who were brought to a Northern photography studio as part of a fund-raising effort to support schools for Louisiana's freedpeople.[106] The adults possess a darker skin color, but most

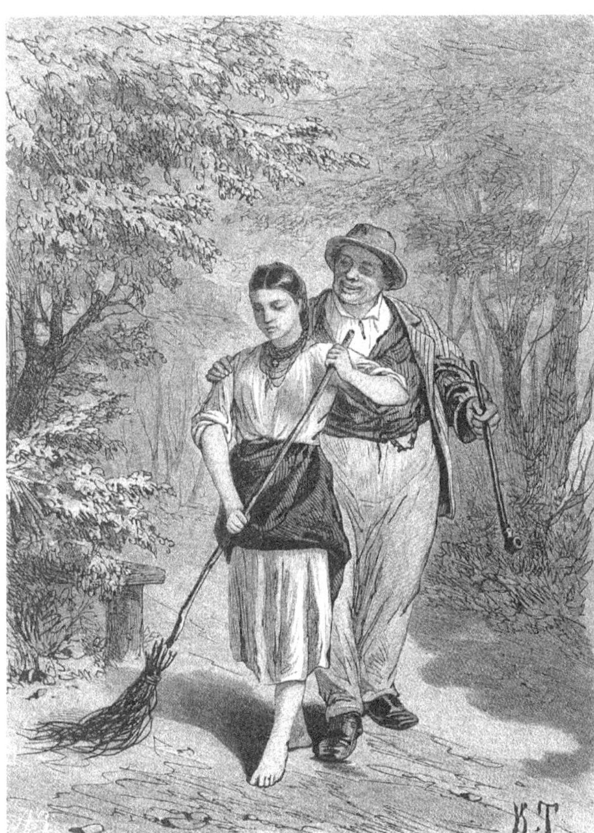

K. A. Trutovskii, "The Intimacy of the Estates," *Vsemirnaia illiustratsiia*, no. 435 (April 30, 1877): 356.

of the children standing in the foreground of the engraving appear to be white. Although the illustration's heading does not comment on this discrepancy, the implication of the drawing—that white slave owners raped enslaved women—was obvious to nineteenth-century viewers. Furthermore, the sight of enslaved children who appeared as white complicated the race-based justifications of those who supported American slavery.

Decades after emancipation, interracial sexual relations remained a highly controversial subject. During Reconstruction, seven Southern states overturned laws banning interracial marriage, but six reinstated them after Reconstruction's collapse.[107] Antilynching activist Ida B. Wells noted in her groundbreaking publication *Southern Lynch Law in All Its Phases* (1892) that unfounded claims of black sexual assault were often used to justify the white lynching of African American men during the late nineteenth century.[108] Illustrated periodicals largely avoided the topic of interracial relationships, but examples of cartoons addressing sexual relations between whites and

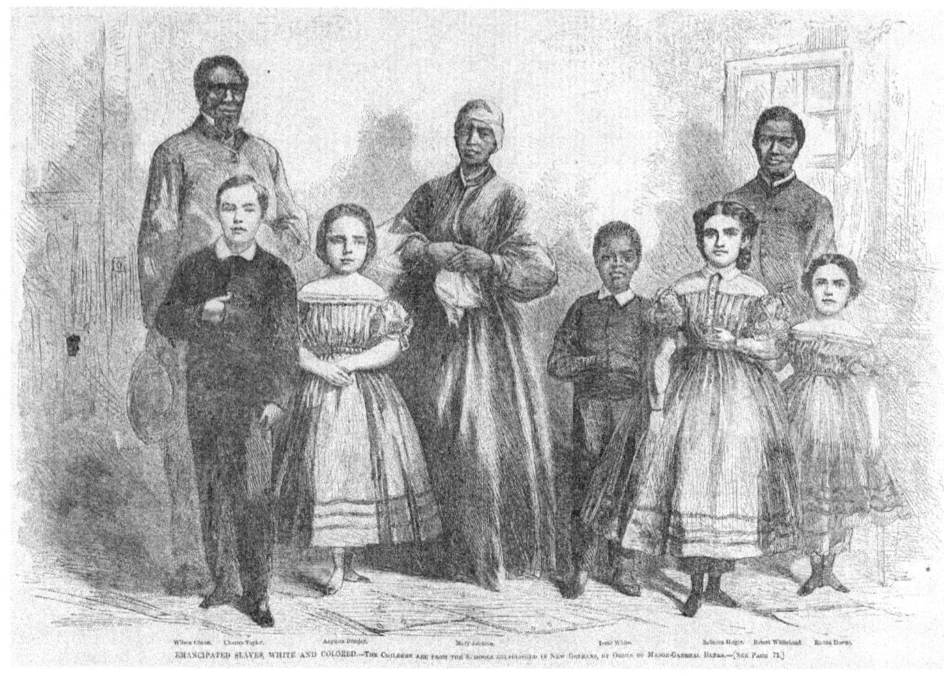

"Emancipated Slaves: White and Colored," *Harper's Weekly*, January 30, 1864, 69.
New-York Historical Society.

blacks can be found. For instance, "Not Particular," a turn-of-the-century cartoon of unknown provenance, features a well-dressed white man embracing and kissing a barefoot African American woman wearing a kerchief, possibly an enslaved laborer or domestic servant. She stands with fists clenched, unsure of how to respond to his unwelcome affections. The rhyme beneath the image reads: "I know you're not particular to a fault / Though I'm not sure you'll never be sued for assault, / You're so fond of women that even a wench / Attracts your gross fancy despite her strong stench."[109] Although the cartoon attempts to shame the predatory white man, it does so through racist language that denigrates the assaulted African American woman.

Illustrations that criticized members of the Russian nobility or white slave owners appeared with far less frequency than images that disparaged peasants and African Americans. Engravings and cartoons alike attributed to formerly bonded laborers traits such as stupidity, ignorance, or laziness. Despite the absence of racism due to shared ethnicities between landowners and peasants in the Russian context, denigrating representations of peasants regularly appeared in periodicals. In both nations, however, landowners' struggle to retain power in the face of transformative social change helps explain the simultaneous production of critical representations that characterized as inferior those engaged in the fight for civil rights, economic mobility, and political recognition.

Self-Representations of African Americans and Peasants in Illustrated Periodicals, *Lubki*, and *Lubochnaia literatura*

In the United States, dignified representations of African Americans in the illustrated periodicals with the widest circulation were uncommon. Although the nation's most popular illustrated journals, *Harper's Weekly* and *Frank Leslie's*, primarily depicted African Americans in sentimental, rural settings or as caricatures, these publications occasionally printed respectful images of African Americans.[110] During Radical Reconstruction, when the Republican-controlled Congress sought to expand rights for African Americans, for instance, both periodicals portrayed freedpeople engaging in political activity and exercising their newfound civil rights. Scholar Joshua Brown notes that these illustrations coexisted with the aforementioned stereotypes and "buffoonish caricatures" that typically appeared on the periodicals' pages, ensuring that neither publication depicted African Americans from what he calls an entirely "unilateral perspective."[111]

By comparison, the first illustrated periodicals with a primarily African American readership and artistic production staff, the *Indianapolis Freeman* and the *Colored American Magazine*, produced an abundance of dignified depictions of African Americans that contrasted sharply with those produced by white-owned publications. Edward Cooper, a native of Tennessee, recognized the demand for illustrated journals in the African American community during the late nineteenth century and established the *Freeman*. Called "the best all-around newspaper man the colored race has yet produced" by the pastor and educator Daniel Wallace Culp in 1902, Cooper achieved success as an entrepreneur.[112] According to Culp, the *Freeman* "quickly jumped into great popularity and soon gained international fame."[113] In 1903, the *Freeman* stated that its circulation reached sixteen thousand, although this number may be overstated.[114] The *Colored American Magazine*, founded by Boston's Colored Co-operative Publishing Company, also specified that its circulation was seventeen thousand at its height, making it the most widely distributed illustrated African American magazine of the era.[115] The *Freeman* maintained an art department composed of black artists who created original engravings and cartoons, while the *Colored American* primarily published photographs of African Americans rather than engravings.[116]

The depictions of African Americans that filled the pages of these popular publications challenged those that appeared in periodicals targeting white audiences. For the most part, representations of African Americans in the *Freeman* and the *Colored American Magazine* were respectful. On the front page of each weekly issue, the *Freeman* published illustrations of prominent African American leaders that included ministers, politicians, journalists, and teachers.[117] Men and women alike were featured, although most of the representations portrayed male community leaders. Depictions of accomplished members of the black professional, urban, middle class differed significantly from the sentimental images of rural African American freedpeople or criminal city dwellers.

The *Colored American*, which called itself "an Illustrated Monthly devoted to Literature, Science, Music, Art, Religion, Facts, Fiction and Tradition of the Negro Race," also regularly portrayed African American professionals. Although prominent African American men dominated the pages of the *Freeman*, many of the individuals depicted in stand-alone photographs in the *Colored American* were women. Elegant, modestly attired female "social leaders" of towns across the nation graced the magazine's pages, offering a visualization of black femininity that contrasted sharply with that of the maternal, asexual mammy or the oversexualized women of Currier and Ives.[118] For example, a photograph titled "Mrs. Johnston: One of the Leaders of Social Life in Pueblo, Col." depicts an African American woman in a dark dress with delicate buttons, sparkling earrings, and elegantly styled hair.[119]

The *Colored American*, like the *Freeman*, also published photographs of black professionals both as stand-alone portraits and as embedded in articles. For instance, in an essay assessing the causes and consequences of the infamous Springfield riot of 1909, author E. L. Rogers surveyed the black professional scene in Springfield. He presented dignified photographs of attorneys, businessmen, firemen, and insurance agents accompanied by biographical, textual information regarding their numerous accomplishments.[120] Together, illustrations and photographs of members of the black middle class in the *Freeman* and the *Colored American* offered an impressive record of the ways in which nineteenth-century African Americans contributed to their communities and achieved upward mobility.

The *Freeman's* representations of African Americans, however, were not all respectful. The publication experienced backlash from some readers for publishing cartoons that employed the visual language of the racial caricatures that appeared in white-owned periodicals of the era. Artist Moses Tucker, hired in 1889, unsettled black readers with cartoons that ridiculed African Americans as inept or foolish. For example, a cartoon from the Septem-

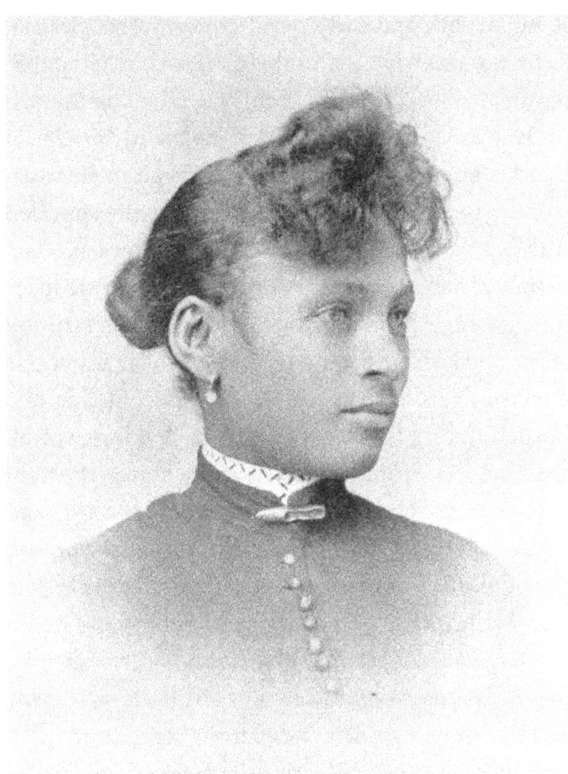

"Mrs. Johnston: One of the Leaders of Social Life in Pueblo, Col.," *Colored American Magazine,* October 1900, 284.

ber 6, 1890, issue of the *Freeman* portrays a conversation between an African American boy, "Little Eboney," and a maternal figure, "Mrs. Eboney." When the boy approaches the woman with his mouth agape and eyes wide, she inquires, "What's de matter chile?" The boy responds nonsensically, "Oh, mammy! I'se done been scared dat bad I can't talk no more. Boo-oo-oo-wah!"[121] Here, the artist adopts strategies of racist humor typically employed by white artists that included the creation of cartoonish physical features and the use of caricatures like the mammy figure. Scholar Andreá N. Williams writes that Cooper, the *Freeman*'s editor, defended his decision to hire Tucker because "when created by and for African American viewers in a black periodical, black caricatures served a self-reflexive, didactic function rather than the denigrating one in white media."[122] Nonetheless, the *Freeman*'s decision to publish such cartoons attests to the pervasiveness and perniciousness of visual stereotypes of African Americans during the late nineteenth century.

Russian peasants also gained increased access to illustrated, mass-oriented publications including *lubki* (popular prints) and *lubochnaia literatura* (popular literature) during the late nineteenth and early twentieth centuries. Scholar Jeffrey Brooks has traced the extensive history of these mass-oriented publications that first appeared in the seventeenth century as religious-themed prints for the nobility.[123] Over the next two centuries, *lubki* and *lubochnaia literatura* evolved in style and content as their subject matter became increasingly secular. By the turn of the nineteenth century, *lubki* primarily appealed to rural and urban peasants, who adorned the walls of their homes and taverns with the colorful illustrated sheets, much as African American freedpeople decorated cabins with engravings from illustrated journals at the turn of the twentieth century. *Lubochnaia literatura* changed in a similar fashion, a transformation that is reflected in its subject matter. Brooks contends that 40 percent of works published during the 1890s related to "folklore, chivalrous tales, instructive works, and tales about merchants," whereas the subjects of "banditry, crime, science, romance, and an admixture of crime and romance" made up 16 percent of works during the same decade.[124] In fact, one of the most successful publishers of mass-oriented literature in the late nineteenth century was Ivan Sytin, a state-owned peasant's son, whose newspaper *Russkoe slovo* had the largest circulation in the nation.[125] Overall, little is known about the authors of *lubochnaia literatura*, but it is likely that many of these works were written by individuals descended from the peasantry.[126]

Two of the most prominent post-emancipation authors of *lubochnaia literatura*, Ivan Semenovich Ivin (1858–1918/1921) and Matvei Ivanovich Ozhegov (1860–1933), heralded from the peasant estate.[127] Ivin was the son of a serf, and Ozhegov descended from state-owned peasants. Brooks has found that both men "shared with other people of peasant origin many of the conflicting and troubling pressures of their times. They may have escaped from their class, but they were deeply marked by its worries and concerns. When they wrote about social mobility and whether or not a person could and should make his way up in the world, they wrote from experience."[128] Ivin dealt with topics including urban migration and the peasantry's homesickness for rural life, while Ozhegov wrote optimistic poems about upward mobility.[129] Other creators of peasant-oriented *lubochnaia literatura* and *lubki* that targeted the peasantry similarly addressed the changes transforming their villages or illustrated the challenges of urban life.[130] Gambling, a risky way of striving to improve one's fortunes, was figuratively demonized in the *lubok* "Demon igry: Kartezhnaia igra ne prineset dobra" (Demon Game: The Card Game Will Not Bring Good Fortune).[131] The print depicts several smaller illustrations that surround an image of a fierce dragon made of cards. Clutching a bag of money, the dragon breathes fire onto the smoldering towns and cities of Russia. Meanwhile, a male peasant shields his son from the dragon, pointing toward the creature as if to warn the child of the dangers of gambling. The smaller illustrations adorning the exterior of the *lubok* depict men who have lost their possessions: one peasant sells his clothing, while another lies bleeding on the ground after having committed suicide from despair. This instructive *lubok* cautioned peasants by urging them to avoid temptations that might bring about their financial ruin. The writers of *lubki* and *lubochnaia literatura* created works that appealed to the peasantry because they comprehended their troubles and the social transformations wrought by abolition, industrialization, and urbanization. Although too little is known about these authors, Brooks notes, they "took their writing seriously" and shared with readers their own experiences with "ambition, success, disappointment, and injustice" through simple, illustrated fictional tales with which peasant readers could directly relate.[132]

The range of visual representations of serfs, enslaved African Americans, peasants, and freedpeople in illustrated periodicals reveals both the multiplicity and evolution of perspectives of peasants and freedpeople during the four decades that followed the abolition of serfdom and slavery. Representational similarities demonstrate parallel responses to the social, economic, and political changes that transformed two predominantly agricultural societies. Postemancipation depictions of liberated peasants and African American freedpeople contentedly continuing to serve their former owners demonstrate artists' and viewers' resistance to changes in historical power dynamics governing relationships, while images portraying freedpeople and peasants as perpetrators of urban disorder serve as additional evidence of nonpeasant and white anxieties about the activities of liberated serfs and formerly enslaved people. Representations of folk culture speak to viewers' curiosity about peasants and freedpeople and their fascination with conceptions of national identity, but they also point to the cultural divisions that separated educated, urban elites from predominantly rural peasants and freedpeople shortly after emancipation. Depictions that demeaned the intellect of former serfs and enslaved African Americans abounded, whereas portrayals critiquing the character of serf and slave owners were in short supply, a discrepancy that indicates a lack of self-reflection and an absence of self-awareness among those who had never personally experienced a life of enslavement or enserfment. Finally, the dignified self-representations of African Americans and peasants in illustrated publications targeting African American and peasant audiences served as essential counterpoints that challenged and expanded the depictions circulating in white-owned periodicals and publishing companies.

CHAPTER FOUR

Oil Paintings

The abolition of Russian serfdom and American slavery heralded enormous societal changes that encouraged the development of national art during the second half of the nineteenth century. In Russia, the political decision to emancipate the serfs occurred at a moment when many artists chafed against the prescripts of aesthetic convention that encouraged the mimicry of European traditions in painting.[1] After the abolition of serfdom, Russian painters grappled with questions pertaining to peasant identity and assimilation in genre paintings that focused on both contemporary and historical Russian topics. Meanwhile, the experience of the U.S. Civil War inspired American artists to paint works depicting slavery, the central cause of the conflict, as well as the war's aftermath. Just weeks after Confederates fired on Fort Sumter, *New York Monthly Magazine* accurately predicted that a new form of American national art would "arise from out of this political chaos . . . and soar aloft on the expanded wing of the American eagle."[2] As in Russia, the abolition of slavery prompted American artists to assess its legacy in genre paintings of African Americans that sparked debate among audiences as they sought to comprehend their changing national identity.

Between 1861 and 1905, American and Russian artists of diverse backgrounds depicted peasants and African Americans in hundreds of oil paintings, a prestigious form of creative expression supported by grand institutions like New York's Academy of Design and St. Petersburg's Academy of Arts. Their compositions of peasants and African Americans differed significantly from pre-emancipation works primarily painted by white and aristocratic artists who typically presented slavery and serfdom through a classical, formal lens that marginalized those who were enserfed or enslaved.[3] These paternalistic representations of plantation and estate life belied the hardships of servitude and denied agency to serfs and enslaved people. By contrast, postemancipation artists, some of whom were African American or came from the peasant estate, portrayed their subjects in a broader range of settings that revealed to viewers the complexity of their experiences. Russian and American painters created thematically similar works that depicted bondage, emancipation, military service, public schooling, and the urban environment. In these paintings, serfs and enslaved African Americans seek freedom, become soldiers, learn to read, or leave the countryside to find employment in cities. While many post-emancipation artists created humanizing portraits of African Americans and peasants that countered the archetypes circulating in mass-oriented publications, some depicted them as contented serfs or enslaved people or as dissolute urban migrants in representations that questioned the benefits of abolition. These compositions collectively served as important visual sources that shaped nineteenth-century viewers' conceptions of freedpeople and peasants during the decades that followed the abolition of serfdom and slavery. Furthermore, these paintings played a critical role in molding Russians' and Americans' sense of national identity as the two countries reconstructed their societies during an era of substantial political and social reform.

Representations of Peasants and African Americans in Russian and American Paintings

Russian and American artists represented peasants and African Americans in paintings in parallel and contrasting ways between 1861 and 1905. Immediately after abolition, Nikolai Nevrev and Thomas Satterwhite Noble reflected on the twin legacies of serfdom and slavery in bold, controversial paintings that sharply criticized landowners in scenes depicting the sale of serfs and enslaved African Americans.[4] Their pictorial condemnations of institutionalized servitude contrasted sharply with nostalgic paintings that portrayed peasants and freedpeople as loyal to their former owners.[5] Such discordant representations suggest that Russian and American artists possessed differing views of serfdom and slavery and strove to shape audiences' historical memories through opposing scenes that depicted owners as callous or clement and serfs and enslaved people as faithful or defiant.

Artists also reflected on notions of citizenship, subjecthood, and duty by depicting African American freedpeople or Russian peasants as enlisted or conscripted soldiers. After the Confederacy's defeat in the Civil War, Northern painters Thomas Waterman Wood and Edward Lamson Henry portrayed African American military service as a noble, liberating endeavor that legitimized their claims to citizenship.[6] In Russia, however, painters including Il'ia Repin, Konstantin Savitskii, and Nikolai Pimonenko depicted military conscription as a fate comparable to enslavement for the peasantry.[7] They did so even after the enactment of the Universal Conscription Act in 1874, a fact that attests to the enduring memory of an era when the peasantry bore the brunt of military service.

Agriculture is another common theme in Russian and American depictions of freedpeople and peasants; artists created numerous scenes in which men and women labored in fields of wheat, corn, and cotton. Russian compositions of this type typically showed serene, lush landscapes where peasants happily engaged in labor that was well suited to their abilities.[8] Such representations encouraged in Russian audiences a sense of national pride in the peasantry's traditional, rural way of life and reflected the ideological sentiments espoused by Slavophiles and proponents of the Populist movement. By contrast, American portrayals of African Americans completing fieldwork, such as Winslow Homer's *The Cotton Pickers* (1876), Thomas Anshutz's *The Way They Live* (1879), and William Edouard Scott's *It's Going to Come* (1916) and *Untitled (Sharecropper)* (circa 1915–1918), criticized the continued confinement of African Americans to Southern farms because of ineffective postemancipation economic and social reforms. As a notable exception to this trend, South Carolinian William Aiken Walker suggested that African Americans could not survive outside the plantation setting in his paintings of impoverished, slovenly African Americans that belittled their physical and intellectual capabilities.[9] Ultimately, the consistency of Russian painters' depictions of agricultural labor and the diversity of comparable American representations attest to the prominent position of the peasants' agrarian tradition in Russia's national identity and to greater ideological conflict and freedom of expression in the United States.

Artists also expressed their fascination with traditional peasant culture in depictions of rituals and ceremonies in works that celebrated traditional aspects of Russia's national heritage. Weddings, holidays, dances, and religious processions were among the most commonly painted events during the second half of the nineteenth century in works by Vasilii Maksimov, Illarion Prianishnikov, Il'ia Repin, Andrei Riabushkin, and others.[10] Like the Russian ethnographers who concurrently traveled to villages to transcribe peasant folk songs, these artists journeyed across the countryside with brushes and paint boxes to record the peasants' disappearing way of life as former serfs left their cohesive communities to pursue job opportunities in expanding cities. Paintings like Maksimov's *The Arrival of a Magician at a Peasant Wedding* (1875) and Repin's *Procession of the Cross in Kursk Province* (1883) particularly thrilled urban audiences, who, increasingly removed from rural life, delighted in seeing the historic customs of Russia's rural folk (*narod*) in large-scale, dramatic paintings. Like their Russian peers, American artists also captured scenes of freedpeople practicing or passing down their musical and religious traditions in respectful illustrations that explained a way of life that was largely unfamiliar to many white Americans.[11] But while depictions of peasant rituals situated the former serfs within Russia's historical narrative, white portrayals of African American traditions positioned formerly enslaved people as exotic outsiders rather than as representatives of America's cultural heritage, a contrast due partly to ethnic differences in the case of the United States. African American artists' depictions of African American culture like Henry Ossawa Tanner's *The Banjo Lesson* (1893), by comparison, highlighted the family connections forged through the sharing of tradition.

Two additional shared themes in Russian and American depictions of peasants and freedpeople relate to educational and economic progress after emancipation. First, artists in both countries created numerous scenes pertaining to the literacy of the formerly bonded laborers. Russian painters took audiences inside rural schoolhouses where earnest children struggled to read or learn arithmetic, while American painters typically connected literacy with Christianity in scenes showing African American adults and children reading the Bible.[12] Both Russian and American artists also expressed doubt about students' advancement in paintings depicting ambivalent pupils or teachers who lack interest in the educational process.[13] Second, in their consideration of increased peasant and African American migration to urban areas during the late nineteenth century, Russian and American artists offered pessimistic assessments of how peasants and freedpeople fared outside of traditional agrarian settings. In these paintings, they frequently met unfortunate ends after leaving the countryside; for instance, a woman weeps over the body of her deceased husband in Sergei Ivanov's *On the Road: The Death of a Migrant* (1889). Unemployed urban African Americans lounge on cotton bales by the waterfront in William Aiken Walker's *Where Canal Meets the Levee* (late nineteenth century), and listless peasants doze in the mud by a ferry port in Sergei Vinogradov's *Without Work (Waiting for the Ferry)* (1888). Together, these representations suggest that some artists harbored mixed feelings about the abolition of serfdom and slavery.

Russian Artists' Depictions of Serfs and Peasants

The movement to paint Russia's *narod* (folk), the peasantry, coincided with the emancipation of the serfs. Prior to this pivotal moment in the history of Russian art, many of the nation's most famous painters received their training at the Imperial Academy of Arts. Located in St. Petersburg and restructured by Catherine the Great in 1764, the academy was a conservative, state-sponsored institution that educated students in the European tradition.[14] During the nineteenth century, the academy encouraged scholars to create neoclassical scenes inspired by Roman or Greek mythology and generally limited students' thematic choices for their works of art.[15] According to one early twentieth-century account of the guiding philosophies of the era, "All Russian, folk, [and] popular [subjects were] considered unworthy of art, [and] the relationship of art to life was professed to be blasphemy, unworthy of the vocation of the artist."[16] In spite of students' nascent interest in painting more diverse subjects, the academy's administration, "abiding by these old-fashioned judgments, led the young artists on this well-worn road, silencing and crushing original talent in the young men."[17] During the mid-nineteenth century, the academy successfully stifled dissent among students from varied backgrounds, who, for the most part, continued to paint scenes inspired by the Bible or by Greek and Roman history and culture.

Significant opposition to the mimicking of European artistic practices arose during the 1850s, when Westernizers argued with Slavophiles about whether Russia should follow Europe's path of development or return to Russia's traditional institutions. In journals, heated discussions among members of the intelligentsia about politics, economics, and society also influenced the public's ideas about literature, art, and culture. Of particular importance was Nikolai Chernyshevskii, author of the influential book *The Aesthetic Relations of Art to Reality*.[18] In it, Chernyshevskii promoted Realism by encouraging artists to create works that explored the tangible world around them rather than illustrated ideals, arguing that "reality is reproduced in art not in order to eliminate flaws, not because reality as such is not sufficiently beautiful, but precisely because it is beautiful."[19] Indeed, Chernyshevskii continues, the central purpose of art is to "reproduce phenomena of real life that are of interest to man" and "to explain life" to audiences by calling "attention to an object . . . in order to explain its significance, or to enable people to understand life better."[20] Realism became increasingly popular in Russia during the mid-nineteenth century, when, according to art historian Molly Brunson, this "pan-European and American movement . . . compel[led] all the arts—literary, visual, musical, and dramatic—to forgo the fantasies and phantasms of romanticism for more sober and democratic subjects with positivist pretensions."[21] The central forces of the movement included industrialization, urbanization, and new developments in the fields of science.[22]

Ultimately, public discussion among intellectuals about works by Chernyshevskii and others led to increasingly widespread changes in attitudes toward

Russian art. For instance, in a scathing critique of an exhibit held in St. Petersburg in 1859, a reviewer for the liberal journal *Sovremennik* (The Contemporary), edited by poet Nikolai Nekrasov, lambasted the lack of originality in contemporary Russian paintings, contending that Russia's artists "must proceed along the path traveled by European art, but not repeat it," because they possess "a different nationality, a different history, [and] different geographical conditions." Speaking about one hackneyed painting, the reviewer despaired, "Why, we have seen all this a thousand times before, not only these circumstances and these costumes, but also these groups and these people!" After criticizing Russia's artists for simply imitating their European peers, the reviewer encouraged the next generation of painters to focus on the study of the human condition and to seek inspiration in the "history and movement of contemporary society, not moribund sentimentalism, life, not the world of fairytales . . . [in order to become] modern artists!"[23]

Just four years after the publication of *Sovremennik*'s review, a group of ambitious young artists at the Imperial Academy answered the journal's call for change. Led by Ivan Kramskoi (1837–1887), fourteen students vigorously protested the institution's constricting adherence to European subjects by withdrawing from the academy. The catalyst for their secession was a gold medal competition in which contestants were required to create paintings relating to one of two themes.[24] The students initially petitioned for the freedom to choose their own subject matter for the competition in October 1863, but the academy rejected their request.[25] On November 9, 1863, the young artists gathered in the academy's Council Hall to learn about the official historical themes for the competition.[26] In a letter to photographer Mikhail Tulinov, Kramskoi excitedly recounted the tense confrontation between faculty and defiant students: "One of us, by the name of Kramskoi, breaks away and offers the following: 'We request consent before the persons of the council to say a few words' (silence, and the gazes of all pierced the speaker)." The students petitioned the academy to "liberate [them] from participating in the competition," but their request was refused and the group decided to disenroll from the institution. Even at the moment of their exodus, however, the pupils were full of hope as they planned their next steps; Kramskoi recorded four days later that many of his compatriots had already "decided to hold on and to collectively form an artistic association . . . [in which they would] work together and live together."[27] The "Revolt of the Fourteen" ultimately altered the trajectory of Russia's artistic development.

Kramskoi and his peers formed the St. Petersburg Artel of Artists, an organization that thrived during the next decade by accepting commissions for paintings and mending its relationship with the academy, where the *artel'*s members even exhibited their works.[28] In 1871, however, four members of the *artel'* and like-minded artists from St. Petersburg and Moscow including Kramskoi, Grigorii Miasoedov (1834–1911), and Illarion Prianishnikov (1840–1894) founded the Society of Traveling Art Exhibitions. The new co-operative differed significantly from its predecessor because, as scholar David Jackson contends, the Society "realised Kramskoy's dream of an independent artistic organisation which, unlike the Artel, was professionally administered and attracted mass popularity."[29] Many of the Society's prolific members, often referred to as "the Wanderers," espoused what scholar Elizabeth Kridl Valkenier calls "morally motivated critical realism" and desired to paint authentic scenes of Russian life that often focused on its common people.[30] Their central aim, however, was not to reproduce scenes they had witnessed but to interpret particular moments or events and to explain their greater meaning through art. In the words of one Russian nineteenth-century critic, the Realist painter "is not a photographic camera; he does not copy nature, but recreates it. [He brings] into it the personal element of his feelings and thoughts."[31] Moreover, paintings in the style of Russian Realism did not embellish nature or mankind but contained components of idealism because painters sought to capture "the highest truth—a truth that is only a manifestation of the laws governing the world."[32]

The Wanderers sought to make the genre paintings that typified Realist art more accessible to the Russian populace by holding exhibitions in cities and villages across the empire and by taking advantage of new technologies that permitted the replication and distribution of their artwork. In the Society's founding statutes, members proclaimed that the organization's central goals were to ensure that residents of the provinces had "the opportunity to become acquainted with Russian art and to keep track of its successes" and to cultivate "a love of art in society."[33] The Society remained true to these aspects of its mission during the fifty-two years of its existence, holding forty-eight separate mobile exhibitions in towns all over the nation. Russian audiences also became familiar with members' most popular works by viewing them on collectible postcards or in widely distributed illustrated journals like *Vsemirnaia illiustratsiia* and *Niva*, where the paintings were frequently reprinted as engravings.

Some of the most beloved artists of the Society of Traveling Exhibitions included Vasilii Maksimov, Il'ia Repin, Abram Arkhipov, and Filipp Maliavin. Each of these artists evinced an interest in painting scenes from Russian peasant life that celebrated the peasantry's emancipation from serfdom, explored their traditions, fulminated against the conditions that kept them in poverty, or humanized them by showing the range of their emotions and experiences. Although several Wanderers came from noble families, the aforementioned painters were born into the peasant estate, a fact that helps explain their special attention to this segment of Russian society. Two of these artists, Maksimov and Repin, depicted the peasantry with an exquisite sensitivity that revealed their deep understanding of village life.

The son of a state-owned peasant, Vasilii Maksimov (1844–1911) was born in the village of Lopino, near Staraia Ladoga. Described by a friend as "homely, pockmarked, with an enormous head of white curly hair . . . [and] the face of a clever *muzhik* [peasant]," Maksimov left the countryside to receive training in icon painting (1855–1862) and to study at the Imperial Academy of Arts in cosmopolitan St. Petersburg between 1863 and 1866.[34] As a member of the Society of Traveling Art Exhibitions, he excelled at creating intimate domestic scenes of cluttered, cozy huts where peasant families shared stories, engaged in age-old rituals, and battled poverty.[35] Maksimov's paintings could be sentimental but were never saccharine; he viewed the peasantry with clear eyes, drew from personal experience, and frequently returned to the countryside for inspiration. According to one friend, Maksimov "engaged [his peasant models] continually in long conversations," and the peasants greatly respected his realist work, telling him, "You are ours . . . and when you paint, it is not for fun."[36] Maksimov's admiration for the peasantry was evident not only in his paintings but also in his deeds, which evoked admiration in the very people he loved to paint. At his wintertime funeral near Staraia Ladoga, a group of peasant mourners risked their lives to ensure that Maksimov received a proper burial by pulling the artist's body on a wooden sledge across the thin ice of the Volkhov River, "lead[ing] their artist to his final sanctuary."[37] Describing Maksimov posthumously, Repin declared that Maksimov was "the flint of the Wanderers, the most indestructible stone of its foundation—inconceivable without Russia, inseparable from his people."[38]

Like Maksimov, Il'ia Repin (1844–1930) was born to a peasant family, but in the village of Chuhuiv (present-day Ukraine).[39] First trained as an apprentice to icon painter I. M. Bunakov (1857–1859), Repin made his way to St. Petersburg, where he studied at the Imperial Academy of Arts for about six years.[40] Icon painting shops provided peasants the unique opportunity to obtain access to education in the arts at a time when rural schools were scarce.[41] According to one critic, Repin was a man who "devoted his entire energy to furthering the cause of national artistic expression"; he joined the Society of Traveling Art Exhibitions in 1878 and became its "dominant figure," presenting "an enthralled public" with numerous paintings in the Realist style that were hailed by audiences as "the evangel of actuality" or greeted as "an incomparable evocation of the past."[42] In spite of his fame, Repin was a modest man; one friend recalled that "humility appeared to be a fundamental and uncontrived trait in Repin's character."[43] The artist's diverse compositions spanned a host of subjects, but his most famous paintings depicted peasant suffering. Excursions to the Volga River inspired Repin's *Barge Haulers on the Volga* (1870–1873), a painting that critic Vladimir Stasov described as a "glorious artistic creation" because of its depiction of men engaging in inhumane labor commonly assigned to Russian serfs before 1861.[44] Several years later, Repin's composition *Seeing off a Recruit* (1879) captured the tragedy of military conscription, an emotionally devastating event that separated male peasants from their parents, wives, and children for years on end. In the words of his former student, Repin's empathetic works earned him a preeminent place in Russian culture as "the most beloved artist of [Russia's] working people."[45] His peasant roots and personal encounters "with grief and need" led him to produce "works that served his native people" and ultimately made his name "the national pride of the Russian folk."[46]

During the late nineteenth century, Wanderer Abram Arkhipov (1862–1930) and Repin's protégé Filipp Maliavin (1869–1940) began experimenting with new artistic techniques to produce joyous, festive paintings of peasants. Born to a peasant family in Ryazan Province, the confident young Arkhipov arrived at the Moscow School of Painting in 1877 with his father, who, according to one observer, was "dressed completely like a rural villager."[47] Arkhipov joined the Society of Traveling Art Exhibitions in 1891 and subsequently produced numerous paintings of the peasantry whom he "so loved," according to one acquaintance, in part because of his awareness of the abuse his father endured as a serf.[48] Arkhipov often depicted the peasantry laboring or relaxing outside in works like *On the Oka River* (1889) and *Easter (Before Mass)* (1892). His works are unsentimental and typically devoid of a storyline; rather, they appear as sun-filled snapshots of peasant life.[49] Peers praised Arkhipov's ability to see joy in simplicity, a trait that ultimately enabled him to "add to the cultural achievements of mankind" through paintings that celebrated Russia's people.[50]

Like Arkhipov, Filipp Maliavin was similarly inspired by his rural upbringing to create vibrant, wild paintings of the peasantry. Born in Kazanki, Maliavin recalled with fondness the sound of pealing church bells and the sight of onion domes in the countryside.[51] After receiving early artistic training in icon painting, he studied under Repin at the Imperial Academy of Arts between 1894 and 1899. Completing school after the peak of Russian Realism's popularity, Maliavin experimented with abstract techniques to create swirling scenes of peasants singing, dancing, and laughing in a blur of color.[52] He unambiguously celebrated peasant culture in kinetic paintings filled with life and activity, earning himself a place as one of Russia's most prominent early twentieth-century artists.[53]

Together, the intellectuals and peasants who united to form the Society of Traveling Art Exhibitions ushered in a new era of artistic production and creativity in Russia. For the first time in Russia's history, its artists turned the nation's attention to the customs and daily lives of the common people: the peasantry. The Wanderers helped humanize the *narod* for a range of citizens either who were unfamiliar with the practices of former serfs or who previously viewed them as property. Ultimately, the Society's dedication to disseminating its artwork through mobile exhibitions, engraving, and photographic reproduction ensured that the widest possible audience viewed its representations.

American Artists' Depictions of Enslaved African Americans and Freedpeople

The nineteenth century was correspondingly a period of national soul-searching for artists who strove to comprehend the American character; indeed, art historian Barbara Novak argues that "it was the nineteenth century when American artistic identity was vigorously formed."[54] Viewers swelled with pride when seeing grand historical works like Emanuel Leutze's *Washington Crossing the Delaware* (1851), and urban dwellers thrilled to view the American wilderness in the stunning landscape paintings of Thomas Cole, Frederic Church, and other Hudson River School artists of the mid-nineteenth century. Like their Russian peers, many antebellum American intellectuals and critics lauded paintings that depicted historical and mythological themes, but they considered genre paintings to be a less sophisticated art form.[55] During the first half of the nineteenth century, these compositions typically showed common people going about their daily lives in quotidian scenes that either conveyed moral lessons to viewers through a story or gently ridiculed the depicted subjects.[56] Early genre paintings served another important purpose by helping viewers comprehend their nation's growing demographic diversity and interconnectedness; according to art historian

Elizabeth Johns, early genre paintings "drew on generalizations about social groups that developed during periods of intense change" to create recognizable visual representations of different people.[57] Consequently, early nineteenth-century audiences living in an era of urbanization, geographic expansion, and immigration slowly began to appreciate paintings that explained their evolving communities and the fluctuating world around them.

The U.S. Civil War transformed Americans' sense of national identity as the country divided and then reunified under new conditions. In 1861, *New York Monthly Magazine* promoted national art as a balm to heal the fresh wounds of disunion, arguing, "Never was there a time in the annals of our country when art held a more important position than it now does."[58] The author distinguishes between different forms of art, praising genre painting and urging American artists to "be National!" and to "depend upon [their] own identity for immortality" rather than mimic their European peers. Calling national art "the wholesome food for the aggregate want of individuals expressed as one grand whole," the author asks the reader, "And is it not a noble work, this catering for the aesthetic food to satisfy the craving ... ineradicable in the hearts of men?"[59] Artists considered such questions relating to national identity in their visual representations of America's new, diverse citizenry.

After the abolition of slavery, many American artists became captivated by the lives of African American freedpeople, who now legally possessed many of the same rights as their former owners. Unlike the Wanderers, however, artists who depicted African Americans had no organization equivalent to the Society of Traveling Art Exhibitions.[60] Instead, American painters independently decided to represent African Americans in distinct ways according to their individual perspectives and experiences.

Henry Ossawa Tanner (1859–1937) and William Edouard Scott (1884–1964), two of the most prominent African American artists of the late nineteenth and early twentieth centuries, created humanizing genre paintings of African Americans that challenged the flat caricatures circulating in mass-oriented publications. Born in Pittsburgh, Pennsylvania, Tanner exhibited artistic talent at an early age. His mother had once been enslaved in Virginia, while his father, a Pennsylvanian, was born free.[61] He studied at the Pennsylvania Academy of Fine Arts in Philadelphia and at the Académie Julian in Paris, France, an institute located far from the confining environment of the Jim Crow South.[62] In the United States, one critic remarked, Tanner was "reminded of his race," but in Paris, he was "treated purely as an artist."[63] There, in the words of an acquaintance, "color was never counted against [Tanner] in the least," and he hoped to "win fame and return to his own land."[64] Tanner's works ranged from religious paintings to genre paintings that offered intimate portraits of his subjects and were often filled with drama and emotion. Described by one critic as a devoted, careful artist who exhibited "faithfulness to drudging detail, as well as the triumph of genius," Tanner achieved great success in his career and was the first African American artist elected as a full member of the National Academy of Design in 1927.[65]

In many ways, William Edouard Scott's educational path paralleled that of Tanner, his peer and mentor. Born in Indianapolis, Indiana, Scott first trained at the School of the Art Institute in Chicago before traveling abroad to Paris. He studied with Tanner in France and was influenced by some of his artistic techniques.[66] Like Tanner, Scott moved between the United States and France, where African Americans were drawn to opportunities that greatly surpassed those of Jim Crow America during the early twentieth century. Scott attended both the Académie Julian and the Académie Colarossi in Paris before the advent of the First World War, when he returned to the United States.[67] Inspired by what he saw during a trip to Alabama, Scott began painting African American sharecroppers living in the rural South. Scott portrayed them as industrious, vigorous, and resilient in works that indicate his sincere admiration and respect. According to one critic, Scott's interest in portraying African Americans stemmed in part from his desire to "creat[e] racial pride which [would] bring about a better understanding between the races."[68] Like Tanner, Scott achieved international recognition for his works, exhibiting paintings in many prominent galleries in Europe and the United States.[69]

Two white artists who created complex, thoughtful portraits of formerly enslaved African Americans through which audiences were encouraged to assess the effects of emancipation were Winslow Homer (1836–1910) and Eastman Johnson (1824–1906). Homer learned to capture the details of a scene under the threat of cannon fire while working as an artist-correspondent for *Harper's Weekly* during the Civil War. The Bostonian's time on Virginia's battlefields and apprenticeship at Bufford's lithography shop in Boston during the height of the abolitionist movement likely stoked his interest in African Americans and inspired his postwar journeys to Virginia, where he painted the upturned lives of freedpeople.[70] In compositions like *The Cotton Pickers* (1876) and *Dressing for Carnival* (1877), Homer displayed a distinctive style that moved audiences, particularly through his representations of African Americans.[71] Indeed, one critic declared in 1880 that Homer "shows his originality in nothing so much as in his manner of painting negroes" and that his talent surpassed that of the creators of "pitiable caricatures of negroes" that "over-[ran]" the pages of late nineteenth-century American illustrated magazines.[72] As a storyteller, Homer continuously strove to create paintings of freedpeople that struck viewers as true to life, an artistic decision that ultimately made him, in the eyes of the critic, "one of the few artists who ha[d] the boldness and originality to make something out of the negro for artistic purposes."[73]

Eastman Johnson, one of Homer's peers, similarly displayed what another nineteenth-century critic called "decided individuality and independence in choice and treatment of subject," especially in his humanistic paintings of middle-class Americans.[74] Like Homer, Johnson was born in the North and also worked at Bufford's lithography shop.[75] Trained in Europe, Johnson returned during the mid-1850s to the United States, where, according to one critic, he "found inspiration in American subjects, which he portrayed to the end of his career."[76] A particular topic of interest for Johnson was African American life; he composed numerous genre paintings featuring enslaved African Americans and freedpeople throughout the second half of the nineteenth century. Johnson's complicated and at times ambiguous works of art such as *Negro Life at the South* (1859), *Fiddling His Way* (1866), and *The Old Stagecoach* (1871) triggered intense debate among critics who strove to comprehend the artist's underlying messages about slavery and freedom.[77] Johnson's thought-provoking works were sometimes displayed alongside those of Homer at events like the American Centennial Exhibition and institutions such as the National Academy of Design, which the *New York Times* described as essential in fostering "the cultivation of a taste for art" among the American populace.[78]

Two white American painters who unequivocally condemned the institution of slavery and lauded freedpeople's achievements were Thomas Satterwhite Noble (1835–1907) and Thomas Waterman Wood (1823–1903). A native of Lexington, Kentucky, Noble was acquainted with the harsh realities of servitude as a consequence of witnessing enslaved African Americans performing manual labor on his father's hemp farm.[79] His abhorrence of slavery and his decision to compose poignant, emotional paintings that denounced the sale of human beings may stem from his personal encounters with the men and women on his father's estate. In his youth, Noble learned about African Americans' folk traditions while visiting their cabins and listening to ghost stories until, he remembered, "night had settled over . . . and the way back to the house seemed long and dark."[80]

In early adulthood, after Noble trained in France under Thomas Couture in the late 1850s and served as a Confederate soldier during the Civil War, he made his way to New York City and produced eight paintings containing representations of enslaved African Americans.[81] His dramatic scenes of auctions of enslaved people and attempted escapes stunned audiences with their brutal authenticity. For instance, one reviewer pronounced that Noble's work *The Modern Medea* (1867), a graphic depiction of a fugitive slave's desperate attempt to murder her own children to keep them from bondage, "illustrated one of the horrors of the institution of Slavery as it formerly existed, and produced a vigorous and interesting work, although it is on a repulsive subject."[82] In fact, numerous critics disapproved of Noble's topical selection; for example, a reviewer from the *St. Louis Times* argued that audiences must "question the propriety of the subject" when considering Noble's *The Last Sale of Slaves* (1870), a portrayal of an auction of enslaved African Americans at the St. Louis courthouse.[83] Such statements testify to some audiences' discomfort with Noble's stark depictions of slavery and the rarity of such representations in American art during the 1860s and early 1870s.

Another opponent of slavery, Vermont native Thomas Waterman Wood was a genre painter interested in quotidian scenes who, according to one contemporary, "forcibly represent[ed] the humble life of the poor with pathos and humor."[84] Wood's portraits of African American freedpeople undeniably praise their post-emancipation achievements. In *A Bit of War History: The Contraband, The Recruit,* and *The Veteran* (1865–1866), arguably Wood's most famous series of paintings, the artist celebrates the military service of a formerly enslaved man who sacrifices his body for his country by serving as a Union soldier. Other paintings depicted freedpeople as integrated citizens exercising their rights. For example, a watercolor titled *American Citizens (To the Polls)* (1867) shows three men standing in line on equal footing to cast their ballots on Election Day. The third man is an African American whose eagerness to vote is palpable; he stands with arms outstretched, as if to hug the man in front of him.[85] Paintings like these not only countered the denigrating cartoons in periodicals that mocked African Americans but also served as important visual examples of harmonious post-emancipation relationships between black and white citizens.

Although late nineteenth-century artists like Homer, Johnson, Noble, and Wood created dignified representations of African Americans, painter William Aiken Walker (1838–1921) produced degrading, cartoonish portrayals of freedpeople that differed markedly from those of his peers. Information about Walker's youth is sparse, but scholars know that the artist was born in

Charleston, South Carolina, and spent time honing his craft in Louisiana, Georgia, North Carolina, and Florida.[86] He painted several works on commission and sold hundreds of collectible, souvenir-size pictures.[87] Although Walker's technique was arguably less sophisticated than that of his peers, his works appeared at national and international exhibitions including the Annual Exhibition of the Artists' Association of New Orleans, Chicago's Columbian Exposition (1893), and the St. Louis World's Fair (1903).[88] Currier and Ives's lithographic reproductions of *The Levee, New Orleans* and *A Cotton Plantation on the Mississippi* also circulated widely in 1884. Walker's name was known across the South during his lifetime because, in the words of one collector, Walker was an artist of "no parallel among American genre painters as a visual recorder and preserver of life in the rural South during the post–Civil War period."[89]

Walker's folksy, stereotypical depictions of freedpeople clad in rags as they toiled on plantations or wandered through cities appealed to some audiences but displeased others. In 1884, a *Daily Picayune* critic praised Walker's "drawings of the Negro in his native cotton and cane field . . . with all the half pathetic ruggedness of costume and love of gay colors that render the darkey such good artistic material for one who has the skill." A year later, however, another *Daily Picayune* critic lambasted Walker's simplistic "negro character sketches," characterizing them as "homely . . . seemingly uninteresting, and often repulsive."[90] These reviews suggest that audiences interpreted Walker's paintings in different ways during the 1880s, when Americans continued to hold divided views about freedpeople.

Together, these artists presented a wide range of representations of enslaved African Americans and freedpeople to postbellum audiences that stimulated debate and elicited criticism. Although American artists' depictions were arguably less sentimental and idealistic than those of the Wanderers, most U.S. painters shared with their Russian counterparts the goal of humanizing formerly enserfed or enslaved people and employed analogous strategies to do so. To fully assess the connections and disjunctures between the ways in which American and Russian artists portrayed enslaved African Americans, freedpeople, serfs, and peasants, however, requires a closer look at representations in individual works of art. An examination of this kind shows that Russian and American paintings fall into six distinct thematic categories: relationships between owners and serfs or enslaved people; peasants and freedpeople in the military; post-emancipation agricultural labor; heritage, religion, and rituals; education; and urban migration. A deeper comparison of these works of art reveals startling similarities and differences between the ways in which artists and audiences imagined and represented African Americans and peasants during the forty years that followed the abolition of serfdom and slavery.

Visualizing Serfdom and Slavery: Relationships between Serfs, Enslaved People, and Owners

Russian and American artists sought to shape the public's memory of serfdom and slavery immediately after emancipation by offering diverse representations of each institution. American painter Thomas Satterwhite Noble and Russian painter Nikolai Nevrev (1830–1904) both condemned the sale of serfs and enslaved African Americans in works that portrayed landowners as heartless and enserfed or enslaved individuals as defiant.[91] A pair of astonishingly similar paintings created just two years apart, Nevrev's *Bargaining. A Scene from Serf Life (from the Recent Past)* (1866) and Noble's *The Price of Blood* (1868), bring the viewer into a private home where a wealthy landowner reclines in his robe and slippers.[92] Both men dispassionately bargain with traders over the price of their human property, a female serf and an enslaved man. Neither Nevrev nor Noble depicts these individuals as weak; rather, the serf stands with arms crossed as she glares at her owner, while the enslaved man, with one hand on his hip, looks into the distance with disgust.[93] Their compositions were two of the most direct denunciations of slavery and its facilitators out of the hundreds of genre paintings produced during the mid- to late nineteenth century.[94]

More frequently, however, artists employed an oblique approach to their depictions of enslaved African Americans and Russian serfs that avoided assigning blame for their maltreatment. American painters Thomas Waterman Wood, Thomas Moran, Eastman Johnson, and Theodor Kaufmann created dramatic scenes that told harrowing stories of enslaved African Americans' attempted escapes from captivity, while Russian painters Boris Kustodiev and Grigorii Miasoedov portrayed the long-awaited moment of the serfs' liberation when they heard the Emancipation Manifesto read aloud for the first time. First, Wood delicately alluded to the historical pattern of enslaved African Americans' northward flight from Southern plantations in *A Southern Cornfield* (1861), a painting that depicts an enslaved man offering water from a gourd to a line of enslaved people that vanishes into the shadows of tall green cornstalks.[95] During the next two years, Moran, Johnson, and Kaufmann

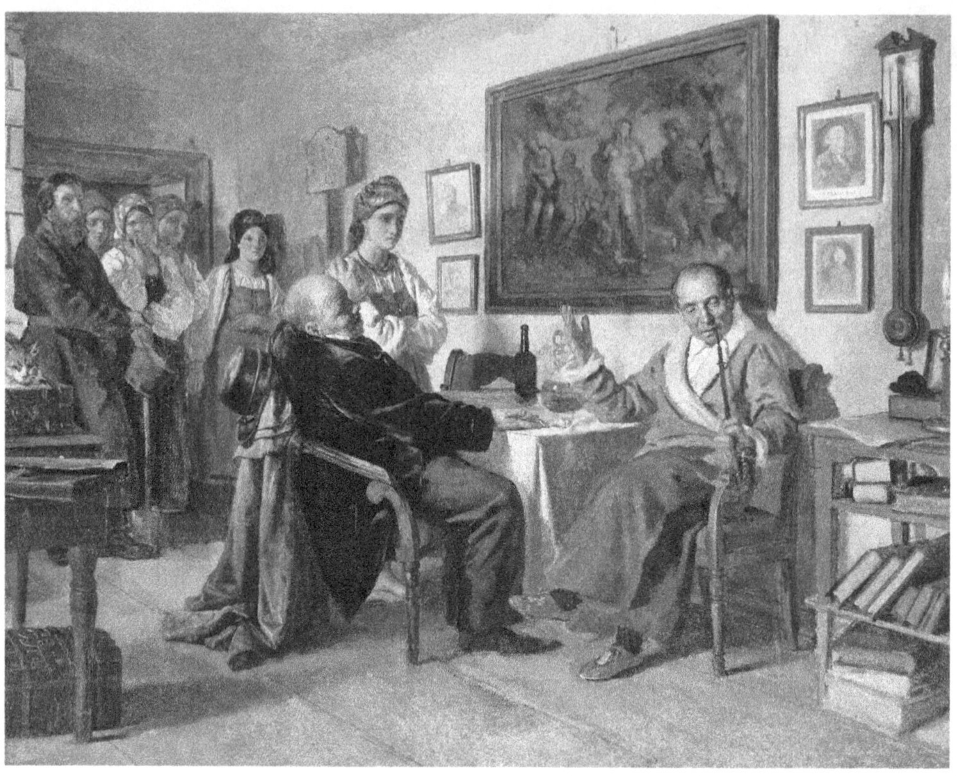

Nikolai Nevrev, *Bargaining. A Scene from Serf Life (from the Recent Past)* (1866). State Tret'iakov Gallery, Moscow.

completed similarly sympathetic compositions portraying enslaved families escaping from captivity to liberty on horseback or on foot, journeying through stygian swamps, forests, and fields as they fled toward freedom's light.[96] As the Civil War raged on, these artists sought to evoke compassion in audiences, without explicitly criticizing slave owners, by humanizing the enslaved African Americans who risked their lives to attain a better future for themselves and their children.

By contrast, Russian painters did not focus on the subject of flight, a difficult task for enserfed peasants residing in a vast empire where serfdom was legal and for whom escape to its distant borderlands, where law enforcement was lax, posed a challenge.[97] Instead, Miasoedov and Kustodiev painted scenes that depicted serfs as passive recipients of freedom after learning of the state's decision to liberate them.[98] In one of Miasoedov's most famous paintings, *Reading the Manifesto of 1861* (1874), illiterate male peasants raptly

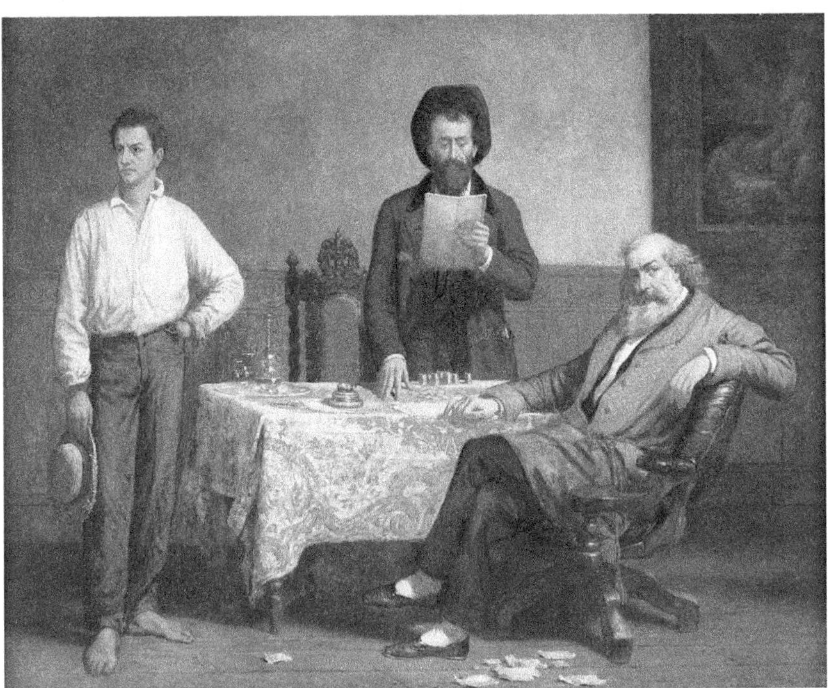

Thomas Satterwhite Noble, *The Price of Blood* (1868). Morris Museum of Art, Augusta, GA.

listen to a peasant child who reads aloud from a copy of the Emancipation Manifesto amid the hay bales of a darkened barn.[99] Kustodiev's *Reading of the Manifesto (Emancipation of the Peasants)* (1907), which was painted more than forty years after emancipation, presented a more humorous view of emancipation in which a male official reads aloud the manifesto from the steps of a country estate to a colorful group of peasants. A woman, presumably the wife of the estate owner, histrionically weeps behind a column. In both works, Miasoedov and Kustodiev portray the serfs as receiving the gift of liberty bestowed on them by the state. By contrast, each of the aforementioned American paintings portrays enslaved people as central actors in the drama of liberation who exercise agency by making the risky decision to run away. These representational contrasts demonstrate important differences in the ways in which Russian and American artists viewed the serfs' and enslaved African Americans' respective roles in bringing about their liberation.[100]

Although several artists criticized the institutions of slavery and serfdom, others created nostalgic paintings that idealized relationships between

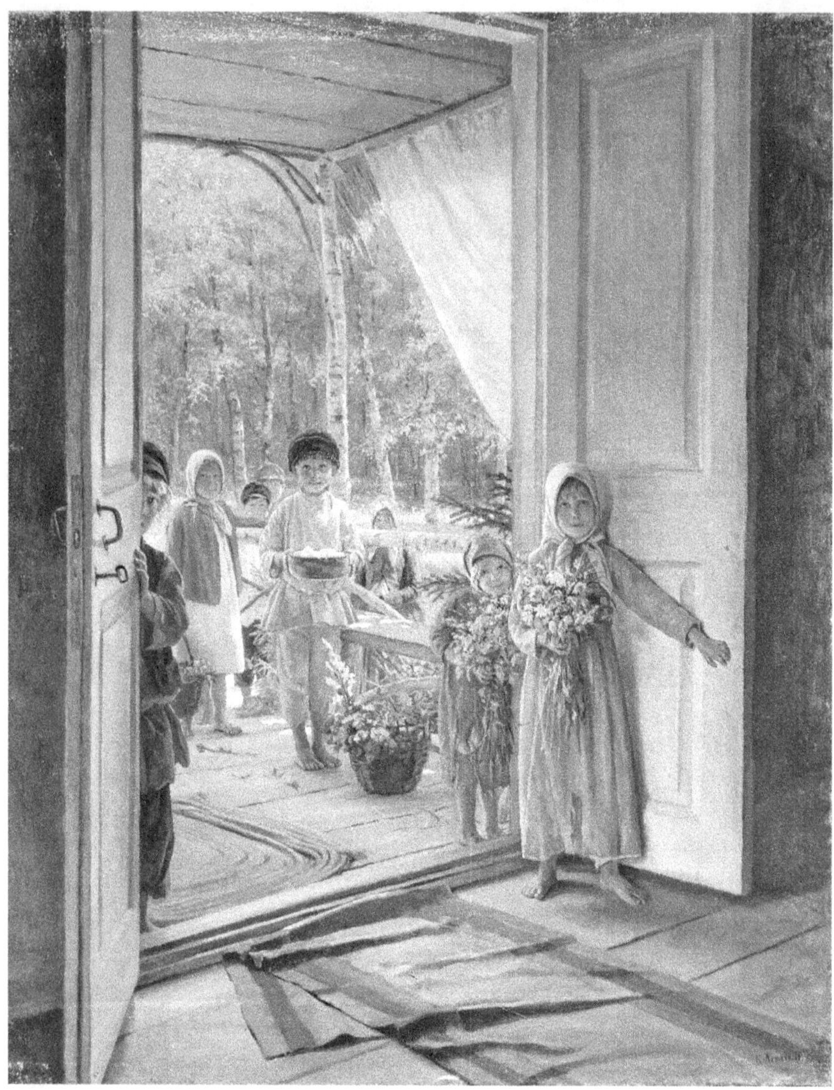

Kirill Lemokh, *Summer (with Congratulations)* (1890). © State Russian Museum, St. Petersburg.

owners and bonded laborers. More than a decade before he completed *Reading the Manifesto of 1861*, Miasoedov, the son of a poor landowner, produced the idealistic *Congratulation of the Betrothed in the Landlord's House* (1861). In this sentimental painting, peasants spill into the parlor of their owner's manor, bringing foodstuffs and merriment to celebrate the engagement of a young peasant couple. The scene is one of domestic bliss; the bride-to-be kisses her groom in a felicitous gesture of goodwill as their owners look on in delight.[101] Wanderer Kirill Lemokh (1841–1910) created a comparable scene in *Summer (with Congratulations)* (1890), a painting in which barefoot peasant children stand nervously on the threshold of an estate house. The girls carry bouquets of wildflowers and a boy holds a large basket of fresh eggs, all gifts for their landowner and his family on an unnamed occasion. These saccharine tableaux offered viewers rosy sketches of landlord-peasant relations where both groups cheerfully celebrated one another's holidays.

Russian compositions depicting contented, loyal serfs and peasants mirror American paintings of enslaved African Americans who faithfully served their owners. Such works were typically produced by American artists who drew inspiration from the Lost Cause mythology, a set of beliefs that defeated Southerners promoted after the Civil War. A central component of the mythology was a revisionist account of antebellum relations between slaveholders and enslaved people in which African Americans cherished their owners and did not desire to be free. One representative painting that visualizes this concept is William D. Washington's *The Burial of Latané* (1864), which depicts the Virginia funeral of Confederate captain William Latané. A group of weeping white Southern women and enslaved African Americans surrounds his coffin, collectively mourning his death. This mawkish image was exceedingly popular among white Southerners not only during the war but also in post-emancipation decades, when Virginian families hung copies of the painting's engraving on their parlor walls.[102]

American artists continued to draw inspiration from the Lost Cause myth nearly half a century later, when Tennessean Carl Gutherz (1844–1907) produced *I Promised the Missus I'd Bring Him Home* (1904).[103] Like Washington, Gutherz used wartime imagery to illustrate the notion of black loyalty; his painting featured an enslaved black man carrying home to his white mistress the corpse of a Confederate soldier, his owner. Ultimately, maudlin representations of enslaved African Americans like those of Gutherz and Washington sought to bolster Southerners' claims that antebellum plantation owners treated their enslaved laborers well and that African American freedpeople would be better-off if they had never been liberated.

Fearing Conscription or Fighting for Freedom:
Peasants and Freedpeople in the Military

Another common theme in Russian and American paintings of former serfs and enslaved African Americans is that of military service; however, while Russian artists consistently depicted peasant conscription as a kind of

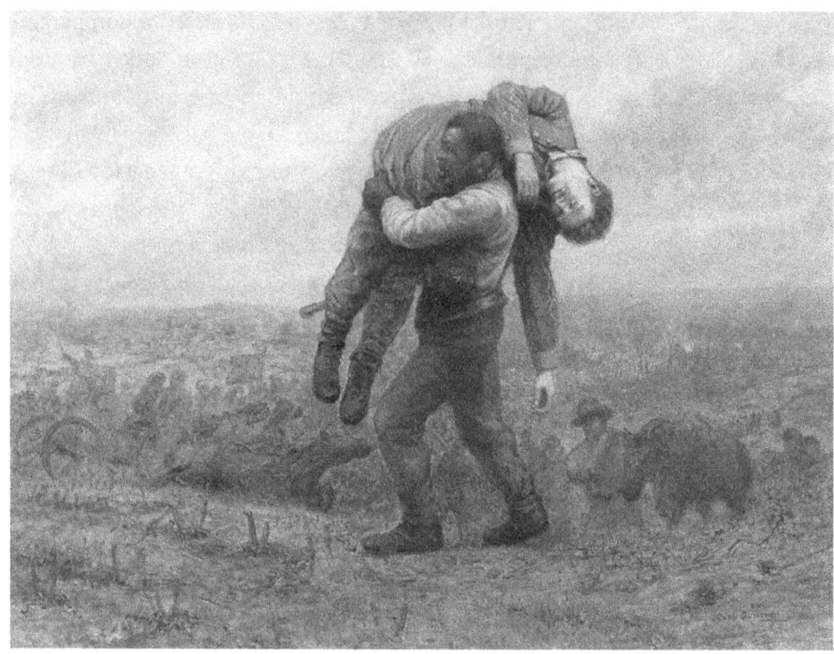

Carl Gutherz, *I Promised the Missus I'd Bring Him Home* (1904). Memphis Brooks Museum of Art, Memphis, Tennessee.

enslavement due to harsh terms of service, American painters portrayed soldiering as an opportunity for African Americans to earn or exercise their freedom. This stark discrepancy between representations comes from differences between the two nations' martial histories. In nineteenth-century Russia, the tsarist government primarily selected recruits from the peasant estate to form its standing army.[104] Male peasants dreaded being called to service for the standard term of twenty to twenty-five years, a period that nearly matched the average peasant's life span of twenty-seven years.[105] Permanently separated from their families, soldiers faced disease, malnutrition, and the prospect of death during battle. Evidence of peasant attitudes toward recruitment appear in myriad nineteenth-century *soldatskie pesni* (soldier songs) in which they characterize military service as a form of servitude. For instance, in one illustrative song recorded in the Voronezh *oblast'* (region), a peasant sings, "My sorrow is great, / my legs do not move from grief / . . . / Your sweet one is in slavery [*v nevole*], / in military conscription."[106] Composing a majority of the total population, peasants also continued to constitute an outsize proportion of the army after War Minister Dmitrii Miliutin enacted the Universal Conscription Act of 1874, an important step in reforming Russia's military after the abolition of serfdom.[107] Likely aware of the burden that peasant soldiers and their families continued to bear during the second half of the nineteenth century, numerous members of the Society of Traveling Art Exhibitions depicted scenes of recruitment in paintings.

Russian painters from the peasant estate like Il'ia Repin comprehended the trauma of military conscription as well as the peasantry's abiding aversion to recruitment even after the state's military reforms. Repin's heartbreaking work *Seeing off a Recruit* (1879) portrays a young male peasant bidding farewell to his bereaved wife and children in a courtyard (*dvor*) located in the village of Bykovo.[108] Repin designed the scene in such a way that the viewer's eyes are drawn toward the empty rural horizon where the painting's planes converge, perhaps in an attempt to convey the fatalistic feeling of finality that enveloped the gloomy recruit and his family. In 1880, the popular magazine *Vsemirnaia illiustratsiia* reprinted Repin's painting, which was also displayed in the Society of Traveling Art Exhibitions' eighth show, and added a short story to bring the image to life. *Vsemirnaia illiustratsiia*'s fictional tale describes how the family of a conscripted peasant responded to the government's unwelcome call: "Mikita was hooked! . . . Matrona, his mother, wailed loudly: what would life be like for Mikita as a soldier, such need, there would be such hunger and cold to endure on campaigns. . . . Woe settled over the family."[109] Together, Repin's painting and *Vsemirnaia illiustratsiia*'s short story likely evoked pity and increased support for Miliutin's policies in audiences who, through these sympathetic representations, began to better understand the peasantry's plight.

Two later works, by Konstantin Savitskii (1844–1905) and Nikolai Pimonenko (1862–1912), echoed and expanded on the themes contained in Repin's *Seeing off a Recruit*. Savitskii's *To War* (1888), featured in the Society of Traveling Art Exhibitions' sixteenth show, is a sprawling work depicting a chaotic scene at a smoke-filled train station where several recruits prepare to depart.[110] At the center of the painting, two recruits lead a fellow peasant to the train, but he gazes back in terror at his grief-stricken wife, who desperately extends her hand toward him. The peasant's forced march to war is like that of a prisoner to his execution; his fate has been determined. Pimonenko's *Seeing off the Recruits* (before 1912) also portrays a conscripted peasant's train station departure. The poses are recognizable; a wife weeps into her husband's chest while children stand around them, but Pimonenko presents the event from a more impressionistic perspective. The anguished peasants' faces are indistinguishable blurs of color, a technique that gives the

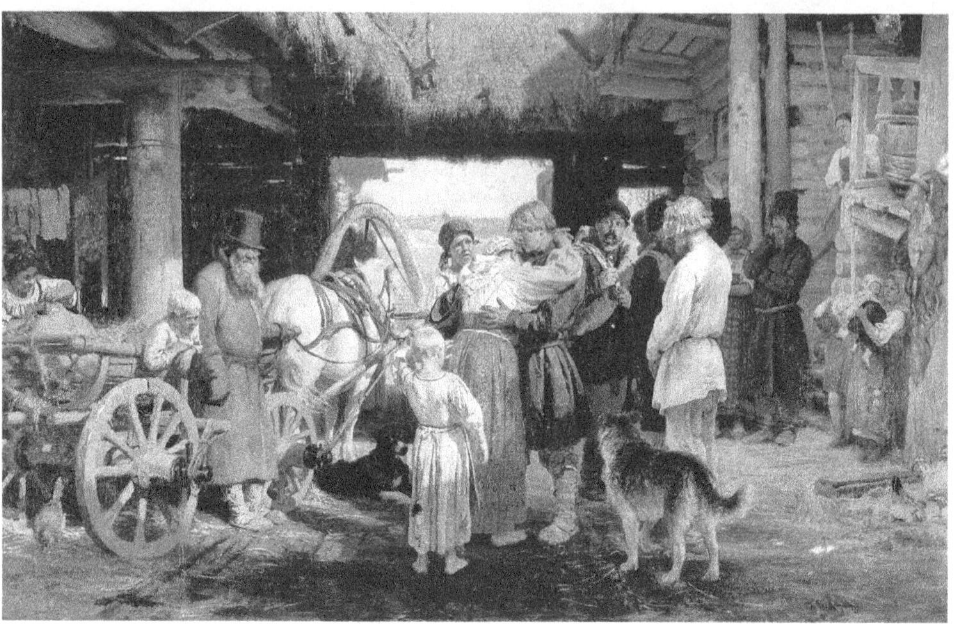

Il'ia Repin, *Seeing off a Recruit* (1879). © State Russian Museum, St. Petersburg.

viewer the sense that the very surface of the painting is damp from the gray mist and violet smoke hanging in the air. Thus, Pimonenko reimagined a tableau now familiar to audiences by emphasizing the melancholic atmosphere and universalizing the peasants' experiences through their anonymity.

Russian artists' depictions of peasant military service differed significantly from those of American painters, who typically portrayed soldiering as a patriotic, heroic endeavor. The Civil War possessed special meaning for enslaved African Americans, whose futures as free men and women largely depended on the conflict's outcome. The Union army did not formally recruit black soldiers prior to 1863, but after President Lincoln's issuance of the Emancipation Proclamation and the formation of the Bureau for Colored Troops in May of that year, tens of thousands of African Americans enlisted. Of the 179,000 who served during the Civil War, 146,000 hailed from Confederate states or from border states, a fact that attests in part to African Americans' desire to eliminate slavery.[111] Two artists whose works lauded African Americans' wartime contributions were Edward Lamson Henry (1841–1919) and Thomas Waterman Wood. Henry's composition *A Presentation of the Colors to the First Colored Regiment of New York by the Ladies of the City in Front of the Old Union League Club, Union Square, New York City in 1864* (1868) was one of the first to celebrate African American military service on a large scale. Henry borrows from modes of representation used in the grand historical paintings of the early nineteenth century to create a magnificent scene that applauds the formation of the Twentieth U.S. Colored Infantry, a regiment solely composed of black soldiers.[112] Crowds of New Yorkers surround the blue-uniformed soldiers in support of their efforts, while nearly a dozen outsize American flags decorate grandstands or wave in the bright sunlight from atop the buildings. This patriotic panorama placed African Americans at the center of the North's effort to preserve the Union.

By contrast, Thomas Waterman Wood praised black military service in a more intimate set of paintings inspired by his observations in wartime Tennessee. Wood's triptych, *A Bit of War History: The Contraband, The Recruit,* and *The Veteran* (1866), tells the story of a formerly enslaved man who enlisted in the Union army during the Civil War. In the first painting, the cheerful man brims with naive optimism upon arriving at the provost marshal's office. After donning the bright blue uniform in the second scene, however, he becomes stoic, suddenly aware of the challenges ahead. Now a soldier, he stands upright with his hand proudly on his hip and his rifle against his shoulder, looking thoughtfully into the distance.[113] The third painting offers a sober conclusion to the formerly enslaved man's story; in his faded and tattered uniform, the soldier leans on crutches and his remaining leg, heroically saluting the viewer.

These radical compositions appealed to many Northern viewers; in one testament to their popularity, *Harper's Weekly* declared that the triptych was "among the most finished and impressive of the paintings on exhibition at the National Academy [in 1867]," calling them "admirable works" that told a "thrilling story" to audiences about a formerly enslaved man's journey from bondage to freedom.[114] The *New York Evening Post* criticized Wood's technical skills but conceded that the paintings' "best qualities consist in the clearness with which they tell their story, and the evident sympathy of the artist with his subject."[115] The triptych continued to fascinate viewers throughout the late nineteenth century; after the Metropolitan Museum of Art acquired the works in 1884, one critic noted that they "attract[ed] much attention" from museumgoers.[116] Indeed, Wood's paintings represented freedpeople in a new light by highlighting their service and bodily sacrifice for a nation that had so often mistreated them. Through their depictions of noble black soldiers, Wood and Henry encouraged American audiences to view African Americans as fellow citizens and as partners in the fight to preserve the Union. Their representations of military service as an emancipating effort contrasted sharply with images of enchaining peasant conscription.

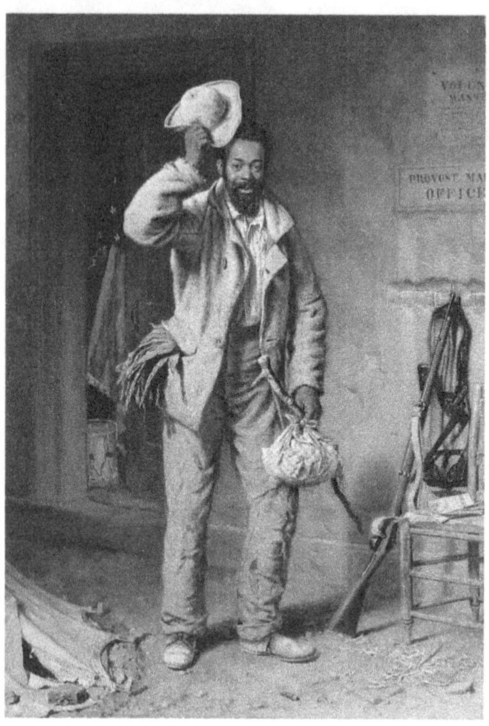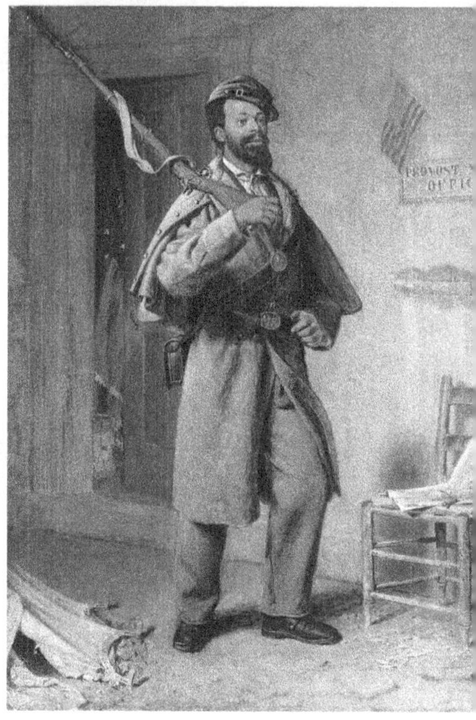

Thomas Waterman Wood, *A Bit of War History: The Contraband, The Recruit,* and
The Veteran (1866). Gift of Charles Stewart Smith, 1884, Metropolitan Museum of Art.

Joy in Suffering? Depictions of Agricultural Laborers in the Post-Emancipation Era

The abolition of serfdom (1861) and slavery (1865) produced post-emancipation
conditions for peasants and freedpeople that overlapped in important ways.
In Russia, serfs were legally freed from bondage but required to pay enormous redemption payments for the right to work the communal land. As a
result, post-emancipation peasant agricultural labor during the 1870s and
1880s looked very similar to that of serfdom. African American freedpeople
faced analogous challenges in the United States, where many freedpeople
were initially unable to purchase their own land. Thousands of families in the
U.S. South participated in the system of sharecropping, renting land from
white farmers and giving up part of their annual harvest in a cycle that kept
many freedpeople, like the Russian peasantry, mired in poverty.

Despite these similar circumstances, Russian and American artists depicted peasant and African American labor in starkly different ways that
indicate divergent perceptions of agriculture's role in the national histori-

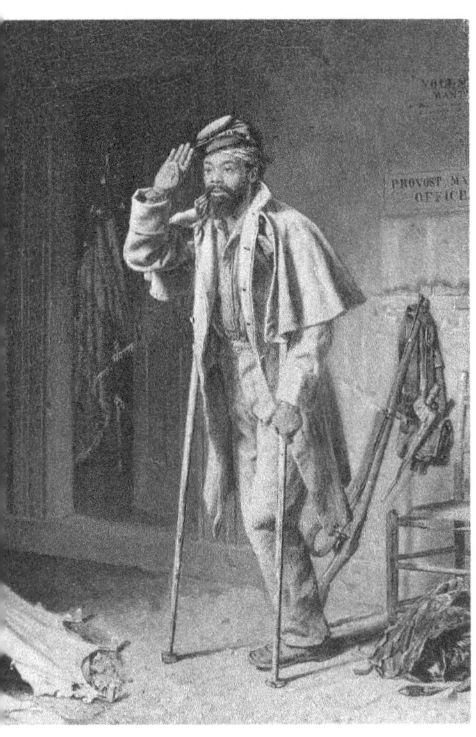

cal narrative. While Russian painters Konstantin Makovskii, Mikhail Klodt (1833–1902), and Grigorii Miasoedov created lush, colorful scenes of peasants working in verdant fields, American painters William Edouard Scott, Winslow Homer, and Thomas Anshutz produced portraits of African American laborers that criticized their working conditions and lack of economic advancement after emancipation. Like his American peers, artist William Aiken Walker portrayed agricultural labor as an inferior occupation, but he suggested through his disparaging representations of African Americans that freedpeople were well suited to this type of work.

Landscape painter Konstantin Makovskii (1839–1915), a founding member of the Society of Traveling Art Exhibitions, created an idyllic agrarian scene in *Peasant Lunch during Harvest* (1871). Under a cloudless azure sky, several peasant families cook their midday meal around a campfire in the green grasses. Dressed in traditional rural attire, female peasants feed their plump-cheeked children in a picture of communal unity and economic stability. Golden wheat fields wave in the breeze behind the close-knit group, a sign of the land's fecundity and the Russian peasantry's fertility. Painted a year later, in 1872, Mikhail Klodt's *Ploughing* similarly represents agricultural labor as an enriching endeavor. Here, a single female peasant in a red headscarf and blue *sarafan* (pinafore), the traditional colors of the garments worn by the Virgin Mary as illustrated in Russian icons, stands erect as she looks across a vast, recently ploughed field. The deep grooves of the upturned earth are rich and black, contrasting sharply with the green grass and bright blue sky. A symbol of purity and fertility, the female peasant seems to assure viewers that Russia's future will be secured through the preservation of its traditional agrarian way of life.

One of the most famous nineteenth-century depictions of agricultural labor was Grigorii Miasoedov's *Harvest Time (Scythers)* (1887). Described by

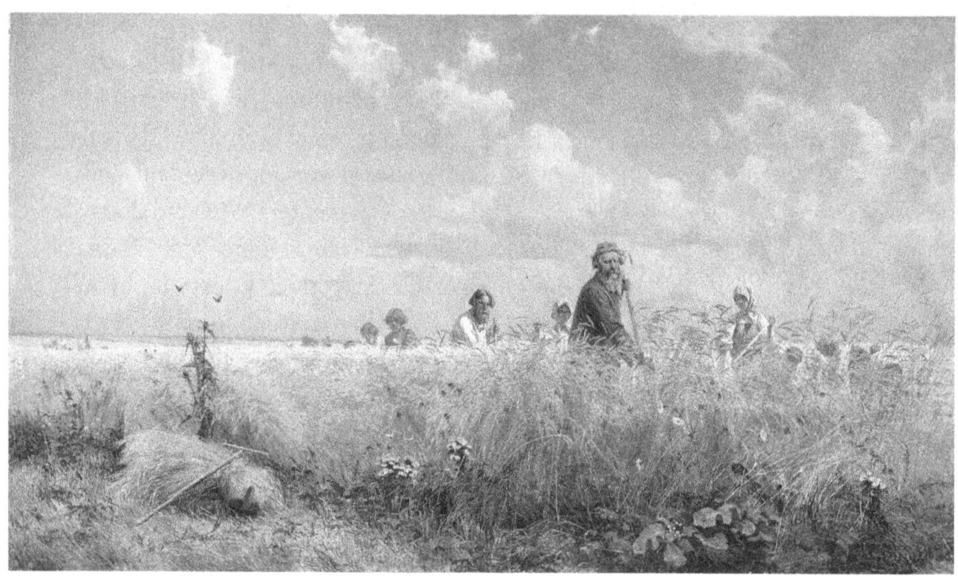

Grigorii Miasoedov, *Harvest Time (Scythers)* (1887). © State Russian Museum, St. Petersburg.

art critic Vladimir Stasov as "full of poetry, light feeling, health, and solemnity," *Harvest Time* is an expansive painting that portrays a group of male and female peasants rhythmically mowing wheat in unison with long-handled scythes.[117] On a beautiful day, the pale pink sunlight warms the backs of the workers, while butterflies dance above the gilded wheat stalks and violet wildflowers. The peasants remain intensely focused on their collective task, however, and follow the lead of a male peasant at the center of the composition. The *muzhik* wears a woven wreath of golden wheat around his head, a symbol that recalls an angelic halo or even the crown of thorns worn by Christ at his crucifixion. After years of bodily sacrifice in these fields, the elderly peasant has gained wisdom and earned his position as head of the group. Miasoedov's pastoral representation offers more than visual beauty; his painting seeks to elevate the Russian peasant because of his work ethic, humility, and dedication to a traditional pastime.

Indeed, *Scythers* recalls several famous passages from Lev Tolstoi's best seller *Anna Karenina* (1877), in which the author describes harvest time as "the most pressingly busy season of the year, when an extraordinary tension of self-sacrificing labor manifests itself among all the peasants, such as is never shown in any other condition of life."[118] According to one of the novel's protagonists, the landowner Constantine Levin, the countryside was where "one rejoiced, suffered, and labored" and where the rural peasantry developed the

Christ-like qualities of "strength, meekness, and justice" through manual toil.[119] Miasoedov's depiction of the humble, laboring peasantry, completed ten years after the publication of *Anna Karenina*, similarly attributes saintly virtues to Russia's *narod*. These three Wanderers collectively viewed Russia's agrarian tradition as an important aspect of their cultural heritage and national future. Their optimistic representations of rural laborers attest to their respect for the peasantry and their knowledge that agriculture remained an essential component of the economy even in a post-emancipation era of increasing urbanization and industrialization.

By contrast, American painters Winslow Homer, Thomas Anshutz, and William Edouard Scott questioned whether agricultural labor benefited or harmed African American freedpeople by restricting their geographic and economic mobility. In his famous work, *The Cotton Pickers* (1876), Homer portrays two contemplative African American women looking into the distance across a cotton field. Their worn clothing and bonnets suggest their modest means, but they appear strong and healthy in body and spirit. The painting's title asks the viewer to consider whether the painting is historical or contemporary: Are the cotton pickers enslaved laborers or freedpeople?[120] In fact, it is almost impossible to answer this question because the composition intentionally offers few temporal or geographic clues. Instead, the painting's intrinsic ambiguity begs the viewer to consider how little conditions had changed for African Americans since their emancipation and to ponder the role of agriculture in uplifting freedpeople from poverty. Exhibited at New York's Century Club, *The Cotton Pickers* was deemed by one reviewer to be a model work for artists who hoped to truthfully represent the African American experience.[121]

Homer also urged readers to consider the post-emancipation relationship between freedpeople and their former owners in his painting *Visit from the Old Mistress* (1876). Completed the same year as the controversial presidential election that led to the Hayes administration's retreat from Reconstruction, *Visit from the Old Mistress* depicts a tense scene in which the mistress of a plantation meets with her formerly enslaved laborers in their home, possibly the old slave quarters. The three adult freedpeople display body language that reveals their discomfort with and resistance to their unwelcome guest; one sits with folded arms, while the others stand. The painting reveals the extent to which emancipation has upended the power dynamics between freedpeople and white Southerners and indicates that uncertainty defined a postbellum era marked by African Americans' struggle for upward mobility and political rights.

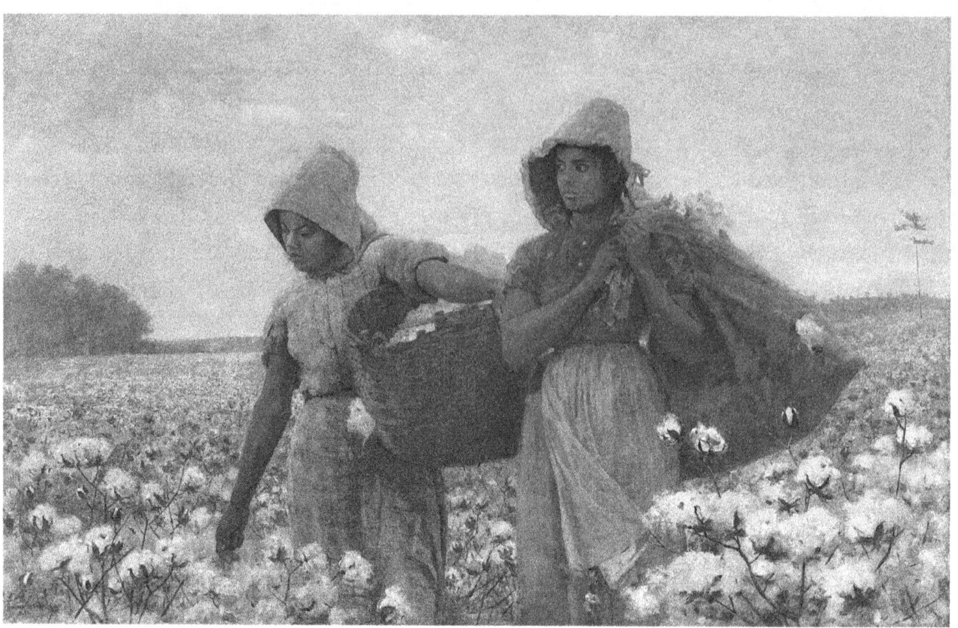

Winslow Homer, *The Cotton Pickers* (1876). Los Angeles County Museum of Art.

Three years after Homer completed his thought-provoking composition, Thomas Anshutz (1851–1912) created a similar painting that subtly critiqued black Americans' continued societal marginalization on secluded rural farms where they struggled to eke out an existence. As an artist, Anshutz strove to capture life as he truly saw it. In 1873, he recorded of his plein air excursions: "[I] get out my materials and make as accurate a painting of what I see in front of me as I can."[122] Indeed, his depiction of an African American mother tending her vegetable garden alongside her children, titled *The Way They Live* (1879), strikes the viewer as a genuine snapshot of African American farm life. The humble family toils on their dry patch of land in the hot sun, focused only on ensuring that their cabbages survive. Although little is known about the scene's geographic location, experts surmise that Anshutz painted the composition at the site of the event, possibly in the mountains of West Virginia.[123] Reviewers praised the work after it was displayed at the Academy of Fine Arts in 1879; one called it "remarkably well painted" and lauded Anshutz's representation of the figures of the black family as "especially good."[124] The artist's compassion for his subjects is apparent in the respectful way in which he portrays them; the industrious mother's calm, serious facial features suggest that she possesses a sober and introspective nature. Finally, the painting's title, *The Way They Live,* likely impressed on viewers the idea that African Americans were economically disadvantaged and lived under difficult conditions in rural communities far from the urban settings where Anshutz's paintings were exhibited. Such sympathetic representations of African American freedpeople may have evoked sympathy in audiences with limited knowledge of how freedpeople struggled to establish new lives after their emancipation.

Fifty years after the abolition of slavery, thousands of African Americans had migrated from the countryside to cities seeking new job opportunities. But in 1915, when artist William Edouard Scott visited Alabama as a guest of Tuskegee Institute founder Booker T. Washington, many African Americans still toiled as sharecroppers in the Jim Crow South.[125] Scott, who had recently completed his training in Paris under the instruction of French artists and mentor Henry Ossawa Tanner, decided to paint Alabama's black rural laborers.[126] Two works, *It's Going to Come* (1916) and *Untitled (Sharecropper)* (circa 1915–1918), portray their experiences with empathy. In the first painting, two women stand in front of their home, which is nestled in a grove of trees. Their poverty is evident from their simple clothing, their bare feet, and the ramshackle cabin behind them. The woman in the foreground of the painting looks stoic as she stands with hands on her hips, determined to overcome her circumstances. The painting's ambiguous title alludes to the family's anticipation of an event that may bring good or harm their way. *Untitled (Sharecropper)* sends a similar message to viewers about the resilience of African American laborers. Here, a young boy stands in bare feet in front of a field bursting with vegetables. The child wears overalls that he has outgrown and carries two large, heavy buckets. There is little opportunity for him on the farm; he works the land instead of attending school and remains mired in poverty. Yet he faces the viewer squarely with an indomitable spirit that indicates his will to survive.

Other American painters of African American laborers lacked the compassion demonstrated by Scott, Homer, and Anshutz in their compositions. For instance, artist William Aiken Walker played on racial stereotypes in his two-dimensional works depicting freedpeople. Walker created many paintings for private buyers or mass audiences instead of submitting them to exhibitions, for example, at the National Academy of Design, a fact that may have contributed to the unsophisticated and shallow nature of his works. In one representative image from the late nineteenth century, *Cotton Pickers,* two African American field-workers stand side by side with vacant expressions on their faces. Their tattered, threadbare clothing and the dilapidated cabin in the background attest to their poverty on an unnamed Southern cotton plantation. But the man and woman seem content in their situation; their placid, empty faces suggest nothing to the viewer about any inner ambitions they might harbor. In another oil painting, *I'll Stick to Cotton as Long as It Sticks to Me* (1886), a bedraggled African American man, likely a freedman, also maintains an air of indifference to his condition. With a hand in his pocket, he leans comfortably against a basket of cotton while smoking a corn-cob pipe. Such flat representations likely appealed to the same white late nineteenth-century audiences who were drawn to the nostalgic short stories of authors like Thomas Nelson Page and Joel Chandler Harris that featured fictional freedmen who preferred life as slaves.[127] Walker's title, *I'll Stick to Cotton as Long as It Sticks to Me*, suggests that the freedman did not care about relocating from the plantation where he had likely resided since before emancipation. Although his unflattering depictions of rural African American freedpeople contrasted with those of Homer and Anshutz, Walker seems to have shared their perception of fieldwork as a limiting, restrictive environment for African Americans. Together, these three artists' unenthusiastic visions of rural America differed substantially from those of Russian painters who saw the peasantry's agricultural labor as an ennobling, purifying endeavor that represented an essential element of Russia's national heritage.

Religion and Ritual in Russian and African American Culture

Members of the Society of Traveling Art Exhibitions also expressed their pride in Russia's history through the creation of paintings depicting peasants passing down folktales, conducting ancient wedding rituals, and participating in religious processions and pilgrimages.

One of Vasilii Maksimov's earliest paintings was *Grandmother's Tales* (1867), a composition that received first prize from the Imperial Society for the Encouragement of Artists.[128] Inspired by Maksimov's memories of his mother, who, according to one friend, "recounted interesting fairy tales and authentic histories to the children on long winter evenings," *Grandmother's Tales* similarly takes place in a candlelit hut where a wise grandmother captivates an audience of children and young adults who surround her as they attentively listen to her stories.[129] This nostalgic, sentimental scene about the role of oral tradition in rural communities resonated with audiences and may have inspired subsequent painters to pursue similar themes.[130]

Numerous Wanderers also revealed to audiences the private rituals of peasant families as they prepared to give away sons and daughters in marriage.

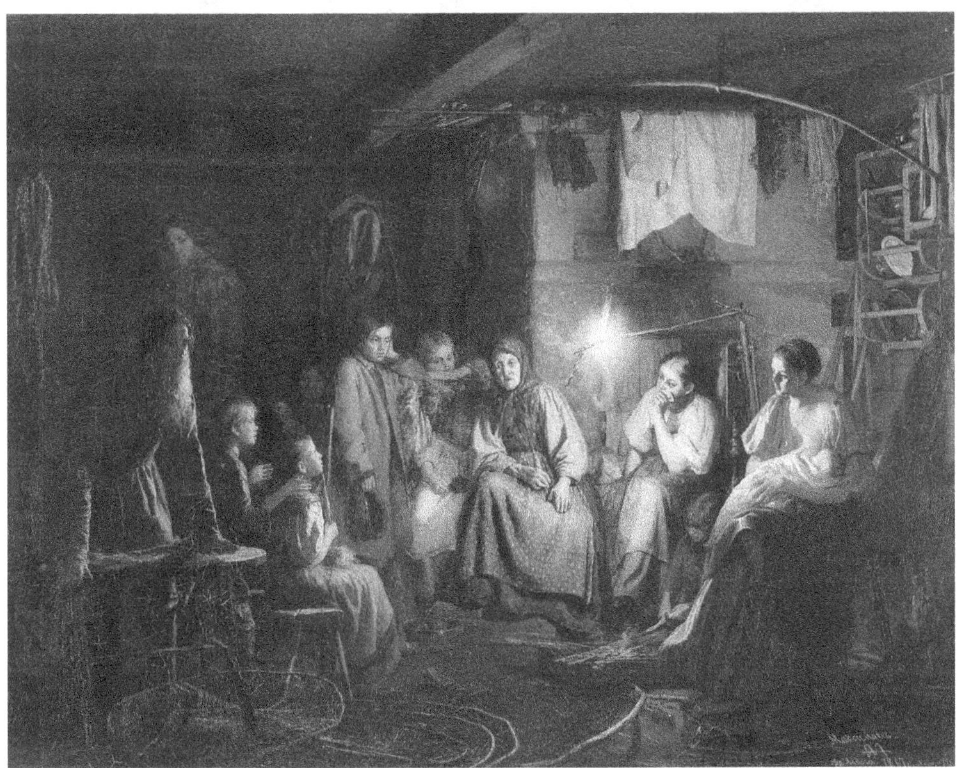

Vasilii Maksimov, *Grandmother's Tales* (1867). State Tret'iakov Gallery, Moscow.

Maksimov's *The Arrival of a Magician at a Peasant Wedding* (1875) depicts a glowing cottage where a wedding party feasts in celebration of a newly married couple.[131] But an unexpected visitor interrupts the gathering; a snow-covered magician stands at the entryway, preparing to either bless or curse the happy couple.[132] Similar works that portrayed ancient peasant wedding rituals through a romanticized or ethnographic perspective include Grigorii Miasoedov's *Examining a Bride* (second half of the nineteenth century), Alexei Korzukhin's celebratory *Hen Party* (1889), and Andrei Riabushkin's *Peasant Wedding in the Tambovskii Province* (1880) and *Awaiting Newlyweds in the Novgorod Province* (1891).[133] Together, these works served as visual records of artists' interpretations of the peasantry's most sacred cultural practices and celebrations of their life in the provinces.

Another popular mode of peasant representation was that of the humble Christian procession (*krestnyi khod*) that occurred on various holy days during the year.[134] In the Russian Orthodox Church, nineteenth-century peasants often collectively displayed their religiosity through public parades and demonstrations during which they carried icons, flags, or holy objects. Artists including Konstantin Savitskii, Leonid Solomatkin, and Illarion Prianishnikov captured these rituals in grand paintings depicting a devoted, faithful peasantry kissing icons, waving banners, and enduring harsh traveling conditions as they participated in religious processions.[135]

Il'ia Repin's *Procession of the Cross in Kursk Province* (1883), inspired by the artist's visit to a region renowned for its pilgrimages, made an especially strong impression on audiences thanks to its scale, level of detail, and representation of different estates.[136] Exhibited at the eleventh show of the Society of Traveling Art Exhibitions, *Procession of the Cross* was primarily a critique of the economic and spiritual divisions among the downtrodden peasantry, the wealthy nobility, and tidy urban merchants who all marched together in a long parade.[137] According to Iakov Minchenkov, a manager of the Society, Repin painted this work for the peasantry; he "saw before him images from the epoch of serfdom, before him stood the living people of this era . . . and he presented them on canvas with all the strength of his talent."[138] Through his condemnation of the material gap between the peasantry and the nobility, Repin sought to impress on audiences the paternalistic idea that, in spite of life's challenges, the peasantry's humble religiosity enabled them to endure poverty and oppression.

In contrast to their Russian peers, most white American artists did not depict black culture as representative of American national culture; instead, they portrayed African American music and religious rituals either as mysterious curiosities or as a bridge that could link two disparate peoples.[139] During the mid- to late nineteenth century, many white Americans saw more differences than commonalities between their religious and secular traditions rooted in western European history and those of the enslaved people who maintained many elements of their heritage after their transport to the United States from different regions in Africa. These ethnic and cultural divisions, partly manifested and enforced in the practice of segregation, were particularly sharp in the South, where, as James C. Cobb aptly puts it, "this definition of southern identity effectively excluded the South's black residents in much the same way that both black and white southerners had been 'othered' out of the construction of American identity."[140]

In American art, George Fuller's (1822–1884) *Negro Funeral, Alabama* (1881) illustrates this white American mentality. Born in Massachusetts, Fuller traveled during the 1850s, to Augusta, Georgia, and Montgomery, Alabama, where he witnessed aspects of enslaved African Americans' culture such as a mass baptism in a nearby river and a burial.[141] Although Fuller did not record his impressions of the funeral in his diary, he completed a sketch in March 1858 that most likely inspired the oil painting he completed more than twenty years later.[142] *Negro Funeral, Alabama* is a stark, impressionistic painting that depicts an undefined crowd of enslaved African Americans surrounding a coffin in a desolate field. Harsh yellow light pierces the clouds, illuminating the figure of a black celebrant whose outstretched arms and tall stature command the attention of his peers. The scene conveys a sense of the exotic rather than the familiar; here, Fuller emphasizes the physical and experiential distances between the enslaved people and the viewer, who is positioned as an outsider.

Other postbellum paintings by white artists portrayed elements of African Americans' culture, particularly that of music, as a link between black and white Americans.[143] One representative composition is Eastman Johnson's *Fiddling His Way* (1866). Portraying a cozy scene inside a rural farmhouse, *Fiddling His Way* exemplifies a style that one critic described as Johnson's original "method of painting . . . [that of] 'the portrait interior' . . . [depicting] a family group assembled in their drawing room," which produced for audiences a familiar and "charming effect of domesticity."[144] In the painting, a well-dressed freedman deftly plays his instrument to the delight of the white family, particularly its youngest members, who respectfully listen to the engaging tune that infuses the dim cottage with vitality and animates its residents. Racial tensions often ran high between impoverished white Americans and black Americans during the nineteenth century, but in Johnson's painting, the formerly enslaved man's music acted as an integrating, unifying force. Although the family invited into their home an unfamiliar itinerant musician, he, in turn, opened the doors of communication between two typically segregated groups through the universal language of music.

Like Johnson, Winslow Homer similarly spanned the gap between white and black Americans in his painting *Dressing for Carnival* (1877), which was exhibited and sold at auction in 1879.[145] The composition, which Homer described as one of his "darkey pictures," shows a complex scene in which a group of freedpeople prepares to celebrate Independence Day.[146] In front of a Virginia plantation's slave quarters, two African American women help prepare the colorful costume worn by an African American man, while children waving American flags watch with great interest. His attire blends American patriotic colors with visual and stylistic elements of the West Indian Jonkonnu festival, a celebration during which the rules governing relations between landowners and enslaved laborers were suspended and costumed men and women engaged in revelry at the owner's expense.[147]

After emancipation, some African Americans observed Jonkonnu on the Fourth of July, presumably the phenomenon that Homer shows in *Dressing for Carnival*. By depicting the melding of two disparate cultural traditions in his painting, Homer alludes to the process of assimilation occurring in many parts of the nation and reminds audiences that freedpeople had a rightful place in American society as citizens who collectively celebrated both national and individual independence.[148] Unlike Fuller, who distanced audiences from the exotic burial, Homer combined an unfamiliar aspect of African American culture with the well-known Fourth of July holiday to encourage mutual understanding between black and white Americans.

By comparison, the work of African American artist Henry Ossawa Tanner displays the spirit of cultural pride that so frequently infused the paintings of the Wanderers, who portrayed peasant rituals and culture as central components of Russia's national heritage. His most famous genre painting of African Americans, *The Banjo Lesson* (1893), celebrates the transmission of musical knowledge from a grandfather to his grandson. Tanner, writing in the third person, described his own interest in depicting African Americans in a statement published between 1893 and 1894:

> Since [Tanner's] return from Europe he has painted many Negro subjects. He feels drawn to such subjects on account of the newness of the field and because of a desire to represent the serious and pathetic side of life among them, and it is his thought that other things being equal, he who has the most sympathy with the subject will obtain the best results. To his mind, many of the artists who have represented Negro life have only seen the comic, ludicrous side of it and have lacked sympathy with and affection for the big heart that dwells within such a rough exterior.[149]

Seeking to improve on the representations of African Americans that typified those of white American artists, Tanner chose to portray black musical heritage in a scene that sharply contrasted with the stereotypical late nineteenth-century image of the comic black minstrel figure.

Drawn in Florida, *The Banjo Lesson* is a sober, intimate portrait of the loving relationship between a grandson and his grandfather.[150] In a peaceful interior illuminated by the light of a fire, the child sits on his grandfather's lap while he carefully strums the musical instrument. The affection between the two figures is palpable; the attentive grandfather supports the heavy banjo while he listens carefully to his grandson's chords. Described by one early twentieth-century critic as a painting that "comes near being the finest piece of work on that subject," *The Banjo Lesson* presented a respectful, admiring

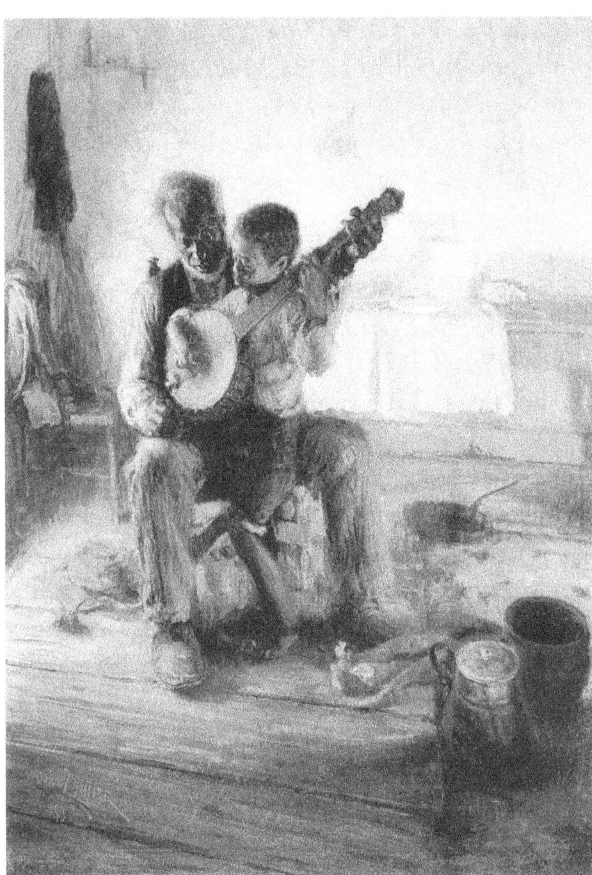

Henry Ossawa Tanner, *The Banjo Lesson* (1893). Hampton University Museum Collection, Hampton University, Hampton, Va.

portrait of African American culture and family life.[151] Furthermore, Tanner's masterpiece was, in the words of scholar Judith Wilson, "a declaration of African American self-esteem that anticipated the twin emphases on racial pride and vernacular culture which would come to characterize the work of numbers of Black artists only in the 20th century."[152] Ultimately, Tanner's empathetic work served as an essential and influential contribution to the growing range of representations of African Americans in genre paintings.

Obtaining an Education: Representations of Peasants and Freedpeople as Students

In Russia and the United States, the abolition of slavery and serfdom paved the way for additional policy reforms that provided freedpeople and peasants with access to education. Emancipated Russian serfs and African American freedpeople generally shared a desire to obtain literacy, but some peasants distrusted advocates of education or worried that schooling might disrupt the peasantry's traditional way of life.[153] In Russia, educational changes quickly followed the abolition of serfdom as part of the Great Reforms that transformed society. Tsar Alexander II's biographer recorded that "the issue of spreading primary education among the people, of teaching the peasants literacy, flowed directly from the changes taking place in their daily lives with the onset of the emancipation from serfdom."[154] Three years after the announcement of the Emancipation Manifesto, the Russian government issued an education statute that encouraged the founding and local management of elementary schools without estate-based barriers to entry and ultimately produced a significant rise in literacy rates among peasant populations.[155] African American freedpeople also learned to read and write in rising numbers after emancipation. At public, statewide conventions, freedpeople urged listeners to support the education of formerly enslaved people, arguing not only that it was their right but also that Southern states would benefit from an educated population.[156] African Americans subsequently created opportunities for children and adults by founding local schools or petitioning state governments to set up public institutions or by attending institutions funded by private charitable organizations or the Freedmen's Bureau.[157] As a result, illiteracy rates among African Americans fourteen years of age and older dropped from 80 percent in 1870 to 30.5 percent in 1910.[158] Although some farming families in Russia and the United States were initially skeptical about the value of education, many peasants and freedpeople quickly realized that literacy could help them succeed in business as well as provide them with the tools to interpret the Bible, enjoy popular literature, or serve in the military.[159]

Most Russian and American artists created compositions that celebrated peasants' and freedpeople's educational achievements, but a handful of artists produced paintings that questioned the former serfs' and freedpeople's commitment to gaining literacy.[160] One of the strongest proponents of peasant schooling was Nikolai Bogdanov-Bel'skii (1868–1945), an artist who, as a peasant child, studied under Moscow University professor Sergei Rachinskii at the elementary school for local children Rachinskii founded in the rural town of Tatevo.[161] Bogdanov-Bel'skii's appreciation for this opportunity, gratitude to Rachinskii, and belief in the merits of education for rural children are evident in numerous sentimental paintings that recall those of an American peer, painter Norman Rockwell (1894–1978). In the work

Mental Calculation: In Public School of S. A. Rachinskii (1895), peasant boys in traditional clothing earnestly struggle to solve a long-division equation that the teacher has drawn on a chalkboard.[162] Their sincere interest in the presented material is evident from the bright, genuine expressions on their faces. Indeed, Bogdanov-Bel'skii may have sought to dispel any doubts the nobility harbored about the former serfs' aptitude and appetite for learning. A later painting, *At the Doors of a School* (1897), further encouraged empathy in educated audiences by placing the viewer in the position of a peasant child who stands in the doorway of a schoolroom as he timidly observes his future classmates. The threshold symbolizes the beginning of an important journey for the child, with walking stick in hand and knapsack on his back, whose path will undoubtedly be altered by the education he will soon receive.

Like Bogdanov-Bel'skii, American painters Winslow Homer, Thomas Waterman Wood, and Eastman Johnson also celebrated African Americans' academic successes in their paintings, but they especially emphasized the religious benefits of literacy. For instance, Homer's *Sunday Morning in Virginia* (1877) and Wood's *Sunday Morning* (1877) both depict African American children reading aloud from the Bible in humble domestic settings. In Homer's composition, a group of children jointly study the precious book in the corner of an empty wooden cabin, while Wood portrays a single female child reading to an elderly woman sitting in a rocking chair. In both paintings, the young children are bathed either in hopeful sunlight or in the glow of an adjacent fire, artistic decisions that reference the figurative power of knowledge and faith to illuminate the mind and soul. In addition, by portraying literate children and adults who had most likely endured decades of enslavement, Wood and Homer conveyed an optimistic message to audiences about the future achievements of the black community's youngest generation.

Although Bogdanov-Bel'skii, Homer, and Wood primarily focused on children, artist Eastman Johnson chose to feature an adult freedman learning to read. *The Lord Is My Shepherd* (1863), painted shortly after Lincoln issued his Emancipation Proclamation, shows a well-dressed young man sitting by the dying embers of a fire as he quietly reads from the Old Testament of the Bible. Art historian Eleanor Harvey contends that the painting contains layers of meaning; at the surface, the image "seems to posit the gentle nature of a formerly enslaved man reading the Psalms as a model of emerging humanity and citizenship."[163] Indeed, the painting's title alludes to the first verse of Psalm 23, a passage that speaks of God's protection on life's difficult journeys,

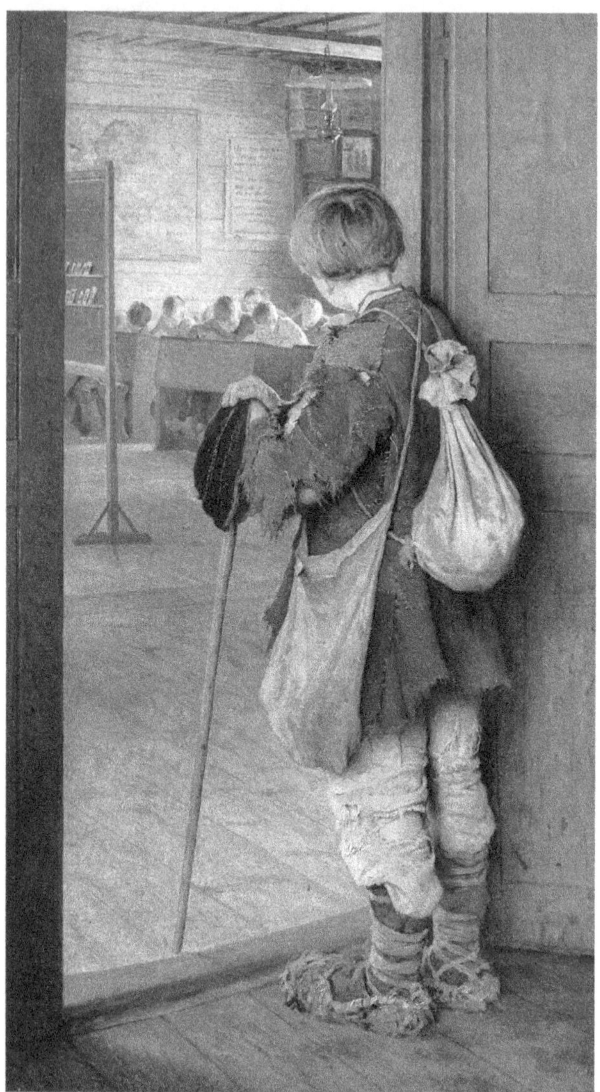

Nikolai Bogdanov-Bel'skii, *At the Doors of a School* (1897). © State Russian Museum, St. Petersburg.

but Harvey argues that the freedman is most likely reading from Exodus, a book that describes the enslaved Israelites' escape from Egypt.[164] Thus, although one critic called Johnson a simple "painter of the fireside," at times the artist's works contained subtle, politically controversial messages that revealed Johnson's personal beliefs about contemporary divisive issues like emancipation and literacy among African Americans.[165]

Other artists including Aleksei Stepanov (1858–1923), Vladimir Makovskii (1846–1920), and Edward Lamson Henry created compositions that questioned peasants' and freedpeople's interest in learning to read and write. In late nineteenth-century Russia, peasant communes in rural villages hired instructors from other regions to teach at local schools, but these itinerant teachers were not paid well and possessed a low social status in the town.[166] Furthermore, the insular residents of isolated villages could be suspicious of outsiders who did not understand their traditions and practices. In addition, some members of the peasantry remained skeptical about the value of education and apprehensive of its potential for social upheaval.[167] Two genre paintings, Stepanov's *Arrival of the Teacher* (1889) and Makovskii's *Arrival of the Teacher in the Village* (1897), depict a town's cold reception of a traveling instructor. Stepanov's work shows a group of apprehensive peasants huddled together by a hut as they watch a horse-drawn wagon carrying an educator enter their little village. The stone-faced men and women stand with arms crossed, uncertain of how this stranger might change their traditional ways. Makovskii's painting plays on the same theme; in it, a female teacher in modern clothing sits soberly at a table outside of her new rural home, while her peasant hosts watch her from a distance. Neither the teacher nor the peasants make eye contact in the composition, a fact that attests to their mutual mistrust and the emotional gulf that separates them.

But while Russian artists Makovskii and Stepanov focused on physical and experiential divisions between peasants and instructors to articulate a degree of skepticism about peasant education, American painter Edward Lamson Henry depicted a young African American girl's schoolhouse infractions. *Kept In* (1888) shows a stubborn child sulking alone in a classroom as she gazes out the window, observing her classmates playing during recess. Her lack of interest in education is apparent in her indifferent posture; she leans back with arms behind her head in feigned relaxation, ignoring the book that she has cast on the floor. Henry's representation of a reluctant black student contrasts sharply with Bogdanov-Bel'skii's sentimental paintings of enthusiastic peasant children, perhaps sending a subtle message to white audiences that African Americans were too undisciplined to thrive in academic settings. Although ambivalent depictions of apathetic African American students and peasants by artists like Henry, Makovskii, and Stepanov remained exceptional examples that did little to discourage peasants and freedpeople from obtaining an education, their representations may have confirmed the views of those who opposed providing African Americans and peasants access to public schools.

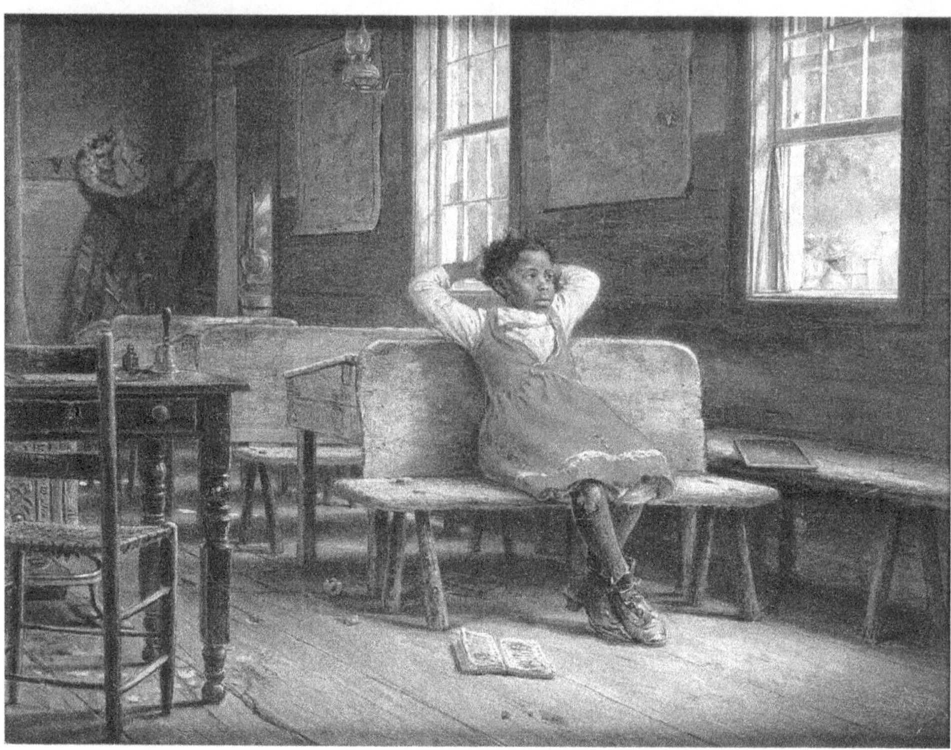

Edward Lamson Henry, *Kept In* (1889). Fenimore Art Museum, Cooperstown, N.Y. Gift of Stephen C. Clark, N0309.1961. Photograph by Richard Walker.

Urban Migration and the Struggle to Survive

A final common theme in representations of peasants and freedpeople is that of urban migration, a phenomenon that transformed the social fabric of the United States and Russia during the late nineteenth century. As discussed in chapter 3, thousands of peasants and African Americans migrated from estates and farms to bustling cities between 1890 and 1910.[168] Reflecting on this massive demographic shift, Russian and American artists created paintings that explored the challenges peasants and freedpeople faced on the road and after arriving in unfamiliar cities. American painter William Aiken Walker and Russian artists Sergei Korovin (1858–1908), Sergei Ivanov (1864–1910), and Sergei Vinogradov (1869–1938) each portrayed phases of these journeys in paintings that illustrate the hardships peasants and freedpeople endured as migrants. Walker's *The Old Traveler* (late nineteenth century) and Korovin's *Peasant on the Road (For Earnings)* (1890s) both depict poverty-stricken men dressed in rags as they make their way on foot across the countryside to un-known destinations. Wizened and sober, the lonely figures carry simple sacks on their backs, symbols of their few worldly possessions. These representa-tions do not inspire hope; rather, they evoke sympathy in the viewer for itin-erants with a grim past and an uncertain future.

Ivanov's *On the Road: The Death of a Migrant* (1889), featured at the seven-teenth show of the Society of Traveling Art Exhibitions, offers more clarity by depicting a migrant's tragic end. A male peasant's body lies stretched across the road in front of his wagon; his face has been covered with a cloth and his arms are folded across his chest. The peasant's wife weeps upon the ground, her tears soaking the dry, desolate path on which she, her husband, and their daughter were traveling in search of a new life. Disastrously, the family's sole provider has perished, and it is unclear how the woman and child will survive on their own.

Ivanov's graphic scene contrasts with idealized depictions of peasants working the land by Grigorii Miasoedov, Konstantin Makovskii, and other Wanderers. As one of the darkest, most pessimistic visual representations of urban migration, *The Death of a Migrant* likely suggested to late nineteenth-century audiences that peasants were better suited to life in traditional agri-cultural settings. Two additional works that convey a similar message to viewers about the former serfs' and enslaved African Americans' ability to survive in urban settings are Vinogradov's *Without Work (Waiting for the Ferry)* (1888) and Walker's *Where Canal Meets the Levee* (late nineteenth century). These compositions are illustrations of migrants who recline against bales of cotton or doze in the mud as they wait for work by the riverside.[169] Both Vino-gradov's peasants and Walker's freedpeople lounge, smoke pipes, and con-verse to pass the time, representations that signaled to late nineteenth-century viewers that the former serfs and freedpeople were not productive members of urban society.

These depictions belie the historical experiences of peasant and African American migrants who had little difficulty obtaining gainful employment in cities including St. Petersburg, Moscow, Philadelphia, and Washington, D.C. Two autobiographies offer firsthand accounts of the job opportunities that awaited migrant workers during the late nineteenth century. African American William Pickens, the son of tenant farmers, described his work experience in Argenta, Arkansas, where his family arrived in the winter of 1890–1891. While studying in high school during the late 1890s, Pickens took up work in a stave factory and copper shop, where he proudly recalled "earning . . . seventy-five cents a day, more money than I had ever received steadily before in my life."[170]

Soon after, Pickens's father, now "a fireman for a sawmill," helped him find additional part-time labor by "securing" for him "the privilege of employing" some of "[his] Saturdays on the lumber yards."[171] Like Pickens's family, thousands of Americans migrated from farms to cities to take advantage of unprecedented prospects of securing regular salaries in thriving industries.

Autobiographical serf narratives also attest to the ways in which industrial development improved the lives of the peasantry. The former serf F. D. Bobkov remembered how the construction of new factories transformed his native village and provided the residents with more wealth, penning, "Yes, there were many changes. Some men, owing to their own laziness and idle life, became impoverished, but the peasants, thanks to their energy, now rejoiced in life."[172] During the late 1870s, Bobkov, who moved several times during his lifetime, recalled working for a factory where he received a salary of 150 rubles per month, a princely sum compared to the 15–20 rubles in net farm income that rural peasant households typically earned in the late nineteenth century.[173] These two testimonies serve as evidence of the new opportunities generated by industrialization, a topic infrequently depicted by Russian and American painters during the late nineteenth century. Their experiences provide an important counterpoint to the pessimistic representations of urban life that many artists produced during this time. Ultimately, the differences between these artistic portrayals and the historical realities suggest that both Russian and American painters felt uncomfortable about emigration trends that saw traditionally agrarian peoples abandoning the countryside for a more unrestricted existence in metropolitan areas.

In Russia and the United States, the abolition of serfdom and slavery triggered decades of reflection among artists who sought to make sense of these transformational events and their enduring consequences. Russian and American genre painters created works of art that visualized the experiences of the peasants and freedpeople who constituted the nations' newest subjects and citizens. In their paintings, artists explored black and peasant experiences of captivity and the processes of their liberation. While some criticized proponents of servitude or portrayed the hardships serfs and enslaved people endured, others created nostalgic images of serfdom and slavery or examined the varied mechanisms of the laborers' liberation.

Russian and American painters also examined the dual roles of military service and education in creating subjects and citizens. While American artists from the North typically depicted soldiering as an act of bodily sacrifice that entitled freedpeople the privileges of citizenship, Russian artists, particularly those from the peasant estate, represented military conscription as an inescapable burden of subjecthood borne primarily by the nation's most impoverished people. For other painters contemplating the idea of national identity, literacy was an additional path to citizenship. While some artists portrayed peasants and freedpeople enthusiastically receiving lessons in newly accessible public schools or learning how to read, works intended to bolster popular support for educational initiatives, others rendered peasants and African Americans uninterested in formal education, depictions that point to underlying societal tensions about providing educational access to former serfs and freedpeople.

Finally, Russian and American painters expressed interest in traditional African American and peasant culture and in the consequences of urban migration. While Russian artists celebrated peasant traditions as representative of their national heritage, American artists created a wider range of representations of black culture. Both Russian and American artists appear to have been doubtful about rural laborers' ability to thrive in urban centers, attitudes manifested in works of art that featured unemployed or even deceased migrants. In each of these categories, ethnicity remained a particularly important consideration for American artists. Although the abolition of serfdom and slavery generated for both countries the comparable challenges of absorbing peasants and freedpeople, notions of racial difference played a greater role in influencing the creation of and responses to works of art depicting African Americans.

CHAPTER FIVE

Advertisements and Ephemera

The metal plough cuts into the rich earth as the Russian peasant guides two horses across a small plot of land. In the distance, birds soar above a river that gently winds toward the green onion domes and thatched roofs of structures in a nearby village. The colorful fin de siècle advertising poster promoting Rudolph Bekher's agricultural equipment offers a vision of rural tranquility as the independent peasant in traditional dress, possibly a former serf, deftly manipulates a modern agricultural tool. Indeed, the sun shines upon the man whose future seems bright.[1] Meanwhile, a contemporaneous advertisement for Durham's "Bull Fertilizer," produced in the United States, similarly draws on pastoral imagery to market a modern product.[2] This illustrated trade card portrays a male African American farmer, perhaps a freedman, struggling to pull two obstinate mules that are hitched to a steel reaper. The card's tagline, "No kicking when 'Bull Fertilizer' is used," mocks the man and subtly alludes to the historical tradition of white landowners' control over black laborers. While the Russian peasant seems to be a successful steward of his property, the African American farmer appears incompetent and foolish.

Although these late nineteenth-century advertisements differ in significant ways, they both reference the legacies of serfdom and slavery. In Russia and the United States, businesses played an important role in shaping attitudes about the processes of social absorption during the decades that followed abolition. Advertisements commonly featured visual representations of serfs and enslaved people that informed consumers' conceptions of peasants and African Americans as new subjects and citizens. A comparative analysis of these carefully crafted scenes sheds light on businesses' marketing strategies and efforts to target specific consumer groups through images of historically subjugated populations.

In late imperial Russia, illustrated advertisements portraying serfs and peasants at once idealized serfdom and post-emancipation agrarianism, promoted new concepts of nationhood and national identity, and, perhaps most important, shaped and reflected broad changes in the nation's social fabric. First, businesses produced nostalgic advertisements targeting nonpeasants that depicted serfs and peasants in positions of subservience as they performed duties for wealthy members of the nobility. Companies also created nationalistic ads that elevated emancipated peasants and their traditional culture as symbols of Russia's collective history and strength. In addition, firms sought to directly capture the attention of Russia's new urban peasantry in advertisements. They employed two distinct strategies. First, they distributed paternalistic advertisements that addressed the anxieties of recent migrants by urging them to buy goods or apparel supposedly deemed essential for their successful assimilation. Second, firms targeted peasant consumers by portraying them in ads as independent, decisive patrons or as integrated citizens who shopped as equals alongside Russia's urban elites.

In the United States, companies produced representations of enslaved African Americans and freedpeople in posters, trade cards, and magazines during the late nineteenth and early twentieth centuries. American businesses developed several marketing strategies that paralleled those of Russian companies; for example, many firms created advertisements depicting African Americans in positions of servitude that appealed to white consumers who were nostalgic for a preindustrial, pre-emancipation era. As in Russia, U.S. businesses also tapped into the apprehensions of a post-emancipation nation adapting to a new social order, while citizens of all backgrounds grappled with changes wrought by rapid industrialization, urbanization, immigration, and geographic expansion.

But while Russian businesses produced a significant number of advertisements depicting peasants in positions of equality relative to other citizens, comparable images of African Americans rarely appeared in U.S. advertisements over the same period. Indeed, one discovers not only the absence of equivalent images of integrated African Americans but also an abundance of demeaning caricatures. Racism and ethnic differences between blacks and whites contributed to the production of advertisements that emphasized rather than minimized perceived dissimilarities, but distinctions between Russian and American population compositions, urban migration patterns, and notions of nationhood also account for the profusion of denigrating advertisements featuring African Americans in the United States and the comparative scarcity of such peasant representations in Russia.

Advertising Ascendant in the United States and Russia

Advertising became increasingly important during the late nineteenth century when Russia and the United States simultaneously underwent manufacturing booms as numerous industries developed and cities expanded.[3] In the United States, manufacturers created a vast array of goods, including clothing, agricultural equipment, automobiles, alcohol, and cigarettes.[4] Many of these commercial items were distributed via the railroad system, which played a critical role in enabling producers to transport materials to geographically distant consumers.[5] Meanwhile, Russia's economic foundations similarly shifted from agricultural labor toward commerce, manufacturing, and textile production, a structural change that mirrored that of France during the first half of the nineteenth century.[6] Improvements to communication systems and infrastructure, such as the government's decision to increasingly invest in railroad construction and supervision in 1880, led to the enhanced flow of information and goods.[7] Russian industries developed further after 1897, when Finance Minister Sergei Witte put the ruble on the gold standard to stimulate foreign investment. As Russia's annual growth rate reached 8 percent during the 1890s, the nation witnessed a new era of production and distribution of material goods, many of which were available for purchase in bustling cities like St. Petersburg and Moscow.[8]

Industrialization, migration, and improvements to national infrastructure enabled Russian and American merchants and manufacturers to reach a wider range of potential customers. Advertising, a nascent industry in each country prior to the late nineteenth century, became an increasingly important component of companies' marketing strategies as they promoted their goods to consumers. As they tried to inform buyers about the products now available to them, Russian and American firms also performed a balancing act by using marketing materials to reassure consumers who were apprehensive about social and economic changes. In Russia, Tsars Alexander III and Nicholas II presided over autocratic regimes with paradoxical policies; although these rulers restricted political activity, they encouraged elements of economic liberalism, albeit under the state's watchful eye. According to historian Sally West, Russian advertising mirrored this contradiction by deliberately promoting "a consumerist ethic at odds with autocratic society" that "spoke in the language of both tradition and change, simultaneously perpetuating and undermining the values of Russian cultural heritage."[9] Ultimately, Russia's rapid economic transformation, inadequate protections for urban workers, and a lack of political rights sowed seeds of discontent that produced labor strikes, rioting, and general upheaval during the Revolution of 1905. Such unrest exceeded the potentially palliative effect of advertisements seeking to diminish the psychological hardships inherent in the process of modernization.

Americans were similarly troubled by the unsettling changes generated by industrialization. Discord was prevalent among laborers who worked long hours in factories and manufacturing plants. In Chicago's Haymarket Square, laborers clashed with police after protesting conditions at the McCormick Harvesting Machine Company plant in 1886, while an 1892 strike at Andrew Carnegie's steel factory in Homestead, Pennsylvania, similarly ended in violence. In 1894, angry Americans marched across the country toward Washington, D.C., as part of labor leader Jacob Coxey's army to encourage the government to enact policies to support unemployed workers. Although the United States did not experience a major revolution comparable to that of Russia at the turn of the twentieth century, these individual examples demonstrate that social unrest was similarly widespread.

During this period of significant change, American and Russian businesses sought to guide apprehensive consumers along the pathway toward modernization through comforting advertisements. Companies blended text and images to create a language of familiar signs and symbols, easily comprehended by viewers, which conveyed information and meaning. Recognizing that an increasing number of people were leaving their rural homes to live in crowded cities, Russian and American companies marketed products of the industrial age through comforting pastoral imagery. For instance, historian T. J. Jackson Lears contends that late nineteenth-century American artists and lithographers "recreated a vision of preindustrial life" in pictures of homes and farms in peaceful agrarian settings that represented "the still point of the turning world."[10] Businesses also joined traditional images with wholly modern ones including sprawling factories or innovative agricultural equipment as part of what Lears calls "an ideology of national progress that merged with technological, intellectual, and spiritual development."[11]

Two well-known images, a chromolithograph of John Gast's *Westward, Ho!* (1872) and a poster for the Mariia Vasil'evna Sadomova factory (1884), present a striking opportunity for comparison.[12] In both illustrations, benevolent, outsize, female figures preside over scenes of industrialization, migration, and national transformation. In the first picture, America's patriotic Columbia leads pioneers and other entrepreneurial groups westward as telegraph lines, trains, ships, and bridges appear in her wake. Meanwhile, the Sadomova advertisement similarly depicts Mother Russia as a patron saint or spirit of industrial progress; she floats serenely above a group of rural and urban peasants who inspect yarn in front of a factory located in a bucolic setting. This advertisement references Russia's industrial and urban transformation through its allusion to the processes of migration and its illustration of a harmonious union between the rural peasantry and modern industrial development.[13] These parallel examples reflect companies' broader strategies of incorporating traditional images in advertisements to habituate consumers to a new, modern world. Moreover, as Russian and American businesses looked to their respective national pasts for inspiration, they both chose to use visual representations of two groups whom consumers definitively associated with agrarianism and rural life: Russian serfs and enslaved African Americans.

U.S. and Russian Advertisements in Daily Life

Russian and American businesses touted the superiority of their wares to urban and rural consumers through textual and visual advertisements in newspapers, journals, catalogs, magazines, ephemera, trade cards, and illustrated posters. Advertisements were especially noticeable in cities, where broadsides brightened the walls of taverns and colorful signs shouted to shoppers through storefront windows, on columns, or on the side of horse-drawn trolleys.[14] Even building facades served as canvases for painted announcements that urged customers to sample the latest consumer products.

In a pamphlet printed in 1909, the American agency J. Walter Thompson Company declared that the rise of advertising was "the permanent result of an economic revolution" and scolded businesses that still hesitated to spend money on marketing, admonishing, "If you have anything worth advertising, and do not advertise it, you are simply keeping yourself out of touch with the world's progress."[15] Responding to the changing times, both American and Russian manufacturers increasingly recognized that advertising was vital to the growth of their businesses and adjusted their budgets accordingly. In the United States, private companies' advertising budgets dramatically increased during the late nineteenth century, with businesses spending $30 million in 1880 and $600 million in 1910.[16] While the practice of advertising among manufacturers and retail stores in Russia initially lagged behind that of Europe by approximately fifteen years, by 1905 a great number of Russian companies' advertising budgets matched those of their Western peers.[17]

In prerevolutionary Russia, advertising agencies did not play a major role in crafting the messages of the advertisements in newspapers and on posters. Rather, businesses of varying sizes often contracted out different advertising needs to placement agents, artists, copywriters, printers, and distributors.[18] By contrast, U.S. advertising agencies played a significant role in creating advertisements for American companies prior to 1914. During the 1890s, ad agencies Lord & Thomas and N. W. Ayer & Son ushered in new business by employing copywriters and artists to design advertisements for customers.[19] In 1905, advertising giant J. Walter Thompson Company touted the skills of its in-house copywriters as essential to businesses prone to producing unattractive or unsophisticated ads, assuring potential clients, "This agency practically insures you against such mistakes. It has writers and designers, trained to the work of telling the merits of goods in the most effective way."[20] Thus, professional copywriters and artists were essential in helping U.S. businesses create engaging marketing content that was more thematically uniform than that of Russia during the late nineteenth and early twentieth centuries.

Advertisements in American and Russian Print Media and Ephemera

Print media effectively disseminated information about new consumer goods in the United States, which possessed an increasingly literate and interconnected populace. The American advertising boom was largely fueled by cost-efficient developments in lithography and transportation that resulted in the production and wide circulation of an abundance of journals and newspapers.[21] Publishers adopted business models that relied on advertising revenue to fund their operational expenses and sold advertising space directly to companies or through placement agencies. In turn, businesses strove to capitalize on the reading habits of a new generation during an age when, as one advertisement put it, there had never been "so many Magazines, Newspapers, and interesting books published, subscribed for, and read."[22]

Numerous businesses competed to place illustrated ads in publications to ensure that information about their products reached the widest possible audience. In the United States, J. Walter Thompson Company responded to growing manufacturer demand by helping firms purchase space in newspapers and journals.[23] In 1889, Thompson claimed to place 80 percent of all ads in the United States and continued to prosper during the last decade of the nineteenth century.[24] The agency succeeded in large part because it targeted varied demographic groups, touting its access to numerous magazines that reached "the homes of well-to-do people who ha[d] the means to purchase and intelligence to appreciate the desirability of an article brought to their notice."[25] Thompson urged clients to establish mutually beneficial relationships with publications, advising, "The illustrated weeklies, the humorous and society papers, the scientific periodicals and trade journals—all have their special clientele, which it is frequently wise to cultivate."[26] As advertisements in newspapers and journals became commonplace, businesses and agencies grew savvier in their marketing decisions. For example, Thompson explained to its potential clients in 1902: "Our intimate and profound acquaintance with newspapers and magazines here give an impressive advantage. . . . We can insure that automobiles shall not be extensively advertised to the working classes nor bargain jack-knives to the well-to-do."[27] These examples show that, with the help of advertising agencies like Thompson, companies could target particular consumer groups with increased precision.

Although literacy rates in Russia were significantly lower than those in the United States, newspapers and periodicals also served as important vehicles for Russian firms hoping to spread information about their products to rural and urban readers.[28] Imperial Russia's most popular publications included *Russkoe slovo* (Russian Word); the nation's largest newspaper, *Peterburgskii listok* (Petersburg Sheet); and *Russkie vedomosti* (Russian News).[29] During the late nineteenth century, the circulation of such printed materials increased dramatically as distribution channels grew and literacy rates increased.[30]

Another way in which Russian and American businesses reached consumers was through illustrated advertising posters. French artist Jules Chéret (1836–1932), the father of commercial art, popularized the poster medium in Paris by creating visually stunning works in the Art Nouveau style that attracted audiences with their strong colors and contrasting images.[31] *Reklamnye plakaty* (advertising posters) first appeared in Russian in 1868, but they were not widely used in Russia or America until the 1880s and 1890s.[32] In the United States, businesses began hiring artists directly to create large-scale works depicting scenes in which men, women, and children sampled their products.[33] As commercial works of art, posters entranced consumers because of their size and exquisite level of detail. Their unique format enabled businesses to develop their brands by crafting narratives about different products that appealed to specific consumer groups separated by class and gender. For instance, American advertisements for luxury goods such as perfume or soap typically featured elegant young women attired in expensive, fashionable clothing. Confectionary advertisements usually depicted well-dressed children indulging in sweets, while the earliest beer and tobacco posters showed working-class men engaging in daring athletic activities or business professionals conversing in upscale restaurants. Ultimately, for large businesses with big advertising budgets, posters presented new opportunities for promoting merchandise to diverse buyers.

Like American illustrated posters, Russian *plakaty* similarly mediated the experience of shopping through representation and constructed narratives that told a complex story through visual elements. For example, an 1899 Laferm advertisement portrays an urban scene in which wealthy men examine an announcement for the company's "Trezvon" cigarettes that had been painted on the cracked plaster covering a brick wall.[34] But an urban peasant clad in a bright red shirt and shiny leather boots, articles of clothing typically used to signify success, stands at the front of the group as he studies the text. Here, the peasant exercises his ability to read, a new skill that allows him to stand among the city's well-dressed businessmen as they collectively interpret the ad. This aspirational poster may have appealed to male peasant consumers who hoped to become integrated into the city's educated upper and middle classes. Thus, the format of the *plakat* also enabled Russian businesses to transmit messages to targeted consumer groups through a language of representation.

A final way in which American and Russian businesses promoted their products was through the creation and distribution of different types of ephemera such as fans, cigar boxes, pamphlets, paper dolls, stamps, calendars, and illustrated cards. Companies frequently incorporated visual imagery into the exterior packaging of products during the late nineteenth century. For instance, Russian confectionary firms adorned candy wrappers with colorful scenes of domestic life relating to the title of a particular series or brand of candy. An African American man and a white woman dance across the cardboard box containing M. Konradi's "Cake-Walk" sweets, while a Native American man rides bareback on a bar of flag-bearing "American Chocolate," examples of Russian ephemera that contain elements of American culture.[35] U.S. tobacco companies also enlivened their products with visual imagery; for example, the American company W. T. Blackwell used illustrated paper labels on its white pouches of dried tobacco and decorated its "Clear Havana" cigar boxes with colorful island scenes that ostensibly referenced the plant's provenance.[36] As tangible objects, illustrated or decorated pieces of ephemera were handled by a range of people, an act that may have legitimized the images and ideas they described or embodied.[37]

Less widely circulated in Russia, the illustrated trade card was one of the most common types of advertising ephemera in the United States.[38] During the mid- to late nineteenth century, American merchants and shopkeepers handed out slim, colorful, paper cards depicting or describing various products in their stores. Large manufacturers could design and print their own materials, while smaller companies often ordered their cards directly from businesses like Sunshine Publishing of Philadelphia, Donaldson Brothers of Five Points, and New York Pictorial Printing, which charged $3.50 per thousand single-sided cards.[39] Businesses eventually improved their marketing strategies by producing sets of between fifteen and ninety-five "collectible" cards that could be exchanged, shared, or displayed rather than tossed into the trash.[40] Tobacco companies employed this advertising tactic during the 1880s, when they repackaged cigarettes by swapping the traditional round bundle design for cardboard boxes, a change that conveniently allowed for the insertion of trade cards.[41] For instance, W. Duke, Sons & Company, a North Carolina–based tobacco giant, produced numerous sets of souvenir cards packed in cigarette boxes depicting U.S. states and their governors, different types of musical instruments, or illustrated cartoons that incorporated wordplay.[42] Overall, the diversity of late nineteenth- and early twentieth-century ephemera attests to the expanding possibilities for businesses striving to capture buyers' attention through the production of creative advertisements that shaped the culture of consumerism through their broad reach.

Street Scenes: Storefronts, Symbols, and State Allegiance

In Russia and the United States, urbanites from many backgrounds purchased their goods from street vendors or shopped in *rynki* (outdoor markets), *lavki* (traditional shops), or a host of new *magaziny* (stores).[43] Many of these businesses described different consumer products through both textual and pictorial signage that informed consumers about the products they stocked inside their shops.[44] Seeking to appeal to both domestic and foreign customers and perhaps to signal higher product quality, Russian businesses frequently printed information about their brand or products in multiple languages including Russian, English, German, and French. American stores also displayed product information in a range of languages to inform and attract immigrants from diverse backgrounds; for example, photographer Joseph Byron captured a Brooklyn street scene from 1899 where women and children lined up for a taste of Horton's Ice Cream in front of a pricing sign printed in Hebrew.[45]

In Russia, however, storefront windows did more than transmit information about the cost or content of merchandise. Historian Marjorie Hilton argues that, prior to the Revolution of 1905, merchants who identified with the Russian state signaled their political views to customers by "symbolically melding their business firms with the imagery and rituals of state power."[46] One way in which they did so was by creating storefront designs that evoked Russia's medieval past. For example, confectionery company George Borman signified its links to the state through a storefront renovation inspired by the patriotic Style Russe, an architectural style influenced by the Silver Age and promoted by the conservative Tsar Alexander III.[47] Drawing from Muscovite Russian architecture as well as nineteenth-century Art Nouveau, the Style

Russe was at once traditional and modern, influencing aspects of Russian culture such as graphic design and building construction.[48] A comparison of photographs taken between 1900 and approximately 1915 reveals that the shop significantly expanded and remodeled the building. While George Borman's 1900 storefront contained unremarkable square glass windows that mirrored those of surrounding shops, its new design included two semicircular glass panels that formed an entryway in the shape of a two-dimensional onion dome and a sumptuous facade with swirling Cyrillic lettering. Two additional storefront symbols alluded to Russian state power: an imperial double-headed eagle perched on the awning over the doorway and a bust of Peter the Great that watched passing shoppers from the window display.[49]

Russian companies also touted their connections to the state through their participation in urban trade fairs or large-scale exhibitions where they vied with one another to win prizes certifying the superiority of their products.[50] One of the most desirable awards, however, was the government's permission to print the imperial seal with its formidable double-headed eagle on products or advertising materials as a sign of the state's endorsement.[51] This noteworthy symbol loomed large in the mind of writer Sergei Gornyi, who recalled from his childhood days in fin de siècle St. Petersburg that "golden eagles were embossed on the [wrapping] of the chocolate of George Borman [in honor of] the exhibition in Nizhni Novgorod."[52] Grand spectacles like that of Novgorod and other cities captivated Russian consumers by enticing them with an enormous display of items. In a description of St. Petersburg's 1870 All-Russia Manufacturing Exhibition, a journalist praised the show's role in allowing inventors to quickly debut their newest creations to the public and for acquainting consumers "with the best and cheapest products" as a "kind of school of the people, which act[ed] through the education of even the masses."[53] Trade fairs and major exhibitions served as important spaces where consumers could learn about the latest goods, but more important, these state-endorsed competitive events promoted the spirit of entrepreneurship in Russia by encouraging manufacturers to compete for consumers' rubles by creating attractive products.

Visual evidence of merchant-state alliances, critical in an autocratic system where government capital played an outsize role in the flowering of industry, was less apparent on product packaging and city streets in the United States. While the nationalistic Style Russe grew increasingly popular in Russian cities, American builders and designers drew not from the country's colonial past, but from eclectic sources of inspiration such as ancient Greece and Egypt or medieval Europe to create urban storefront facades and buildings that revived foreign architectural traditions.[54] Lears argues that "this jumble of pseudohistorical styles" produced "a new and bewilderingly various visual environment" for late nineteenth-century urban residents.[55] He posits that, ironically, architectural disunity in America's sprawling cities contributed to Americans' heightened sense of national interconnectedness. In cities dominated by miscellaneous structures, supported by a complex market economy, and populated by immigrants from around the globe, Americans felt less autonomous and increasingly interdependent as they observed changes that challenged historic, classical, and liberal notions of "independent selfhood."[56] Ultimately, late nineteenth-century urban development contributed to changing conceptions of American identity not through singular emphasis of a particular national style, but through the amalgamation of a widening range of diverse peoples and ideas.

Analyzing Images of Serfs and Enslaved African Americans in Russian and American Advertisements

Both Russian and American businesses and ad agencies employed similar strategies to market goods to consumers. A close analysis of advertisements in newspapers, posters, and ephemera reveals that companies selected text and images that spoke to different consumer groups in distinct ways. To sell products to American and Russian consumers of all backgrounds, companies frequently used pictorial representations of serfs, peasants, enslaved African Americans, and freedpeople that were endowed with meaning through signifying functions such as clothing, shoes, facial features, hairstyles, body language, surrounding environment, and activities.[57] As Victoria E. Bonnell argues in her examination of Soviet political posters, such images constitute a "visual language (with a lexicon and syntax)" that viewers interpret through the act of seeing.[58] In both imperial Russia and the postwar United States, as in the Soviet period that Bonnell studies, such representations conveyed a great deal of information about social status, ethnicity, gender, and more.[59] Both Russian and American companies used visual depictions to assign to peasants and freedpeople varying positions in rural and urban social hierarchies. For example, Russian advertisements used different representations of rural peasants to either denigrate or elevate former serfs. While some images of rural peasants signaled their lack of sophistication and subordinate relationship to sophisticated city dwellers, others glorified their agrarian lifestyle and culture as symbolic of traditional Russia's beauty and strength. By comparison,

American advertisements targeting white, middle-class, female consumers repeatedly featured images of female African Americans wearing red kerchiefs or headscarves. These symbolic articles of clothing became associated with the notion of servile black women, representations that created and reinforced stereotypes. In order to efficiently transmit information to consumers about the intended use or quality of the promoted product, businesses used images whose symbolism became increasingly recognizable over time.

Landowner-Serf Relationships in Russian Advertisements

An examination of late nineteenth- and early twentieth-century Russian posters, ephemera, newspapers, and illustrated journals reveals that businesses depicted serfs and peasants as distinct archetypes: servant of the aristocracy, preserver of traditional Russian culture, benighted migrant, and shrewd urbanite. First, companies created nostalgic scenes referencing pre-emancipation Russia that depicted peasants in positions of servitude in relation to landowning noble families or overseers. Several advertisements marketing tea portray female peasants offering the beloved drink to wealthy aristocratic families. A colorful wrapper for F. Turbin's "Folk Tea" presents a picturesque scene in which a father, a mother, and their son sit around an enormous brass samovar atop a parlor table. The family's wealth is evidenced by the blue and yellow wallpaper, the embroidered tablecloth, their shining leather shoes, and their fashionable Western clothing. The father relaxes in his chair, holding a teacup in one hand and a newspaper in the other, watching as a peasant dressed in traditional folk attire offers tea to the family. She displays her subservient position through her demure gaze, focusing intently on her task and bowing her head respectfully.[60] In a comparable advertisement for Pavel Gorbunov's "Fruit Tea and Coffee," this time in poster form, a mother wearing Western clothing sits with her two children on the sunny porch of a country estate. A female peasant dressed in traditional folk costume, her head adorned with a sumptuous jeweled *kokoshnik* (headdress), looks upward toward her mistress while serving the family tea from a brass samovar.[61]

In advertisements such as these, the servant's status as a serf or a peasant is ambiguous, but the allusions to an idealized vision of serfdom are clear. The scene occurs on a rural estate, the servant women wear the attire of rural peasants that differentiates them from the aristocratic families adorned in luxurious Western clothing, and their body language reveals the unequal power dynamics.[62] It is improbable, however, that such advertisements solely targeted members of Russia's elite. Although tea was unaffordable for most of the Russian population at the turn of the nineteenth century, prices halved between 1885 and 1900, resulting in increased consumption across a broader range of socioeconomic groups.[63] Consequently, late nineteenth-century advertisements depicting nostalgic images of servitude sent aspirational messages to nonpeasant, middle-class consumers seeking to position themselves in the new social order. By purchasing and drinking fruit tea or folk tea, they could imagine themselves engaging in an exclusive and refined activity formerly restricted to the landowning nobility of the pre-emancipation era.

Another category of advertisements alludes to pre-emancipation landowner-serf relationships through the juxtaposition of tradition and modernity in depictions of peasants engaging in mechanical fieldwork under the watch of a *nachal'nik*, or "boss." Merchant Andrei Gustavovich Gendune's firm marketed its portable field engines and peat machines in a 1900 issue of *Russian News* through an illustration in which a group of peasants works alongside a Gendune machine.[64] Dressed in Western clothing and standing atop the enormous piece of equipment, an overseer presides over the scene, keeping an attentive eye on the peasants, who are operating the machinery. *Plakaty* and trade cards depict the rural peasantry in a similar fashion; for example, a colorful poster for Henry Lantz's portable engines shows female peasants in headscarves and male peasants in archetypical red *rubashki*, or blouses, feeding wheat into an enormous threshing machine. In the foreground, however, stands the *nachal'nik*, who sports a coat and bow tie and holds a small book. He alone looks directly at the viewer as if to affirm his authority and control.[65] Finally, a trade card for I. B. Pappe's tobacco firm presents a highly idealized and anachronistic scene of peasants harvesting tobacco. Clad in colorful costumes reminiscent of the medieval attire of Muscovite Rus', male and female peasants pick and bundle the plant's green leaves before hauling them onto a waiting train. These diminutive peasants are the least threatening of those portrayed in the three advertisements; they appear as child-like adults, docile and obedient.[66]

Drawn from different types of advertising media, a common theme of peasant servitude nonetheless emerges from these representations. In the first two examples, peasants appear as subordinate to an authoritative boss who manages their labor and oversees the operation of the sophisticated ma-

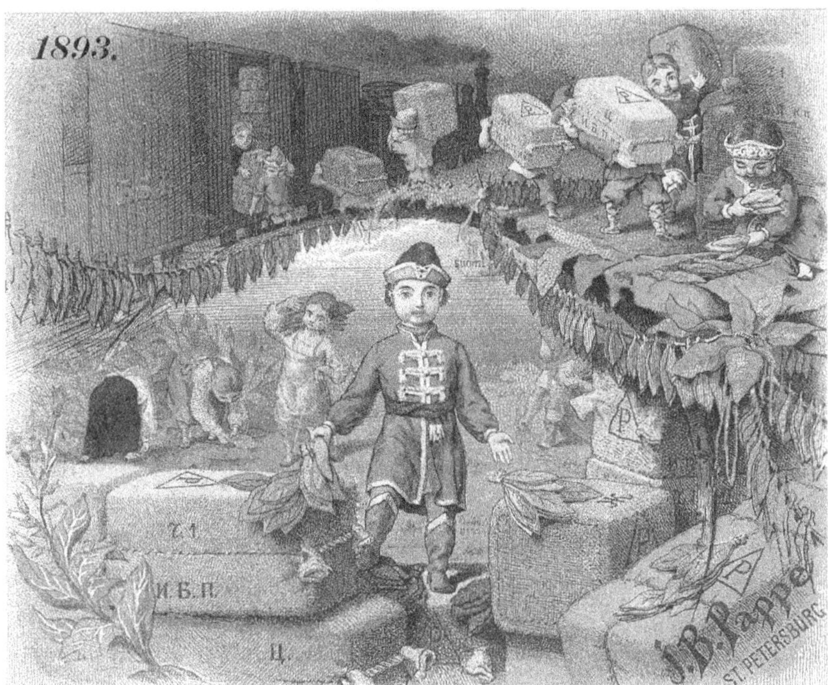

I. B. Pappe, untitled trade card, published November 20, 1893. Russian National Library
Ephemera Collection.

chinery. The Pappe trade card goes a step further by depicting the peasantry
as infantilized, costumed serfs who cheerfully complete their fieldwork without objection. In addition, all three advertisements blend elements of the old
and new in a reassuring combination: railroad tracks and trains appear alongside peasants harvesting tobacco in traditional dress or the smoke from a noisy
threshing machine billows into the blue sky above an idyllic wheat field.[67]
Such images may have appealed to a Russian population wary of change and
slow to use mechanized farm equipment that would improve laborers' productivity.[68] Seeking to capture market share in a difficult environment, manufacturers of agricultural machinery may have produced these advertisements
to target gentry landowners, who collectively possessed 79.9 percent of private land in 1877 and 52.7 percent in 1905.[69] Property owners with large holdings
likely had the capacity to make significant capital investments in expensive
equipment to increase agricultural output on their land. Thus, advertisements that marketed newfangled machinery using traditional imagery and
deferential peasant workers may have made the transition more palatable to
members of the nobility.

Peasants as a National Symbol

Images of peasants in advertisements also served a second, related purpose during the late nineteenth century, when many Russians struggled with the changes wrought by industrialization, geographic expansion, and the incorporation of new ethnic groups into their empire. Russia's military defeat in the Crimean War (1853–1856) prompted intellectuals to reconsider and redefine the nation's character and collective identity. Many intellectuals, including the politically oriented Populists of the 1870s, promoted the concept of a national metamorphosis achieved through the reinterpretation of the principles of the Slavophile movement by emphasizing "a fictive ethnicity," in the words of Étienne Balibar, or a romanticized vision of the Russian folk.[70] As Russia's expanding borders absorbed new ethnic groups, some intellectuals believed that the nation's Slavic citizens were the true descendants of Muscovite Rus' and deserved to stand as Russia's "politically and culturally dominant group."[71] Furthermore, as Cathy Frierson explains, the image of the "communal peasant" as a "moral actor for whom not the survival of the fittest but the survival of the community and its cultural heritage" particularly resonated during the era of Great Reforms when intellectuals debated "questions of Russia's development."[72]

Advertisements sought to address this collective anxiety about national identity and expansion through images of the peasantry positioned as primary symbols of Slavic identity and history. Consider a turn-of-the-century poster for E. I. Mel'goze's Kharkov-based agricultural machinery manufacturing firm, which one contemporary described as known for its "efficient, durable [equipment] . . . that perfectly meets the requirements of Russian peasants and landowners in possession of small-to-medium sized holdings."[73] The Mel'goze poster depicts a peasant in a conventional red *rubashka* driving a seeding machine across a spherical map of Russian territory. A crowd of men and women of different ethnographic backgrounds wearing their respective traditional costumes reach longingly upward toward the peasant, arms outstretched, from their positions in Central Asian and eastern European territory.[74] In banner form, a slogan splashed across the globe declares, "All require only a Mel'goze seeder." While the peasant's literal job is that of a farmer, his figurative role is to sow his seeds for future generations of Slavic people and their traditions to flourish across the empire. Indeed, the Slavic peasant's preeminent position in relation to other ethnic groups is unmistakable.

Other advertisements depicting the peasantry as a national symbol employed a nostalgic approach. For example, an 1888 poster for Shapshal "Conversation" cigarettes shows a peasant couple, an accordion-playing boy in a red *rubashka* and a girl in a yellow headscarf and *lapti* (bast shoes), strolling through a rural village.[75] Saccharine images of young peasants were particularly common in confectionary ephemera. Packaging for George Borman's candies and chocolates features sentimental portraits of peasant children building snowmen in villages, sledding, playing the accordion, or holding dolls.[76] Other products incorporated historical elements of peasant culture; for example, Borman's chocolate bar series "Russian Songs in Faces" shows at least ten distinct village scenes of peasant life that illustrated the lyrics of traditional Russian folk songs.[77]

Finally, advertisers depicted the peasantry as the protagonists of Russian myths and folktales. For instance, Borman's "Golden Fish" candies presented an image of a peasant casting his net in the story of the omnipotent fish who possessed the ability to grant any wish to the poor *muzhik* (peasant) and his greedy wife.[78] Meanwhile, confectionary firm M. Konradi's "Konek-Gorbunok" candy showed colorful scenes from the fairytale "The Little Humpbacked Horse," a story in which a cunning peasant surmounts numerous obstacles to win the hand of the tsar's daughter, while the "Krylov's Fables" series depicted peasants as the leading characters in tales like "The Hermit and the Bear" and "The Miser and the Chicken."[79] Sweet treats such as these were likely marketed to upper- or middle-class children and their parents, who possessed the means to purchase little indulgences. Together, advertisements that presented appealing illustrations of the peasantry through fables and folktales solidified their position as inheritors and preservers of traditional Russian culture.

Country Bumpkin to City Slicker:
The Education of the Peasant Migrant

Peasants who migrated to urban centers from the countryside exercised a newfound sense of autonomy and joined communities of people from across the Russian Empire. In cities, traditional relationships based on *sosloviia* (estates) changed in important ways. Although the 1897 census found that 84 percent of Russia's male population self-identified as members of the peasantry, a category that traditionally described agricultural laborers who resided on private or state-owned lands in semiautonomous village communities, this classification did not capture the experiences of urban peasants who worked in newly constructed factories, sold newspapers, or performed other kinds of urban services.[80] No longer constrained by historic landowner-serf relationships, urban peasants strolled along boulevards and window-shopped beside merchants, intellectuals, and members of the aristocracy.

Exercising their newfound purchasing power, male peasants frequently bought manufactured products to bring as gifts when they returned to rural villages to visit their parents, wives, and children. Stories from popular nineteenth-century periodicals offer a human portrait of this common occurrence. One fictional tale printed in the supplement to *Moskovskii listok* (Moscow Sheet), a publication that targeted working-class readers, recounts the adventures of a male peasant, Ivan Artemov, who migrated to a city in order to support his family members living in a nearby village.[81] For fourteen years, Ivan "had worked hard in the factory. During this time he built himself a new hut, dressed himself as a city dweller . . . and dressed up his [wife] Mar'ia."[82] Reflecting on his successes, Ivan proudly creates a mental inventory of the goods he acquired for the family's *izba* (hut). He recalls how, having obtained "two samovars, small and everyday, and big and celebratory, for guests, he set out chairs, and Mar'ia hung curtains on the windows and put flowers in broken jugs, and he whitened the stove with chalk."[83] Ivan's story reflected the experiences of urban peasants who sought to transform their homes and physical appearances through the purchase of newly accessible consumer products at the turn of the twentieth century. Thousands of rural peasants like the fictional character Ivan faced an unfamiliar world in cities like Moscow and St. Petersburg. They quickly learned, however, that it was important to follow new rules of decorum and dress. Stories like that of Ivan Artemov suggest that urban peasants learned to outfit themselves *po gorodskomu*, as city dwellers, by replacing their worn bast shoes and *valenki* (felt boots) with polished black leather boots and sporting smart short-brimmed caps.[84]

Manufacturers recognized the opportunity for capturing urban peasants' attention through advertisements intended to edify buyers who sought to learn how to dress *po gorodskomu*. For example, in 1904, the Russian-American Association of Rubber Manufacturing printed a poster that portrayed a stylish urban peasant speaking with a witless rural peasant wearing tattered clothing and dilapidated bast shoes.[85] The well-groomed urban peasant points to a pair of new rubber-soled footwear, teaching the country bumpkin about the shoes' merits. This advertisement likely resonated with recent migrants who were hoping to assimilate into city life and who dreaded a scenario in which their peers pointed out their ignorance about urban dress codes. Manufacturers also encouraged parents to buy appropriate products for their children in order to conform to metropolitan mores. In another 1904

Russian-American Association of Rubber Manufacturing poster that employed such a tactic, a well-to-do urban peasant woman wearing colorful necklaces and an embroidered blouse bends down to show her son the black rubber sole of a shoe.[86] Like parents instructing their children, manufacturers similarly coached and encouraged recent migrants to buy their goods. Through didactic posters like these, businesses tapped into consumers' latent apprehensions about the transition from rural to city life.

Manufacturers that produced aspirational advertisements sought to capture peasants' attention by highlighting the benefits of metropolitan consumer culture. *Papirosy*, or imperial-era cigarettes, were popular among city dwellers who wanted an inexpensive, efficient tobacco product suited to their fast-paced lives.[87] Tobacco advertisements often targeted peasants by depicting cigarettes as an affordable and essential part of urban life. For example, Laferm's "Trezvon" cigarettes produced a paper cutout figure depicting an archetypal urban peasant. Wearing sleek leather boots, a red shirt, a neatly trimmed beard, and a jaunty cap, the tidy peasant smokes as he gazes assuredly at the viewer. His socioeconomic position is evident not only in his dress and stature but also in his apparent ability to afford the eight boxes of cigarettes he carries in his arms.[88] The subtleties of Laferm's message about materialism and urban integration contrast sharply with the overt nature of A. N. Shaposhnikov's provocative-for-its-day poster "Tary-Bary," or "Chit-Chat," cigarettes. As they converse and smoke, two urban peasants clad in boots and red blouses look with great interest at a man dressed in flamboyant Western clothing. Holding a cane, wearing a top hat, and smoking a cigarette, the gentleman cuts a stylish figure. The poster's slogan, "Papirosy Tary-Bary zakurili dazhe bary," references the class division between the men; *bary* is a plural form of the word *barin*, which meant "nobleman" or "master" during the pre-emancipation era.[89] Therefore, this advertisement's urban peasants are pleased to discover that members of the nobility smoke Tary-Bary cigarettes, a brand that they, too, can afford to enjoy. In posters like these, manufacturers presented to peasants a vision of upward social mobility that appeared within their reach through material consumption.

Another aspirational poster, tobacco factory S. Gabai's "How Van'ka Arrived in Moscow and Came to 'Fame'" serves as an additional example of an ad that addressed peasant fears about urban assimilation and promoted personal transformation through the purchase of goods. Designed as a pictorial narrative akin to a comic strip, the poster features twelve individual scenes with text that recount the humorous story of the hapless migrant Van'ka.[90]

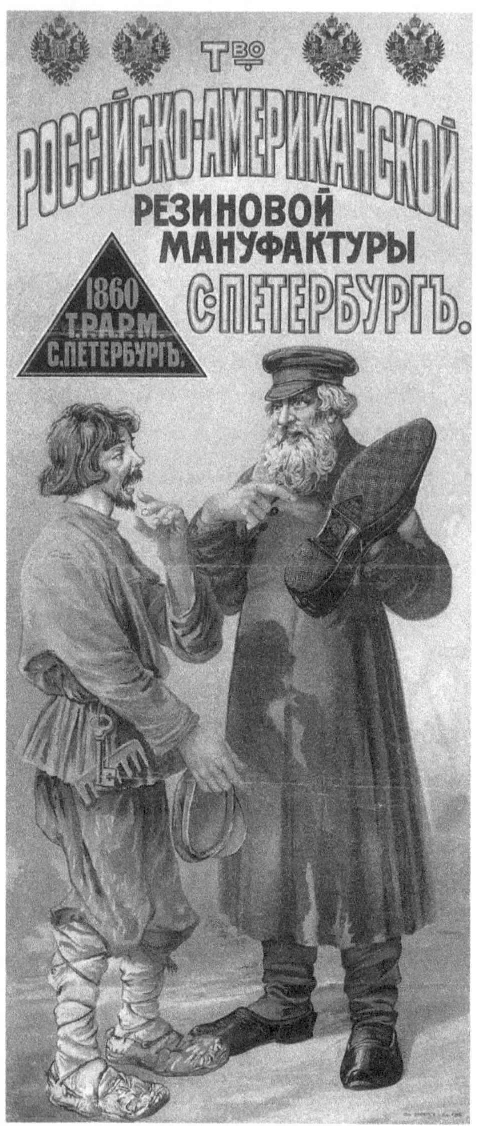

Russian-American Association of Rubber Manufacturing, St. Petersburg, 1904. Russian National Library Poster Collection.

This unique format permitted the artist to convey a considerable amount of information to the intended viewer, likely an urban mobile peasant, through the comic strip's elaborate storyline. Upon arriving at the outskirts of a city with his worldly possessions on his back, Van'ka, a scruffy peasant wearing worn bast shoes and a red shirt, stands aghast at the impressive sight of palaces and factories. After he reaches the city, however, Van'ka does not quite fit in; he is nearly run over by a horse-drawn carriage and finds himself uncomfortable among unfamiliar people, dreaming instead of his village. Suddenly shaken from his homesick reverie by the comforting voice of another recent migrant, Van'ka strikes up a new friendship, but finds himself in trouble once again after getting drunk with his coarse compatriot in a local tavern. Finally, a well-dressed urban peasant approaches the weeping Van'ka, whose remorse for his follies renders him open to advice about how to properly assimilate to urban life. Van'ka subsequently cleans himself up, acquires stylish urban clothing, and buys "Fame" cigarettes. In the closing image, Van'ka is surrounded by sophisticated urban peasants as he smokes and converses with the members of his new community.[91]

S. Gabai's poster shares many thematic elements with the advertisements produced by tobacco firms Laferm and A. N. Shaposhnikov. But this poster is highly unusual in its representation of Van'ka's transformation from rural villager to urban peasant. While other ads primarily depict this shift through the adoption of new types of clothing, S. Gabai's comic strip portrays Van'ka's metamorphosis in physical, bodily terms. Early images of Van'ka as a benighted villager appear as caricatures in which his nose and lips are exaggerated in form and size. After Van'ka's urban transformation through the purchase of snappy clothing and cigarettes, however, his visage is unrecognizable. Van'ka's formerly black hair becomes blond and his mouth and nose shrink significantly. This remarkable poster distinguishes between rural and urban peasants by portraying the former group as possessing intrinsic physical characteristics that recall the racist tropes employed by U.S. companies to disparage African Americans in advertisements. Such an example suggests that in Russia, as in the United States, advertisers constructed imaginary racial and ethnic physiognomies in order to convey ideas about bodily differences between sets of people.

One of the Crowd: The Urban Peasant's Assimilation

As businesses attempted to sell modern products like rubber-soled shoes and cigarettes to an emerging consumer group, they created advertisements that addressed urban peasants' anxieties about the new world. Most manufacturers marketed a metropolitan way of life characterized by modes of dress and behavior that they deemed essential to a migrant's successful assimilation. However, some businesses rejected the strategy of portraying urban peasants as outsiders; instead, they depicted them as fully integrated members of city society capable of selecting and purchasing certain products. Numerous newspaper advertisements and posters position peasants alongside wealthier

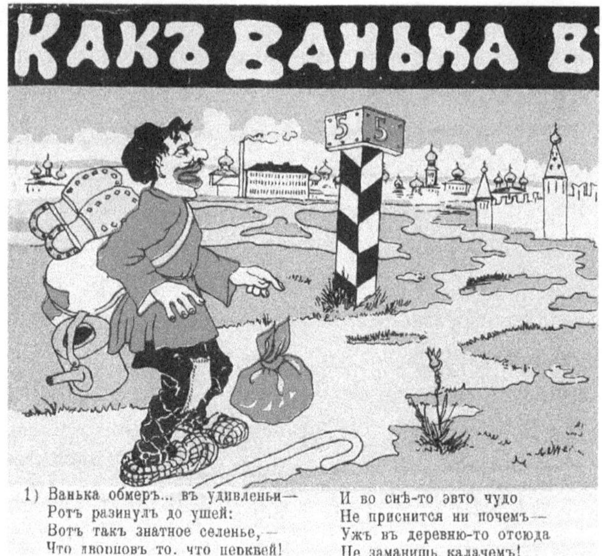

1) Ванька обмеръ... въ удивленьи—
Ротъ разинулъ до ушей:
Вотъ такъ знатное селенье,—
Что дворцовъ то. что церквей!

И во снѣ-то эвто чудо
Не приснится ни почемъ—
Ужъ въ деревню-то отсюда
Не заманишь калачемъ!

Van'ka approaches Moscow. S. Gabai, "How Van'ka Arrived in Moscow and Came to 'Fame'" (1900). © State Historical Museum, Moscow.

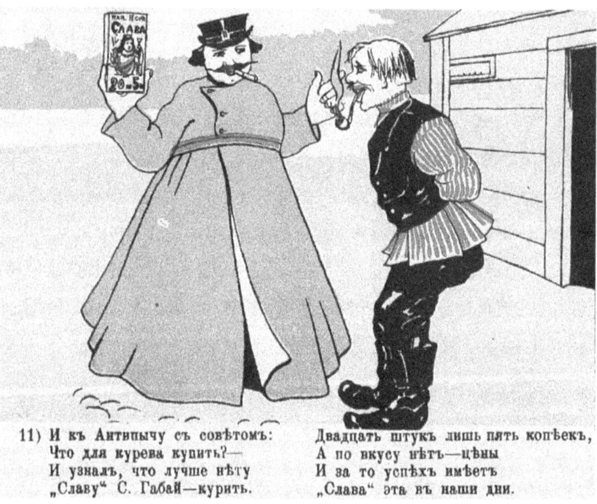

11) И къ Антпычу съ совѣтомъ:
Что для курева купить?—
И узналъ, что лучше нѣту
„Славу“ С. Габай—курить.

Двадцать штукъ лишь пять копѣекъ,
А по вкусу нѣтъ—цѣны
И за то успѣхъ имѣетъ
„Слава“ эта въ наши дни.

After Van'ka's transformation. S. Gabai, "How Van'ka Arrived in Moscow and Came to 'Fame'" (1900). © State Historical Museum, Moscow.

members of Russian society with whom they would not typically associate. These advertisements contain striking, radical representations of the peasantry, who appear as social equals to merchants, civil servants, and members of the nobility. For example, in one lighthearted newspaper advertisement for the Moscow-based company "Gramophone," several children hold hands, spinning in a circle as they dance to music. Four of the five children wear expensive Western clothing, but a fifth child sports black leather boots and a flowing blouse that recall the costume of an adult male urban peasant.[92] Although advertisements for products like gramophones targeted urban dwellers with the means to afford such luxuries, nonthreatening representations of young peasants as part of an assimilated group created a harmonious image that delicately referenced broader societal changes.

Most posters depicting integrated urban peasants were published after 1900, when the number of migrants had skyrocketed in cities. Recognizing a new demographic opportunity, manufacturers spoke directly to adult male urban peasants in advertisements promoting affordable products like beer and cigarettes. For instance, A. N. Bogdanov's tobacco factory, one of nine in St. Petersburg at the turn of the century, produced a poster for its "Kapriz" cigarettes in 1904 that featured a range of urban residents all smoking the same brand.[93] A soldier, a professional, a child in a sailor suit, and two urban peasants stand shoulder to shoulder as they collectively enjoy Bogdanov cigarettes. The advertising slogan explains the price and offers an egalitarian message: "'Harmless and cheap'—that's the motto. . . . They offer 'Caprice' [cigarettes] to the old and young and even children and even the ill."[94]

A poster for Saatchi and Mangubi's "Zoria" cigarettes employs a similar tactic through its depiction of a crowd of city dwellers rushing to buy cigarettes from a peddler. The urban denizens form a line; gentlemen in top hats stand at the front and the back, while a bearded urban peasant in a red blouse waits in the middle, extending his arm toward the peddler's golden cigarette box.[95] Beer and mead manufacturers like the Kalashnikov Brewery also created inclusive advertisements that sought to attract a wide range of consumers. Its poster for Kalashnikov beer presents four men drinking out of glass steins; two bearded men in traditional costumes represent urban peasants, while a third gentleman wearing a red bow tie and spectacles appears to be a member of the nobility. Its slogan, "Kalashnikov Brewery beer—caters to every taste," offered textual validation of the beer's supposedly universal appeal.[96] Together, these posters reveal that manufacturers of nondurable goods like beer and cigarettes sought to transcend traditional economic and estate boundaries in their marketing materials through depictions of the urban peasantry as socially integrated, knowledgeable consumers. Furthermore, it is notable that some of the most egalitarian images of the peasantry were produced not by sympathetic intellectuals or idealistic Populists, but by profit-driven businessmen who recognized the vast collective purchasing power of urban peasant workers and who strove to sell as many products as possible through the creation of advertisements that encouraged consumption across all estates.

Representations of African Americans in American Advertisements

While pictures of serfs and peasants flooded Russian posters, newspapers, and product packaging during the late nineteenth and early twentieth centuries, American advertisers from all parts of the country similarly incorporated images of enslaved African Americans and freedpeople in broadsides, trade cards, and ephemera that primarily targeted white consumers. As in Russia, businesses deployed archetypal representations of African Americans to convey messages to buyers about social hierarchies, gender roles, and conceptions of perceived racial traits. African Americans appeared in advertisements as wizened faithful servants, loyal mammies, impoverished sharecroppers, garishly dressed urban dwellers, or even unsuspecting victims of violent actions perpetrated by white people. Speaking about depictions of African Americans in early twentieth-century films, scholar Lawrence D. Reddick describes many of the stereotypical characteristics attributed to them in late nineteenth-century advertisements; these included "ignorance, superstition, fear, servility, laziness, clumsiness . . . [and] a predilection for eating fried chicken and sliced watermelon."[97] African Americans rarely appeared in positions of equality relative to whites or figured as symbols of national identity; rather, businesses in the United States disparaged formerly enslaved laborers to a degree and with a frequency that far exceeded that of Russian companies.

As in the nostalgic Plantation School literature of the late nineteenth and early twentieth centuries, sentimental visions of the antebellum South and the Civil War era pervaded contemporaneous advertisements. Realizing that white Americans' fascination with the "Old South" transcended regional boundaries, Northern, Southern, and Midwestern businesses alike employed imagery and language relating to the antebellum era in advertisements. Companies recognized that, in the words of historian Karen L. Cox, urbanites across the country "felt an antipathy toward modernity and longed for a return to America's pastoral and romantic past," viewing a mythical South as the perfect escape from city life.[98] Like Russian businesses, Southern companies were "keenly aware of consumers' anxiety about modernization, and they cleverly linked their products" to an imagined past in the hopes of enticing nervous customers.[99] For instance, the Southern Manufacturing Company's advertising card for "Good Luck Baking Powder" features the visage of a genteel white Southern woman and is titled "A Belle of the Old South," while J. H. McElwee's card for "Ante-Bellum Smoking Tobacco" pictures a white gentleman enjoying his "North Carolina sun-cured tobacco" from a long pipe.[100] The Boston-based company Potter & Wrightington even marketed "Old South Brand Baked Beans," which it claimed were "baked the old fashioned way not *stewed* or *boiled*."[101]

Businesses also carefully referenced the Civil War in advertisements that deferred to white Americans' growing desire for national reunification. During the late nineteenth century, scholar David Blight posits, many white Americans ignored the pressing racial problems of the post-emancipation era, focusing instead on reconciliation and consequently sacrificing "the civil and political liberties of African Americans . . . on the altar of reunion" in the process.[102] Indeed, several advertisements alluding to the war illustrate this trend. A card for Richmond-based Myers Brothers & Company's "Love Tobacco," produced in the late nineteenth century by a lithographer in Detroit, Michigan, and distributed in Bangor, Maine, depicts a Union soldier and a Confederate soldier pausing from battle to exchange precious goods. The Union soldier asks, "Haloo Johnny! Got any tobacco want to swap for coffee?" "All right, Yank!" he replies. "Pass over the coffee; I've got the best tobacco made in the world."[103] This idealized vision of wartime fellowship spoke more to the nation's postwar desire for reunification than to wartime realities. Furthermore, such a harmonious vision of compromise between whites submerged slavery's role as the central cause of the Civil War and disregarded important questions about integration for freedpeople. Other advertisements were more explicit in their preference for a specifically white process of reunion. For example, the company Spicers & Peckham, based in Providence, Rhode Island, promoted a stove in its card titled "The New 'Model Grand' Portable Range." In the illustration, Uncle Sam sits at a table across from the stove, waiting for an African American waiter to serve his dinner. Uncle Sam's message of reconciliation, achieved at the expense of freedpeople, is clear through his declaration to the servant: "Let us have *piece!*"[104]

Freedpeople as Faithful Servants

Although some businesses ignored African Americans in advertisements, many others deployed distinct representations of enslaved African Americans and freedpeople intended to attract white consumers. One of the most prevalent images was that of the submissive servant, typically an enslaved person or a freedperson, who maintained an unwavering loyalty to his former owners.[105] Some advertisements, like the trade card for Boston-based Chase & Sanborn's "Seal Brand" java and mocha, marketed as the "Aristocratic Coffee of America," merely indicated the presence of a mistress. The card depicts a

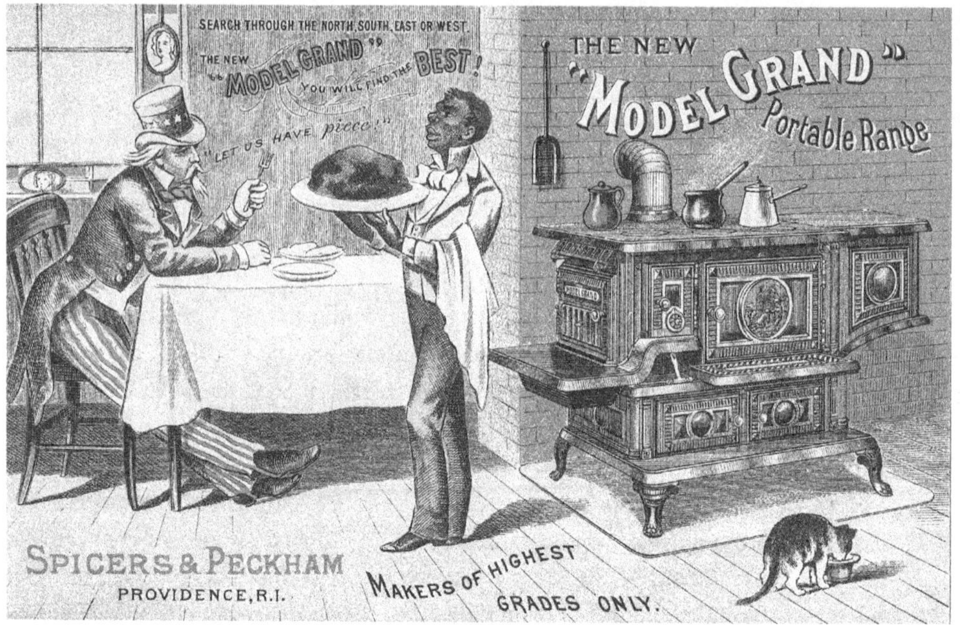

Spicers & Peckham, "The New 'Model Grand' Portable Range" (after 1876).
American Antiquarian Society.

toothless African American man who holds up a can of coffee, saying, "My
missus says dar's no good coffee in these yer parts. Specs she'll change 'er
mine when she drinks SEAL BRAND."[106] Chase & Sanborn likely used this image of a nonthreatening, loyal black servant to draw in white female customers who might have imagined themselves in a position of a well-to-do lady.
Other manufacturers created colorful pictures of African American men and
women serving white families. For instance, a trade card for H. E. Taylor's
furniture polish features a black servant rubbing a brass lamp, while her
white female employer polishes a handsome upright piano. The scene is one
of upper-middle-class domestic serenity; a fire glows brightly, a dog wanders
about, and a young girl watches while the adult women complete the
housework.[107]

By contrast, other advertisements overtly place African American servants
in positions of inferiority relative to white women who do not toil alongside
them. Enoch Morgan's Sons Company's pamphlet for "Sapolio" soap tells the
story of a "lady" who "much discomfort knew" because her "pots and pans,
and kettles too, / Were never bright and shining; / Her servants at the labor
hard / Were all the while repining." The pamphlet portrays an African Ameri-

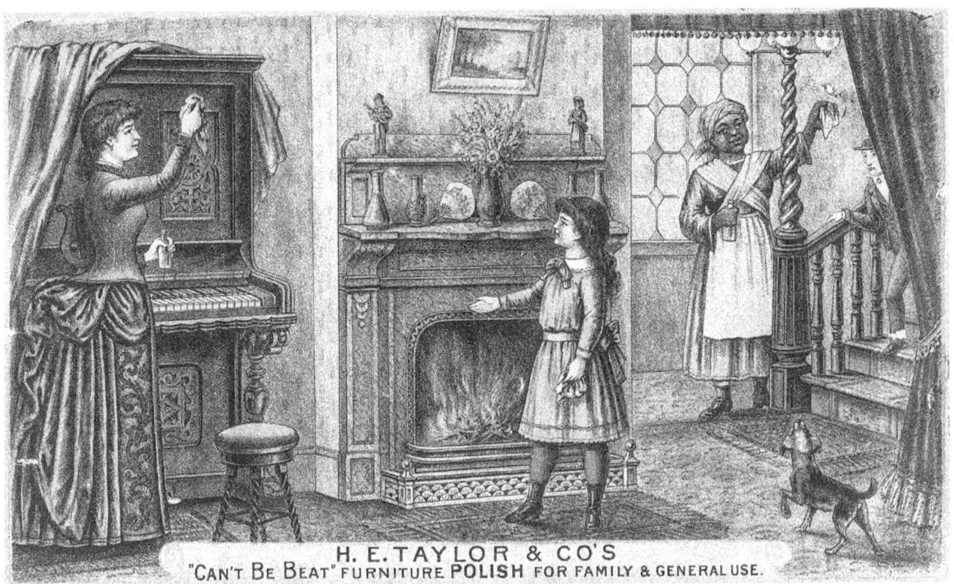

H. E. Taylor & Company, "'Can't Be Beat' Furniture Polish for Family and General Use" (after 1876). American Antiquarian Society.

can female servant kneeling before her white employer, unable to clean the kitchen accoutrements until the employer's introduction of Sapolio soap. The advertisement concludes by reinforcing the supposed superiority of whiteness, as the "tablet white as snow" ensures that "uncleanliness quick fades away" from the woman's kitchen.[108]

Businesses also exploited the exceedingly popular image of the mammy in their representations of African American servants. Late nineteenth- and early twentieth-century Americans viewed the mammy, an enslaved woman in the household who helped raise white children, as a maternal, loving, and loyal figure.[109] Children of planters, including author John Esten Cooke, recalled their mammies fondly in adulthood, but the notion of a mammy also suffused the collective mentality of the many white Southerners who recognized that having a mammy was a kind of status symbol.[110] Images of servile African Americans were an essential component of aspirational advertisements because, as historian Kenneth Goings asks, "what better way to ... provide the consumer with a sense of racial superiority than the stereotypical Old South / New South myth of the loyal, *happy* servant just waiting to do the master's—now the consumer's—bidding?"[111] Businesses that deployed images of mammies in late nineteenth-century advertisements tapped into middle-class consumers' yearning to belong to a kind of American nobility and their nostalgia for a romanticized antebellum South, a place that seemed evermore distant as the United States marched down the path of industrialization and urbanization. In addition, representations of mammies engaging in domestic labor for white families sought to reinforce the idea that black women possessed an inferior social and racial status. As scholar Satyasikha Chakraborty convincingly argues in her comparative study of visual depictions of racialized nursemaids, "Normalizing the labors of non-White women, objects like racialized postcards, perhaps, acted as tools of domestic and social control, legitimizing the nonextension of political rights and social equality to 'colored' and colonized people, particularly women."[112] Ultimately, portrayals of mammies faithfully serving white families sought to assure audiences that African American women were content as domestic helpers.

Trade cards and pamphlets featuring mammies caring for white children on behalf of their parents abounded at the turn of the twentieth century. The cover of Walter A. Taylor's riddle book promoting the use of "Dr. Biggers' Huckleberry Cordial" portrays a mammy wearing a red kerchief with a white child on her lap, while an interior image depicts the same woman holding the ill child while the white mother, dressed in fine clothing, offers a spoonful of medicine.[113] A similar representation on a trade card for "Excelsior Metal Polish" portrays a mammy, hair tied back under a crimson scarf, scrubbing pots in the kitchen alongside a white woman while children play underfoot.[114] Some businesses even incorporated anachronistic images of mammies into advertisements; for example, a 1908 magazine advertisement for Colorado's "Rock Island [Railroad] Lines" depicted a white family in a horse-drawn carriage accompanied by a mammy who looked after the children on their mountain adventure.[115] Finally, additional advertisements excluded white parents from their illustrations in order to highlight the fond relationship between mammies and their young charges. One notable example appears on a card for Dixon's Stove Polish, where a smiling mammy gently cleans the greasy polish off a white child. The young girl's affection for her mammy is evident in her gestures; she lovingly gazes at the African American woman while tenderly stroking her cheek with one hand.[116]

In sum, numerous American businesses created representations of African Americans as caretakers and faithful servants in advertisements intended to attract white customers. Their strategy mirrored that of Russian manufacturers, who similarly developed aspirational marketing materials using the image of the submissive peasant to evoke in customers nostalgia for a genteel, pre-emancipation age. By deploying illustrations of African Americans and peasants as loyal servants, both Russian and American businesses sought to convince consumers that they, too, could participate in a post-emancipation version of a past aristocratic tradition if they simply purchased the right products.

The African American Farmer Ridiculed

The passage of the Thirteenth, Fourteenth, and Fifteenth Amendments granted citizenship to freedpeople and gave African American men the right to vote, but Congress passed no national legislation that provided freedpeople with land in the form of private property on a widespread basis. During the decades that immediately followed the abolition of slavery, many freedpeople entered into a system of sharecropping in which black laborers farmed land owned by whites and paid rent in the form of seasonal surplus. By 1900, however, African Americans had made significant progress on the path to becoming independent farmers. Claude F. Oubre, in his study on black landownership, analyzes census data to evaluate change over time and discovers that while the percentage of African American farmers who owned their own farms varied by state, ownership rates increased on the whole across the South between 1865 and 1900, when 25.2 percent of all Southern black farmers owned the land upon which they labored.[117] In states like Virginia, where enslaved African Americans once supported numerous tobacco plantations, 59.2 percent of African American farmers owned the land upon which they worked in 1900.[118]

American manufacturers of sewing materials, farm equipment, and tobacco products responded to black progress by creating racist advertisements that mocked the efforts of African American farmers. An advertising card for J & P Coats Thread contains an unflattering illustration of rural farm life in which an African American couple struggles to train a donkey. The stubborn animal resists the wife's best efforts to control him, while her husband watches bemusedly, whip in hand, as he scratches his head. This scene of emasculation sent the paternalistic message to viewers that African American men and women were unable to manage farms without white guidance.[119] Indeed, a card for Durham Bull Fertilizer printed just six years later depicts a portly white overseer holding a wooden staff while he looks down on a black laborer working in his field.[120] Other advertisements presented infantilized representations of African American farmers; an undated trade card for Jacob G. Shirk's "Homestead" cigars features an African American with a boyish face smoking a cigar and pointing to a tobacco field where other diminutive figures pick leaves.[121] Such demeaning portrayals of African Americans gave white viewers the impression that these laborers were non-threatening. American advertising cards similarly spoke to white landowners through subtle references to authority and power.

Ambition and Entrepreneurship: Resisting African American Progress

After emancipation, African Americans sought to exercise their newfound liberties by running their own households without landowner interference, purchasing fine clothing, or founding businesses or community organizations like churches and schools. Some white Americans were discomfited by the formerly enslaved African Americans' independence and clung to the paternalistic idea that they required white support in order to survive. Manufacturers of products like stove polish, ovens, cleaning chemicals, food products, and cigarettes recognized white anxieties about black self-determination and created numerous advertisements that denigrated African Americans who sought to create autonomous lives for themselves.

For instance, businesses portrayed African Americans as incapable of understanding basic household tasks like cooking. An advertising card for the Massachusetts-based Weir Stove Company depicts a cartoonish man with exaggerated facial features holding up a kitten. It appears as though a nearby cat has delivered her litter of kittens inside of the man's oven, but he expresses his total confusion about the situation, asking the viewer in broken English, "Uf de ole cat hab kittens in de ubben doant it make um biskit."[122] Such disparaging images reinforced white perceptions of African Americans as helpless, naive, and unable to manage their households after emancipation. Additional advertisements mocked African Americans who purchased expensive clothing, characterizing those who did so as uncouth mimickers of white Americans. Before emancipation, some enslaved people who acquired new outfits deliberately showed off their finery, an action that whites interpreted as unsuitable for their station and even defiant.[123] White attitudes about black fashion persisted after emancipation and manufacturers played on these sentiments in advertisements. For instance, a series of cards marketing "Boraxine" toilet soap depicted black monkeys dressed in fine clothing as they courted, painted, danced, hunted, or fished.[124] Meanwhile, trade cards for companies like Clarence Brooks portrayed African Americans dressed in garish clothing and fanciful hats engaging in foolish behavior.[125]

Many advertisements were particularly critical of African Americans' attempts to form community organizations or start new businesses. An elaborate ad from 1886 for Dixon's Stove Polish titled "Brother Gardner Addresses the Lime Kiln Club on the Virtues of Dixon's Stove Polish" portrays a meeting of the "Lime Kiln Club," whose twelve African American members sport colorful, mismatched suits and whimsical accessories. The club's headquarters are modest, but members are nonetheless enthusiastic about discussing the mundane topic of stove polish. The back of the advertising card contains the text of club leader Brother Gardner's humble speech touting Dixon's polish as well as the signatures of all twelve members, which included "Bro. Shindig," "Give-a-dam Jones," "Accordingly Davis," and "Trustee Pullback."[126] Together these details presented a ridiculous portrait of black civic life in which African Americans convened to discuss unimportant ideas and bestowed on themselves nonsensical honorifics. Advertisements such as these not only spoke to white racism but also reflected Americans' latent fears about freedpeople's independence and their ability to organize and exercise power.

Manufacturers similarly produced illustrations lambasting African American entrepreneurs. For instance, Boston's Henry Mayo & Company created a card marketing its "Codfish Balls" that portrayed an African American man in a top hat and ill-fitting suit marching toward Liberia alongside his wife, who sports a sky-high hairstyle and house slippers. The advertisement's caption describes their ambitions: "We's gwine back to our old ancestral halls, to make our fortune sure on dees codfish balls."[127] The insulting advertisement, produced by a Northern company, ridiculed entrepreneurial African Americans by depicting them as incompetent, naive, and possessing unattainable desires. Like the illustration for Dixon's Stove Polish, Henry Mayo's trade card similarly reflected white resistance to black progress.

"I'd Get That Coon": Violence against African Americans

A final category of advertisements marketed to white Americans contained violent, disturbing images in which African Americans were physically threatened, beaten, or even killed. The prevalence of these vicious representations in American advertisements and their absence in Russian commercial materials speaks to the dehumanization of freedpeople that was specific to the American context. Some manufacturers paired friendly imagery and intimidating text to subtly communicate a menacing message. For example, an advertisement for Seneca Falls–based Rumsey & Company's pumps features a racist caricature of an African American couple preparing to carve a watermelon as they sit on a fence in the country. Text below the image, however, ominously alludes to the man's knife and to the broader tradition of violence against African American men: "We'll cut you deep," the caption reads.[128]

Other advertisements presented brutal scenes of violence against African Americans that masqueraded as humor. In an illustrated trade card for "Alden Fruit Vinegar," a cartoonish African American man stealing two chickens looks in horror at a white farmer, presumably the birds' owner, who points a gun in his direction.[129] Such an image may have affirmed late nineteenth-century perceptions of African Americans as criminals and offered a justification of white men's extralegal attempts to police communities. A comparable trade card for "Merrick's Thread" depicts a white dog lunging at a African American child stealing a chicken. Attached to his doghouse with thread, the hound is unable to reach his target and moans with disappointment, "If this was not Merrick's Thread I'd get that coon."[130] Rawson's Railroad and Steamship company produced an especially gruesome advertisement in 1882. Titled "(Going to Camp Meeting), Gone to Meet the Angels Peaceful Evermore," the illustration depicts a white engineer driving a train called the "Sunny South" across the countryside. The train suddenly rams into an African American family, their dogs, and their mule. Blood splatters against the front of the train as the disembodied figures fly through the air. A child is beheaded, while another child's leg is broken into pieces.[131]

Graphic images like these reflected the normalization of violence against African Americans during the late nineteenth century, when instances of lynching and other forms of white violence against African Americans reached their apex.[132] Such atrocities occurred in part as a response to post-emancipation black advancement. Despite the fact that African Americans faced racism, obstacles to political and economic gains, and threats of bodily harm in the 1880s and 1890s, freedpeople and their descendants continued to make progress by purchasing private land, accumulating capital, gaining education, and strengthening their communities. But the question remains: Why did not more businesses create advertisements that celebrated black achievement or social integration as Russian companies did by depicting former serfs as symbols of national heritage or assimilated members of urban society?

Even late nineteenth- and early twentieth-century advertisements in newspapers targeting African American readerships including the *Savannah Tribune,* the *Washington Bee,* and the *Kansas Baptist Herald* typically featured

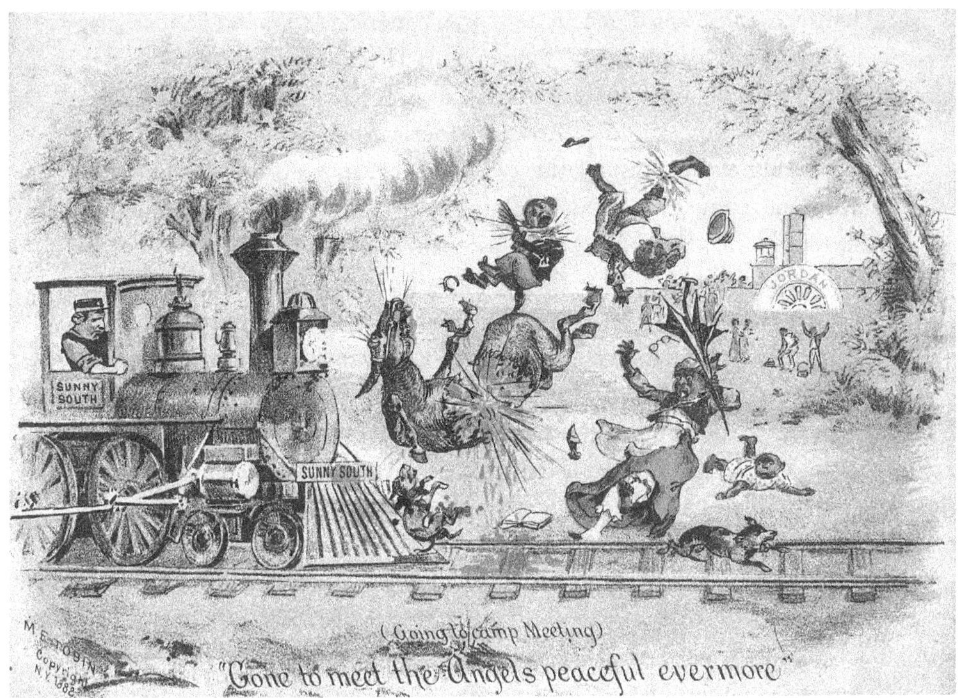

Rawson's Railroad and Steamship, "(Going to Camp Meeting), Gone to Meet the Angels Peaceful Evermore" (1882). American Antiquarian Society.

the visages of white Americans to market services like embalming or products like soap and sewing machines.[133] Indeed, socially integrated scenes depicting black and white Americans were rare. When African American figures did emerge in early twentieth-century advertisements, they appeared in ads for African American–owned companies, representations that contrasted with those produced by white-owned businesses. For instance, advertisements for insurance companies like the North Carolina Mutual and Provident Association or the hair-care products of successful black entrepreneurs such as Madame C. J. Walker and G. A. Morgan featured dignified images of African Americans in sophisticated clothing.[134] Targeting black customers, firms owned by African Americans created respectful representations that differed significantly from the caricatures of white-owned businesses that dominated the broader marketplace. Advertisements like these paved the way for the surge of commercial marketing materials targeting African Americans from the 1930s and onward following the National Negro Business League's publication of an influential analysis of African Americans' purchasing power, which encouraged entrepreneurial African Americans to found popular magazines and advertising agencies targeting black readers and consumers.[135]

Ultimately, dignified images of African Americans made up a small percentage of all illustrations of African Americans appearing in national advertisements at the turn of the twentieth century. As in Russia, where nonpeasants owned most Russian businesses, white Americans owned and managed the majority of U.S. businesses through the turn of the twentieth century. By contrast, however, these companies largely ignored African American consumers in part because they composed a minority of both the total and the urban populations.[136] Furthermore, an examination of U.S. census data between 1860 and 1920 shows that the share of African Americans as a percentage of the total population steadily declined by an average of 0.7 percent each decade.[137] U.S. businesses focused on creating advertisements that attracted the white consumers who composed a majority of the total national and urban populations during the late nineteenth and early twentieth centuries. Firms managed by white citizens essentially disregarded the black minority, choosing instead to deploy denigrating images of African Americans in advertisements to entice white consumers. By contrast, large-scale manufacturers selling products in Russia were likely incentivized by the peasants' national demographic majority to produce representations of former serfs in positions of equality relative to other social groups. Indeed, most Russian firms could not afford to offend the peasantry, a group of potential consumers with growing purchasing power who made up approximately 40 percent of urban residents in 1897.[138]

American and Russian businesses sought to attract a wide range of potential consumers through advertisements portraying serfs, peasants, enslaved African Americans, and freedpeople during the late nineteenth and early twentieth centuries. However, while Russian firms sometimes depicted peasants as symbols of traditional culture or assimilated members of society, American businesses portrayed African Americans as outsiders at the turn of the twentieth century. Nonetheless, these differences in representation point to a common strategy: both U.S. and Russian companies recognized that strong nationalistic and nostalgic undercurrents coursed through both populations. Many Russians and Americans desired to strengthen their respective countries through retrospective policies. But while Russians influenced by Slavophilism and Populism believed that the peasants' traditions and institutions were essential to national advancement, most white Americans continued to view the formerly enslaved through the lens of race. Rather than including freedpeople in their plans for reconstruction, they saw African

Americans as impediments to national reunion. Thus, Russian and American businesses' distinct portrayals of the peasants and freedpeople both reflected and shaped popular views about nation building and collective identity. But while U.S. advertisements depicting violence against African Americans foreshadowed the nation's continued social upheaval, depictions of assimilated peasants gave no indication of the bloody revolution that would bring about Russia's political, economic, and social transformation in 1917.

CHAPTER SIX

Literature and Visual Culture at the Turn of the Twentieth Century

[The mice] scent for themselves new abundance:
Soon the Master will die of decline,
The heir will abandon the Manor,
Where lived his illustrious line,

And the house will for ever be empty,
The overgrown steps out of sight . . .
And to think about this is so mournful
While it blows and it rains in the night.

—Alexei Tolstoi, 1840s, trans. M. Baring

In the poem "Outside It Is Blowing and Raining," Russian nobleman Alexei Tolstoi laments the deterioration of a *barskii dom* (manor house) during a nighttime storm in the 1840s. He conjures an image of a once prosperous estate that falls into ruin when it ceases to serve as a productive institution that relies on the enforced labor of the peasantry and the stewardship of the nobility. More broadly, however, Tolstoi's prescient lines foreshadowed the impending decline of the aristocracy after the abolition of serfdom. Between 1861 and 1905, a host of political and economic changes resulted in the Russian nobility's forfeiture of power and the peasantry's gradual attainment of increased geographic and social mobility. By the turn of the twentieth century, Russian landlords had lost control of nearly one-third of their collective property and estates across the country had fallen into disrepair.[1] At the same time, many former serfs purchased land or relocated to urban centers where they sought opportunities and encountered challenges. Similar dynamics transformed the post-emancipation United States during the late nineteenth century, when freedpeople made strides in acquiring acreage, while white landownership rates decreased.[2] Like the peasantry, African Americans concurrently relocated to metropolitan areas in search of jobs and increased autonomy, an emigrational shift that altered the demographic compositions of rural and urban areas. Consequently, these phenomena upended the social structures that had long defined Russian and American society, changes that produced new dynamics between different groups of people.

At this historical moment, an increasingly diverse set of Russians and Americans reflected on their changing worlds in literature and visual culture. As men and women considered the decline of the landowning class and the rise of formerly bonded laborers, they produced competing representations of serfs, enslaved African Americans, peasants, and freedpeople that alternately idealized and criticized the pre- and post-emancipation eras. While some authors and artists were white citizens or members of the nobility, others were descended from enserfed or enslaved individuals. They grew up as subjects and citizens with no firsthand knowledge of servitude, but they still carried the weight of their familial histories. Perhaps unsurprisingly, their representations often contrasted sharply with those of white or nonpeasant authors and artists who continued to sentimentalize serfdom and slavery in literature and art.

In early twentieth-century literature, elite American and Russian writers including Joel Chandler Harris, Thomas Nelson Page, Evgenii Opochinin, and A. Gorskii continued to create nostalgic representations of former serfs and enslaved African Americans. During a period characterized by industrialization, national soul-searching, and interracial or inter-estate violence, these men produced mass-oriented stories that depicted peasants and freedpeople as faithful servants who remained loyal to their former owners long after their emancipation. These tales, culturally hegemonic during the 1880s, continued to appeal to some readers but appeared stale and out of touch to others in an increasingly modern era. More often, forward-looking audiences found themselves captivated by fresh literary and artistic representations of the post-emancipation era that boldly acknowledged the rise of African Americans and the peasantry, and the decline of Russian noblemen and white Southern landowners.

In short stories, authors Anton Chekhov, Kate Chopin, Charles Waddell Chesnutt, and others addressed complex issues including racial identity, urban and rural poverty, violence, and interracial or inter-estate relationships. Their realistic portrayals of African Americans and peasants striving to uplift their families and exercise their free will during the post-emancipation era contrasted with images of nostalgic former serfs and enslaved African Americans in historical fiction and illustrated periodicals. Such nuanced depictions subtly encouraged white and nonpeasant audiences to adopt a more empathetic perspective toward the two historically marginalized groups. In the United States, African Americans faced the particular challenge of combating racist representations of freedpeople in literary works by the controversial author Thomas Dixon Jr. Photographs of America's growing black middle class in cartes de visite and in W. E. B. Du Bois's "American Negro" exhibit at the Paris Exposition of 1900 served as effective visual counterpoints to Dixon's portrayals of aggressive, violent freedmen that were designed to stoke racial tensions. Ultimately, however, new forms of cultural production could prevent neither the continued race riots that plagued American cities in the early twentieth century nor the 1905 and 1917 revolutions that led to the downfall of Russia's autocracy.

The Continued Idealization of Slavery and Serfdom

After acquiring worldwide fame for their sentimental stories during the late nineteenth century, Thomas Nelson Page, Evgenii Opochinin, and Joel Chandler Harris continued to produce early twentieth-century literature that propagated stereotypes about loyal freedpeople and former serfs who preferred slavery to freedom. In 1903, Harris published *Told by Uncle Remus: New Stories of the Old Plantation*, a collection of folktales that transmits black culture through the voice of a faithful freedman speaking to a young white child.[3] In *Told by Uncle Remus*, Harris attempts to engage a new generation of readers with the character of the kindly freedman, Uncle Remus, who imparts his wisdom and good humor to his former owner's family through stories about the anthropomorphic "Brer Rabbit," "Brer Fox," "Brer Gator," and others. In the book's introduction, he describes how Uncle Remus travels with his former owner's family to Atlanta, where he longs to return to the plantation from his days as an enslaved man. Uncle Remus's dream comes true when, Harris writes, the entire family moves back to the countryside, "much to the delight of the old negro," and Uncle Remus reprises his role as storyteller to his past owner's own young son.[4]

Over the course of the novel, Uncle Remus and "this latest little boy" develop a tender relationship in which he faithfully guides and cares for his young charge. The white child is fragile, sickly, and possesses inherently old-fashioned tendencies; indeed, he is a "source of perpetual wonder" to "the old negro" because of his "large, dreamy eyes, and the quaintest little ways that ever were seen."[5] The two characters seem to be living relics of a bygone age because they exhibit traits and tendencies from the antebellum era. On the plantation, where the child's health begins to improve, Uncle Remus uses didactic stories to teach the boy about discipline and self-control. Under Remus's supervision, he grows up to be independent and strong-willed, a development that subtly attests to the purported salubriousness of the rural plantation environment and the old-fashioned care he receives from the formerly enslaved man.

Reviewers from numerous journals praised Harris's latest collection of folktales but repeatedly commented on Uncle Remus's job of sharing stories from the pre-emancipation era with a twentieth-century reader. For instance, the Atlanta-based *Southern Cultivator*, a journal whose audience largely comprised members of the planter class, described Uncle Remus as a "genial old darling" who sought to convey his "quaint and humorous philosophy" to a "youngster of the modern school."[6] Critics writing on behalf of the *Congregationalist and Christian World* and the *Dial* also remarked on the significance of Remus's task; the first observed that Remus's "process of getting acquainted with a shy and repressed modern youngster colors the stories and brings out Uncle Remus's tact and humor in a fresh way," while the second wrote that Harris's explanation of why Uncle Remus began telling his stories once again was "ingenious and convincing[,] as if an excuse for such a proceeding was really needed."[7] Thus, although reviewers viewed the newest iteration of *Uncle Remus* favorably, their commentary about Remus's goal of engaging young, modern readers suggests Harris's stories may have begun to appear outdated to twentieth-century audiences.

Thomas Nelson Page similarly depicted freedpeople as yearning to return to the pre-emancipation era in his collection of short stories titled *Bred in the Bone* (1904). "Bred in the Bone," the tale after which the book is named, recounts the postwar relationship between an elderly freedman and the white grandson of his former owner. The freedman, the stable boss of the local jockey, is known to all as "Colonel Theodore Johnston's Robin, of Bullfield, suh," a relational title that identifies him as the former property of a white slaveholder. Robin recalls with great fondness his life prior to emancipation, an era that Page describes as perpetually dwelling in his mind "with tender memory."[8] He frequently speaks with colleagues about his days as an enslaved man, asserting that no contemporary horse race could match those of the past and vehemently disputing the claims of the stable boy, who insists that "freedom's better 'n befo' de wah."[9]

As in his previous short stories about freedpeople, Page characterizes Robin as intensely loyal to his former owner's family. During a scene in which Robin is reunited with his past owner's adult grandson, Theodoric Johnston, Page describes how the elderly man greets him as his "young master," a designation that reflects his self-perception as the Johnston family's lifelong servant. Theodoric's appearance also brings back Robin's memories of the pre-emancipation era. After gazing at Colonel Johnston's grandson, Robin remembers his former owner, a gentleman who stood as "the leader of men; whose graciousness and princely hospitality were in all mouths; whose word was law; whose name no one mentioned but with respect."[10] Here, Page's favorable description of Colonel Johnston serves two purposes. First, it helps assure readers that slave owners were venerable people, and, second, it reveals the depths of Robin's admiration of and devotion to his former owner. Indeed, Robin is so dedicated to the Johnston family that he sells his most prized possession, a gold watch, to ensure that Theodoric can participate in an important horse race. By the end of the story, the freedman and his former owner's grandson have become "great friends" and formed a relationship that will flourish in the years ahead.[11]

A second story within Page's collection, "Old Jabe's Marital Experiments," depicts another freedman so attached to his former owner's family that he refuses to depart from the plantation of his youth. The paternalistic story begins with a brief history of the formerly enslaved man's origins; Jabe "belonged to the Meriweathers, a fact which he never forgot or allowed anyone else to forget."[12] The reader immediately learns that Jabe may not have been the hardest worker, but he argued that his worth rested in his faithful service because he "had been on the plantation before any overseer had put his foot there, and he would outstay the last one of them all, which proved to be true."[13] After emancipation, many of his formerly enslaved peers departed to make new lives for themselves, but Jabe purchased land on the plantation so that he could remain close to his former owners. In Page's perspective, Jabe "had all the privileges of a freedman, but lost none of a slave. He was free, but his owner condition remained unchanged: he still had to support him, when [Jabe] chose to call on him, and [Jabe] chose to call often."[14] Thus, like Robin and Uncle Remus, Jabe remains perfectly loyal to his former owner's family and even chooses to perform the duties of an enslaved laborer to receive what Page deems to be its advantages: food, material support, and white companionship.

Reviews of *Bred in the Bone* were ambivalent, and critics concurred that Page's best days were behind him. The *New York Times* argued that while Page exhibited "the same evidence here of intimate knowledge of the proud old Southern gentry and an understanding of the negro character," there seemed to have been "something vital missing from 'Bred in the Bone,' and its loss has a perceptible effect on one's interest."[15] Reflecting on the issuance of a new collection of Page's works that included the short story "Bred in the Bone," a reviewer for the *Independent* expressed an opinion that mirrored that of the

New York Times. He admitted that although not much time had elapsed since Page "first began his dialect stories, the most prominent of which are 'Meh Lady' and 'Marse Chan,'" he doubted "whether any of [Page's] later tales equal[ed] those in freshness of narration or quaintness of idea."[16] He argued that Page's stories in *In Ole Virginia*, one of the most popular assemblages of fiction during the late nineteenth century, would always be "far ahead of any story in such a collection as *Bred in the Bone*."[17] Even the *Congregationalist and Christian World*, which favorably reviewed Harris's *Told by Uncle Remus*, lamented that the stories contained in *Bred in the Bone* did not "represent the high-water mark of his accomplishment" despite their "qualities of humor and delightful local color."[18]

Together, these reviews suggest that early twentieth-century critics found Page's short stories about the South and its African American population less appealing than others did during the 1880s, when the author was hailed as an innovative chronicler of antebellum Southern mores and social relations. While Page's earlier tales inspired nostalgia in readers, stories of the same genre seemed antiquated during the early twentieth century. Although Page's and Harris's representations of loyal, formerly enslaved African Americans appealed to millions of readers two decades after the Civil War ended, they conflicted with the modern realities of American life that included African American advancement in the fields of education, business, and the arts. A return to the pre-emancipation era seemed increasingly unlikely, and Page's retrospective fiction largely failed to acknowledge these contemporary social changes.

As in the United States, some Russian authors of historical fiction continued to promote idealistic visions of the pre-emancipation era through literary depictions of faithful former serfs at the turn of the early twentieth century. For instance, the aristocratic novelist Evgenii Opochinin published his story "The Last Soul," an account of an emancipated peasant who takes care of his impoverished owner, in the supplement to the popular journal *Moskovskii listok* (Moscow Sheet) in 1905.[19] Another story published in *Moskovskii listok* by a lesser-known writer, A. Gorskii, portrays a nostalgic former serf whose life has been bleak and miserable since his liberation from bondage.[20] In "Blizzard: A New Year's Story," Gorskii begins by introducing the reader to Dem'ian, a former serf who looks out across the landscape through the snow-covered window of his hut. The elderly peasant "had not always lived in such a tiny, half-sunken hovel," and he reflected on bygone days when "all of his fellow villagers, from small to great, with sighs of relief spoke about the great event of the liberation of serfs from bondage."[21] But Dem'ian remembered and honored the past differently. Every year, he visited his local church on All Saints' Day, the eighth of November, a holiday marked by the commemoration of beloved deceased friends and family by Russian Orthodox Christians. There, he would take "communion for the soul of his former landowner, and to this day, if he had extra change, he would offer it to the church in commemoration of [Romanov dynasty founder] boyar Mikhail and his kin."[22] In this scene, Dem'ian appears as a traditional peasant who remains devoted to his former owner and who espouses Russia's patriarchal hierarchy comprising the paternal figures of God, the tsar, and one's father or landowner. He believes that his "deceased *barin* [landlord] was kind to him and trusted in his faithful Dem'ian," and the former serf "sincerely and deeply" mourned his passing.[23]

After his former owner's death and the collapse of the estate under the "new order" of the post-emancipation era, Dem'ian's life took a turn for the worse.[24] First, his son was conscripted into the military and subsequently died in a hospital. Next, his daughter, for whom "he could not find in the entire township a decent groom," married, "without her parents' consent," "a puny urban philistine who called himself a merchant," and their wedding "was a harbinger of new storms and grief for Dem'ian and his wife."[25] Gorskii's description of Dem'ian's hardships during the late nineteenth century and his continued loyalty to his former owner present the abolition of serfdom as an event that diminishes the quality of the emancipated peasant's life. Dem'ian seems to yearn for a simpler age and misses the paternalistic figure of his former owner, a literary portrayal that sentimentalizes the relationship between the nobility and their human property. Although Gorskii's mild idealization of serfdom mirrors that of predecessors Vsevolod Solov'ev, Evgenii Salias, and Grigorii Danilevskii, his emphasis on the unique hardships that the former serf Dem'ian faces after emancipation signaled a transition to a new type of representation that permeated Russian and American literature in the late nineteenth and early twentieth centuries.

Post-Emancipation Social Change in Russia

A diverse cadre of writers and artists hailing from different estates, classes, and ethnic backgrounds addressed the complex topic of post-emancipation social absorption in thoughtful short stories that substituted realism for sentimentalism. Their African American and peasant characters no longer yearned for the pre-emancipation era; rather, they strove to achieve economic mobility and join urban societies during the late nineteenth and early twentieth centuries. Some achieved these goals, while others could not overcome the obstacles of poverty and social prejudice. Ultimately, the authors and artists of these new works presented the struggles of African Americans and peasants with an unflinching candor that raised awareness of the difficulties faced by two historically oppressed groups of people.

Playwright Anton Chekhov's short story "Muzhiki" (The Peasants) was one of the first works of fiction to depict the impoverished peasantry using literary realism.[26] As discussed in chapter 5, industrialization transformed the Russian nation during the late nineteenth and early twentieth centuries, when migration from rural villages to metropolitan centers dramatically increased. Peasant laborers, typically men, sought work in factories and shops and often sent money home to support the families they left behind. Despite their efforts, both urban and rural peasants alike continued to fight poverty, a phenomenon documented by *zemstvo* commissions, government-sponsored censuses, and individual observers interested in social reform.[27] In fiction, however, Chekhov captured the spirit of the peasantry's dire situation and made it palpable to readers in a way that data could not.

The son of a serf, Anton Chekhov (1860–1904) indirectly understood the experience of servitude through his family's history.[28] He received educational opportunities that were unavailable to his parents prior to the abolition of serfdom, completing coursework at a *gimnaziia* (high school) and studying at the Moscow University Medical School.[29] Although Chekhov originally intended to practice medicine, he began writing short stories as a student and, as the author of his obituary in *Niva* put it, ultimately "became a doctor of men's souls, not so much as a pathologist, but as a skilled and very profound diagnostician . . . [a profession to which] he devoted himself completely."[30] He was a creator of short stories and plays that were published in journals including *Severnyi vestnik* (Northern Messenger), *Russkie vedomosti* (Russian News), *Novoe vremia* (New Time) *Budil'nik* (Alarm Clock), and *Strekoza* (The Dragonfly).[31] Chekhov revealed to readers his understanding of human nature and psychology through literary works written in the style of realism. He drew inspiration from his diverse experiences exploring his native country and its people; Chekhov visited a penal colony in Siberia, aided villagers during the famine of 1891–1892, and helped conduct the first Russian census of 1897 by gathering information from impoverished peasant families living in Moscow.[32] Through his encounters with Russians from a range of backgrounds, he gained an awareness of the conditions in which differing groups of people lived and the social dynamics that shaped post-emancipation Russian society.

Chekhov's "Muzhiki" recounts the story of the Chikil'deev family, a group of peasants living in abject poverty in the village of Zhukovo. The story begins with the arrival of Nikolai Chikil'deev, a male peasant who returns to his home in Zhukovo from Moscow, where he worked as a waiter. Here, Chekhov refers to a common late nineteenth-century practice: male heads of household often worked in factories or shops for a portion of the year and returned to the countryside during the other portion, engaging in a sort of cyclical work that mimicked that of the traditional agricultural season.[33] Nikolai had long supported his family through his work at Moscow's Slavianskii Bazar (Slavic Bazaar) restaurant, but he took ill and was forced to return to Zhukovo with his wife and daughter. The present condition of his family's abode contrasted sharply with the cozy *izba* (hut) of his memories; upon arriving there Nikolai is shocked to find that it is "dark, cramped, and filthy," the stove is "covered with soot and flies," and the structure verges on collapse.[34] The Chikil'deevs' house is but one of several homes in the village set apart from the neighboring five-domed church and manor house. Reflecting on their new situation, Nikolai and his family feel "perplexed" and unable to fully comprehend "the poverty, the poverty!"[35] Although the countryside is beautiful, the idyllic scenery cannot mitigate the misery of the Chikil'deev family's circumstances.

Nikolai quickly realizes that his parents, brother, and sisters-in-law suffer from physical and spiritual impoverishment. His parents are starving, his brother Kir'iak drinks himself into an abusive rage, and his sisters-in-law are "extremely ignorant and could not understand anything at all."[36] Their financial situation, like that of the other peasants in the village, is dire thanks to the burdensome taxes they are unable to pay each year. In one poignant scene, the village elder removes the family's samovar from their hut after they fail to provide the bailiff with the requisite amount of money, an event that Chekhov describes as "something degrading, injurious . . . as if the *izba* had been stripped of her honor."[37] Natural phenomena further exacerbate the village's poverty; for instance, a domestic fire devastates a neighboring family's home and increases the Chikil'deev family's sense of helplessness.[38]

As they assess their calamitous situation, they recall the days of serfdom in a passage that offers a more balanced account of the institution than that of Chekhov's literary predecessors. Conversing about their past, Osip, an elder member of the Chikil'deev family, asserts that food had been plentiful and that there was a comforting rhythm to life. He remembers that one only had to "work, and eat, and sleep" and that justice was meted out accordingly when "the evil were punished with rods or banished to the Tver' estate, while the good serfs were rewarded."[39] But the matriarchal grandmother recalls that their owner was "a carouser and a libertine" whose daughters "married a drunkard . . . and . . . a petty urban bourgeois."[40] Here, Chekhov's peasants discuss what they perceive to be the benefits and flaws of the pre-emancipation era, viewing the past critically and with less of the sentimentalism that permeated the stories of authors like Salias and Opochinin. Despite all the hardships of the post-emancipation era, they conclude that a life in which they can exercise free will is superior to a life of enserfment.[41]

By the end of the short story, however, the reader realizes that although the peasants believe themselves to be liberated, their choices are in fact constrained by their poverty. Burdened by crushing taxes and subsisting in a desolate village far removed from modern Moscow, they cannot escape from their circumstances. Unlike the period immediately following the abolition of serfdom, when everyone "spoke about partitioning, new lands, of treasures," now "their lives were as clear as daylight, in full view, and they could only speak about need and food."[42] They await death expectantly, even hopefully, as an event that will finally alleviate the sufferings of their miserable lives. Through these passages, Chekhov conveys the gravity of the peasants' condition using realistic descriptions rather than the lachrymose prose employed by authors like Harriet Beecher Stowe, whose novel depicting the plight of enslaved African Americans, *Uncle Tom's Cabin* (1852), produced in Chekhov "an unpleasant sensation which mortals feel after eating too many raisins or currants."[43] Using stark, spare language, Chekhov produces a bleak picture of rural life at the turn of the twentieth century that effectively evoked sympathy in readers, who may have found themselves as surprised as Nikolai to learn about the deterioration of rural peasant life.

"Muzhiki" made a powerful impression on Russian audiences, stirring up controversy even before its publication. For instance, Chekhov recorded in a letter to writer Mikhail Men'shikov that censors had "snatched a sizable piece out of 'Muzhiki,'" a section that amounted to twenty-seven lines, and even threatened his arrest if he failed to comply with their exacting demands.[44] Despite the Censorship Committee's efforts to remove troubling material from the short story, however, readers were still taken aback by the realistic tale. Some critics argued that the story was imbued with pessimism and that Chekhov had deliberately created a disturbing "portrait of human zoology, or even rural brutality" that depicted the transformation of "man into animal."[45] Others marveled at Chekhov's ability to write fiction that effectively re-created life; for example, the publicist Petr Struve, writing under the pseudonym "Novus," observed in *Novoe slovo* (New Word) that Chekhov's descriptions "produced a powerful impression of their remarkable veracity."[46]

But the truth of the rural peasantry's condition was unsettling, and readers were discomfited by what Novus called Chekhov's representation of a people living in an "endless struggle against want, not illuminated by any glimmer of consciousness or hope for a better future."[47] "Muzhiki" drew attention to the former serfs' troubles during an era of transformation that benefited those in urban areas but left behind many of Russia's rural people. Ultimately, Chekhov's prescient short story captured the sense of malaise and hopelessness that permeated the peasant population at the turn of the twentieth century, sentiments that produced in them a deep-rooted longing for radical change manifested during the Revolutions of 1905 and 1917.

After the publication of "Muzhiki," several lesser-known authors expanded on Chekhov's endeavor by producing short stories in *Moskovskii listok* that addressed the experiences of peasants seeking to adapt to metropolitan life. Their pessimistic tales provided similar representations of peasants as individuals who were ambivalent about urban living but dreaded returning to the villages of their pasts. One poignant tale, "Soshnikov," written by an author only known as "P.B.," recounts the tragic history of an emancipated serf through the perspective of a literate, educated narrator.[48] A talented violinist in his seventieth decade, Soshnikov impresses the narrator when he plays for customers in a tavern located near Moscow. Broad in stature, the performer wears a shirt of "rustic homespun peasant cloth" in the traditional rural style of the nineteenth century.[49] His music attracts customers' attention because of its soulful nature, a characteristic born from Soshnikov's painful experiences as a serf.

Through the narrator's questioning, Soshnikov reveals to the reader his unfortunate past and inability to find happiness in the present. He recounts how he received musical training from his former owner, a rural nobleman who drove his orchestra of serfs to St. Petersburg and Moscow, where they performed for "astonished" audiences.[50] Eventually he fell in love with a female serf named Tanya, but his jealous owner succeeded in keeping them apart. Soshnikov received his freedom, but Tanya was sent abroad, where she unexpectedly died. As a result, Soshnikov became depressed and lost his will to succeed in life; he was demoted from his position as a soloist in Moscow's orchestra to "the ranks, from which [he was] soon kicked out," and found himself scrounging for a living playing in local taverns.[51] Haunted by his past, Soshnikov plays sorrowfully for the narrator, who describes the sound emanating from his violin as "snow during a blizzard, hovering, swirling, writhing, moaning, like old spruces bending from the pressure of the wind."[52] This metaphor effectively captures the experiences of the emancipated serf whose life has been determined in part by powerful external forces. The story concludes on a pessimistic note, with the author remarking that Soshnikov "fell ill and died in the hospital, forgotten by all."[53] Like Chekhov's *muzhiki*, Soshnikov cannot lift himself from his lowly circumstances and is destined to suffer a tragic, lonely end as an impoverished peasant.

Two additional short stories published in *Moskovskii listok* at the turn of the twentieth century tackle the topics of urban peasant assimilation and economic mobility in representations of peasant factory workers. The first, "Razdum'e" (Thoughts), written by M. Bylov, tells the tale of Ivan Artemov, a male peasant who migrated from his village to an urban area where he found employment in manufacturing.[54] Like Chekhov's Nikolai Chikil'deev, however, Ivan suddenly finds himself out of work and "home in his native village," which appears more dismal than the town of his childhood memories.[55] During the fourteen years he spent working in the factory he transformed himself into an urban peasant by dressing as a city dweller, and he brought material goods to his family in the countryside to improve their lives as well.[56] At first, Ivan enjoyed urban life; he recalls how "the factory exhilarated him," and he spent time among his "circle of noisy friends."[57]

At the age of forty, however, Ivan grew tired and weak with age; his "right shoulder sort of fell apart, aching in the weather, then in the morning [he developed] some kind of cough . . . and he himself became . . . angry at the hoots and noises" of factory life.[58] Upon returning to rural Russia, however, Ivan becomes despondent and discovers that he is deeply conflicted about the choices that will determine the course of his life. The story concludes with Ivan's final, depressing realization, posed as a question to readers: "The past—repugnant, but the future—terrifying! How would it be possible to continue living?"[59] On the whole, "Thoughts" is a remarkable work of fiction because it serves as a psychological portrait of a peasant striving to adapt to urban life and improve his family's financial circumstances. While "Muzhiki" and "Soshnikov" assess the experience of the peasantry from an outsider's viewpoint, "Thoughts" brings the reader into the mind of Ivan Artemov, a novel literary strategy that encouraged early twentieth-century audiences to empathize with the peasantry by figuratively walking in their shoes.

"Za chuzhie den'gi" (For Other People's Money), by N. Afanas'ev, similarly portrays an ambitious peasant who leaves his rural village in search of opportunity; however, it offers an even darker representation of urban assimilation.[60] Lukin, the tale's protagonist, lives in an apartment with his wife and three small children, near the factory where he has worked as the *artel'shchik* (member of the cooperative) by collecting money.[61] Although he had already spent ten years in the position, when he "thought about his service, about his life," he realized it was characterized by disquiet.[62] Lukin knew of other people in his position who had been killed while they delivered or collected money on behalf of their bosses, an awareness that produced in him "severe anxiety."[63] One night, Lukin journeys to the post office to collect a significant amount of money and his worst fears are realized: two former colleagues murder him.[64]

Immediately after Lukin's death, the reader is brought to a new scene in the peasant's apartment, where his wife anxiously awaits his return. She paces around the apartment, reheating the samovar and reflecting on their recent conversation about moving back to the countryside. Fed up with the uncertainty and danger of her husband's job, she had discussed with him the possibility of returning to the countryside, where they owned land and would live "in poverty, but peacefully."[65] However, Lukin delayed their departure, and she in turn "didn't want him to give up a good income," in spite of what she called their "eternal anxieties."[66] Her thoughts are interrupted when a group of men suddenly arrives at the apartment with the body of her deceased husband. The children are awakened by the commotion, and the oldest exclaims in horror, "Mama! Mama! They brought our Papa!"[67] Lukin's wife sees "the pale, set face of her husband," with eyes that remain open, "as if they were asking [her], 'For what?' 'For what?'"[68]

"Za chuzhie den'gi" presents a pessimistic vision of urban life through its realistic descriptions of factory work and its portrayal of a conflicted peasant family. Like "Razdum'e," "Za chuzhie den'gi" gives readers the opportunity to consider the difficult choices facing peasants like Lukin and his wife, who were torn between their desire to live in the familiar quiet of rural Russia and the necessity of earning money to support their families. Ultimately, "Za chuzhie den'gi" conveys a subtle message to readers through its somber conclusion: rural peasants ought not to change their traditional ways of life by migrating to metropolitan areas where they would surely struggle, and perhaps even perish.

Post-Emancipation Social Change in the United States

While a host of Russian authors confronted the obstacles facing peasants at the turn of the twentieth century, American writers Charles Waddell Chesnutt and Kate Chopin similarly created groundbreaking works of fiction that candidly acknowledged the problems African Americans encountered in the 1890s and 1900s. Like the peasantry, they also fought against poverty and strove to become integrated into urban populations. But African Americans, even those who had never experienced slavery, faced the unique obstacle of racism, a phenomenon that affected their quality of life in many ways. For example, whites excluded African Americans from public spaces through laws enforcing segregation, refused to pay them fair wages for their labor, and prohibited interracial sexual relations through discriminatory state laws that were notably upheld by the Supreme Court during landmark cases including *Pace v. Alabama* (1883) and *Plessy v. Ferguson* (1896). During the 1890s, whites committed horrific acts of violence against blacks including lynching, a phenomenon that W. Fitzhugh Brundage describes as "systematic political terrorism."[69] Through a wide range of endeavors, white Americans effectively pushed back against African Americans' ability to exercise their civil rights at the turn of the twentieth century.

The topics of interracial marriage, segregation, and lynching infrequently appeared in popular fiction during the decades immediately following the abolition of slavery. Although sentimental literary representations of slavery dominated the genre during the 1880s, a new cohort of Southern writers, one of whom was biracial, brought these issues to the forefront of the public mind through realistic short stories and novels that addressed these subjects and more during the 1890s and 1900s. The first of these authors is Kate Chopin (1850–1904), a woman of French and Irish descent whose depictions of African Americans in post-emancipation Louisiana raised readers' awareness of issues pertaining to racial identity and integration. Chopin was a native of St. Louis, Missouri, but she relocated with her husband to Louisiana, where she resided for nearly fifteen years. Familiar with the institution of slavery from her childhood experience of growing up in a household with enslaved laborers, Chopin sensitively treated African Americans in her writing.[70] Like Page and Harris before her, Chopin attained a degree of authorial expertise through her lineage; critics believed that a central reason for the "facility and directness with which Mrs. Chopin handle[d] the Creole dialect and the fidelity of her descriptions of that strange, remote life on the Louisiana bayous" was that "Mrs. Chopin herself [was] a Creole and . . . lived much of her life in New Orleans and on her Natchitoches plantation."[71] However, her work differed from that of Harris and Page through what scholar Richard H. Potter calls "her departure from the traditional stereotypes" and her "realistic and humanistic" representations of African Americans living in Louisiana.[72]

Chopin began writing for the public after her husband's untimely death from malaria in 1882. She captivated readers with her stories about the lives of Louisiana's diverse residents.[73] Her collection of short stories, *Bayou Folk* (1894), focuses on the wide-ranging experiences of African Americans in rural Louisiana, with fifteen of the twenty-three tales featuring African American men and women.[74] One story, "In and out of Old Natchitoches," offers a glimpse of the tense post-emancipation racial relations between white and black Louisianans. Readers meet a progressive landowner, Mr. Alphonse Laballière, who purchases an old plantation where he intends to grow cotton. He befriends the plantation's residents, the members of the mixed-race Giestin family, who had never been enslaved, but white society immediately criticizes him for appearing "entirely too much at home with the free mulattoes."[75] Nonetheless, Laballière persists in his attempts to establish good relations by taking "his meals at the free mulatto's, quite apart from the family, of course; and they attended, not too skillfully, to his few domestic wants."[76] Talk around town continues, however, with neighbors remarking that Laballière "had more use for a free mulatto than he had for a white man," but the forward-thinking landowner insists that it is his own business if he chooses to "hobnob with mulattoes, or negroes or Choctaw Indians or South Sea savages."[77]

When Laballière brings one of the family's children to the local school, an institution for white children that is led by his love interest, Suzanne, he is warned by the female instructor that it is "not a school conducted fo' the education of the colored population."[78] Laballière leaves the boy there anyway in an act of defiance. Reflecting later on Suzanne's anger at his audacity, however, Laballière abruptly abandons his principled stance. Blinded by love, he decides that he would like to "exterminate the Giestin family, from the great-grandmother down to the babe unborn," a sentiment that the family perceives and which motivates them to relocate to a segregated area called l'Isle des Mulâtres.[79] After the Giestinses depart from his plantation, Laballière apologizes to Suzanne and woos her back.

Some readers may have found themselves surprised by the ease with which Laballière abandons his advocacy of improving race relations between whites and blacks, while others harboring racial prejudices of their own may have empathized with him. Nonetheless, "In and out of Natchitoches" clearly illustrates the pervasiveness of a rural community's belief in segregation through their rejection of an outsider's attempts to alter traditional race relations. Chopin does not directly criticize Laballière through her description of his character, but she gives readers the opportunity to draw their own conclusions about his actions.

A second short story in *Bayou Folk*, "Désirée's Baby," also reveals to readers the embeddedness of prejudice toward biracial Americans in late nineteenth-century Louisiana. After the abolition of slavery, white Southerners feared the destruction of the existing racial order and, as historian Martha Hodes argues, believed that "it was crucial that both elite and nonelite white women minded the boundaries of the color line" by avoiding interracial sexual relations.[80] The notion of white female purity, typically applied to upper-class women, pervaded popular culture during the late nineteenth century and shaped public opinion about proper codes of behavior.[81] According to historian Philip Alexander Bruce (1856–1933), white women who engaged in sexual intercourse with African American men were looked down on. White society also condemned, in Bruce's words, the "few white women who have given birth to mulattoes," a group that he claimed had "always been regarded as monsters; and . . . belonged to the most impoverished and degraded caste of whites, by whom they are scrupulously avoided as creatures who have sunk to the level of the beasts of the field."[82] Late nineteenth-century Americans even adhered to a principle called the "one-drop rule" that defined individuals with one or more ancestors of African descent as black.

White Americans denigrated those whom they believed possessed African American blood. Furthermore, many people thought that, as Edward B. Reuter explained in his 1918 book *The Mulatto in the United States*, "any person bearing the physical marks of the lower group . . . embod[ied] the traits that are supposed to be typical of the lower race."[83] For most white Southerners, Reuter argued, the dark color of a person's skin represented "a symbol of [the race's] inferior culture . . . [standing for], in the thinking of the culturally superior group . . . poverty, disease, dirt, ignorance, and all the undesirable concomitants of a backward race."[84] Biracial men and women drew particular scorn from their peers because, in Reuter's view, their distinctive appearances "separate[d] them from both groups and [made] them alien in both."[85]

Writing at a time when public disapproval of interracial sexual relations reached its apex, Chopin published a provocative short story that challenged readers to reassess their biases against women who gave birth to mixed-race children. Her tale, "Désirée's Baby," takes place in antebellum Louisiana on a plantation owned by a man of French descent, Armand Aubigny, where he lives with his wife, Désirée. An orphan with unknown familial origins, Désirée grew up to be a "beautiful and gentle, affectionate and sincere" woman who instantly captured her future husband's attention.[86] Aubigny doted on Désirée throughout their marriage and after the birth of their newborn son, two events that tempered the slave owner's "imperious and exacting nature greatly."[87] A few months after the child's birth, however, Chopin describes how there was "an awful change in [Aubigny's] manner, which [Désirée] dared not ask him to explain."[88] Both Aubigny and Désirée realize that the growing child's appearance suggested that he possessed African heritage, a revelation that moves Aubigny to accuse his wife of lacking the white racial purity that he assumed she possessed. Estranged from her husband and in total despair, Désirée takes her baby and kills herself and the child by walking into the "deep, sluggish bayou," perhaps a metaphor for the oppressive environment women in her predicament faced during the late nineteenth century.

Reviews of "Désirée's Baby" and the other stories in *Bayou Folk* were generally favorable; critics found Chopin's stories thought-provoking, authentic, and, in the words of one columnist, "absolutely true to nature."[89] Rather than creating stock characters that resembled those found in the tales of Page and Harris, Chopin developed multifaceted literary protagonists whose circumstances, sometimes troubled, reflected those of white, black, and biracial Southerners living in the late nineteenth century. For instance, a reviewer writing for the *Critic* praised Chopin for the "photographic realism" with which she represented the residents inhabiting Louisiana's bayous and for the "shrewdness of observation" she exhibited through her stories.[90] He found "Désirée's Baby" to have been "flooded with more color" than many of the other sketches and delicately commented that Chopin's "keen eyes see through the glooms of her prairies and cane brakes, and see things well worth bringing into the light."[91] Like most late nineteenth-century reviewers of *Bayou Folk*, the *Critic's* columnist did not directly reference Chopin's careful descriptions of racial integration or interracial sexual relationships in her short stories; rather, he merely alluded to the controversial topics therein. Ultimately, Chopin's short stories did not revolutionize public opinion about late nineteenth-century race relations, but they served as some of the first works to cast a soft light on shadowed subjects that were seldom seen in popular fiction.

Chopin's *Bayou Folk* set the stage for a new set of fictional tales that boldly put forth controversial questions about the social absorption of freedpeople and biracial identities in a society that prohibited interracial sexual relations. The author of these controversial works was Charles Waddell Chesnutt (1858–1932), a man whose own experiences living in turn-of-the-century North Carolina informed his literature. Chesnutt was born in Cleveland, Ohio, but migrated to Fayetteville, North Carolina, as a child with his parents after the conclusion of the Civil War.[92] Chesnutt descended from individuals whose familiarity with the institution of slavery differed; his father was the son of a white slaveholder and his African American housekeeper, while his black mother was never enslaved.[93]

Growing up in the South during Reconstruction, Chesnutt witnessed the transformation of a former slaveholding state. He attended the Howard School, a public school for African Americans founded by the Freedman's Bureau, and worked alongside his father in the grocery store he owned in Fayetteville.[94] During his adolescence, Chesnutt taught at several public schools and published his first short story in order to generate additional income for his family.[95] Although African Americans like the Chesnutts made great strides in business, education, and politics during this era, they also experienced episodes of violence that served as reminders of the precariousness of their societal positions. For instance, as a child Chesnutt saw three white men publicly murder an African American man in downtown Fayetteville for what they claimed was the crime of rape, a traumatic occurrence for the young boy.[96] Although the murderers were convicted, President Andrew Johnson pardoned them in 1868, an event that Chesnutt biographer William L. Andrews argues taught the young boy how "the subversion of law [was] a fact of life for the Afro-American in the postwar South."[97] Events like these were frightening, but the Chesnutts did not waver in their decision to make a life for themselves in North Carolina.

As a young adult, Charles Chesnutt became increasingly aware of his unique situation as a biracial man living in the South and lamented the isolation he experienced as a result. In a diary entry from 1881, he reflected on how his identity made him feel as though he was "neither fish[,] flesh, nor fowl—neither 'nigger,' poor white, nor 'buckrah.'"[98] Furthermore, he continued, both black and white Americans excluded him from their communities; he was "too 'stuck up' for the colored folks, and of course, not recognized by whites."[99] Although he was frustrated by his inability to find social acceptance, Chesnutt drew inspiration from his personal circumstances that would inform his works of fiction.

After marrying and starting a family, Chesnutt settled down in Cleveland and began writing in the hope of achieving literary success akin to that of Albion Tourgée, an Ohioan whose popular novel *A Fool's Errand* (1879) depicted African American life in Reconstruction-era North Carolina.[100] Chesnutt's first collection of short stories, *The Conjure Woman* (1899), mirrored the tales of white author Joel Chandler Harris. *The Conjure Woman* was composed of a series of African American folktales told in black dialect through the character of an elderly freedman named Uncle Julius. One early twentieth-century reviewer astutely observed, however, that although "the trade edition of Chesnutt's book bore a picture of an aged Negro and a pair of rabbits, obviously designed to make those who were enraptured by Joel Chandler Harris' stories think that here was another book they would like … there are only two points in common between Chessnut's [*sic*] and harris' [*sic*] books, really—both are filled with folktales told by an aged Negro narrator; and both are in Negro dialect."[101] Indeed, Chesnutt voiced his desire to distinguish his work from the nostalgic tales of white authors, writing in a letter to educator Booker T. Washington, "It has been the writings of Harris and Thomas Nelson Page and others of that ilk which have furnished my chief incentives to write something upon the other side of this very vital question."[102] Unlike Remus, Chesnutt's Uncle Julius was hardly nostalgic for the antebellum era. By contrast, Chesnutt informs the reader, Uncle Julius's stories were always characterized by "the shadow, never absent, of slavery and of ignorance; the sadness, always, of life as seen by the fading light of an old man's memory."[103]

The Conjure Woman sold well enough that Chesnutt was confident in continuing to pursue his career in writing, and he subsequently published his second collection of short stories, *The Wife of His Youth, and Other Stories of the Color Line* (1899). These short stories differed significantly from those of *The Conjure Woman*, however, because of their emphasis on the contentious topics of interracial relationships and biracial identities. But Chesnutt was firm in his resolve to bring these subjects to public attention because, as one reviewer noted, "his sympathies [were] all with the race which suffers so grievously from Anglo-Saxon pride and prejudice both North and South."[104]

"The Wife of His Youth," the first story in Chesnutt's collection, recounts a biracial man's crisis of identity as he struggles to reconcile his past decisions with his dreams for the future. Chesnutt describes the protagonist, Mr. Ryder, as possessing "features … of a refined type, his hair was almost straight; he was always neatly dressed; his manners were irreproachable, and his morals above suspicion."[105] A member of the middle class with aspirations for increased social mobility, Mr. Ryder lived in an African American community but surrounded himself with light-skinned men and women whom he subconsciously believed to be superior to those with darker complexions. As a bachelor approaching middle age, Mr. Ryder planned to host a ball for the woman he hoped to marry.

The object of his affection was a widow named Mrs. Dixon, and Mr. Ryder found many of her qualities appealing; she "was whiter than he, and better educated. She had moved in the best colored society of the country, at Washington, and had taught in the schools of that city."[106] Indeed, Mr. Ryder believed that his marriage to Mrs. Dixon would help fulfill his social aspirations by "further[ing] the upward process of absorption he had been wishing and waiting for."[107] Although he claimed to lack any form of "race prejudice," he sincerely believed that his destiny rested in assimilation by "the white race and extinction in the black."[108] Through his description of Mr. Ryder's fears and aspirations, Chesnutt revealed to readers the difficulties experienced by biracial American citizens. Men like Mr. Ryder found themselves caught between two worlds, a phenomenon that few white Americans understood or sympathized with during the late nineteenth century.

Through a remarkable plot twist, however, Chesnutt embedded a radical message about racial identity in "The Wife of His Youth." On the day of the ball, Mr. Ryder receives a visit from a "little woman" who was "very black, —so black that her toothless gums . . . [were] blue," who appeared as "a bit of the old plantation life, summoned up from the past by the wave of a magician's wand."[109] He pities the woman, who narrates her sad history to him. A formerly enslaved woman, she had spent her life searching for her long-lost love from whom she had been separated when she was sold downriver by her owner. For twenty-five years she faithfully searched for him in vain, convinced that he, too, longed to be reunited with her. Through Chesnutt's vignette, a revisionist version of tales of faithful, formerly bonded laborers like Page's "Ole 'Stracted" or Salias's "The Last Soul," the once enslaved woman demonstrates her fidelity to the man with whom she hopes to be "as happy in freedom as [they were] in de ole days befo' de wah."[110] Mr. Ryder promises to look into the matter for the woman before she departs to continue her search.

In the story's final pages, Mr. Ryder and the members of his community come to terms with their biracial identities and the burden of history as the descendants of enslaved African Americans. During the tale's concluding scene, set during the ball hosted by Mr. Ryder, Chesnutt emphasizes the perceived distance between emancipation and the late nineteenth century by focusing on black achievement. He describes how the guests comprised "a number of school teachers, several young doctors, three or four lawyers, some professional singers, an editor, [and] a lieutenant in the United States army," a list that likely impressed on white readers the extent to which African Americans had advanced in their careers since the abolition of slavery.[111] Indeed, for the guests themselves, the pre-emancipation era seemed far removed from their present circumstances.

Mr. Ryder calls up their memories through his retelling of the visit from the elderly, formerly enslaved woman, revealing that he was in fact her long-lost love before introducing the woman to the waiting crowd. Chesnutt describes how the story "awakened a responsive thrill in many hearts" because "there were some present who had seen, and others had heard their fathers and grandfathers tell, the wrongs and sufferings of this past generation, and all of them still felt, in their darker moments, the shadow hanging over them."[112] Thus, the woman's appearance changes Mr. Ryder's aspirations; he gives up his dream of becoming increasingly integrated into the white community through his marriage to Mrs. Dixon and decides to fulfill his promise to "the wife of his youth." Furthermore, the formerly enslaved woman's visit alters the way in which the members of the mixed-race community perceived themselves by forcing Mr. Ryder's guests to recall and internalize the difficult elements of their collective history. The "wife of his youth" may even have served as a metaphor for the freedpeople whom Chesnutt urged a younger generation of African American readers to remember as they assimilated into a modernizing nation.

Reviewers remarked on the sensitivity with which Chesnutt depicted the characters of "The Wife of His Youth." A critic writing for the *Bookman* commented that Chesnutt had "a firmer grasp than any preceding author has shown in handling the delicate relations between the white man and the negro from the point of view of the mingling of the races," an observation that reveals Chesnutt's efficacy in using fiction as a vehicle to gently bring controversial subjects to public attention. The reviewer also praised Chesnutt's literary talents and expressed his hope that the author's "philosophical grasp[,] . . . imaginative power and literary skill may combine to give us an expression of the life of his people not yet realised by any writer either white or coloured in the States" in a forthcoming novel.[113] A second critic, writing on behalf of the *Worcester Evening Gazette*, acknowledged how Chesnutt's story "brought into high relief" for readers "the effects of the ante-bellum days upon the lives of the negro, in the tragedies for which the war was directly responsible."[114] Unlike the fictional works of Page and Harris that portrayed freedpeople longing to return to the pre-emancipation era, "The Wife of His Youth" demonstrated that the legacy of bondage still affected members of the African American middle class as they sought to advance their careers and assimilate into the nation that had once enslaved them. In this way, Chesnutt's story mirrored that of Russian author "P.B.," whose peasant protagonist Soshnikov wrestles with the memories of his troubled past and long-lost love, reminiscences that prevent him from becoming fully absorbed into post-emancipation Russia as a liberated serf.

Additional stories within Chesnutt's collection similarly gave voice to the unique experiences of biracial African Americans during the late nineteenth century. Two tales, "Her Virginia Mammy" and "The Sheriff's Children," received particular attention from reviewers who praised their subject matter and Chesnutt's skill in crafting emotionally complex portraits of biracial characters. The first, "Her Virginia Mammy," describes the dilemma faced by a young woman, Clara, who wishes to marry her lover. Orphaned during a steamboat accident that took the life of her parents, Clara hesitates to marry without knowledge of her familial roots for fear of embarrassing her future husband. Through a conversation with an acquaintance, the maternal Mrs. Harper, Clara learns of her supposed parents' origins. Mrs. Harper claims that she served as Clara's former mammy, that Clara's father was "a Virginia gentleman," and that her mother was "a Virginia belle."[115] Overjoyed, Clara shares the news with her future husband, who congratulates her but does not admit that he has "noticed the resemblance between [Mrs. Harper and Clara]," a likeness that points to Clara's mixed-race parentage.[116] Indeed, Mrs. Harper's own intense love for Clara, a feeling only visible to the reader, confirms Mrs. Harper's status as Clara's birth mother. Like "The Wife of His Youth," "Her Virginia Mammy" challenges readers' assumptions about what it means to have white and black parents by blurring the "color line." For the better part of the story, Clara appears as a middle-class white woman who harbors her own prejudices toward "the dark faces of whom Americans always think when 'colored people' are spoken of."[117] Although Clara never learns the truth of her own background, readers are encouraged to confront their own assumptions about the protagonist's familial origins and her character.

A second story, "The Sheriff's Children," similarly addresses the subject of racial identity, but it does so through a dramatic plot that prompts readers to sympathize with biracial Americans who had limited choices during the late nineteenth century. Set in a rural town in North Carolina, Chesnutt's harrowing tale depicts a white sheriff who strives to carry out his legal duty by defending a biracial prisoner named Tom. Accused of murdering a Confederate veteran, Tom awaits his trial in jail but is confronted by an angry mob of white men who threaten to hang him. Although the sheriff protects Tom, he attempts to kill the sheriff in an effort to escape after the mob departs. During the stirring confrontation between the two men, Tom reveals that he is the sheriff's son; decades ago the sheriff raped his mother, a formerly enslaved woman, before selling her. Tom explains to his father how slavery had "crushed" his "spirit" and that in the post-emancipation era he was "free in name, but despised and scorned and set aside" by white Americans.[118] Fearing a trial that would find him guilty in spite of his claim that he did not kill the Confederate veteran, Tom believes he has no choice but to escape from prison. Seething with resentment toward his father, Tom prepares to kill him but is instead wounded by the sheriff's daughter, Polly. The sheriff subsequently locks Tom in prison for the night, but when he returns the next day, filled with guilt for his past crime of rape, he discovers that Tom has committed suicide.

"The Sheriff's Children" contained several unusual elements that made a powerful impression on readers. First, Chesnutt addressed the controversial topic of lynching, a subject primarily reported in newspapers or criticized by courageous activists like journalist Ida. B. Wells during the late nineteenth century. Chesnutt's description of the white mob's attempted murder in a new medium, fiction, drew attention to a phenomenon that plagued the nation at the time of the collection's publication. In addition, "The Sheriff's Children" is unique in its fictional portrayal of the numerous hardships facing African Americans, difficulties Chesnutt knew well from his own experiences. In a notable scene, Tom confesses to his father that he believes "no degree of learning or wisdom will change the color of [his] skin and that [he] shall always wear what in [his] own country is a badge of degradation."[119] By listening to his son's explanation of his situation, the sheriff begins to understand his predicament and ultimately repents for his own misdeeds. Alas, the sheriff's revelation comes too late, and he is unable to prevent his son from killing himself out of desperation. Chesnutt may have hoped that, like the sheriff, readers would similarly increase their comprehension of how white society's exclusion of African Americans could produce tragic consequences.

According to reviews printed in numerous journals, Chesnutt successfully raised awareness about the plight of African Americans through fiction. For instance, the *Boston Courier* declared that "the color problem is one that demands grave consideration and even apprehension for the future" and that "the color line is as strong, or almost as strong as when the Dutch brought the first cargo of blacks to be sold as slaves."[120] Chesnutt effectively tackled this problem by showing that "the Negro is a being with emotions, even as is the white man, that for all the prejudice against him, he has within him, sympathies, affections, which can be utilized to his improvement better than the White man's perpetual menace."[121] Other critics agreed with the *Boston Courier*'s assessment that Chesnutt's representations evoked empathy in readers;

for example, the *St. Louis Globe-Democrat* observed that "there is a pathos to the life of these people, with whom the author is in such kindly sympathy. . . . The agoni[zi]ng of [the] 'Old Mammy,' the dispair [*sic*] of the black son of the white sheriff[,] makes one feel that after all the world is akin in that a matter of emotion is not dependent upon the pigment of one's skin."[122] Ultimately, Chesnutt's depictions of African American men and women did much to challenge the flat, stereotypical representations of enslaved African Americans and freedpeople that gained so much popularity during the 1880s. As the *Cambridge (MA) Tribune* put it, "Heretofore we have been dependant [*sic*] for any knowledge . . . of the negro in the South . . . from the pens of Mrs. Stowe, Thomas Nelson Page, Hopkins Smith, Joel Chandler Harris, or some other writer of the Caucasian race. . . . But with the advent in literature of . . . Chesnutt . . . the romantic and dramatic darkey, so long familiar to us, is to be displayed by the real flesh and blood negro, with his own thoughts and aspirations, his joys and sorrows, as he is known to those of his own race."[123]

The achievements of individual members of the burgeoning black middle class reinforced Chesnutt's literary depictions of autonomous, thriving African American communities through visual culture. During the early twentieth century, factors including increased opportunities for educational advancement, urbanization, job differentiation, and access to capital enabled African Americans to purchase property, establish businesses, and form social organizations in all-black neighborhoods.[124] In cities, Southern whites perceived as threatening middle-class blacks' desire to exercise their purchasing power and obtain what Grace Elizabeth Hale calls "unmediated access" to previously restricted goods and services, but African Americans remained undaunted in their pursuit of a better life.[125]

One way in which members of the black middle class sought to visually represent themselves was through their cartes de visite. Dressed in elegant clothing, they visited photography studios, where they commissioned self-portraits printed on small cards that could be exchanged with friends and family.[126] In cartes de visite from the late nineteenth century, African American men and women appear in smartly tailored jackets, fur-trimmed coats, delicate hats, and elbow-length gloves, finery that signified their social status and material wealth.[127] These modern, aspirational images contrasted sharply with concurrent white literary portrayals of melancholic freedpeople who waxed nostalgic for their lives as slaves.

Sociologist and activist W. E. B. Du Bois played an important role in presenting photographs of black, middle-class Americans to the nation and to the world. A graduate of Fisk University and Harvard, where he completed his dissertation on the history of the slave trade in 1896, Du Bois committed his life to the study of African Americans. He published countless books and essays that challenged existing historical narratives, discussed racial identity, and made policy recommendations.[128] Du Bois opposed the accommodationist approach advocated by his contemporary, educator Booker T. Washington, and championed efforts to challenge discrimination against African Americans by co-founding the National Association for the Advancement of Colored People in 1909.[129] At the start of his career, Du Bois was charged with providing images to illustrate statistics on African American life for the "Negro Exhibit" in the Palace of Social Economy at the 1900 Paris Exposition. He produced what the *Colored American Magazine* described as "a series of charts giving statistics with reference to the status of the Negro in the United States" as well as 363 photographs of dignified, well-dressed African Americans.[130] In his essay reporting on the exhibit, Du Bois wrote that his photographs depicted "typical Negro faces, which hardly square with conventional American ideas," a statement that alludes to his goal of defying contemporary stereotypes of African Americans as an impoverished, uneducated, and unaccomplished group of people.[131] His objective, Shawn Michelle Smith contends, was to "disrupt the images of African Americans produced 'through the eyes of others,'" particularly depictions of individuals as violent criminals.[132] Photographed by Thomas Askew, the men and women of the Paris Exposition sit in formal poses in sophisticated clothing that mirrored that of contemporaneous cartes de visite.[133] They appear not as farmers, beggars, or urban lawbreakers, but as refined members of metropolitan society. As evidenced by his receipt of a gold medal, Du Bois succeeded in capturing the attention and admiration of judges through his creative, radical challenge to white-produced representations of African Americans.

Racist Representations and Urban Violence

While realistic early twentieth-century portrayals of African Americans and peasants successfully countered many of the nostalgic or cartoonish depictions of previous decades, racist representations of African Americans posed a particular challenge in the battle to shape public perceptions of freedpeople and their descendants in the United States. The provocative author Thomas Dixon Jr. most effectively turned public opinion against African Americans through his inflammatory depictions of freedpeople as a violent group that threatened white society. In Russia's literary history, no author with corresponding effectiveness fortified the existing divisions between former serfs and members of other estates during the post-emancipation era.

Dixon, a North Carolinian, lawyer, and prolific writer, is best known for his popular trilogy about the Ku Klux Klan that was published between 1902 and 1907.[134] The three novels portray the post-emancipation South as a place in which savage African Americans, freed from the restraints of slavery, disrupted white Americans' way of life and endangered the purity of white Southern women. The second novel in the series, *The Clansman* (1905), was adapted into film as David Wark "D. W." Griffith's controversial production, *Birth of a Nation* (1915), a pro-Klan movie that shattered records as the highest-grossing silent film of its day.[135] Dixon's crude representations of African Americans in his literary trilogy exacerbated racial tensions and sparked significant debate among critics and readers during the early twentieth century.

There is little evidence of Dixon's animosity toward African Americans prior to the publication of the first book in the Klan trilogy, *The Leopard's Spots: A Romance of the White Man's Burden, 1865–1900* (1902).[136] Dixon worked as a lawyer and a Baptist minister during the 1880s and 1890s, but changed course by devoting his energies to the production of literature that criticized race relations in the post-emancipation United States. *The Leopard's Spots* thrust Dixon into the national spotlight as a divisive figure whose political and racial views appealed to some but repelled others. An examination of correspondence and reviews pertaining to *The Leopard's Spots* reveals that Dixon's writing struck a powerful chord among Americans who believed the social absorption of African Americans was an undesirable solution to the problems of the post-emancipation era.

Disguised as a romance, *The Leopard's Spots* is in fact a condemnation of black civil rights and interracial sexual relations. An examination of the book's original, unpublished introduction reveals that Dixon intended that his work would serve as the mouthpiece of "the Silent South," a voice that "scorns public opinion, defies proper laws, and lives her own life."[137] The novel takes place in rural North Carolina, where carpetbaggers, planters, and freedpeople vie for wealth and political power. The story centers on the relationship between two white Southerners, Sallie Worth and Charlie Gaston, but also describes dramatic events such as the lynching of a black man who raped a white woman, a crime that Dixon claimed was "unknown absolutely under slavery."[138] Dixon's freedpeople confirmed early twentieth-century white Americans' worst prejudices and fears: they behaved brutishly after emancipation by "terrorising the country, stealing, burning and murdering"; by raping white women; and by working with the Republican Party to reduce whites' political and economic power.[139] As a result, *The Leopard's Spots* resonated not only with disaffected white Southerners who mourned their loss of societal influence but also with white Northerners and immigrants who resented the African American migrants with whom they competed for jobs and political and social status in the nation's growing metropoles.

Reviews from a host of newspapers reveal that Dixon's representations of the postwar era deeply appealed to Southerners and Northerners alike. Numerous critics particularly admired the supposed verisimilitude of Dixon's South: the *Nashville American* declared that "it is his intentness, his earnestness, and the simple truths he tells which hold us spellbound"; Chicago's *Evening Post* called the work "so obviously sincere, so undeniably true . . . , so righteously wroth, so passionately prophetic"; and the *Atlanta Journal* argued that it was "true to the very letter."[140] One explanation for the geographically diverse reviewers' shared opinions lies in the way Dixon deceitfully blended fact and fiction to appeal to readers' emotions. As the *San Francisco Chronicle* explained, Dixon produced a love story that was "a welcome relief in its spiritual beauty from the realistic passion seen in so many novels of the day," a tale devoid of "that realism which coarsens."[141] In one sense, Dixon's representations appealed to readers because he pursued a strategy employed by literary predecessors Page and Harris, that of using historical fiction that eschewed literary realism to shape popular memories of the South. But while Page and Harris encouraged readers to adopt a more sentimental view of the past, Dixon sought to deepen contemporary divisions between blacks and whites. The book was indeed, as one reviewer warned readers, "a live wire; mind how you tread on it."[142]

The Leopard's Spots was but the first of three novels by Dixon that made a powerful impact in American popular culture during the early twentieth century. One of the most controversial authors in U.S. history, Dixon played on Americans' deepest anxieties about perceived racial differences to sell millions of books that both exacerbated and reflected rising tensions in American cities, where many white Americans viewed African Americans with fear or resentment.[143] Race riots broke out during the late nineteenth and early twentieth centuries in cities like Wilmington (North Carolina), Brownsville (Texas), New York City, and Atlanta, where angry white mobs murdered African Americans and destroyed black businesses and homes. While some Americans acknowledged that antiblack racism played a central role in the outbreaks of violence, others placed the blame on African Americans for the chaos. For instance, in his analysis of the causes of the Atlanta race riots of 1906, Georgian A. J. McElway described local African Americans as Atlanta's "criminal class," listing black-on-white offenses that preceded the eruption of violence.[144] He concluded his essay with an ominous prediction about the consequences of the race riots spreading across American cities, warning, "There has been but one white man killed in Atlanta. There was none in Wilmington. In anything like a race war the negro has everything to lose. It means for him, not battle, but extermination."[145]

By contrast, Russian peasants were not the victims of racist acts of physical brutality in urban centers at the turn of the twentieth century. Demeaning literary and visual representations of peasants pervaded illustrated periodicals and advertisements of the era, but these depictions did not produce aristocratic mob violence against peasant communities. As in American cities where race riots exploded, however, strained class dynamics produced comparable forms of upheaval in Russian cities. Growing peasant discontent in urban centers and rural villages stemmed largely from the economic hardships that former serfs and their descendants faced after the abolition of serfdom and the enstatement of redemption payments.[146] As the peasant population increased during the late nineteenth century, so did their demand for land, which became increasingly expensive to purchase. Industrialization and urban migration also exposed peasants to the broader world, leading to a growing awareness of life beyond their traditional villages.

The eruptions of violence during the Russian Revolutions of 1905 and 1917 differed in significant ways from the American race riots of the same era, but they shared as contributing causes class tensions that exacerbated existing divisions between the descendants of serfs and elites. Lacking a political voice in the form of the right to vote and facing high prices for material goods during the Russo-Japanese War (1904–1905) and World War I (1914–1918), Russian peasants expressed their grievances through organized protests, strikes, and the seizure of the gentry's property in rural areas.[147] Data from a survey taken after the 1905 revolution suggest that peasants harbored a sense of injustice about the economic disparities that existed between different estate groups and contributed to their decision to revolt. The report noted that migrant peasants who returned to the Pskov Province after working in St. Petersburg encouraged their peers to participate in the revolt, arguing that "only thus could [they] achieve equal rights with members of the other legal estates."[148] The peasantry and the nobility may have shared the same ethnicity, language, and religion, but countless economic, social, and cultural factors still separated the two groups fifty years after the abolition of serfdom. As in the United States, the post-emancipation social absorption of formerly bonded laborers and their descendants remained incomplete on the eve of World War I.

Epilogue

The fiftieth anniversaries of the abolition of Russian serfdom and American slavery provided two disparate nations with opportunities to reflect on their twin legacies of bonded labor. In 1911, Russia celebrated Tsar Alexander II's issuance of the Emancipation Manifesto with ceremonies, the construction of monuments, the production of commemorative objects, and the publication of books and articles about serfdom. Just two years later, Americans similarly observed President Abraham Lincoln's issuance of the Emancipation Proclamation through public celebrations, exhibitions, and special publications.

Russia's rural and urban subjects alike observed the fiftieth anniversary of the abolition of serfdom in 1911. Manufacturers produced colorful candy wrappers depicting a benevolent Tsar Alexander II surrounded by his grateful peasant subjects and collectible mugs featuring quotations from the Emancipation Manifesto.[1] On February 20, *Moskovskii listok* (Moscow Sheet) published a special issue commemorating emancipation in which journalists reported that crowds of city dwellers had gathered around the Kremlin's cathedrals. There, banner-bearers laid wreaths at the foot of a monument to the "Tsar-Liberator," Alexander II.[2] Nearby, the merchants of Okhotnyi Riad, a central street in Moscow, dedicated a statue to Alexander II. Adorned with the images of Orthodox saints, the monument displayed an inscription that clearly marked the occasion, which read, "This holy icon is built by the traders of Okhotnyi Riad in memory of the realization of the fiftieth anniversary of the liberation of the peasants from serfdom by the Emperor Alexander II on February 19, 1861–1911."[3] *Moskovskii listok* also featured striking images of statues honoring Alexander II that were erected by peasants from the Lublin Province, which is situated in present-day Poland.[4] The body of Christ hung from one of the three crosses that ornamented the bases of the monuments, a symbol that connected Alexander II's bodily sacrifice to that of Jesus in the way sympathetic Americans similarly linked President Lincoln's death to that of Christ.

Commentators and scholars also publicly engaged in historical reflection about the abolition of serfdom in books and articles. During the Revolution of 1905, Tsar Nicholas II issued a document known as the October Manifesto that promised, among other concessions to a discontented populace, "to grant to the people the inviolable framework of civil liberty on the basis of the integrity of the individual, freedom of conscience, speech, assembly, and association."[5] In the years that followed, intellectuals and journalists enjoyed the increased ability to freely express themselves in the public sphere about controversial topics including the consequences of the abolition of serfdom. While some spoke positively of emancipation, others focused on its shortcomings. Illustrated magazines like *Novoe vremia* (New Time) and *Golos Moskvy* (Voice of Moscow) approached the occasion from a historical perspective by featuring photographs of former serfs, or "living witnesses of the era of serfdom," that were accompanied by text describing their prior positions or current occupations.[6] Additional publications crafted a narrative of national advancement that touted Russia's progress. For example, the popular St. Petersburg daily newspaper *Gazeta-kopeika* (Kopek Gazette) argued that emancipation helped enserfed individuals and strengthened the country.[7] It was necessary to free the serfs "from the darkness of ignorance," the publication contended, so the peasantry could "find themselves" and bring about Russia's subsequent development as a modern nation.[8] Furthermore, the newspaper characterized the liberation of the serfs as "an important turning point" in the fields of "industry, commerce, law, science, and art, all areas that could only develop on the basis of free labor and humanity." Ultimately, *Gazeta-kopeika* concluded, the emancipation of the serfs led to the creation of a "new Russia," a country that could follow the path of modernization "traversed by the other civilized peoples of the world."

The elaborately illustrated jubilee album *Krepostnichestvo i volia* (Serfdom and Freedom), produced by the A. A. Levenson publishing house in 1911, similarly promoted a narrative of national advancement.[9] In the album's introduction, the anonymous author praised Tsar Alexander II for his beneficence in liberating the serfs.[10] He declared that the nineteenth of February "has been and will always remain in the eyes of the Russian people a day of the manifestation of the greatest care and love of the Russian monarch for his people, a day of mercy, of humaneness, the dawn of happiness, when a ray of progress and culture penetrated through the fog and darkness of the prereform era."[11] Here, the author characterized the abolition of serfdom as an act of generosity that not only brought joy to the peasantry but also ushered in a new age of modernity that benefited the entire nation. Reflecting on the peasantry's condition in 1911, the author saw the present moment as one of opportunity. He encouraged Russia's rural residents to adopt new habits by investing their labor in their land and exercising their newfound political freedoms in Russia's "highest state legislative institutions" in order to successfully "embark on the broad path of free labor in union with knowledge and culture!"

By contrast, other educated Russians plainly refuted the optimistic, teleological narrative that portrayed Russia as steadily advancing toward a brighter future. For instance, Muscovite Ivan Sytin, a publishing entrepreneur who heralded from the peasant estate, released a six-volume history of serfdom and its abolition in 1911 to mark the fiftieth anniversary.[12] Titled *Velikaia reforma: Russkoe obshchestvo i krest'ianskii vopros v proshlom i nastoiashchem* (The Great Reforms: Russian Society and the Peasant Question in the Past and Present), the illustrated work described the conditions peasants endured during serfdom and the post-emancipation era. Its editors, however, commissioned essays by liberal scholars who presented a critical view of serfdom and argued that the tsar's post-emancipation reforms failed to secure for the peasantry a good quality of life.[13] In the introduction to the first volume, editors A. Dzhivelegov, S. Mel'gunov, and V. Picheta explicitly condemned the peasantry's condition in 1910, arguing that the abolition of serfdom led to "an increase in the shortage of arable land . . . [and] the acceleration of starvation, which became constant companions of village life." Furthermore, they lamented the fact that these events had not been historically connected to the "foundations of the reforms, with their vagueness and cowardice, with their stingy philanthropies and their thoughtful attention to landowners."[14] By directly criticizing the government's inability to uplift the peasantry after emancipation and by linking the abolition of serfdom to the more recent problems that still plagued Russian society, particularly evident in the Revolution of 1905, they offered an alternative historical narrative to that which idealized the emancipation of the serfs.[15] *Velikaia reforma* was ultimately a financial success for Sytin, who considered the project to be one of his most significant and personally meaningful endeavors.[16]

A final way in which Russians interpreted the abolition of serfdom in 1911 was by politicizing the occasion to advocate radical change. Revolutionary activist Vladimir Lenin, writing from abroad, addressed readers in the *Rabochaia gazeta* (Workers' Gazette) in an article titled "The Fiftieth Anniversary of the Fall of Serfdom." He criticized the tsarist government for promoting only "the most reactionary views regarding the so-called 'emancipation' of the peasants" in schools and churches out of fear that "the mere mention of the fact that fifty years ago the abolition of serfdom was proclaimed" might provoke the "people repressed by the Duma of the landlords, of the nobility, people who are suffering more than ever before from the petty tyrannies, violence and oppression of the feudal-minded landowners and of their police and bureaucrats." By contrast, Lenin presented a more radical interpretation of the events of 1861, arguing that they served as a kind of failed revolution. He contended that the peasantry, "who had for centuries been kept in slavery by the landowners, were unable to launch a widespread, open and conscious struggle for freedom" and the government manumitted them from one form of slavery to another in which their subjugation by landlords persisted. Fortunately, Lenin believed, the peasantry's migration to urban centers provided them with a new self-consciousness and enabled them to "straighten their backs and cast off serf habits." Led by "the Russian working class," he continued, the peasantry participated in 1905 in an unfinished revolution. Lenin presciently predicted that the "Revolution of 1905 would be followed by a new, a second, revolution" and concluded that "the anniversary of the fall of serfdom serve[d] as a reminder of, and a call for, this second revolution."[17]

The diversity of opinions that Russian intellectuals expressed about the causes and consequences of emancipation suggests that the meaning of abolition remained contested in 1911. Despite their differing perspectives, Lenin, Sytin, and others similarly recognized that the fiftieth anniversary provided an essential opportunity for the promotion of revisionist historical narratives, the critiquing of contemporary governmental policies, and the encouragement of reform or revolution in Russia. Tsar Alexander II's liberation of the enserfed population ultimately generated significant problems that remained unsolved five decades later and contributed to the government's downfall during the Revolution of 1917.

Shortly after Russians engaged in their retrospective exercise, Americans similarly cast a critical eye toward the events of the past half century. Although African Americans had historically celebrated "Juneteenth" or "Freedom Day" during the years following their emancipation, the fiftieth anniversary of the issuance of President Lincoln's Emancipation Proclamation and its enactment prompted celebrations on an even larger scale.[18] The *New York Times* reported that African Americans gathered at the Metropolitan African Methodist Episcopal Church in Washington, D.C., where they participated in a choral jubilee on September 22, 1912.[19] In New York City, the Philharmonic Society commemorated the enactment of the Emancipation Proclamation with a special concert on New Year's Day during which it played pieces by Antonín Dvořák and Samuel Coleridge-Taylor, works that the *Times* argued "incorporate[d] into artistic music the spirit of the negro folk-song."[20]

Elaborate celebrations were also held between 1913 and 1916 in Chicago, Philadelphia, New York City, Richmond, and Louisville.[21] In New York City, sociologist W. E. B. Du Bois and a group of New York State commissioners staged the Emancipation Proclamation Exposition to celebrate black progress in innovative ways.[22] Held October 22–31, 1913, the exposition featured exhibits that explored African history as well as the lives of African Americans.[23] A rare archival photograph from the exhibition reveals the construction of a massive Egyptian temple surrounded by palm trees and covered in hieroglyphs, a display that likely connected the history of black Africans to that of ancient Egypt.[24] The highlight of the exposition was Du Bois's pageant, "The Star of Ethiopia," an artistic depiction of transnational black history that incorporated African American spirituals and honored prominent abolitionists like Frederick Douglass and Sojourner Truth.[25] Approximately 350 actors performed the pageant for 14,000 audience members over the course of three days. Although critics produced mixed reviews of Du Bois's pageant, "The Star of Ethiopia" traveled to Washington, D.C., and Philadelphia for additional performances in subsequent years. New York City's Emancipation Proclamation Exposition and other pageants across the country primarily attracted African American visitors, many of whom used the occasion to reflect on the gains and losses in the struggle for liberty during the preceding half century. The lack of white participation, by contrast, signaled whites' unwillingness to publicly remember the abolition of slavery and the pervasiveness of racist attitudes during the Jim Crow era.[26]

Whites' focus on national reconciliation at the expense of black civil rights also resulted in a dearth of statues dedicated to the abolition of slavery, particularly when compared to the proliferation of monuments depicting Confederate generals and soldiers during the early twentieth century.[27] Monuments to President Lincoln, however, were more common. Proposed in 1909, one hundred years after his birth, Nebraska's Lincoln Monument was unveiled in September 1912 on the grounds of the state capitol in Omaha, where a crowd of people gathered.[28] The sculpture depicts the figure of Lincoln standing alone, with head bowed; no figures of African Americans were included in the design. Like the Russian monuments commemorating serfdom's abolition through representations of the Tsar-Liberator rather than through depictions of the peasantry, most American sculptures of Lincoln similarly depict him as a redemptive figure. Consider, for instance, Thomas Ball's *Freedmen's Memorial* (1876), which depicts a partially dressed enslaved man stooping beneath Lincoln's outstretched hand.[29] Although

African Americans raised the funds for its construction, white Americans chose its paternalistic, subordinating design, one that Kirk Savage aptly describes as an "unfortunate juxtaposition" that is "not really about emancipation but its opposite—[white] domination."[30] Indeed, whites' efforts to resecure their control over the black population through political legislation, intimidation, and outright violence at the turn of the twentieth century help explain the absence of monuments commemorating the fiftieth anniversary of slavery's abolition. The construction of statues praising black advancement would have been at odds with whites' goal of retaining power over African Americans in a changing nation.

Americans also saw the fiftieth anniversary of the issuance of the Emancipation Proclamation as a chance to promote dueling narratives about the meaning of emancipation, Reconstruction, the social absorption of African Americans, and black achievements. Newspapers and journals like the *New York Times* and the *Outlook* printed special articles that touted black advancement, citing an abundance of data relating to property ownership rates, aggregate wealth, and literacy.[31] Writing for the nation's first illustrated black periodical, the *Indianapolis Freeman*, journalist Dr. M. A. Majors lauded the progress African Americans made during the half century that followed the abolition of slavery. He praised black advancement in the fields of education, business, and politics, declaring, "As we gaze through the dark gloom into the past . . . and offer comparisons with other races condemned as [the African American] has been to a life of serfdom, all history suffers for a single sentence to prove that any other race so enchained . . . to all the graces . . . in fifty years challenge[d] . . . the makers of civilization themselves."[32]

Educator Booker T. Washington, president of the National Negro Business League in 1912, similarly commended black progress by promoting "Fiftieth Anniversary Week," a time when states could host expositions revealing what the league called "the progress in commercial, professional, moral, intellectual, and religious directions made by the race."[33] Acutely sensitive to the racial tensions of the era, however, Washington sought to balance his twin goals of highlighting African American achievements and achieving interracial harmony. He described the fiftieth anniversary of emancipation as an occasion for "the kind of celebration that will [not] exasperate the white people of the South or remind them in an offensive way about slavery . . . [but] a celebration so conducted that both races will feel interest in it."[34] Washington's words indicated his fear that whites might perceive the idea of black progress as threatening; therefore, he urged readers not to disrupt the unequal racial status quo that defined Jim Crow America.

But the more optimistic narratives offered by men like Majors and Washington did not go unchallenged. Indeed, other commentators reflecting on the occasion emphasized the ways in which African Americans living in the United States remained oppressed. For example, author James Weldon Johnson lamented the injustices of Jim Crow America and referenced the sacrifices African Americans had made since slavery's abolition in his poem "Fifty Years: Written on the Fiftieth Anniversary of Lincoln's Emancipation Proclamation."[35] Published in the *New York Times* on January 1, 1913, the popular composition was reprinted in the *New York Age* one month later. In it, Weldon urged African Americans to claim the rights of citizenship that were not only delineated in the Fourteenth Amendment but also earned through centuries of toil, arguing, "This land is ours by right of birth, / This land is ours by right of toil; / We helped to turn its virgin soil, / Our sweat is in its fruitful soil."[36] Johnson concluded his poem by adopting a hopeful tone; he encouraged readers to strive for freedom and equality in an era of segregation, disfranchisement, and violence: "Full well I know the hour when hope / Sinks dead, and round us everywhere / Hangs stifling darkness, and we grope / With hands uplifted in despair. / Courage! Look out, beyond, and see / The far horizon's beckoning span! / Faith in your God-known destiny! / We are a part of some great plan."[37]

Other writers similarly acknowledged the social injustices African Americans still faced in the early twentieth century. The anonymous author of an editorial in New York's *Independent*, a progressive magazine that supported the abolition of slavery during the mid-nineteenth century, argued that while the Emancipation Proclamation "opened an era of national history," the document "did not immediately give to the freedmen an equality of privilege, and it has not yet wholly done so."[38] William H. Lewis, the first black assistant attorney general and the son of a freedman, argued that it was imperative for early twentieth-century Americans to continue fighting to secure civil rights for African Americans. In a speech to the Massachusetts General Assembly in 1913, Lewis contended that African Americans' transition from slavery to freedom was incomplete. He asserted that Americans still viewed one another through the lens of race, a category enshrined in law that produced for African Americans what Lewis understatedly called "vexatious annoyances of color" that contributed to their "present disadvantages and inequalities."[39] As a result, he boldly proclaimed, "The duty of the hour is to unshackle [the Negro] and make him wholly free."[40] For Lewis, Johnson, and others, the fiftieth anniversary of emancipation served as a moment to call for action.

Americans viewed the fiftieth anniversary of emancipation as an occasion during which they could connect the past to the present. While some emphasized a narrative of progress and achievement, others identified the problems that still plagued the nation. As in Russia, different groups of people disputed the meaning of emancipation and advanced particular visions of abolition in writing and art that alternately ignored, celebrated, or critiqued the reforms of the Civil War and postbellum era. Their viewpoints subtly lent support to or undercut the political policies of the era that helped or hindered black advancement and effective social absorption.

The sudden advent of World War I (1914–1917) forced Russia and the United States to quickly turn their attention from history and their present domestic affairs to the conflict that engulfed Europe. With great effort, both nations mobilized their subjects and citizens in the fight to defeat the Central Powers, although the fall of the tsarist government during the October Revolution of 1917 resulted in Russia's exit from the global fight and descent into bitter civil war. After Russian and American troops returned home from abroad, they entered societies that had changed in their absence. The Bolshevik Party consolidated its power in 1922 and established the Soviet Union, a socialist country founded on a new class system based on Marxist principles that replaced the estate system of the previous centuries. Traditional divisions between peasants, clergy, and the nobility were exchanged for new hostilities between impoverished peasants and wealthy peasants, Communist Party members, workers, and police.[41] By contrast, social divisions in the United States continued to fall in part along racial lines, but African Americans' experiences serving their country abroad produced in many renewed passion in the fight to exercise their civil rights at home.[42] White Americans responded to challenges to their political, economic, and social control with violence during the "Red Summer" of 1919, when race riots and other forms of brutality engulfed cities like Chicago and Washington, D.C. Thus, racial prejudice continued to impede the processes of social absorption and the attainment of rights for African Americans in the United States, whereas the Soviets' new focus on Marxist class categories tore down old estate barriers but created new allies and enemies out of different social groups.

After World War I, cultural production played as much of a role in the reconstruction of two disparate countries as it did during the years following the abolition of serfdom and slavery. But the modes of representation differed significantly from those previously employed by Russians and Americans. During the late 1850s and early 1860s, Russian and American poets, authors, and playwrights incorporated sentimental themes into their respective genres of literature to rouse ambivalent populations to action in the fight to abolish serfdom and slavery. Two decades later, when the descendants of landowners and slaveholders came of age, these writers produced an abundance of historical fiction that idealized relations between serfs, enslaved African Americans, and owners and defended the prior generation's enserfment or enslavement of large segments of the population. Artists visually represented peasants and freedpeople in periodicals and oil paintings to deliver messages to audiences about national identity and notions of citizenship, while businesses incorporated images in advertisements to convince particular consumer groups to buy their products. By the turn of the twentieth century, peasants and African Americans took on a growing role in crafting and disseminating self-representations in literature and visual culture that drew from firsthand experience.

During World War I, however, the U.S. and Russian governments recognized the power of cultural representations and strove to generate support for civic causes through wartime propaganda. In the postwar era, the state-controlled Soviet government sought to achieve its goal of creating new identities for its citizens by deploying idealized representations of peasants and workers in visual culture.[43] At the same time, Americans and Russians of all backgrounds increasingly represented themselves and others in new forms of technology such as radio, television, and film that offered exciting audio-visual possibilities. While shows and movies featured new portrayals of peasants and African Americans, many nineteenth-century archetypes reemerged as well, a phenomenon that attests to the durability of earlier cultural representations. The abolition of serfdom and slavery may have seemed increasingly distant after World War I, but Russians and Americans continued to grapple with questions of race, class, and national identity through cultural production.

Notes

Abbreviations in the Notes

RGALI   Russian State Archive of Literature and Art
OR GTG   State Tret'iakov Gallery Archive
d.   file(s)
f.   fond
l., ll.   page(s)
n.   number
o.   index

Introduction

1. Burbank and Cooper, *Empires in World History*, 282.

2. Comparative historian Peter Kolchin has argued that while the Russian nobility viewed peasants as composing "the lowest level of [Russian] society rather than outcasts from it," white American landowners considered enslaved African Americans to be "outsiders" and disparaged their ethnicity and cultural practices. Kolchin, *Unfree Labor*, 44.

3. These included the *gosudarstvennoe krest'ianstvo* (state peasantry), the *dvorianstvo* (nobility), members of the *dukhovnoe soslovie* (clerical order), and the *kupechestvo* (merchantry). As the property of landowners, serfs were known as *pomeshchich'i krest'iane*. Wirtschafter, *Social Identity in Imperial Russia*, 3–4, 170; Pipes, *Russia under the Old Regime*, 144.

4. As Marina Mogilner argues, this "sociocultural gap stood in the way of the homogenization of the population into the 'social mass' of the 'national body,' which was needed to enable racial imagination." Mogilner, *Homo Imperii*, 4.

5. "Polozhenie 19 fevralia i voprosy krest'ianskogo samoupravleniia," *Nedelia*, February 14, 1871, 1.

6. "The Fourth of July, 1865," *Harper's Weekly* 9, no. 445 (July 8, 1865): 418.

7. U.S. Department of Commerce, *Historical Statistics of the United States*, 26–27.

8. U.S. Department of Commerce, 26.

9. Both Russia and the United States experienced a period of societal reconstruction after the abolition of serfdom and slavery. During the decade that followed emancipation, Tsar Alexander II implemented additional reforms that modernized the nation. In the United States, the twelve-year period following emancipation and the end of the Civil War became known as Reconstruction. The states ratified the Thirteenth, Fourteenth, and Fifteenth Amendments to expand and redefine citizenship, while Congress passed legislation in an effort to rebuild and reunite the war-torn nation.

10. Marc Bloch advocated the comparative methodology, describing how it allowed scholars to identify "two or more phenomena that appear, at first glance, to present

between them certain analogies, to describe the curve of their evolutions, to note the resemblances and differences, and, where possible, to explain them both." Bloch, "Pour une histoire comparée," 17.

11. Skocpol and Somers, "Comparative History in Macrosocial Inquiry," 175.

12. Skocpol and Somers, 178.

13. In 1619, the first enslaved Africans arrived in Jamestown, Virginia. In Russia, the *Sobornoe ulozhenie* (Law Code) of 1649 officially established serfdom.

14. The earliest comparative studies of New World slavery include Tannenbaum, *Slave and Citizen*; Klein, *Slavery in the Americas*; and Degler, *Neither Black nor White*. Comparative studies of global slavery include Patterson, *Slavery and Social Death*; Bergad, *Comparative Histories of Slavery*; Dal Lago and Katsari, *Slave Systems*; and Dal Lago, *American Slavery, Atlantic Slavery*. However, the foremost work of scholarship comparing Russian serfdom and U.S. slavery is Kolchin, *Unfree Labor*.

15. See Kolchin, *Sphinx on the American Land*; and "Empires across Continents: The United States and Russia," chap. 9 in Burbank and Cooper, *Empires in World History*. For a comparative study of Prussian landowners and U.S. slave owners, see Bowman, *Masters and Lords*.

16. Brundage, "Reconstruction in the South"; Prior, *Reconstruction in a Globalizing World*; Richardson, *West from Appomattox*; Gleeson and Lewis, *Civil War as Global Conflict*; Nagler, Doyle, and Gräser, *Transnational Significance*; Doyle, *Cause of All Nations*; Summers, *Ordeal of the Reunion*; Brown, *Reconstructions*; Thomas, *Literature of Reconstruction*.

17. For an assessment of the radical and conservative features of the emancipation of Russian serfs and enslaved African Americans, see Kolchin, "Reexamining Southern Emancipation" and "Comparative Perspectives on Emancipation in the U.S. South." The latter essay, according to Kolchin, "draw[s] from research for a [forthcoming] book . . . [about] emancipation in the southern United States and Russia" that will expand on the research presented in *Unfree Labor: American Slavery and Russian Serfdom* (1987). Kolchin, "Emancipation in the U.S. South," 220n2. Other proponents and practitioners of comparative emancipation studies include Dal Lago, *American Slavery, Atlantic Slavery*; Hahn, "Class and State"; Cooper, Holt, and Scott, *Beyond Slavery*; Kerr-Ritchie, *Freedom's Seekers*; and Holt, "'Empire over the Mind.'"

18. In 1955, Hannah Goldman published her dissertation comparing representations of Russian serfs and enslaved African Americans in pre-emancipation literature. For more information, see Goldman, "American Slavery and Russian Serfdom." John MacKay, in 2013, published a transnational study assessing the impact of Harriet Beecher Stowe's antislavery novel *Uncle Tom's Cabin* (1852) in imperial Russia and the Soviet Union. See MacKay, *True Songs of Freedom*.

19. Frierson, *Peasant Icons*, 3; Brooks, "Russian Nation Imagined."

20. Donskov, "Changing Image of the Peasant." For analyses of urbanization and commercialism in fin de siècle Russia, see Hilton, *Selling to the Masses*; and West, *I Shop in Moscow*. For illustrated compilations of Russian *reklamnye plakaty* (advertising posters), see Glinternik, *Reklama v Rossii*; Snopkov, *Reklama v plakate*; and Zolotinkina and Polikarpova, *Reklamnyi plakat v Rossii*.

21. Brunson, *Russian Realisms*; Valkenier, *Russian Realist Art*; Jackson, *Wanderers and Critical Realism*.

22. Blight, *Race and Reunion*; Brundage, *Southern Past*; Janney, *Remembering the Civil War*; Cook, *Civil War Memories*; Foster, *Ghosts of the Confederacy*; Savage, *Standing Soldiers, Kneeling Slaves*; Harris, *Across the Bloody Chasm*; Silber, *Romance of Reunion*; Wilson, *Baptized in Blood*.

23. For recent assessments of photography during the Civil War era, see Rosenheim, *Photography and the American Civil War*; Willis and Krauthamer, *Envisioning Emancipation*; and Wilson, *Hidden Witness*. For visual representations of the Civil War and slavery in paintings, see Harvey, *Civil War and American Art*. Recent studies assessing representations of African Americans in advertisements include Cox, *Dreaming of Dixie*; McElya, *Clinging to Mammy*; and Goings, *Mammy and Uncle Mose*. Finally, for representations of the Civil War in literature and journals, see Thomas, *Literature of Reconstruction*; Prince, *Stories of the South*; Griffin, *Ashes of the Mind*; Fahs, *Imagined Civil War*; and Brown, *Beyond the Lines*.

24. Confino, "Collective Memory and Cultural History," 1386. Confino notes that the phrase "vehicles of memory" was coined by Yosef Yerushalmi, *Zakhor: Jewish History and Jewish Memory* (Seattle: University of Washington Press, 1982).

25. Confino, "Collective Memory and Cultural History," 1386.

26. French philosopher Victor Cousin is credited with creating the phrase *l'art pour l'art*, or "art for art's sake," in his book *Du vrai, du beau et du bien* (Paris: Didier, 1853). See Françon, "Poésie pure et art pour art," 15.

27. For instance, see Pisemskii, *Gor'kaia sud'bina*; Nekrasov, "Zabytaia derevnia" and "Na Volge"; and Alcott, "M.L.," "Brothers / My Contraband," and "An Hour."

28. In the United States, Reconstruction lasted from 1865 to 1877, while Russia's era of Great Reforms primarily spanned the 1860s.

29. Rates of settlement hovered between 1 percent and 2 percent per year between 1840 and 1910, when 75.6 percent of U.S. territory consisted of settled counties. In 1790, settled counties made up just 28.3 percent of U.S. territory. Otterstrom and Earle, "Settlement of the United States," 75, 78.

30. One such policy was the General Allotment (Dawes) Act of 1887, which split reservations into private tracts of land that Native Americans and pioneers subsequently farmed or settled. Carlson, "Dawes Act," 274.

31. Kappeler, *Russian Empire*, 188, 195, 204, 205.

32. Between 1462 and 1914, the Russian Empire grew from 24,000 to 13.5 million square kilometers. Lieven, *Empire*, 262, 264.

33. Kollmann, *Russian Empire*, 454.

34. Kollmann, 206–207.

35. Russia's landowners sought to maintain a firm grip on land production on their estates, while intellectuals known as Narodniki (Populists) believed that the Emancipation Manifesto did not sufficiently improve the peasantry's circumstances. They championed the *mir* (rural commune) and the *artel'* (cooperative association) as historical institutions that ought to be adapted for modern times to increase peasant autonomy. In the United States, federal troops withdrew from former Confederate states in 1877. In their absence, white Southerners strove to increase their political and economic positions through the passage of discriminatory laws that restricted African Americans' rights. White Southerners also used violence as part of a concerted effort to subjugate and control them.

36. For instance, see Gorskii, "Metel'," 2, 3, 6; P.B., "Soshnikov"; Opochinin, "Posledniaia 'dusha'"; Danilevskii, *Kniazhna Tarakanova*; Solov'ev, *Staryi dom*; Page, "Marse Chan"; and Harris, "Free Joe."

37. Moon, *Abolition of Serfdom*, 116–118.

38. Moon, 119.

39. Neuberger, "Stories of the Street," 177.

40. Wormser, *Rise and Fall of Jim Crow*, 105.

41. Blackmon, *Slavery by Another Name*, 53.

42. Gates, *Stony the Road*, 50.

43. Soule, "Populism and Black Lynching," 431.

44. Chekhov, "Muzhiki."

45. Bylov, "Razdum'e"; Afanas'ev, "Za chuzhie den'gi."

46. Chopin, *Bayou Folk*, 53; Chesnutt, *Wife of His Youth*.

Chapter One

1. Addison, *Lucy Larcom*, 87.

2. Addison, 87.

3. Stauffer, *Black Hearts of Men*, 2.

4. Varon, *Disunion!*, 1–2.

5. Varon, 1–2.

6. Freehling, *Road to Disunion*, 1:286, 536.

7. Beckert, *Empire of Cotton*, 219.

8. Schermerhorn, *Business of Slavery*, 63. For additional studies of the connections between American slavery and capitalism, see Baptist, *Half Has Never Been Told*; and Ruef, *Between Slavery and Capitalism*.

9. "Better than Dollars," *Harper's Weekly*, April 20, 1861, 242.

10. Sinha, *Slave's Cause*, 3.

11. Harrold, *Rise of Aggressive Abolitionism*, 8–9.

12. Reid, *Origins of the American Civil War*, 196.

13. Reid, 196.

14. Smith, *Stormy Present*, 3–4.

15. Smith, 17, 19.

16. Guelzo, "Lincoln and the Abolitionists," 63.

17. President Abraham Lincoln and Secretary of War Simon Cameron urged Americans to join the Union army with a formal appeal to the public on April 15, 1861. Victor, *History, Civil, Political and Military*, 81–82; Gallagher, *Union War*, 2.

18. McPherson, *For Cause and Comrades*, 20.

19. Moon, *Abolition of Serfdom*, 53; Easley, *Emancipation of the Serfs*, 12.

20. This committee was later called the Chief Committee on Peasant Affairs. Moon, *Abolition of Serfdom*, 57; Seton-Watson, "Preparation of the Reform," 58, 60; Field, *End of Serfdom*, 107.

21. David Moon points out that Tsar Alexander's bureaucrats "sideline[d] the nobles' provincial committees" in order to "impose [their] programme" in shaping the terms of abolition. Moon, *Abolition of Serfdom*, 85; Seton-Watson, "Preparation of the Reform," 60.

22. Farah, "Autocratic Abolitionists," 97.

23. Seton-Watson, "Preparation of the Reform," 57.

24. Moon, *Abolition of Serfdom*, 63.

25. L. Ruskin, "Noch' na 19-e fevralia 1861 g. v kazarmakh (so slov ochevidtsa)," *Nedelia* 7, (February 15, 1881): 247.

26. A. I. Levshin, "Zapiska A. I. Levshina," *Russkii arkhiv* 8 (1885): 528.

27. Nekrasov, *Sobranie stikhotvorenii*, tom 1; Nekrasov, *Stikhotvoreniia*; Pisemskii, *Gor'kaia sud'bina*; Browne, *Autobiography of a Female Slave*; Alcott, "M.L." and "My Contraband."

28. Sarah Elbert's introduction to her collection of Alcott's short stories, *Alcott on Race, Sex, and Slavery*, stands as the first comprehensive examination of Alcott's short stories pertaining to slavery. Karen Sands-O'Connor discusses the absence of slavery in *Little Women* in "Anything to Suit Customers"; while Augusta Rohrbach, in "Profits of Protest," assesses Alcott's sales tactics.

29. For instance, see Moser, *Pisemsky*; and Peppard, *Nikolai Nekrasov*.

30. One of the only monographs that examines fictional slave narratives is Laura Browder's *Slippery Characters*. For a survey of fictional slave narratives, see Amanda Brickell Bellows, "Author, Author!," *New York Times*, March 16, 2012, https://opinionator.blogs .nytimes.com/2012/03/16/author-author/.

31. For a detailed analysis of the growth of print industries in Russia and the United States, see McReynolds, *News under Russia's Old Regime*; and Kaestle and Radway, *Print in Motion*. Works that assess rising literacy rates in Russia and the United States include Zboray, *Fictive People*; Brooks, *When Russia Learned to Read*; and Eklof, *Russian Peasant Schools*.

32. Rolf Engelsing, a German historian, wrote about the *Leserrevolution*, or reading revolution, in his seminal work *Der Bürger als Leser*. Hochman, *Reading Revolution*, 7; Kaestle, *Literacy in the United States*, 52; Davidson, "History of Books and Readers," 12; Anikst, Baburina, and Chernevich, *Russian Graphic Design*, 12.

33. Anikst, Baburina, and Chernevich, *Russian Graphic Design*, 12; Casper et al., *Industrial Book*, 239.

34. Zboray, *Fictive People*, 196.

35. Casper et al., *Industrial Book*, 280.

36. Brooks, *When Russia Learned to Read*, 4.

37. Basker, introduction to *American Antislavery Writings*, xxvii–xxviii.

38. Turner, "Tampered Truths," 1; William L. Andrews, "An Introduction to the Slave Narrative," Documenting the American South, http://docsouth.unc.edu/neh/intro.html, accessed May 31, 2019.

39. John MacKay recently translated and published four of these accounts in his book *Four Russian Serf Narratives*, 5.

40. Belasco, *Stowe in Her Own Time*, xvii.

41. Belasco, 208.

42. Belasco, 208. Bailey edited the *National Era*, the antislavery journal that published Stowe's story "The Freeman's Dream: A Parable" (1850) and *Uncle Tom's Cabin* (1851–1852) in serialized form.

43. Gossett, *"Uncle Tom's Cabin" and American Culture*, 164; "Uncle Tom's Cabin," Harriet Beecher Stowe Center, https://www.harrietbeecherstowecenter.org/harriet-beecher -stowe/uncle-toms-cabin/, accessed July 12, 2015.

44. "Uncle Tom's Cabin," *Southern Literary Messenger*, December 1852, 12.

45. Review of *Uncle Tom's Cabin; or Life among the Lowly*, by Harriet Beecher Stowe, *Christian Inquirer*, April 10, 1852, 27.

46. MacKay, *True Songs of Freedom*, 26.

47. Nikolai Nekrasov to Ivan Turgenev, December 25, 1857, in *A Russian Discovery of America*, ed. A. N. Nikoliukin and trans. Cynthia Carlile and Julius Katzer (Moscow: Progress, 1986), cited in MacKay, *True Songs of Freedom*, 26–27. The letter was originally published in *Vestnik Evropy* 12 (1903): 637–639.

48. Nikolai Turgenev, "Russia and the Russians," in *The Liberty Bell: By Friends of Freedom* (Boston: National Anti-Slavery Bazaar, 1853), 210–225, cited in MacKay, *True Songs of Freedom*, 16.

49. Boyd, *Aspects of the Russian Novel*, 68–69.

50. Boyd, 68–69.

51. Funke, *Krepostnichestvo i volia*, 270.

52. Goldman, "American Slavery and Russian Serfdom," 24.

53. Hanne, *Power of the Story*, 51.

54. Dupuy, *Great Masters of Russian Literature*, 159.

55. "N. A. Nekrasov," *Vsemirnaia illiustratsiia*, no. 470 (December 1878): 27.

56. "N. A. Nekrasov," 27.

57. "N. A. Nekrasov," 27.

58. Birkenmayer, "Peasant Poems of Nikolaj Nekrasov," 167.

59. Golubev, *Nikolai Alekseevich Nekrasov*, 3; S. Sh., "N. A. Nekrasov," *Delo*, no. 1 (1878): 48; Mirsky, *History of Russian Literature*, 229.

60. Iakubovich, *Nikolai Nekrasov*, sec. 3.

61. A. F. (Aleksandr Fedorovich) Nekrasov, "Moi vospominaniia o N. A. Nekrasove i ego blizkikh," late nineteenth century, RGALI, f. 338, o. 1, n. 35, d. 92, ll. 3–4.

62. Nekrasov, l. 3.

63. Mirsky, *History of Russian Literature*, 229.

64. Golubev, *Nikolai Alekseevich Nekrasov*, 5.

65. S. Sh., "N. A. Nekrasov," 48.

66. Peppard, *Nikolai Nekrasov*, 27.

67. Peppard, 27–28.

68. Nekrasov became editor of the *Contemporary*, a journal founded by famed poet Aleksandr Pushkin, in 1847.

69. Peppard, *Nikolai Nekrasov*, 29–30.

70. Nekrasov, *Stikhotvoreniia*, 51.

71. Konstantin Dmitrievich Bal'mont, "Skvoz' stroi: Pamiati Nekrasova," *Novyi put'*, February 19, 1903, http://az.lib.ru/b/balxmont_k_d/text_1903_skvoz_stroy.shtml.

72. Nekrasov, "Zabytaia derevnia."

73. Nekrasov.

74. Nekrasov.

75. Nekrasov.

76. Kolchin, *Unfree Labor*, 59.

77. Kolchin, 59.

78. Roosevelt, *Russian Country Estate*, xii.

79. Birkenmayer, "N. A. Nekrasov," 189.

80. Nekrasov, "Na Volge."

81. Nekrasov.

82. Prokhorov, *Russian Folk Songs*, 105.

83. Nekrasov, "Na Volge."

84. Nekrasov. This poem also brings to mind Langston Hughes's "The Negro Speaks of Rivers" (1920).

85. V. Chuiko, "N. A. Nekrasov," *Pchela*, no. 2 (January 7, 1878).

86. S. Sh., 55–56.

87. S. Sh., 56.

88. S. Sh., 56.

89. I. Kubikov, "K 50-letiiu so dnia smerti," *Krasnaia niva*, no. 1 (January 1, 1928): 2.

90. "N. A. Nekrasov," *Vsemirnaia illiustratsiia*, no. 435 (April 30, 1877): 350.

91. "N. A. Nekrasov," *Vsemirnaia illiustratsiia*, no. 471 ([1878]): 46.

92. "N. A. Nekrasov," 46.

93. "N. A. Nekrasov," 46.

94. "N. A. Nekrasov," 46.

95. Basker, introduction to *American Antislavery Writings*, xxxv–xxxvi.

96. Lystar, "Perspectives on the Slave Family," 24.

97. William L. Andrews calls the slave narrative a "fiction of factual representation." Andrews, *To Tell a Free Story*, 20.

98. The real price of a commodity worth $1.00 in 1850 would be $33.20 in 2018. See Measuring Worth, http://www.measuringworth.com/calculators/uscompare/relativevalue.php; and Nichols, "Who Read the Slave Narratives?," 149–150.

99. Carey, "Arguing in Prose," 46.

100. The article first appeared in 1856 in the *National Anti-Slavery Standard*, quoted in Lystar, "Perspectives on the Slave Family," 22.

101. Review of "The Self Instructor, a Monthly Journal Devoted to Southern Education and to a Diffusion of Knowledge of the Resources and Power of the South, as Represented by the Negro, the Rail, and the Press," *New Englander* 12, no. 47 (August 1854): 480–482.

102. Review of "The Self Instructor," 480.

103. William L. Andrews, "Martha Griffith Browne," Documenting the American South, http://docsouth.unc.edu/neh/browne/bio.html, accessed June 1, 2019.

104. Browder, *Slippery Characters*, 20.

105. See Pryor, "Anomalous Person," 388; and Wiethoff, *Insolent Slave*, 69.

106. Lydia Maria Child, "How a Kentucky Girl Emancipated Her Slaves," *The Tribune*, reprinted in the *Independent* 14, no. 695 (March 27, 1862); Lystar, "Perspectives on the Slave Family," 107.

107. *Autobiography of a Female Slave*'s sales did not ultimately cover the cost of the enslaved African Americans' liberation, and Browne subsequently received funds from the American Anti-Slavery Society to ensure their freedom.

108. Child, "Kentucky Girl Emancipated Her Slaves."

109. Child.

110. Child.

111. Child.

112. Child.

113. According to an advertisement in the *Liberator* from 1858, readers could purchase *Autobiography of a Female Slave* for one dollar, one of the four highest-priced works on a list of twenty-five books, tracts, reports, and reviews. "Anti-Slavery Publications," *The Liberator* 28, no. 15 (April 9, 1858).

114. Lystar, "Perspectives on the Slave Family," 29.

115. Browne, *Autobiography of a Female Slave*, 86.

116. Browne, 9–10.

117. Browne, 397.

118. Browder, *Slippery Characters*, 31, 26.

119. Browder, 33.

120. Lystar, "Perspectives on the Slave Family," 101; Browder, *Slippery Characters*, 321; "Autobiography of a Female Slave: Redfield," *New York Evangelist* 27, no. 50 (December 11, 1856).

121. Lystar, "Perspectives on the Slave Family," 102–103.

122. Browne, *Autobiography of a Female Slave*, 194.

123. Fredrickson, *Black Image in the White Mind*, 49.

124. Browne, *Autobiography of a Female Slave*, 86.

125. Browne, 399.

126. Browne, 36, 38.

127. Browne, 327.

128. Browne, 13.

129. Browne, 102.

130. Browne, 303.

131. Stanton, *Leopard's Spots*, vii.

132. Smith, *How Race Is Made*, 41.

133. For recent discussions of race as a social construction, see Smith, *How Race Is Made*; Coates, Ferber, and Brunsma, *Matrix of Race*; and Ore, *Difference and Inequality*.

134. Browne, *Autobiography of a Female Slave*, 56.

135. Paul Finkelman contends that the "largest single body of proslavery literature is based on religious defenses of slavery." The most common argument was that Africans descended from Noah, whose grandson Canaan was relegated to the position of a servant, as were his subsequent generations. By contrast, abolitionists often referenced the theology of Christ from the New Testament in their criticisms of slavery's cruelty. See Finkelman, *Defending Slavery*, 26–27.

136. Review of *Autobiography of a Female Slave*, by Martha Griffith Browne, *National Era* 11, no. 545 (June 11, 1857).

137. Pisemskii, *Gor'kaia sud'bina*. Although Lev Tolstoi finished his play *The Power of Darkness* in 1886, it was banned from publication until 1902. See Freeborn, "Nineteenth Century," 274.

138. Moser, *Pisemsky*, 37; Steussy, "Bitter Fate of A. F. Pisemsky," 171, 177.

139. Moser, *Pisemsky*, 2–4; "Biografiia Pisemskogo Alekseia Feofilaktovicha: Rukopis' neustanovlennogo litsa," undated, RGALI, f. 375, o. 1, d. 22, l. 2.

140. B. N. Alzamov claimed that, in a student presentation of Nikolai Gogol's *The Marriage* in 1844, Pisemskii "interpreted the character [of Podkolesin] better than Shchep-

kin," the "great comic" who played the role in St. Petersburg's imperial theater at that time. "A. F. Pisemskii," *Vsemirnaia illiustratsiia*, no. 630 (February 7, 1881): 110; Moser, *Pisemsky*, 5.

141. "A. F. Pisemskii," *Vsemirnaia illiustratsiia*, 110.

142. Moser, *Pisemsky*, 95–96.

143. S. Dudyshkin, "Dve novye narodnye dramy," *Otechestvennye zapiski*, no. 1 (1860): 37.

144. Unnamed author, "Teatral'naia khronika," *Otechestvennye zapiski*, nos. 11–12 (1863): 77.

145. The female protagonist's name, Lizaveta, recalls that of the heroine in Nikolai Karamzin's short story "Poor Liza" (1792), a peasant girl who commits suicide after sleeping with her owner. Ananii Iakovlev's character reminds the reader of another jilted husband, Alexei Karenin, whose rigid morality leads him to punish his wife, Anna, by refusing to let her leave him, in Tolstoi's novel *Anna Karenina* (1877).

146. Tolstoi, *Plays*, 2:ix.

147. Pisemskii, *Gor'kaia sud'bina*, act 1, scene 4.

148. Pisemskii, act 2, scene 2.

149. Pisemskii, act 4, scene 8.

150. Aleksei Pisemskii to Ivan Vasil'evich Pavlov, 1860, RGALI, f. 375, o. 1, d. 10, l. 1.

151. Unnamed author, "Teatral'naia khronika," 77.

152. Unnamed author, "Teatral'naia khronika," 77.

153. Avdeev, Blum, and Troitskaia, "Peasant Marriage," 722; Worobec, *Peasant Russia*, 13.

154. Pisemskii, *Gor'kaia sud'bina*, act 3, scene 7; and act 2, scene 2.

155. Women from the noble and merchant estates also experienced forced marriages. Worobec, *Peasant Russia*, 135; Bushnell, "Serf Marriage," 419.

156. Worobec, *Peasant Russia*, 200–205. Worobec describes how, in the post-emancipation period, "it was more usual for a community to punish an adulterous wife than an adulterous husband" (203).

157. Pisemskii, *Gor'kaia sud'bina*, act 1, scene 4.

158. Pisemskii, act 1, scene 4; Rosslyn and Tosi, *Women in Nineteenth-Century Russia*, 229.

159. Pisemskii, *Gor'kaia sud'bina*, act 2, scene 3.

160. Pisemskii, act 1, scene 4.

161. Pisemskii, act 3, scene 6.

162. Pisemskii, act 2, scene 4.

163. Konstantin Aksakov, "O drame g. Pisemskogo 'Gor'kaia sud'bina,'" *Russkaia beseda*, no. 19 (1860): 133.

164. Aksakov, 134.

165. Mikhail Saltykov-Shchedrin, "Peterburgskie teatry: Gor'kaia sud'bina," *Sovremennik* 99, no. 12, sec. 2 (1863): 95.

166. Saltykov-Shchedrin, 95.

167. Pisemskii, *Gor'kaia sud'bina*, act 2, scene 2.

168. Pisemskii, act 2, scene 1.

169. Pisemskii, act 2, scene 4.

170. Pisemskii, act 2, scene 4.

171. Saltykov-Shchedrin, "Peterburgskie teatry," 101.

172. The document went into effect on January 1, 1863.

173. President Abraham Lincoln, Emancipation Proclamation, January 1, 1863, transcript, National Archives, https://www.archives.gov/exhibits/featured-documents/emancipation -proclamation/transcript.html, accessed May 2, 2019.

174. Lincoln, Emancipation Proclamation.

175. Congress passed the act on July 6, 1861, formally permitting the army's practice of protecting escaped enslaved people. See Wartman, "Contraband, Runaways, Freemen," 122.

176. "Kind Words from [Oliver Wendell] Holmes [Sr.]," *New York Herald*, March 6, 1888, folder 280, MS Am 800.23, Houghton Library, Harvard University.

177. Elbert, *Alcott on Race, Sex, and Slavery*, x.

178. Reverend Edward S. Towne, "A Concord Hillside," unknown newspaper clipping, late nineteenth century, folder 280, MS Am 800.23, Houghton Library, Harvard University.

179. "Letters to the Author of Little Women," unknown newspaper clipping, late nineteenth century, folder 281, MS Am 800.23, Houghton Library, Harvard University.

180. From a Special Correspondent, "Letter from Cultured Concord," unknown newspaper clipping, December 12, 1887, folder 280, MS Am 800.23, Houghton Library, Harvard University.

181. Elbert, *Alcott on Race, Sex, and Slavery*, xxi, xxiv.

182. Alcott was also influenced by Stowe's *Uncle Tom's Cabin*, putting it on her "List of Books I Like" in a journal entry from 1852. Alcott, "Sketch of Childhood, by Herself," in Cheney, *Life of Louisa May Alcott*, 19, 54; Stern, *Louisa May Alcott*, 91, 97.

183. One of Alcott's favorite proverbs was an antiserfdom Russian peasant saying collected by the nineteenth-century lexicographer Vladimir Dal': "The bird is well enough in a golden cage, but he is better on a green branch." MS Am 1817.35, Houghton Library, Harvard University.

184. Elbert, *Alcott on Race, Sex and Slavery*, xxxvii; Alcott, "M.L.," 3.

185. Elbert, *Alcott on Race, Sex, and Slavery*, xxxix; Alcott, "M.L.," 26.

186. Alcott, "M.L.," 4–7.

187. Alcott, 18.

188. Alcott, 18.

189. Alcott, 19.

190. Stern, *Louisa May Alcott*, 93; Stern, "Louisa M. Alcott in Periodicals," 378.

191. Louisa May Alcott's Diary, January 1863, MS Am 1130.13, Houghton Library, Harvard University.

192. Louisa May Alcott's Diary, Monday [January] 4, 1863, MS Am 1130.13, Houghton Library, Harvard University.

193. Phelps, *Our Famous Women*, 41.

194. Louisa May Alcott, Journal and Account Book, 1850–1885, MS Am 1130.13, Houghton Library, Harvard University. "Hospital Sketches" was published in the *Commonwealth* 1, no. 38 (May 22, 1863); no. 39 (May 29, 1863); no. 41 (June 12, 1863); and no. 43 (June 16, 1863). See Stern, *Louisa May Alcott*, 128–130, 335.

195. Louisa May Alcott's notes on herself, titled "Odds and Ends," MS Am 1817, Houghton Library, Harvard University.

196. "Women of History: Louisa May Alcott, 1832–1888," *Daily News*, December 3, 1912, folder 283, MS Am 800.23, Houghton Library, Harvard University.

197. Diary of Abigail May Alcott, August 23, 1863, box 4, MS Am 1817, Houghton Library, Harvard University.

198. "Miss Louisa May Alcott," *Hearth and Home* 8, no. 3 (January 16, 1875): 42; F.B.S., "Miss Alcott: The Friend of Little Women and Little Men," clipped article from *St. Nicholas Magazine*, 1877, 131, folder 283, MS Am 800.23, Houghton Library, Harvard University.

199. "Miss Louisa May Alcott," *Hearth and Home*, 42.

200. For an analysis of sentimental representations of the white soldier, see Fahs, *Imagined Civil War*, chap. 3, "The Sentimental Soldier."

201. Elbert, *Alcott on Race, Sex, and Slavery*, xxxi.

202. The story was first published in the *Atlantic Monthly* in November 1863.

203. Alcott earned $50 for the publication of "My Contraband." Alcott, Journal and Account Book.

204. Alcott, "My Contraband," 70.

205. Alcott, 73.

206. Alcott, 72.

207. Alcott, 83.

208. Alcott, 83.

209. Alcott, 79.

Chapter Two

1. I believe this rare serf narrative is largely unknown to Russian and Western scholars. Klimenov, *Prazdnichnye vospominaniia dlia krest'ian*, 5.

2. Klimenov, 7.

3. Klimenov, 7.

4. Burbank, *Russian Peasants Go to Court*, 3.

5. Burbank, 3.

6. Burbank, 3; Dennison, *Institutional Framework of Russian Serfdom*, 6–7.

7. Moon, *Russian Peasantry*, 343; Kingston-Mann and Mixter, *Peasant Economy, Culture, and Politics*, 98–99.

8. Burbank, *Russian Peasants Go to Court*, 3, 4.

9. Moon contends that abolition "left largely unchanged and unchallenged the rural economy and the peasants' basic units of social organisation, households and communes." Moon, *Russian Peasantry*, 343.

10. Fedor Pavlovich Elenev, "Pervye shagi osvobozhdeniia pomeshchich'ikh krest'ian v Rossii," *Russkii arkhiv* 7 (March 1886): 354.

11. Gorshkov, *Peasants in Russia*, 130.

12. Nikitenko, *Diary of a Russian Censor*, 361.

13. Klimenov, *Prazdnichnye vospominaniia dlia krest'ian*, 4.

14. Nikitenko, *Diary of a Russian Censor*, 219.

15. Ascher, *Revolution of 1905*, 28.

16. Ascher, 28.

17. Mazour, "Economic Decline of Landlordism," 156.

18. Kantrowitz, *More than Freedom*, 313.

19. Manning, *Troubled Refuge*, 263.

20. Kennedy-Nolle, *Writing Reconstruction*, 81, 241.

21. Fitzgerald, *Splendid Failure*, 36.

22. "What Causes Anarchy?," *Harper's Weekly*, September 19, 1868, 594.

23. "What Causes Anarchy?," 594.

24. Native Americans were excluded from the amendment's guarantee of citizenship to those born in the United States. In 1924, Congress offered citizenship to Native Americans through the Indian Citizenship Act. Zuckert, "Completing the Constitution," 69–70.

25. Such cases include the *Slaughter-House Cases* (1873), *United States v. Cruikshank* (1876), the *Civil Rights Cases* (1883), and *Plessy v. Ferguson* (1896).

26. Foner, *Forever Free*, 83.

27. Foner, 82; Ruef, "Demise of an Organizational Form," 1369–1370.

28. Lowery, *Life on the Old Plantation*, 125.

29. Lowery, 125.

30. Lowery, 161.

31. Foner, *Freedom's Lawmakers*.

32. Foner, *Short History of Reconstruction*, xv.

33. Bruce, *New Man*, 119. For an analysis of nineteenth-century Irish–African American relations, see Ignatiev, *How the Irish Became White*.

34. Roark, *Masters without Slaves*, 200.

35. Rosen, *Terror in the Heart of Freedom*, 187.

36. Wormser, *Rise and Fall of Jim Crow*, 25–26.

37. White, *Republic for Which It Stands*, 336.

38. Hahn, *Nation without Borders*, 376.

39. Mizruchi, *Rise of Multicultural America*, 2, 3.

40. Walter Hines Page, "Literature in the South," *Evening Post*, reprinted in the *Critic*, June 25, 1887, 182.

41. Page, 182.

42. Prince, *Stories of the South*, 8.

43. Prince, 8.

44. Nolan, "Anatomy of the Myth," 12.

45. McWhirter, "Introduction: Rethinking Southern Studies," 1.

46. Laura F. Edwards, "Southern History as U.S. History," *Journal of Southern History* 75, no. 3 (2009): 535, cited in Prince, *Stories of the South*, 7. See also Nolan, "Anatomy of a Myth," 12.

47. Vrangel', *Vospominaniia*. Vrangel''s memoir traces Russia's development during the post-emancipation era and recalls his life growing up on a rural estate. Vrangel''s son, Petr Vrangel', served as a commanding officer of the White Guards during Russia's civil war (1918–1921). Many members of Vrangel''s family were killed during the war, but others escaped by fleeing the country.

48. Vrangel', *Vospominaniia*.

49. Vrangel'.

50. Vrangel'.

51. Vrangel'.

52. Vrangel'.

53. Vrangel'.

54. Vrangel'.

55. Vrangel'.

56. Kropotkin, *Memoirs of a Revolutionist*, 158.

57. Vrangel', *Vospominaniia*.

58. Late nineteenth-century public library statistics show that Salias was the most widely read writer in the nation, a man whose works surpassed in popularity those of other favored writers including Danilevskii and Solov'ev. See Beliaev, "Liubimets chitaiushchei Rossii." For references to the aforementioned authors in overviews of Russian literature, see Hapgood, *Survey of Russian Literature*; Terras, *Handbook of Russian Literature*; Mirsky, *History of Russian Literature*; and, for fuller treatment, Ungurianu, *Plotting History*.

59. Bartlett, *Tolstoy*, 3.

60. Bartlett, 3.

61. Knowles, "Tolstoy's Literary Reputation," 628.

62. These authors were likely influenced by writers of the Romantic tradition, including Sir Walter Scott, Alexandre Dumas, and Victor Hugo. Russian readers also became increasingly interested in their national history thanks to the appearance of Nikolai Karamzin's groundbreaking twelve-volume set, *Istoriia gosudarstva rossiiskogo* (History of the Russian State) (1818–1829). See Ungurianu, *Plotting History*, 14. For an analysis of literature's influence in nineteenth-century Russia, see Reitblat, *Ot Bovy k Bal'montu*.

63. Ungurianu, *Plotting History*, 5.

64. Maiorova, *From the Shadow of Empire*, 3.

65. Maiorova, 8.

66. Maiorova, 8.

67. Engelstein, *Slavophile Empire*, 11.

68. Knight, *Empire on Display*, iii, 25; Kalashnikova, "Russia's First Ethnographic Exhibition," 11.

69. While striving to show off the empire's diversity, exhibition organizers simultaneously struggled to emphasize their view that the Russian people remained "the undisputed master ethnicity of the Empire." Thirty years later, when Tsar Alexander III founded the Russian Ethnographic Museum in 1895, the institution's curator grappled with the same problem of embracing diversity while displaying Russian ethnic dominance. Knight, *Empire on Display*, 20; "Collections," Russian Ethnographic Museum, http://eng.ethnomuseum.ru/node/38, accessed 2015 (link now inactive).

70. Ungurianu, *Plotting History*, 136.

71. Ungurianu, 126.

72. Kokorev, "Salias-de-Tournemir."

73. Kennedy, *Swallow Barn*.

74. Rose, "Image of the Negro," 218–219.

75. For more information about antebellum plantation literature, see Taylor, *Cavalier and Yankee*, 148–150.

76. Stampp, "Rebels and Sambos," 372.

77. Stampp, 374.

78. McClurg was a bookseller who resided in Chicago, where the *Dial* was headquartered.

79. Alexander McClurg, "Old-Time Plantation Life," *Dial* 8 (June 1892): 46.

80. McClurg, 46.

81. McClurg, 46.

82. Thomas Nelson Page, "Recollections and Reflections," 3, box 17, Thomas Nelson Page Papers, 1739–1927, and undated bulk, 1885–1920, David M. Rubenstein Rare Book and Manuscript Library, Duke University; C. W. Coleman Jr., "The Homes of Some Southern Authors, IV, V, VI," *Chautauquan*, March 1888, 8.

83. Page, "Recollections and Reflections," 14.

84. Rosewell was five years younger than Thomas. Rosewell Page, "When I Was a Little Boy," ed. Harriet Holman (Field Research Projects, Coconut Grove, FL, 1970), 1, 24, 25, box 14, Page Papers.

85. Page, "Old-Time Negro," 307.

86. Page, 313, 314.

87. McElya, *Clinging to Mammy*, 44–45.

88. "Two Southern Humorists: Their Appearance at the Author's Readings in New York," *Macon Telegraph*, December 29, 1887, 4.

89. "Two Southern Humorists," 4.

90. "The Plantation Edition of Thomas Nelson Page," *Book Buyer*, approximately 1908, 210, box 17, Page Papers.

91. Harris, *Joel Chandler Harris*, 4, 7.

92. Julia Collier Harris was Joel Chandler Harris's daughter-in-law. Harris, 3.

93. Harris, 8.

94. Joel Chandler Harris, "An Accidental Author," *Lippincott's Monthly Magazine*, April 1886, 37.

95. Harris, 37.

96. President Theodore Roosevelt was a great admirer of Harris, inviting him to the White House in the winter of 1902. "Joel Chandler Harris," *Greater Pittsburg Magazine*, undated, 2, Series 4: Printed Materials about Harris, folder 3, Joel Chandler Harris Papers, Stuart A. Rose Manuscript, Archives, and Rare Book Library, Emory University; "'Uncle' George Terrell," photograph, 1880s, Atlanta Rail Corridor Archive, http://atlrailcorridorar chive.org/items/show/272, accessed December 8, 2015.

97. R. Bruce Bickley, "Joel Chandler Harris (1845–1908)," *New Georgia Encyclopedia*, July 18, 2002, http://www.georgiaencyclopedia.org/articles/arts-culture/joel-chandler-harris -1845-1908.

98. Harris, *Uncle Remus*.

99. Harris attributed his good treatment in part to his friend "Mink," a slave fugitive who hid in the woods nearby and who encouraged the plantation's other enslaved people to be kind to him. Harris, *On the Plantation*, 33.

100. Harris, 230.

101. Thomas Nelson Page to Joel Chandler Harris, December 28, 1883, Page–Harris Correspondence, Harris Papers; Thomas Nelson Page, "Literature in the South since the War," *Lippincott's Monthly Magazine*, December 1891, 740, American Periodicals, ProQuest.

102. Page, "Literature in the South," 740.

103. Joel Chandler Harris to Ambrose Bierce, July 16, 1896, Atlanta, GA, Bierce-Harris Correspondence, Harris Papers.

104. Andrew Carnegie to Joel Chandler Harris, March 19, 1907, Carnegie-Harris Correspondence, Harris Papers.

105. Kokorev, "Salias-de-Tournemir."

106. Beliaev, *Evgenii Salias*. For an analysis of Tur's writing, see Gheith, *Finding the Middle Ground*, 35.

107. Beliaev, *Evgenii Salias*.

108. Beliaev.

109. Beliaev. *Peterburgskoe deistvo* was published in 1880, while *Arakcheevskii synok* appeared in 1888.

110. Nikolaev, *Russkie pisateli*, tom 2 (G–K), 80, 741.

111. Nikolaev, tom 4 (M–P), 441.

112. Nikolaev, 441; "Grigorii Petrovich Danilevskii (nekrolog)," *Istoricheskii vestnik* 43, no. 1 (1891): 209; Vasil'eva, *Belletristika Vs. S. Solov'eva*, 15.

113. Danilevskii's *Mirovich* was published in 1879, and *Kniazhna Tarakanova* appeared in 1883. Solov'ev's chronicles appeared between 1881 and 1886. "Grigorii Petrovich Danilevskii (6 dekabria 1890 g.)," *Niva*, no. 50 (December 15, 1890): 1279.

114. Nikolaev, *Russkie pisateli*, tom 5 (P–M), 441; Gavrilova, "K 150-letiiu so dnia rozhdeniia Evgeniia Opochinina."

115. Nikolaev, *Russkie pisateli*, tom 5 (P–M), 441–442.

116. Vasil'eva, *Belletristika Vs. S. Solov'eva*, 17.

117. Ungurianu, *Plotting History*, 126.

118. Ungurianu, 126.

119. See S. F. Gorianskaia, "Pervye besplatnye gorodskie chital'ni v St. Peterburge (Organizatsiia ikh i itogi deiatel'nosti za 1888 god)."

120. Mankov, "Le Comte de Salhias-Tournemire"; Beliaev, *Evgenii Salias*.

121. Beliaev, *Evgenii Salias*.

122. Beliaev; Ungurianu, *Plotting History*, 126.

123. Beliaev, *Evgenii Salias*; Ungurianu, *Plotting History*, 126.

124. Izmailov, *Sviatochnye rasskazy*.

125. P. P. Sokal'skii, "Mirovich," *Russkaia mysl'*, no. 11 (June 10, 1880), http://az.lib.ru/s/sokalxskij_p_p/text_1880_mirovich_oldorfo.shtml.

126. A. I. Vvedenskii, "'Graf' Evgenii Andreevich Salias," *Istoricheskii vestnik*, no. 8 (1890): 393.

127. Solov'ev, *Staryi dom*.

128. Solov'ev.

129. Solov'ev.

130. Solov'ev.

131. Danilevskii, *Kniazhna Tarakanova*.

132. Danilevskii.

133. Page, "Marse Chan," 1.

134. Page, 6.

135. Page, 34.

136. Page, 5.

137. Page, 10.

138. Page, 109.

139. Excerpts of reviews of *In Ole Virginia: Marse Chan, and Other Stories*, collected by Charles Scribner's Sons, 1887, in "Miscellaneous Printed Material; Circulars, etc.," box 17, Page Papers.

140. Harris, "Free Joe."

141. Harris, 2.

142. Harris, 1.

143. Harris, 8.

144. Theodore Roosevelt to Joel Chandler Harris, October 12, 1901, Washington, DC, Roosevelt-Harris Correspondence, Harris Papers.

145. Harris, "Free Joe," 8.

146. Roosevelt to Harris, October 12, 1901.

147. Page, "Marse Chan," 141, 144.

148. Page, 152.

149. Page, 153.

150. Page, 158.

151. Page, 161.

152. Opochinin, "Posledniaia 'dusha,'" 2–10.

153. Opochinin, 2–10.

154. Opochinin, 2–10.

155. Opochinin, 2–10.

156. Opochinin, 2–10.

157. Opochinin, 2–10.

158. Opochinin, 2–10.

159. Opochinin, 2–10.

160. Opochinin, 2–10.

161. David Blight posits that Northern and Southern writers alike flooded national periodicals with "sentimental reconciliationist literature," producing a new genre of American literature and altering the nation's collective memory of the Civil War era. See Blight, *Race and Reunion*, 217.

162. Opochinin, "Posledniaia 'dusha,'" 2–10.

163. Page, "Unc' Edinburg's Drowndin,'" 39.

164. Page, 41.

165. Page, 41.

166. In Europe's royal courts of the sixteenth, seventeenth, and eighteenth centuries, the presence of dwarf servants or enslaved people was common. These men and women were a source of entertainment for members of the nobility. See Ravenscroft, "Invisible Friends," 32–34.

167. Solov'ev, *Staryi dom*.

168. Solov'ev.

169. Solov'ev.

170. Solov'ev.

171. Solov'ev.

172. Salias, *Arakcheevskii synok.*

173. Salias.

174. Salias.

175. Salias.

176. Harris, *Balaam and His Master.*

177. Harris, 170, 172.

178. Harris, 172.

179. Harris, 172, 174.

180. Harris, 173, 174.

181. Harris, 175.

182. Harris, 173.

Chapter Three

1. The amount of leisure time in the average five- and six-day workweeks grew from 2.3 hours per day in 1850 to 3.1 hours per day in 1870. Kaplan, *Leisure Time in America*, 37–40.

2. Britain's *Illustrated London News*, France's *L'Illustration*, and Germany's *Leipziger illustrierte Zeitung* were the first three European magazines to use both pictures and text. David H. Tucker, George Unwin, and Philip Soundy Unwin, "History of Publishing," in *Encyclopaedia Britannica*, https://www.britannica.com/topic/publishing/Magazine-publishing, accessed January 4, 2017.

3. Jaque, "The Fireside: About Reading Books," *Cultivator and Country Gentleman*, September 29, 1892, 736.

4. Boris Sadovskii, "Vstrecha s Repinym, vospominaniia," undated (before 1952), RGALI, f. 842, o. 1, d. 63, l. 1.

5. Brown, *Beyond the Lines*, 48. Nationwide, white-collar workers made approximately between $1,000.00 and $5,500.00 in annual income in 1860, which resulted in daily earnings of $1.00 to $15.00 per day. Men and women working in manufacturing or as domestic laborers made as little as $0.04 per day. Data and estimates from a research project by Peter H. Lindert and Jeffrey G. Williamson, http://gpih.ucdavis.edu/tables.htm, accessed January 4, 2017.

6. Brown, *Beyond the Lines*, 119.

7. Culp, *Twentieth Century Negro Literature*, 347–348.

8. Yukiko, "Russian Illustrated Journals," 164–165.

9. The average skilled laborer in St. Petersburg made approximately nine rubles per week in the 1890s. Ekaterina Khaustova, "Pre-revolution Living Standards: Russia, 1888–1917" (paper prepared for the 2013 Annual Conference of the Economic History Society), http://www.ehs.org.uk/dotAsset/62d8a367-8beb-4dd0-b21f-d98b425c6ef3.pdf, accessed January 4, 2017.

10. Anikst, Baburina, and Chernevich, *Russian Graphic Design*, 19–20.

11. William Bissing, "Rotary Printing Presses," *New England Printing Trades Journal*, October 1, 1901, 1.

12. Moran, *Printing Presses*, 207; Tucker, *Illustration of the Master*, 3.

13. "Fate of the Etching: Peril of Over-Production; New York Sun," *Current Literature* 16, no. 1 (1894): 47.

14. "Reading Trash," *Littell's Living Age* 116 (1872): 62.

15. Le Beau, "'Colored Engravings for the People,'" 131; Selcer, *Civil War America*, 338.

16. Le Beau, "Currier and Ives's America," 74.

17. Le Beau, 71.

18. Brown, *Beyond the Lines*, 68.

19. Brown, 68.

20. For example, Brown argues in his study of illustrations of African Americans in periodicals that "the illustrated press did not take the single-minded racist course suggested in most scholarship." Brown, 113.

21. Shafer contends that there are ten central attributes of nationalism, including the two listed in the text discussion. Shafer, *Faces of Nationalism*, 18–19.

22. During the imperial era, Dominic Lieven argues, members of the Russian ruling elite "drew on European models for everything from literary culture to fashionable dress," making them "more 'European' than many of their peers in western and central Europe." Lieven, "Elites," 237.

23. *Vsemirnaia illiustratsiia*, no. 565 (October 27, 1879): 358–360.

24. Waud, a British immigrant, served as an artist-correspondent with the Union army for the *New York Illustrated News*. Alfred R. Waud, "Scenes on a Cotton Plantation," *Harper's Weekly*, February 2, 1867, 72–73.

25. A. Muratov, "Staryi barin," *Niva*, no. 36 (1889): 892.

26. Descriptive text for the illustration "Staryi barin," *Niva*, no. 36 (1889): 906.

27. "V svoikh vladeniiakh," *Ogonek*, no. 18 (1882): 356–357.

28. Philip Poindexter, "An Easter Visit to Mammy," *Frank Leslie's Weekly*, March 30, 1893, 205.

29. Koonen, *Stranitsy zhizni*.

30. Drawing no. 8, untitled, unknown publication, 1874, box 1, folder 7, "Children" (pp. 1–90), PR 17, Leslie Dorsey Collection, New-York Historical Society.

31. Howard Helmick, "Christmas in the South: Old Mammy's Christmas Cake," *Frank Leslie's Weekly*, December 14, 1893, 11.

32. Poindexter, "Easter Visit to Mammy," 205.

33. U.S. Department of Commerce, *Historical Statistics*, Series J 1–12, "Manufactures—General Statistics for All Manufacturing Industries: 1849 to 1939," 179.

34. Whereas approximately 28 percent of Americans lived in cities in 1880, 51 percent of Americans lived in urban areas by 1920. U.S. Department of Commerce, *Historical Statistics*, Series B 145–159, "Population—Urban Size-Groups and Rural Territory: 1790 to 1940," 29.

35. U.S. Department of Commerce, 29.

36. B. N. Mironov, *Sotsial'naia istoriia Rossii perioda imperii (XVIII–nachalo XX v.)*, 2 vols. (St. Petersburg, 1999), cited in Eltis, *Coerced and Free Migration*, 344.

37. The majority of peasant migrants were men, a phenomenon that initially created a gender imbalance in cities like St. Petersburg at the turn of the twentieth century. West, *I Shop in Moscow*, 95.

38. Johnson, "Peasant Migration," 652.

39. Gregory, *Before Command*, 41–42; Chernina, Dower, and Markevich, "Property Rights and Internal Migration," 3.

40. Johnson, "Peasant Migration," 654.

41. Moon, "Peasant Migration," 346; Moon, "Estimating the Peasant Population," 151.

42. U.S. Department of Commerce, *Historical Statistics*, Series B 13–23, "Population, Decennial Summary—Sex, Urban-Rural Residence, and Race: 1790 to 1940," 25; Painter, *Creating Black Americans*, 174.

43. Work, *Negro Year Book*; U.S. Department of Commerce, *Historical Statistics*, Series B 13–23, "Population, Decennial Summary—Sex, Urban-Rural Residence, and Race: 1790 to 1940," 25; Painter, *Creating Black Americans*, 174.

44. Weissman, "Rural Crime in Tsarist Russia," 229.

45. Neuberger, "Stories of the Street," 177.

46. Neuberger, *Hooliganism*, 113.

47. Weissman, "Rural Crime in Tsarist Russia," 230.

48. Alaniz, *Komiks*, 30.

49. "Zlobodnevnye terminy," *Strekoza*, no. 42 (October 16, 1905): 8–9.

50. "Sposoby lecheniia," *Strekoza*, no. 15 (April 15, 1890): 5.

51. "Sravitel'no," *Strekoza*, no. 21 (May 21, 1895): 6.

52. Henze, *Disease, Health Care and Government*, 4, 11.

53. Frieden, *Russian Physicians*, 284.

54. "Antikholernye mery," *Strekoza*, no. 39 (September 25, 1905): 8–9.

55. "Antikholernye mery," 8.

56. "Antikholernye mery," 9.

57. "Antikholernye mery," 9.

58. "It's a Sure Thing," Currier and Ives, 1884, flat file D, folder "Caricatures 1884," PR10-1, Caricature and Cartoon Collection, New-York Historical Society.

59. "All Broke Up," Currier and Ives, 1884, flat file D, folder "Caricatures 1884," PR10-1, Caricature and Cartoon Collection, New-York Historical Society.

60. William McAdoo, "Experiences of a Police Commissioner," *Harper's Weekly*, May 26, 1906, 741.

61. Thomas Nelson Page, "The Great American Question: The Special Plea of a Southerner," *McClure's Magazine* 28, no. 5 (March 1907): 565, American Periodicals, ProQuest.

62. "De Lime Kiln Club: A Temperance Racket," Currier and Ives, 1883, Subject Files, New-York Historical Society.

63. Frances Kellor, "The Criminal Negro: Childhood Influences," *Arena* 26, no. 3 (September 1901): 304, American Periodicals, ProQuest; "Insanity in the American Negro," *Phrenological Journal and Science of Health*, no. 2 (February 1892): 89, American Periodicals, ProQuest.

64. "Insanity in the American Negro," *Phrenological Journal and Science of Health*, 89.

65. "The Darktown Fire Brigade—Slightly Demoralized," Currier and Ives, 1889, Caricature and Cartoon Collection, New-York Historical Society.

66. "The Darktown Fire Brigade—Under Full Steam," Currier and Ives, 1887, Gail and Stephen Rudin Slavery Collection, 1728–1973, Cornell University Library Digital Collections, https://digital.library.cornell.edu/catalog/ss:21813357.

67. "A Darktown Law Suit—Part Second," Currier and Ives, 1887, Caricature and Cartoon Collection, New-York Historical Society.

68. For fuller treatment of this topic, see Aguilar, "Construction of National Identity."

69. Mogilner, "Beyond, against, and with Ethnography," 82.

70. By comparison, in the late nineteenth-century United States, there were two competing systems of racial classification. George Fredrickson posits that the first was "based primarily on colour—white over black, brown and yellow"; the second "associated the cultural characteristics of certain European nationalities with their genetic makeup and also at times found a physical correlative in non-chromatic features like head shape," and it "won less popular adherence and had a more limited impact." These ideas about race shaped both domestic legislation and immigration laws. Fredrickson argues that "more than the nations of Europe, [America] has made physical race, especially as represented by differences in skin colour, a determinant of civic and social status." Fredrickson, "Race and Citizenship," 1, 3.

71. Old Believers, a religious sect of Orthodox Russians, bestowed the name *devitsy-starchiki* on these women. "Russkie tipy: Zhenshchina Saratovskoi gubernii," *Niva*, no. 46 (November 13, 1878): 848–851.

72. Farnsworth, *Russian Peasant Women*, 35.

73. Farnsworth, 40–43.

74. "Pskovitianki," *Niva*, no. 16 (April 15, 1874): 250–252.

75. "Gadan'e na suzhenogo," *Ogonek*, no. 52 (1882): 1037; M. Dal'kevich, "Sviatki v derevne," *Vsemirnaia illiustratsiia*, no. 625 (January 1, 1881): 12; "Russkaia maslenitsa—Maslenitsa obriady v XVII veke," *Vsemirnaia illiustratsiia*, no. 1358 (February 4, 1895): 1.

76. Brooks, "Russian Nation Imagined," 550.

77. Brooks, 55.

78. "Narody Rossii—Tatary," *Niva*, no. 22 (May 27, 1874): 347–348. The illustration, by Aleksandr de Bar', is titled "Tatarskaia arba" (Tatar Cart).

79. "Narody Rossii—Tatary," 347–348.

80. "Narody Rossii—Tatary," 347–348.

81. Allen, Ware, and Garrison, *Slave Songs*, iii.

82. Allen, Ware, and Garrison, iii.

83. Newman, *Go Down, Moses*, 26.

84. Newman, 26.

85. *Scribner's Monthly* was an illustrated periodical published monthly from 1870 to 1881. Afterward, it became known as *Century Magazine*.

86. "Terpsichore in the Flat Creek Quarters," *Scribner's Monthly*, no. 21 (1881): 488.

87. Richard B. Kimball, "Story of an Old Traveler," *Frank Leslie's Illustrated Newspaper*, June 7, 1873, 202.

88. "In Ole Virginny," *Harper's Weekly*, 1876, box 1, folder 8, "Children," PR 17, Leslie Dorsey Collection, New-York Historical Society.

89. "Market-Day in a Southern City," *Harper's Weekly*, May 5, 1883, 277–278.

90. "Opytnaia niania," *Strekoza*, no. 22 (May 21, 1895): 1.

91. "Poniala," *Strekoza*, no. 48 (December 1, 1885): 8.

92. "Stumped," *Harper's Weekly*, June 25, 1887, 463.

93. "Putting It Clearly," *Daily Courier* (Evansville, IN), 1914, http://www.ebay.com/itm/Newspaper-Cartoon-Darktown-Rastus-Racist-Colored-Black-Americana-Comic-4-1914-/150833676315, accessed February 3, 2017.

94. Untitled, undated illustration (after 1861), Subject Files, New-York Historical Society.

95. Culbertson, "Illustrated Essay," 277–278.

96. Culbertson, 279.

97. Thomas Nast, "The Union as It Was / The Lost Cause, Worse than Slavery," *Harper's Weekly* 18 (October 24, 1874): 878, New-York Historical Society.

98. Thomas Nast, "Is *This* a Republican Form of Government? Is *This* Protecting Life, Liberty, or Property? Is *This* the Equal Protection of the Laws?," *Harper's Weekly*, September 2, 1876, 712, Library of Congress, http://loc.gov/pictures/item/96509623/, accessed May 2, 2019.

99. "Oblomki prezhnego velichiia: Matushka barynia," *Vsemirnaia illiustratsiia*, no. 557 (September 1, 1879): 201.

100. N. Karazin, "Ostatki proshlogo velichiia," *Ogonek*, no. 44 (1882): 853.

101. The literature of Alcott and Pisemskii is discussed in chapter 1; Noble's painting is discussed in chapter 4.

102. Cruz and Berson, "American Melting Pot?," 81.

103. Roosevelt, *Russian Country Estate*, 225–226; Kolchin, *Unfree Labor*, 112.

104. K. A. Trutovskii, "Sblizhenie soslovii," *Vsemirnaia illiustratsiia*, no. 435 (April 30, 1877): 356.

105. "Emancipated Slaves: White and Colored," *Harper's Weekly*, January 30, 1864, 69, New-York Historical Society.

106. Willis and Krauthamer, *Envisioning Emancipation*, 49.

107. Wallenstein, "Reconstruction, Segregation, and Miscegenation," 57.

108. Wells, *Southern Lynch Law*.

109. "Not Particular," unknown origin, turn of the twentieth century, Jim Crow Museum of Racist Memorabilia, Ferris State University, https://ferris.edu/HTMLS/news/jimcrow /mammies/more/mammy-image-gallery-02.htm, accessed May 3, 2019.

110. For example, see "Electioneering in the South," *Harper's Weekly*, July 25, 1868, and "The Operations of the Registration Laws and Negro Suffrage in the South," *Frank Leslie's Illustrated Newspaper*, November 30, 1867, cited in Brown, *Beyond the Lines*, 118, 120–121.

111. Brown, *Beyond the Lines*, 122.

112. Culp, *Twentieth Century Negro Literature*, 464.

113. Culp, 464.

114. Thornbrough, "American Negro Newspapers," 475.

115. Dahn and Sweeney, "History of the *Colored American Magazine*."

116. Williams, "Cultivating Black Visuality," 124.

117. See the front page of the *Indianapolis Freeman*, August 30, 1890; September 6, 1890; November 8, 1890; November 15, 1890; December 20, 1890; December 27, 1890; January 3, 1891; March 21, 1891; and April 4, 1891.

118. *Colored American Magazine*, October 1900, 269, 284, 299.

119. *Colored American Magazine*, October 1900, 284.

120. *Colored American Magazine*, February 1909, 75–80.

121. *Indianapolis Freeman*, September 6, 1890, 5.

122. Williams, "Cultivating Black Visuality," 124.

123. Brooks, *When Russia Learned to Read*, 63.

124. Brooks, 68–69.

125. Sytin was also known for his publication of colorfully illustrated calendars depicting rural life and aimed at peasant consumers. He began printing his Great Russian Calendar in 1884. Ruud, *Russian Entrepreneur*, 7, 28.

126. Ruud, 80; Brooks, *When Russia Learned to Read*, 80.

127. Ruud, 82; Brooks, 82.

128. Ruud, 85; Brooks, 85.

129. Ruud, 86, 88; Brooks, 86, 88.

130. Ruud, 289; Brooks, 289.

131. "Demon igry: Kartezhnaia igra ne prineset dobra," April 1881, *lubok* from the Museum of Wooden Architecture and Peasant Life, Suzdal, Russia.

132. Brooks laments, "Unfortunately, we know nothing of their lives." Brooks, *When Russia Learned to Read*, 91.

Chapter Four

1. Katia Dianina argues that "a remarkable transformation took place . . . [when] art became a familiar marker of national belonging" due to the introduction of public art exhibitions and their widespread coverage in newspapers. Dianina, *When Art Makes News*, 12.

2. Unknown author, "American Art," *New York Monthly Magazine* 58, no. 1 (July 1861).

3. Guided by Sentimentalism and Romanticism, Russia's Alexei Venetsianov produced idyllic scenes of rural life; in his works, serfs clad in sumptuous traditional dress rest in the sun or stroll barefoot through the fields as they obediently complete their fieldwork. See Alexei Venetsianov, *Harvest, Summer* (1827) and *In the Ploughed Field, Spring* (1820s). Kruglov, "Peasantry in Russian Painting," 33–35. American paintings that exemplify this genre include Edward Beyer's *Bellevue, the Lewis Homestead* (1855) and Marie Adrien Persac's *St. John, St. Martin Parish* (1861). These two paintings glorified grand plantation homes but diminished the role of enslaved African Americans, who, in Persac's painting, appear as specks toiling in the fields.

4. Nikolai Nevrev, *Bargaining. A Scene from Serf Life (from the Recent Past)* (1866); Thomas Satterwhite Noble, *The Price of Blood* (1868).

5. Grigorii Miasoedov, *Congratulation of the Betrothed in the Landlord's House* (1861); William D. Washington, *The Burial of Latané* (1864); Kirill Lemokh, *Summer (with Congratulations)* (1890); Carl Gutherz, *I Promised the Missus' I'd Bring Him Home* (1904).

6. Thomas Waterman Wood, *A Bit of War History: The Contraband, The Recruit,* and *The Veteran* (1866); Edward Lamson Henry, *A Presentation of the Colors to the First Colored Regiment of New York by the Ladies of the City in Front of the Old Union League Club, Union Square, New York City in 1864* (1868).

7. See Il'ia Repin, *Seeing off a Recruit* (1879); Konstantin Savitskii, *To War* (1888); and Nikolai Pimonenko, *Seeing off the Recruits* (before 1912).

8. See Konstantin Makovskii, *Peasant Lunch during Harvest* (1871); Mikhail Klodt, *Ploughing* (1872); and Grigorii Miasoedov, *The Road in the Rye* (1881), *Harvest Time (Scythers)* (1887), and *The Sower* (1888).

9. For example, see William Aiken Walker, *The Cotton Field* (1880s), *Cotton Pickers* (late nineteenth century), *Sharecroppers in the Deep South* (late nineteenth century), and *I'll Stick to Cotton as Long as It Sticks to Me* (1886).

10. Vasilii Maksimov, *The Arrival of a Magician at a Peasant Wedding* (1875); Il'ia Repin, *Evening Party* (1881) and *Procession of the Cross in Kursk Province* (1883); Illarion Prianishnikov, *Resurrection Day in the North* (1887) and *Procession* (1893); Andrei Riabushkin, *Peasant Wedding in the Tambovskii Province* (1880), *Divination at Yuletide* (1881), and *Awaiting Newlyweds in Novgorod Province* (1891).

11. For example, see Eastman Johnson, *Fiddling His Way* (1866); Frank Buchser, *Guitar Player* (1867); Winslow Homer, *Dressing for Carnival* (1877); Thomas Eakins, *The Dancing Lesson* (*Negro Boy Dancing*) (1878); George Fuller, *Negro Funeral, Alabama* (1881); and Henry Ossawa Tanner, *The Banjo Lesson* (1893).

12. Eastman Johnson, *The Lord Is My Shepherd* (1863); Winslow Homer, *Sunday Morning in Virginia* (1877); Thomas Waterman Wood, *Sunday Morning* (1877); Vladimir Makovskii, *In a Village School* (1883); Nikolai Bogdanov-Bel'skii, *Mental Calculation: In Public School of S. A. Rachinskii* (1895) and *At the Doors of a School* (1897).

13. Vladimir Makovskii, *Arrival of the Teacher in the Village* (1897); Aleksei Stepanov, *Arrival of the Teacher* (1889); Edward Lamson Henry, *Kept In* (1888).

14. Valkenier, *Russian Realist Art*, 3–4.

15. "Stat'ia G. N. Iakovleva, V. Sekadkova, bibliograficheskii ukazatel' literatury, sostavlennyi Litvinovym V. V. i Kramskim I. N.," 1908, OR GTG, f. 16, o. 1, d. 422, l. 7.

16. "Stat'ia G. N. Iakovleva," l. 7.

17. "Stat'ia G. N. Iakovleva," l. 7.

18. Jackson, *Wanderers and Critical Realism*, 23.

19. Chernyshevskii, *Aesthetic Relations of Art to Reality*, 17.

20. Chernyshevskii, 24.

21. Brunson, *Russian Realisms*, 2.

22. Brunson, 2–3.

23. Mikhail Larionovich Mikhailov, "Khudozhestvennaia vystavka v Peterburge," *Sovremennik* 76 (July 1859): 105–115.

24. The two themes were "The Liberation of the Serfs" and "The Feast of the Gods at Valhalla." Stites, *Serfdom, Society, and the Arts*, 418.

25. Steiner, "Pursuing Independence," 256.

26. The students protested the "Valhalla" topic, which was derived from a Norse mythological tale that Kramskoi later described as "nonsense."

27. "Pis'mo Kramskogo Ivana Nikolaevicha k Tulinovu Mikhailu Borisovichu," November 13, 1863, RGALI, f. 783, o. 2, d. 3, n. 219, eg. xp. 3, ll. 1–3.

28. Steiner, "Pursuing Independence," 258–259.

29. Jackson, *Wanderers and Critical Realism*, 27.

30. Valkenier, "Peredvizhniki," 247.

31. Untitled clipping from *Khudozhestvennye novosti* 5, no. 7 (April 1, 1887), "Gazetnye vyrezki o Kramskom I. N.," OR GTG, f. 16, o. 1, d. 430, l. 54.

32. Untitled clipping from *Khudozhestvennye novosti*, "Gazetnye vyrezki o Kramskom I. N.," l. 54.

33. "Ustav Tovarishchestva peredvizhnykh khudozhestvennykh vystavok," http://tphv .ru/ustav.php, accessed May 2, 2019.

34. "Vospominaniia M. V. Iamshchikovoi-Altaevoi o khudozhnike V. M. Maksimove," May 30, 1940, OR GTG, f. 81, o. 1, d. 24, l. 2.

35. Vasilii Maksimov, *Grandmother's Tales* (1867), *The Arrival of a Magician at a Peasant Wedding* (1875), and *Sick Husband* (1881).

36. "Biografiia V. M. Maksimova, sostav. M. V. Iamshchikovoi-Altaevoi," undated, OR GTG, f. 81, o. 1, d. 22, l. 9.

37. "Vospominaniia M. V. Iamshchikovoi-Altaevoi," OR GTG, f. 81, o. 1, d. 24, l. 51.

38. "Vstupitel'naia stat'ia I. E. Repina Khudozhnik-narodnik k avtobiograficheskim zapiskam Maksimova," 1913, OR GTG, f. 81, o. 1, d. 17, l. 1.

39. "Pis'mo Repina I. E. k Isaevu Petru Fedorovichu," October 19, 1876, RGALI, f. 842, o. 4, d. 7, l. 1.

40. Christian Brinton, "Russia's Greatest Painter: Il'ia Repin," *Scribner's Magazine* 40, no. 5 (1906): 518.

41. The peasantry's access to icon painting workshops helps explain their outsize contribution to the arts rather than literature in the mid- to late nineteenth century.

42. Brinton, "Russia's Greatest Painter," 518.

43. Boris Sadovskii, "Vstrecha s Repinym, vospominaniia," undated (before 1952), RGALI, f. 842, o. 4, d. 63, l. 4.

44. Thanks to advancements in printing technology, Repin's painting was reproduced and widely distributed, reaching thousands of Russians. Vladimir Stasov, "Il'ia Efimovich Repin," *Pchela*, no. 3 (January 19, 1875): 41.

45. I. C. Goriushkina-Sorokopudova, "Vospominaniia o Repine," early twentieth century, OR GTG, f. 50, o. 1, d. 412, l. 3.

46. Goriushkina-Sorokopudova, l. 3.

47. Arkhipov was also wearing traditional attire; the observer noticed he had on a long peasant coat. "Vospominaniia khudozhnika V. A. Lukina o A. E. Arkhipove," May 14, 1927, OR GTG, f. 47, o. 1, d. 12, l. 1.

48. Arkhipov's lifelong affection for the *narod* may even have contributed to his decision to sell his work to arts patron Pavel Tret'iakov rather than to the tsar. "Al'bom pamiati Abrama Efimovicha Arkhipova s avtograficheskimi zapisiami khudozhnikov," 1931, OR GTG, f. 47, o. 1, d. 15, l. 3.

49. Lykova, *State Tret'iakov Gallery*, 234.

50. "Al'bom pamiati Abrama Efimovicha Arkhipova," OR GTG, f. 47, o. 1, d. 15, ll. 1, 3.

51. "Vospominaniia F. A. Maliavina i soprovoditel'naia zapiska O. A. Zhivovoi," undated, OR GTG, f. 41, o. 1, d. 25, l. 2.

52. See Filipp Maliavin, *Laughter* (1898) and *Whirlwind* (1906).

53. "Pis'mo Iaremicha Stepana Petrovicha k Maliavinu Filippu Andreevichu," October 3, 1912, OR GTG, f. 41, o. 1, d. 21, l. 1.

54. Novak, *American Painting*, 10.

55. Johns, *American Genre Painting*, 3.

56. Lubin, *Picturing a Nation*, 205.

57. Such "types" included New England farmers, merchants, the urban poor, or African American laborers. Johns, *American Genre Painting*, 7, 12.

58. Unknown author, "American Art," *New York Monthly Magazine* 58, no. 1 (July 1861).

59. Unknown author, "American Art."

60. Some of the American artists exhibited their work at institutions like New York's National Academy of Design, an organization comparable to the Russian Imperial Academy of Arts.

61. Wilson, "Lifting 'The Veil,'" 33.

62. Harrisburg and Binstock, *African American Art*, 50.

63. Elbert Francis Baldwin, "A Negro Artist of Unique Power," *Outlook* 64, no. 14 (1900): 792.

64. William E. Barton, "An American Painter of the Resurrection," *Advance* 65, no. 2472 (1913): 2011.

65. Barton, 2011.

66. Harrisburg and Binstock, *African American Art*, 46.

67. Harrisburg and Binstock, 46.

68. "William E. Scott, Artist, Gets Rosenwald Fellowship," *Chicago Defender*, January 1931, 3.

69. "William E. Scott, Artist," 3.

70. Wood and Dalton, *Winslow Homer's Images of Blacks*, 16.

71. Unfortunately, scholars do not know of any existing correspondence from Homer during his time in Virginia. Cato, "Winslow Homer's Visits to Virginia," 12.

72. "Artists and Their Work: Pictures in the Academy," *New York Times*, April 9, 1880, 5.

73. "Artists and Their Work," 5.

74. U.S. Centennial Commission, *International Exhibition, 1876*, 29.

75. Johnson was born in Lovell, Maine, in 1824.

76. *The Boy Lincoln*, 2.

77. Davis, "Eastman Johnson's Negro Life," 67.

78. "The Academy of Design," *New York Times*, November 17, 1874.

79. Boime, *Art of Exclusion*, 125–126.

80. Boime, 125–126.

81. Couture's works reveal his abiding interest in depicting the impoverished and the oppressed, a characteristic he may have passed on to his student, Noble. Boime, 130; Furth, "'Modern Medea' and Race Matters," 37, 46.

82. *The Modern Medea* exhibited at the National Academy of Design in 1867. "The Modern Medea," *Harper's Weekly*, May 18, 1867, 318.

83. Alfred Jingle, "Fine Arts: Noble's 'Last Sale,'" *St. Louis Times*, August 12, 1866, quoted in Boime, *Art of Exclusion*, 135.

84. "Thomas W. Wood," in Benjamin, *Our American Artists*, unpaginated.

85. The other two white voters represent an Irishman and a Dutchman. See McElroy, *Facing History*, 50.

86. "Exhibition of Southern Genre Paintings by William Aiken Walker" (New York: Bland Gallery, 1940), Frick Art Reference Library, Manuscript Collection.

87. Seibels, *Sunny South*, 83, 92.

88. Trovaioli and Toledano, *William Aiken Walker*, 113.

89. "Artist Receives Late Recognition," *Charleston (S.C.) Post*, January 24, 1941, clipping, William Aiken Walker Papers, Metropolitan Museum of Art, Watson Library; Trovaioli and Toledano, *William Aiken Walker*, 3.

90. "Seebold's Art Gallery: A New Orleans Exhibition of Oil Paintings," *New Orleans Daily Picayune*, November 30, 1884, and "Art Talk: The Brush and Pencil in New Orleans," *New Orleans Daily Picayune*, July 26, 1885, quoted in Seibels, *Sunny South*, 113–114.

91. Nevrev joined the Society of Traveling Art Exhibitions in 1881.

92. Many thanks to Maurie McInnis for referring me to Noble's painting. For more background on these paintings, see Nesterova, *Itinerants*, 37–38; and Boime, *Art of Exclusion*, 147–148.

93. The enslaved young man is the illegitimate son of the slaveholder, a fact referred to by the painting's title, *The Price of Blood.*

94. One critic alludes to the controversial reception of Nevrev's painting, contending that although the composition won first prize from the Moscow Society of Art Lovers, an organization supported by future Society of Traveling Art Exhibitions patron Pavel Tret'iakov, hardly any reviews appeared in the press. In addition, the painting was supposed to be sent to an artistic exhibition in Vienna, but its content was deemed to be too "uncomfortable." A.P., "Nikolai Vasil'evich Nevrev," *Pchela*, no. 5 (March 28, 1878): 15.

95. Due to its shape and function, the gourd symbolized the Big Dipper, a constellation that served as a navigational guide for runaways making the journey northward. Harvey, *Civil War and American Art*, 182.

96. See Thomas Moran, *Slave Hunt, Dismal Swamp, Virginia* (1862); Eastman Johnson, *A Ride for Liberty: The Fugitive Slaves* (1862); and Theodor Kaufmann, *On to Liberty* (1867).

97. The notion of liberation through escape did not figure prominently in peasants' autobiographical narratives or folk traditions; instead, many serfs believed that emancipation would come through legal avenues. Scholar John MacKay posits that serfs thought liberation would be "linked to the category of the *state*," for example, through a "hypothetical meeting with the Tsar." MacKay, "'And Hold the Bondman Still,'" 118.

98. Kustodiev was not a member of the Society of Traveling Art Exhibitions, which was founded in his youth, but he studied under Repin in St. Petersburg (1896–1903).

99. "Rukopis' Kovalenko A. I.—Ivan Miasoedov, Zhizn' v tvorchestve i bor'be," undated, OR GTG, f. 133, o. 1, d. 187, l. 1.

100. Russian artists also faced unique censorial challenges that might have made it more difficult to paint scenes of peasant flight or rebellion.

101. Miasoedov exhibited this painting at the Imperial Academy of Arts in St. Petersburg in 1861 and earned a gold medal. *World of the Peasantry*, 131.

102. "Original Found in N.J. of 'Burial of Latané,'" *Richmond News-Leader*, February 2, 1939, clipping, William D. Washington Papers, Metropolitan Museum of Art, Watson Library; Harvey, *Civil War and American Art*, 14.

103. Gutherz helped smuggle contraband for the Confederate army during the Civil War. According to one reviewer, he combated postwar change through his art by "pulling the mantle of the past over the rapidly advancing age of industrialization" during the late nineteenth century. See exhibition catalog *Carl Gutherz: Designs for Memphis, 1873–1877*, copyrighted by Joseph S. Czestochowski Jr., 1974, Carl Gutherz Papers, Metropolitan Museum of Art, Watson Library.

104. Wirtschafter, *From Serf to Russian Soldier*, 9–11.

105. Wirtschafter, 9–11.

106. Propp, *Narodnye liricheskie pesni*, 445.

107. Fuller, *Civil-Military Conflict*, 11.

108. Repin drew inspiration for this painting from the recruitments that occurred during the Russo-Turkish War (1877–1878). *World of the Peasantry*, 141.

109. Ar. Eval'd, "Provody novobrantsa: K kartine I. E. Repina," *Vsemirnaia illiustratsiia*, no. 617 (November 1, 1880): 337–338.

110. Savitskii studied at the Imperial Academy of Arts during the 1860s and early 1870s, joining the Wanderers in 1891.

111. Lee, "Black Union Soldiers," 430.

112. Harvey, *Civil War and American Art*, 203.

113. One contemporary review noted that "nothing could well be better than the quiet self-conceit developed in every line of Sambo's face, after he has donned Uncle Sam's uniform." "National Academy of Design," *New York Leader*, May 11, 1867, Object Files for Thomas Waterman Wood's *A Bit of War History*, Metropolitan Museum of Art, Watson Library.

114. "The Contraband, Recruit, and Veteran," *Harper's Weekly*, May 4, 1867, 284.

115. "The Academy of Design," *New York Evening Post*, May 2, 1867, 1, Object Files for Thomas Waterman Wood's *A Bit of War History*, Metropolitan Museum of Art, Watson Library.

116. Frank Weitenkampf, "Fine Arts: The Negro in Art," *Independent*, August 26, 1897, 9.

117. *World of the Peasantry*, 92.

118. Tolstoi, *Anna Karenina*, 717.

119. Tolstoi, 216.

120. Viewers may also have asked the same question of *Scythers*, in which the peasants' status as enserfed or free is ambiguous.

121. The reviewer believed that too many artists focused on the "comical features" of "negro life." "The National Academy Exhibition, 1877," *Scribner's Monthly* 14, no. 2 (June 1877): 263; Downes, *Winslow Homer*, 3:89.

122. Thomas Anshutz, "Discourse on Art," ca. fall 1873, microfilm roll 140, Archives of American Art, quoted in Griffin, *Thomas Anshutz*, 28.

123. H.B.W., "Notes," *Metropolitan Museum of Art Bulletin* 35 (1940): 118, Object Files for Thomas Anshutz's *The Way They Live*, Metropolitan Museum of Art, Watson Library.

124. "The Fine Arts," *Philadelphia Daily Evening Telegraph*, November 10, 1879, clipping, Object Files for Thomas Anshutz's *The Way They Live*, Metropolitan Museum of Art, Watson Library.

125. Warkel, "Image and Identity," 22.

126. Warkel, 22.

127. See Page, *In Ole Virginia*, and Harris, *Balaam and His Master*.

128. Maksimov spent time working in the countryside in 1866 and subsequently produced *Grandmother's Tales* (1867). "Biografiia V. M. Maksimova," OR GTG, f. 81, o. 1, d. 22, ll. 2–3.

129. "Biografiia V. M. Maksimova," l. 3.

130. See Konstantin Makovskii, *Stories of Grandfather* (1881), and Nikolai Bogdanov-Bel'skii, *A New Fairy Tale* (1891).

131. This painting was exhibited in the fourth show of the Society of Traveling Art Exhibitions (1875–1876).

132. Russian peasants sometimes worried that village magicians or sorcerers would cast a spell on a bride and groom, causing unhappiness, illness, or even death. For more

information about the numerous rituals surrounding betrothal and matrimony, see Worobec, *Peasant Russia*, chap. 5.

133. See *World of the Peasantry*, 132.

134. This ceremonial ritual dates to the fourth century A.D. and is common to both the Eastern Orthodox and Roman Catholic traditions.

135. See Konstantin Savitskii, *Meeting the Icon* (1878); Leonid Solomatkin, *Religious Procession* (1882); and Illarion Prianishnikov, *Resurrection Day in the North* (1887) and *Procession* (1893).

136. Critics gave the painting mixed reviews. Many conservative journals saw the work as destabilizing, liberal, and unartistic. See Valkenier, *Ilya Repin*, 93–94.

137. Valkenier, 93–94.

138. "Minchenkov, Iakov Danilovich: Vospominaniia o peredvizhnikakh," Klassika, Lib. ru, http://az.lib.ru/m/minchenkow_j_d/text_0180.shtml, accessed May 2, 2019.

139. Throughout the nineteenth century, popular minstrel shows portrayed African American culture as exotic through highly disparaging, racist performances by white musicians in blackface.

140. Cobb, *Away Down South*, 5.

141. Burns, "Images of Slavery," 35–36.

142. Burns, 49–50.

143. See Frank Buchser, *Guitar Player* (1867), and Thomas Eakins, *The Dancing Lesson (Negro Boy Dancing)* (1878).

144. Edgar French, "An American Historical Portrait Painter of Three Historical Epochs," *World's Week*, December 1906, clipping, Eastman Johnson Papers, Metropolitan Museum of Art, Watson Library.

145. This painting, likely inspired by Homer's trips to Petersburg, Virginia, may also have been shown under the title *Sketch—Fourth of July in Virginia* in 1877. *Catalogue for the American Collection of Paintings*, Kurtz Gallery Auction Catalogue, April 8–9, 1879, photocopy, Object Files for Winslow Homer's *Dressing for Carnival*, Metropolitan Museum of Art, Watson Library; Harvey, *Civil War and American Art*, 234.

146. Winslow Homer to Thomas B. Clarke, April 23, 1892, Winslow Homer Papers, Archive of American Art, photocopy from the Object Files for Winslow Homer's *Dressing for Carnival*, Metropolitan Museum of Art, Watson Library.

147. JBHE Foundation, "Jonkonnu," 70.

148. Harvey, *Civil War and American Art*, 233–234.

149. Files from Pennsylvania School for the Deaf, Philadelphia, quoted in Woods, *Henry Ossawa Tanner*, 75.

150. "FRENCH: Nation Bought Pictures of Henry Tanner, an American Colored Artist," *Cincinnati Enquirer*, January 13, 1900, 10.

151. "FRENCH: Nation Bought Pictures," 10.

152. Wilson, "Lifting 'The Veil,'" 31.

153. Eklof, *Russian Peasant Schools*, 50.

154. Eklof, 257–258.

155. Literacy rates among rural peasants increased from 6 percent in the 1860s to 25 percent in the 1910s. Brooks, *When Russia Learned to Read*, 4; Eklof, *Russian Peasant Schools*, 52–54.

156. Williams, *Self-Taught*, 71–72.

157. Williams, 69.

158. National Center for Education Statistics, "120 Years of Literacy," http://nces.ed.gov/naal/lit_history.asp, accessed May 3, 2019.

159. Brooks, *When Russia Learned to Read*, 9, 13, 18, 22–24; Williams, *Self-Taught*, 81, 147, 169.

160. For additional depictions of peasant education in paintings, see Aleksandr Morozov, *Village Free School* (1865), and Nikolai Bogdanov-Bel'skii, *Sunday Reading in the Rural School* (1895), *At the Sick Teacher's House* (1897), and *Schoolgirls* (1901).

161. Lykova, Volchenkova, and Cook, *Masterpieces of the State Tretyakov Gallery*, 194.

162. This painting was displayed at the twenty-fourth show of the Society of Traveling Art Exhibitions.

163. Eleanor Harvey, "Painting Freedom," *New York Times*, October 30, 2013.

164. This biblical story was very familiar to enslaved African Americans, who drew parallels between their experience and that of the Israelites. Harvey, "Painting Freedom." The freedman's Bible in Johnson's painting appears to be opened to either Genesis or Exodus.

165. Eugene Benson, "Eastman Johnson," *Galaxy* 6, no. 1 (July 1868).

166. Brooks, *When Russia Learned to Read*, 37.

167. Eklof, *Russian Peasant Schools*, 259.

168. Urban migration began before 1850 but significantly increased during the late nineteenth century. Painter, *Creating Black Americans*, 174.

169. These men may have been looking for employment as dockworkers or longshoremen, who assisted in loading or unpacking cargo from incoming boats at urban ports. For a discussion of waterfront labor during the nineteenth century, see Arnesen, *Waterfront Workers of New Orleans*.

170. Pickens, *Heir of Slaves*, 64.

171. Pickens, 71.

172. "Iz zapisok byvshego krepostnogo cheloveka," *Istoricheskii vestnik*, no. 5 (1907): 446–474; no. 6 (1907): 734–764; no. 7 (1907): 143–164, http://dugward.ru/library/alexandr2/bobkov_iz_zapisok_byvshego_krepostnogo.html, accessed May 3, 2019.

173. "Iz zapisok byvshego krepostnogo cheloveka"; Dennison and Nafziger, "Micro-Perspectives on Living Standards."

Chapter Five

An early version of this chapter, titled "Selling Servitude, Captivating Consumers: Images of Bondsmen in Russian and American Advertisements, 1880–1915," was published in the *Journal of Global Slavery* 1, no. 1 (2016): 72–112.

1. Rudolph Bekher, "Luchshie plugi v mire," undated (likely produced at the turn of the twentieth century), Russian National Library Poster Collection.

2. "Durham Bull Fertilizer," 1884, box 16, c. 1, Advertising Ephemera Collection, David M. Rubenstein Rare Book and Manuscript Library, Duke University.

3. U.S. census data show that national indexes of industrial production quadrupled between 1880 and 1920. Over the same period, the value of finished commodities and construction materials output grew over nine times in real-dollar terms, with the largest area of

growth in the food and kindred products industries. U.S. Department of Commerce, *Historical Statistics*, Series J 13–14, "Manufacturing Production—Indexes of Total Production: 1863 to 1939," and Series J 97–148, "Value of Output—Finished Commodities and Construction Materials at Producers' Current Prices: 1869–1919," 179, 183.

4. "37 Companies in 1869, 15 Companies in 1914," box JW1, c. 1, J. Walter Thompson Company, Domestic Advertisements Collection and Publications Collection, Rubenstein Library, Duke University (hereafter Thompson Collections).

5. More than 290,000 miles of track were added between 1880 and 1920, enabling trains to bring agricultural equipment, livestock, and manufactured goods year-round to millions of Americans living in urban and rural areas. U.S. Department of Commerce, *Historical Statistics*, Series K 1–17, "Railroads before 1890—Mileage, Equipment, and Passenger and Freight Service: 1830 to 1890," and Series K 28–42, "Railroads—Mileage, Equipment and Passenger Service; Operating Steam Railways: 1890 to 1945," 200, 202.

6. Russia also increasingly focused on the extraction of iron, coal, and oil. Kahan, *Russian Economic History*, 16; Waldron, *Between Two Revolutions*, 17. Paul Gregory asserts that the amount of structural change in the development of Russian industries was "average or slightly below average when compared to [other Westernized countries]." See Gregory, *Before Command*, 28–29.

7. Under Sergei Witte, a former railroad official, track mileage increased by 40 percent. Waldron, *Between Two Revolutions*, 17.

8. Waldron, 17.

9. West, *I Shop in Moscow*, 4.

10. Lears, *Fables of Abundance*, 103.

11. Lears, 109.

12. George A. Crofutt produced the chromolithograph, *American Progress*, of Gast's *Westward, Ho!* in 1873. Lears, *Fables of Abundance*, 109–110.

13. West, *I Shop in Moscow*, 198.

14. See "Nevskii prospekt: Uglovoi fasad doma 36" (1908), in Ozerov, *Nevskii prospekt*, 134; and West, *I Shop in Moscow*, 3, 29.

15. *Advertising as a Selling Force* (New York: J. Walter Thompson Company, 1909), JWT box DG5, c. 1, Thompson Collections.

16. Leach, *Land of Desire*, 42.

17. Glinternik, *Reklama v Rossii*, 62; West, *I Shop in Moscow*, 52.

18. As West points out, evidence reveals "the continuation of merchant/manufacturer control of advertising content up to the First World War, whether through direct composition or the hiring of independent writers and artists." West, *I Shop in Moscow*, 41, 54.

19. Sivulka, *Soap, Sex, and Cigarettes*, 84.

20. *The Thompson Blue Book on Advertising 1904–1905* (New York: J. Walter Thompson Company, 1905), 13, box DG4, c. 1, Thompson Collections.

21. In the 1880s, millions of Americans learned about current events, religion, science, and art from daily newspapers or from some of the ten thousand different periodicals in existence. Sivulka, *Soap, Sex, and Cigarettes*, 29–30; Kaestle and Radway, *Print in Motion*, 29.

22. Acetylene Jones, "That Health Light for Homes," box 35, c. 1, Advertising Ephemera Collection, Rubenstein Library, Duke University.

23. The company's strategy was to purchase large amounts of advertising space and to resell it to interested businesses.

24. By 1900, the agency's portfolio of clients surpassed eight hundred. Excerpted from "1889 Hubbard's Blue Book," box JW1, c. 1, and *Blue Book on Advertising* (New York: J. Walter Thompson Company, 1901), 7, box DG4, c. 1, Thompson Collections.

25. They charged businesses between $12 and $15 per line for advertisements placed in popular publications like the *Century, Fireside Monthly, Harper's,* and *Scribner's.* Excerpted from "1889 Hubbard's Blue Book," box JW1, c. 1, Thompson Collections.

26. *The Thompson Blue Book on Advertising* (New York: J. Walter Thompson Company, 1905), 14, box DG4, c. 1, Thompson Collections.

27. *The Thompson Blue Book on Advertising* (New York: J. Walter Thompson Company, 1902), 8, box DG4, c. 1, Thompson Collections.

28. According to the 1897 census, 21 percent of the total population was literate. See Brooks, *When Russia Learned to Read,* 4.

29. McReynolds, *News under Russia's Old Regime,* 9.

30. For example, between 1870 and 1916, circulation of *Peterburgskii listok,* the "boulevard" newspaper, grew by 1,000 percent, from a circulation of 9,000 to 128,500. West, *I Shop in Moscow,* 31.

31. Feyel, "Presse et publicité en France," 864.

32. The Russian terms are of German and French provenance; *plakat* is derived from the German word for poster, *Plakat,* as well as the French verb *plaquer,* which means "to apply or attach" something to a surface. The French term *réclamer* can mean "to call for." Zolotinkina and Polikarpova, *Reklamnyi plakat v Rossii,* 7; Barkhatova et al., *Le premier âge d'or,* 11; Snopkov, Snopkov, and Shkliaruk, *Reklama v plakate,* 9.

33. Sivulka, *Soap, Sex, and Cigarettes,* 86.

34. *Trezvon* has several meanings, including a "ringing" noise, gossip, or rumors. "Papirosy 'Trezvon,' Tovarishchestvo 'Laferm,'" St. Petersburg, February 5, 1899, Russian National Library Poster Collection.

35. M. Konradi, "Kek-Uok," St. Petersburg, undated; "Amerikanskii shokolad, Factory in Moscow," 1898. Russian National Library Poster Collection.

36. W. T. Blackwell & Company, Blackwell's Durham Clear Havana [Cigar Box], box 4, c. 1, Tobacco Collection, Rubenstein Library, Duke University.

37. For example, Kenneth Goings, in his study of black collectibles in late nineteenth-century American ephemera, finds that "objects of material culture gave a physical, tangible reality to the idea of racial inferiority" because those who used these items "consciously or unconsciously accepted the stereotypes they presented." Goings, *Mammy and Uncle Mose,* xiii.

38. Trade cards were less widely distributed in Russia, where businesses mailed notices, letters, or visiting cards to selected members of Russia's elite. West, *I Shop in Moscow,* 29.

39. Roy Alquist, "Sewing Machine Tradecards," *Paper Collector's Marketplace,* undated, 14, 16, box 49, Advertising Ephemera Collection, Rubenstein Library, Duke University.

40. Lou McCulloch, "On Paper: Of Generals, Dukes, and Tobacco Cards," *American Collector,* February 1982, 7, box 4, W. Duke, Sons & Company Advertising Materials, Rubenstein Library, Duke University.

41. McCulloch, 7.

42. See collections in boxes 2 and 3, W. Duke, Sons & Company Advertising Materials, Rubenstein Library, Duke University.

43. See Hilton, *Selling to the Masses*, 22.

44. For early twentieth-century photographs of storefront windows and shops on Nevskii Prospekt, a major thoroughfare in St. Petersburg, see "Fasad doma 1 po Nevskomu prospektu" (1901), in Ozerov, *Nevskii prospekt*, 11.

45. "Brooklyn, 1899," in Byron, *New York Life*, image 29.

46. Hilton, *Selling to the Masses*, 9; West, *I Shop in Moscow*, 77.

47. Anikst, Baburina, and Chernevich, *Russian Graphic Design*, 17–19; Brumfield, *Modernism in Russian Architecture*, xx–xxi.

48. Anikst, Baburina, and Chernevich, *Russian Graphic Design*, 17–19; Brumfield, *Modernism in Russian Architecture*, xx–xxi.

49. See "Fasad doma 21 po Nevskomu prospektu" (1900) and "Vitrina magazina tovarishchestva 'Zhorzh Borman' (Nevskii prospekt, 21)," in Ozerov, *Nevskii prospekt*, 50–51.

50. Businesses that amassed prizes at numerous competitions displayed these circular golden emblems on advertising materials; for example, international florist T. Gerstner appears to have exhibited no fewer than eight awards in its storefront windows in 1903. See "Zdanie Peterburgskogo obshchestva strakhovaniia (Nevskii prospekt, 5)," in Ozerov, *Nevskii prospekt*, 14.

51. Hilton, *Selling to the Masses*, 80; West, *I Shop in Moscow*, 68–69.

52. Gornyi, *Al'bom pamiati*, 36.

53. An additional article outlining the rules for visitors indicates the popularity of such exhibitions; it warns overeager consumers not to directly handle the products on display or to carry away their purchased items from the exhibition until its official closing. "Pravila dlia posetitelei Vserossiiskoi manufakturnoi vystavki," from the "Illiustrirovannoe opisanie: Vserossiiskoi manufakturnoi vystavki 1870 g.," *Vsemirnaia illiustratsiia* 74, nos. 1–2 (1870): 1–2.

54. Lears, *No Place of Grace*, 33.

55. Lears, 33.

56. Lears, 34.

57. Barthes, "Myth Today," 415.

58. Bonnell, *Iconography of Power*, 10.

59. Bonnell, 10–11.

60. F. Turbin, "Narodnyi chai," late nineteenth century, Russian National Library Ephemera Collection.

61. Pavel Gorbunov, "Fruktovyi chai i kofe iz vinnykh iagod," in Glinternik, *Reklama v Rossii*.

62. These advertisements portray peasant women in ornate costumes that would have been worn only on special occasions, not for work. This mode of representation links the women to traditional Russian culture and offers a paternalistic view of serfdom as an institution that provided to peasants not only necessities but also expensive clothing.

63. Yoder, "Russian Tea Culture," 2; Sokolov, "Rossiiskaia 'chainaia skazka,'" 20.

64. *Russkie vedomosti*, no. 254 (1900): 4; *Vestnik finansov, promyshlennosti i torgovli*, no. 5 (1903): 80.

65. Henry Lantz, "Lokomobili i molotilki," likely produced during the late nineteenth century, Russian National Library Poster Collection.

66. I. B. Pappe, untitled card, published November 20, 1893, Russian National Library Ephemera Collection.

67. This strategy relates to what Sally West describes as advertisers' awareness of their role in "facilitating the modern" through "the language of both tradition and change." West, *I Shop in Moscow*, 4.

68. Between 1883 and 1915, crop production grew by approximately 2.3 percent annually across all of Russia. The use of mechanized agricultural equipment was not widespread even by the turn of the twentieth century. Goldsmith, "Economic Growth of Tsarist Russia," 442, 447.

69. Spulber, *Russia's Economic Transitions*, 74.

70. See Maiorova, *From the Shadow of Empire*, 12, 13.

71. Here, Olga Maiorova refers to the viewpoint of intellectuals like Mikhail Katkov (1818–1887), editor of *Moscow News*, whose newspaper advocated the unification of "the heterogeneous state on the basis of, and for the benefit of, the 'ruling nationality.'" Maiorova, 21.

72. Frierson, *Peasant Icons*, 101.

73. Dmitriev-Mamonov, *Ukazatel' deistvuiushchikh*, 2:326.

74. E. I. Mel'goze, "Zavod zemledel'cheskikh mashin," undated, Russian National Library Poster Collection.

75. Br. Shapshal, "Beseda papirosy," St. Petersburg, September 16, 1888, Russian National Library Poster Collection.

76. See George Borman, "Shokolad druz'ia," after 1896, and George Borman, untitled prerevolutionary wrapper, Russian National Library Ephemera Collection.

77. George Borman, "Russkie pesni v litsakh," undated, Russian National Library Ephemera Collection.

78. George Borman, "Zolotaia rybka," undated, Russian National Library Ephemera Collection.

79. M. Konradi, "Konfety Konek-Gorbunok," undated, and "Basni Krylova," undated, Russian National Library Ephemera Collection.

80. Wirtschafter, *Social Identity in Imperial Russia*, 101–102.

81. Brooks, *When Russia Learned to Read*, 129.

82. Bylov, "Razdum'e," 12.

83. Bylov, 12.

84. Bylov, 12.

85. Russian-American Association of Rubber Manufacturing, St. Petersburg, 1904, Russian National Library Poster Collection.

86. Russian-American Association of Rubber Manufacturing, St. Petersburg, 1904, Russian National Library Poster Collection.

87. Starks, *Smoking under the Tsars*, 7.

88. Laferm, "'Trezvon'" Cigarettes," undated, Russian National Library Poster Collection.

89. In English, the slogan reads, "Chit-Chat cigarettes—even noblemen smoke them." A. N. Shaposhnikov, "'Tary-Bary' Cigarettes," approximately 1914, Russian State Historical Museum Archive.

90. Van'ka is a name that connotes the idea of the "everyman," or the common peasant.

91. S. Gabai, "Kak Van'ka v Moskvu prishel i do 'Slavy' doshel" (How Van'ka Arrived in Moscow and Came to "Fame"), May 20, 1900, Russian State Historical Museum Archive.

92. "Kompaniia 'Grammofon,'" *Russkie vedomosti*, no. 353 (1900): 3.

93. Bogdanov, *Dym otechestva*, 129.

94. A. N. Bogdanov, "Kapriz," December 19, 1904, Russian National Library Poster Collection.

95. Saatchi i Mangubi, "Zoria," January 27, 1900, Russian National Library Poster Collection.

96. Kalashnikov Brewery, "Vkusu kazhdogo ugozhdaet," 1900s, in Snopkov, Snopkov, and Shkliaruk, *Reklama v plakate*, 60.

97. Reddick, "Educational Programs," 369.

98. Cox, *Dreaming of Dixie*, 3.

99. Cox, 4.

100. Southern Manufacturing Company, "Good Luck Baking Powder," Richmond, VA, 1907, box 17, c. 1, Advertising Ephemera Collection, Rubenstein Library, Duke University; J. H. McElwee, "Ante-Bellum Smoking Tobacco," Statesville, NC, box 1, c. 1, Tobacco Collection, Rubenstein Library, Duke University.

101. Potter & Wrightington, "Old South Brand Baked Beans," Boston, MA, after 1880, box 17, c. 1, Advertising Ephemera Collection, Rubenstein Library, Duke University.

102. Blight, *Race and Reunion*, 139.

103. Myers Brothers & Company, "Love Tobacco," Richmond, VA, late nineteenth century, box 22, Trade Cards and Pamphlets, Ephemera Collection, American Antiquarian Society.

104. This advertisement references Ulysses S. Grant's campaign slogan, "Let us have peace," from the 1868 presidential election. Spicers & Peckham, "The New 'Model Grand' Portable Range," after 1876, Ephemera Late Trade Cards not in ABE 17976, American Antiquarian Society.

105. McElya, *Clinging to Mammy*, 3–4.

106. Chase & Sanborn, "Seal Brand Java & Mocha Coffee," Boston, MA, 1888, Folio Trade Cards—Late, box 2, American Antiquarian Society.

107. H. E. Taylor & Company, "'Can't Be Beat' Furniture Polish for Family and General Use," after 1876, Folio Trade Cards—Late, box 1, American Antiquarian Society.

108. Enoch Morgan's Sons Company, "Sapolio Soap," New York, NY, Trade Cards Late—Pamphlets Post 1876, American Antiquarian Society.

109. McElya, *Clinging to Mammy*, 82.

110. Remembering his mammy, Cooke wrote, "God forbid that I should ever be anything but proud of that old negro's affection. Not so long as I live." See Beaty, *John Esten Cooke, Virginian*, 10. Jessie W. Parkhurst notes, "In order to be recognized as belonging to the aristocracy of the Old South it was necessary to say that one had been tended by a 'Black Mammy' in youth." Parkhurst, "Role of the Black Mammy," 351.

111. Goings, *Mammy and Uncle Mose*, 11.

112. Chakraborty, "Mammies, Ayahs, Baboes," 26.

113. Walter A. Taylor, "Taylor's Riddle Book," Atlanta, GA, after 1876, Trade Cards Late Pamphlets—Post 1876, American Antiquarian Society.

114. "Excelsior Metal Polish," Boston, MA, undated, box 18, Ephemera Collection, American Antiquarian Society.

115. Rock Island Lines, 1908, box 8, c. 1, Roy Lightner Collection of Antique Advertisements, Rubenstein Library, Duke University.

116. Dixon Crucible Company, "Dixon's Stove Polish," Jersey City, NJ, after 1880, Ephemera Late Trade Cards not in ABE 17976, American Antiquarian Society.

117. Oubre, *Forty Acres and a Mule*, 180.

118. Oubre, 180.

119. J & P Coats' Thread, "Ef Dis Don't Fetch You NOTHING Will," 1881, box 20, Ephemera Collection, American Antiquarian Society.

120. Durham Bull Fertilizer, "Makes Me Grow," Durham, NC, 1887, box 16, c. 1, Advertising Ephemera Collection, Rubenstein Library, Duke University.

121. Jacob G. Shirk, "'Homestead' Cigars," Lancaster, PA, likely late nineteenth century, box 2, c.1, Tobacco Collection, Rubenstein Library, Duke University.

122. Weir Stove Company, "Glenwood & Elmwood Ranges & Parlor Stoves," Taunton, MA, after 1876, Ephemera Late Trade Cards not in ABE 17976, American Antiquarian Society.

123. As scholars Shane White and Graham White explain, enslaved African Americans with access to costly items publicly constructed a "vivid, visual presence . . . [as] an emphatic repudiation of their allotted social role." White and White, "Slave Clothing and African-American Culture," 184.

124. J. D. Larkin & Company, "Boraxine," Buffalo, NY, 1882, box 18, Ephemera Collection, American Antiquarian Society.

125. Clarence Brooks & Company, "The Rivals Embrace" and "Why Does He Want to Shine 'Em Up for Nothing?," after 1876, box 18, Ephemera Collection, American Antiquarian Society.

126. Dixon Crucible Company, "Dixon's Stove Polish," Jersey City, NJ, 1886, "Susan Paine Gift in Process Not Dig Not Cat," Late Trade Cards Folio, American Antiquarian Society.

127. Henry Mayo & Company, "Boston Codfish Balls," Boston, MA, after 1876, box 5, Ephemera Collection, American Antiquarian Society.

128. Rumsey & Company, "Pumps," St. Louis, MO, after 1876, Folio Trade Cards—Late, box 1, American Antiquarian Society.

129. "The Alden Fruit Vinegar," sold in Hartford, CT, after 1876, box 6, Ephemera Collection, American Antiquarian Society.

130. "Merrick's Thread," after 1876, box 21, Ephemera Collection, American Antiquarian Society.

131. Rawson's Railroad and Steamship, "(Going to Camp Meeting), Gone to Meet the Angels Peaceful Evermore," 1882, Folio Trade Cards—Late, box 1, American Antiquarian Society.

132. Between 1880 and 1930, 4,697 lynching cases were recorded, an estimate that may not account for unreported instances. Apel and Smith, *Lynching Photographs*, 15; Brundage, *Civilizing Torture*, 222.

133. "Cuticura Soap," *Savannah Tribune*, February 24, 1900, 4; "Santa Fe Watch Co.," *Kansas Baptist Herald*, December 9, 1911, 4; "S. H. Hines, Undertaker and Embalmer," *Washington*

Bee, September 16, 1905, 5; "New Home Sewing Machine," *Washington Bee*, November 23, 1907, 7.

134. "The North Carolina Mutual and Provident Association," *American Citizen*, May 6, 1911, 1, box 69, c. 1, North Carolina Mutual Life Insurance Company Archives, Rubenstein Library, Duke University.

135. African Americans were largely disregarded as a potential consumer group until the 1930s, when demographic trends reversed and African Americans began constituting a growing percentage of the total population. African Americans made up 9.8 percent of the total population in 1940 and 12.1 percent of the population in 1990. See U.S. Census Bureau, "Table 1. United States—Race and Hispanic Origin: 1790–1990"; and Brown and Stentiford, *Jim Crow Encyclopedia*, 6.

136. African Americans made up less than 12 percent of the total U.S. population in 1900, while white Americans composed about 88 percent. "U.S. Census Bureau, "Table 1. United States."

137. African Americans constituted 14.1 percent of the population in 1860 and just 9.9 percent in 1920. "U.S. Census Bureau, "Table 1. United States."

138. In 1897, the peasantry formed 84 percent of the Russian population. Wirtschafter, *Social Identity in Imperial Russia*, 101–102.

Chapter Six

1. Ascher, *Revolution of 1905*, 28.

2. Between 1880 and 1910, statistics suggest that overall black farm ownership increased while white ownership rates fell. Alston, "Issues in Postbellum Southern Agriculture," 217.

3. Harris, *Told by Uncle Remus*.

4. Harris, 4.

5. Harris, 4.

6. "New Uncle Remus Stories," *Southern Cultivator*, November 15, 1905, 63.

7. "Folk and Fairy Tales," *Congregationalist and Christian World*, November 18, 1905, 90; "Holiday Publications, II," *Dial* 39 (December 16, 1905).

8. Page, "Bred in the Bone," 6.

9. Page, 4.

10. Page, 15.

11. Page, 29.

12. Page, "Old Jabe's Marital Experiments," 171.

13. Page, 171.

14. Page, 172.

15. "Mr. Page's Novel," *New York Times*, June 25, 1904, 25.

16. "The Works of Thomas Nelson Page," *Independent*, December 6, 1906, 61.

17. "Works of Thomas Nelson Page," 61.

18. "Short Stories," *Congregationalist and Christian World*, August 6, 1904, 89.

19. This story is discussed in further detail in chapter 2. Opochinin, "Posledniaia 'dusha.'"

20. I am unable to find information about this writer's background. Gorskii, "Metel'," 2, 3, 6.

21. Gorskii, 2.

22. Gorskii, 2.

23. Gorskii, 2.

24. Gorskii, 2.

25. Gorskii, 2.

26. Chekhov, "Muzhiki."

27. Gregory, *Before Command*, 38.

28. "Konchina A. P. Chekhova," *Niva*, no. 28 (July 10, 1904): 560.

29. "Konchina A. P. Chekhova," 560.

30. "Konchina A. P. Chekhova," 560.

31. D. Gorodetskii, "Iz vospominanii o A. P. Chekhove," *Ogonek*, no. 29 (1904): 213.

32. Coope, *Doctor Chekhov*, 14; Figes, *Natasha's Dance*, 256–257.

33. Confino, *Russia before the "Radiant Future,"* 173.

34. Chekhov, "Muzhiki."

35. Chekhov.

36. Chekhov.

37. Chekhov.

38. Here, Chekhov draws readers' attention to an important late nineteenth-century problem for the peasantry: fires plagued their towns, causing billions of rubles' worth of destruction and exceeding famines in their degree of frequency. Educated urban Russians became increasingly aware of the problem of rural fires through the efforts of authors like Chekhov and artists Leonid Solomatkin, Illarion Prianishnikov, and Nikolai Dmitriev-Orenburgskii, who visually represented burning villages and soot-covered, grieving peasants in dramatic oil paintings. For examples of nineteenth-century paintings depicting rural fires, see Leonid Solomatkin, *Pozhar v derevne* (Fire in the Countryside; 1870); Illarion Prianishnikov, *Pogorel'tsy* (Fire Victims; 1871); and Nikolai Dmitriev-Orenburgskii, *Pozhar v derevne* (Fire in the Countryside; 1885). Frierson, *All Russia Is Burning!*, 3; Chekhov, "Muzhiki."

39. Chekhov, "Muzhiki."

40. Chekhov.

41. Chekhov. The peasant Mar'ia exclaims at the end of the passage about the pre-emancipation era, "Net, volia luchshe!" This translates to "No, freedom is better!"

42. Chekhov.

43. Quoted in Foote, introduction to *Anton Chekhov*, xvi.

44. Anton Chekhov to Mikhail Men'shikov, April 16, 1897, in Yarmolinsky, *Letters of Anton Chekhov*, 286.

45. Novus (pseudonym of Petr Struve), "Na raznye temy: 'Muzhiki' g. Chekhova," *Novoe slovo*, no. 8 (February 8, 1897): 45.

46. Novus, 45.

47. Novus, 46.

48. P.B., "Soshnikov," 4, 6, 7, 10, 11.

49. P.B., 4. This image recalls the resolute figure in Solomatkin's painting *Brodiachii muzykant* (The Wandering Musician), which was completed in 1871. For a discussion of the characteristics of male peasant attire, see Parmon, *Russkii narodnyi kostium*, 168–186.

50. P.B., "Soshnikov," 10.

51. P.B., 10.

52. P.B., 11.

53. P.B., 11.

54. This story is also referenced in chapter 5. Bylov, "Razdum′e," 12–16.

55. Bylov, 12.

56. Bylov, 12.

57. Bylov, 15.

58. Bylov, 15.

59. Bylov, 15.

60. Afanas′ev, "Za chuzhie den′gi."

61. Afanas′ev, 12.

62. Afanas′ev, 12.

63. Afanas′ev, 12.

64. Afanas′ev, 13.

65. Afanas′ev, 13.

66. Afanas′ev, 14.

67. Afanas′ev, 14.

68. Afanas′ev, 14.

69. Lynching rates rose during periods of economic hardship such as the depression of 1893–1898. Brundage, *Lynching in the New South*, 6; Senechal de la Roche, "Sociogenesis of Lynching," 60.

70. "Mrs. Kate Chopin: Author of Bayou Folk," *Current Literature* 16, no. 2 (August 1894): 106, American Periodicals, ProQuest; Seyersted, *Kate Chopin*, 93; "Biography," Kate Chopin International Society, http://www.katechopin.org/biography/, accessed May 3, 2019.

71. "Mrs. Kate Chopin," *Current Literature*, 106.

72. Potter, "Fiction of Kate Chopin," 42.

73. "Biography," Kate Chopin International Society.

74. Potter, "Fiction of Kate Chopin," 46.

75. During the nineteenth century in antebellum Louisiana, black Catholic slave-owning Creoles inhabited the Isle Brevelle, amassing land, wealth, and status. Chopin, "In and out of Old Natchitoches," 53; Nagel, *Race and Culture*, 126.

76. Chopin, "In and out of Old Natchitoches," 54.

77. Chopin, 56.

78. Chopin, 57.

79. Chopin, 60.

80. Hodes, *White Women, Black Men*, 202.

81. Apel, *Imagery of Lynching*, 28.

82. Bruce, *Plantation Negro as a Freeman*, 55.

83. Reuter, *Mulatto in the United States*, 18.

84. Reuter, 18.

85. Reuter, 19.

86. Chopin, "Désirée's Baby," 148.

87. Chopin, 151.

88. Chopin, 152.

89. "Fiction," *Art Amateur*, June 1894, 31.

90. "Bayou Folk," *Critic*, May 5, 1894, 21.

91. "Bayou Folk," 21.

92. Chesnutt, *Charles Waddell Chesnutt*, 1–4. The book's author, Helen M. Chesnutt, is the daughter of Charles Waddell Chesnutt.

93. Brodhead, *Journals of Charles W. Chesnutt*, 2; Andrews, *Charles W. Chesnutt*, 1–2.

94. Chesnutt, *Charles Waddell Chesnutt*, 5.

95. Chesnutt, 8–10.

96. Chesnutt, 5–6; Andrews, *Charles W. Chesnutt*, 2.

97. Andrews, *Charles W. Chesnutt*, 3.

98. Diary entry from January 3, 1881, in Brodhead, *Journals of Charles W. Chesnutt*, 157.

99. Diary entry from January 3, 1881, 158.

100. Andrews, *Charles W. Chesnutt*, 10.

101. Elrick B. Davis, "Du Bose Heyward's 'Mamba's Daughters' and Republication of Chesnutt's 'The Conjure Woman' Makes This 'Negro Literature Week,'" *Cleveland Press*, February 2, 1929, 10, box 1, folder 9, PC7, Charles W. Chesnutt Archive, Fayetteville State University.

102. Charles W. Chesnutt, *To Be an Author: The Letters of Charles W. Chesnutt, 1889–1905*, ed. Joseph R. McElrath Jr. and Robert C. Leitz (Princeton, NJ: Princeton University Press, 1997), 167, quoted in Thomas, *Literature of Reconstruction*, 30.

103. Chesnutt, *Conjure Woman*, 168.

104. William Hudson, "A New Delineator of Southern Life," *Self Culture Magazine*, no. 11 (July 1900): 409–411, Charles Chesnutt Digital Archive, https://chesnuttarchive.org /Reviews/OthersReviews/other7.html, accessed May 3, 2019.

105. Chesnutt, "Wife of His Youth," 102.

106. Chesnutt, 103.

107. Chesnutt, 104.

108. Chesnutt, 104.

109. Chesnutt, 105.

110. Chesnutt, 107.

111. Chesnutt, 109.

112. Chesnutt, 110.

113. Review of "The Wife of His Youth" and bio note, in Chronicle and Comment, *The Bookman*, 7 (August 1898): 452, Charles Chesnutt Digital Archive, http://www.chesnut tarchive.org/Reviews/WifeReviews/wife2.html, accessed May 3, 2019.

114. "Tales of Negro Life," in "Reviews of Many New Books That Are Well Worth Reading," *Worcester Evening Gazette*, December 11, 1899, 4, Charles Chesnutt Digital Archive, http://www.chesnuttarchive.org/Reviews/WifeReviews/wife39.html, accessed May 3, 2019.

115. Chesnutt, "Her Virginia Mammy," 126, 127.

116. Chesnutt, 129.

117. Chesnutt, 118.

118. Chesnutt, "The Sheriff's Children," 144.

119. Chesnutt, 147.

120. Review of *The Wife of His Youth*, Books and Authors, *Boston Courier*, January 21, 1900, 2, Charles Chesnutt Digital Archive, http://www.chesnuttarchive.org/Reviews/Wife Reviews/wife22.html, accessed May 3, 2019.

121. Review of *The Wife of His Youth*, *Boston Courier*, 2.

122. Review of *The Wife of His Youth*, Notes on New Books, *St. Louis Globe-Democrat*, December 16, 1899, 13, Charles Chesnutt Digital Archive, http://www.chesnuttarchive.org /Reviews/WifeReviews/wife25.html, accessed May 3, 2019.

123. Review of *The Wife of His Youth*, Among the Books, *Cambridge (MA) Tribune*, December 23, 1899, 2, Charles Chesnutt Digital Archive, http://www.chesnuttarchive.org /Reviews/WifeReviews/wife6.html, accessed May 3, 2019.

124. Durant and Louden, "Black Middle Class in America," 254–255.

125. Hale, *Making Whiteness*, 128.

126. Wallace and Smith, *Pictures and Progress*, 4, 330.

127. "To Am Meer from Canzonnetta. 'Canzonetta' died Aug. 30th 1897, on verso," Cartes-de-visite Collection, Schomburg Center for Research in Black Culture, Photographs and Prints Division, New York Public Library Digital Collections, http://digital collections.nypl.org/items/510d47e1-cdbd-a3d9-e040-e00a18064a99, accessed May 3, 2017; "Unidentified young woman wearing gloves, leaning on prop fence," Cartes-de-visite Collection, http://digitalcollections.nypl.org/items/510d47e1-cde9-a3d9-e040-e00a1 8064a99, accessed May 3, 2017; "Your friend, Jno. H. Smith," Cartes-de-visite Collection, http://digitalcollections.nypl.org/items/510d47e1-cda3-a3d9-e040-e00a18064a99, accessed May 3, 2017.

128. Some of Du Bois's most influential works include *The Philadelphia Negro* (1899), *The Souls of Black Folk* (1903), and *Black Reconstruction* (1935).

129. Later in his life, Du Bois became a Soviet sympathizer and joined the Communist Party at the age of ninety-three. Peter Kihss, "Dr. W. E. B. Du Bois Joins Communist Party at 93," *New York Times*, November 23, 1961.

130. Morris Lewis, "Paris and the International Exposition," *Colored American Magazine*, October 1900, 295.

131. W. E. B. Du Bois, "The American Negro at Paris," *American Monthly Review of Reviews* 22, no. 5 (1900): 575.

132. Smith, "'Looking at One's Self,'" 581.

133. African American Photographs Assembled for 1900 Paris Exposition, Library of Congress, http://www.loc.gov/pictures/collection/anedub/dubois.html, accessed May 3, 2017.

134. Together the novels sold millions of copies. Wells, *White Man's Burden*, 112.

135. Okuda, "'A Nation Is Born,'" 218.

136. Kinney, "Rhetoric of Racism," 146.

137. "To the Reader," original sketch of title page, preface, and dedication of *The Leopard's Spots*, Thomas Dixon Papers, Stuart A. Rose Manuscript, Archives, and Rare Book Library, Emory University.

138. Dixon, *Leopard's Spots*, 381.

139. Dixon, 100.

140. "The Points of View: What Is Said about 'The Leopard's Spots,' by Thomas Dixon, Jr.," clipping, box 1, folder 2, #23, "Miscellaneous Items: Photos, Clippings, 1902–1903," Dixon Papers.

141. "What Is Said about 'The Leopard's Spots.'"

142. "What Is Said about 'The Leopard's Spots.'"

143. In New York, a *Harper's Weekly* article explored the attitudes of different ethnic groups toward African Americans, remarking on the "natural antipathy" of the Irish toward blacks and the hostility of the countless "native Americans" who celebrated the 1900 New York City race riots. Gilmer Speed, "The Negro in New York: A Study of the Social and Industrial Condition of the Colored People in the Metropolis," *Harper's Weekly*, December 22, 1900, 1249.

144. A. J. McElway, "The Atlanta Riots: A Southern Point of View," *Outlook*, November 3, 1906, 557, American Periodicals, ProQuest.

145. McElway, 562.

146. Perrie, "Russian Peasant Movement," 124–125.

147. Moon, *Abolition of Serfdom*, 123–124.

148. *Agrarnoe dvizhenie v Rossii v 1905–1906 gg.*, cited in Perrie, "Russian Peasant Movement," 136.

Epilogue

1. S. Siu i Ko., "Shokolad iubileinyi v pamiat' osvobozhdeniia krest'ian, 1861–1911," Moscow, Russian National Library Ephemera Collection; Inna Kerasi, "Hermitage Volunteers and the Abolition of Serfdom," State Hermitage Volunteer Service, http://benevole.ru/en/2016/03/03/hermitage-volunteers-and-the-abolition-of-serfdom/, accessed May 9, 2017.

2. Supplement to *Moskovskii listok*, no. 8 (February 20, 1911): 3.

3. Supplement to *Moskovskii listok*, no. 9 (February 27, 1911): 2.

4. Supplement to *Moskovskii listok*, no. 8 (February 20, 1911): 7.

5. "17 oktiabria posledoval manifest," Runivers, https://www.runivers.ru/Runivers/calendar2.php?ID=61707&month=&year=, accessed September 8, 2018.

6. *Novoe vremia* 40 (February 19, 1911): 18; supplement to *Golos Moskvy*, February 19, 1911, 8.

7. "19 fevralia 1861 g.–19 fevralia 1911 g.," *Gazeta-kopeika (St. Petersburg)*, no. 929 (February 19, 1911): 1.

8. "19 fevralia 1861 g.–19 fevralia 1911 g.," 1.

9. Funke, *Krepostnichestvo i volia*.

10. The unsigned introduction may have been published by the editor, V. V. Funke.

11. Funke, *Krepostnichestvo i volia*, 5.

12. Carla Cordin, "1861 as a Russian and Soviet 'Lieu de mémoire,' Narrating and Commemorating the Abolition of Serfdom" (talk delivered at a conference at the University of Basel, October 28–30, 2011).

13. Cordin, "1861."

14. Dzhivelegov, Mel'gunov, and Picheta, *Velikaia reforma*, 1:3.

15. Cordin, "1861."

16. Cordin.

17. V. I. Lenin, "The Fiftieth Anniversary of the Fall of Serfdom," *Rabochaia gazeta*, no. 3, (February 8 [21], 1911), trans. R. Cymbala, Lenin Internet Archive, https://www.marxists .org/archive/lenin/works/1911/feb/08.htm, accessed May 3, 2019.

18. "Juneteenth" celebrations originated in Galveston, Texas, in 1866, when formerly enslaved African Americans celebrated Union major general Gordon Granger's announcement of their liberation on June 19, 1865.

19. "Negroes Celebrate: Attend Services throughout the Country on Emancipation Anniversary," *New York Times*, September 23, 1912, 3.

20. "The Philharmonic Concert: Commemoration of Emancipation—Brahms's Double Concerto Played," *New York Times*, January 3, 1913, 9.

21. Kachun, *Festivals of Freedom*, 247, 249.

22. Kachun, 247.

23. Quirin, "Du Bois, Ethiopianism and Ethiopia," 6.

24. "New York Exposition 1913," box 14, folder 152, Photographs of Prominent African Americans Collection, Beinecke Rare Book and Manuscript Library, Yale University.

25. W. E. B. Du Bois, "The National Emancipation Exposition," *Crisis*, November 1913, 339–341.

26. Kachun, *Festivals of Freedom*, 252.

27. For a comprehensive analysis of the number and type of Confederate monuments erected in North Carolina between 1890 and 1930, see Commemorative Landscapes of North Carolina, Documenting the American South, University of North Carolina at Chapel Hill, https://docsouth.unc.edu/commland/, accessed May 2, 2019.

28. "Standing Abraham Lincoln Sculpture," Nebraska State Capitol, https://capitol .nebraska.gov/standing-abraham-lincoln-sculpture, accessed May 3, 2019.

29. For further analysis of this sculpture and others, see Savage, *Standing Soldiers, Kneeling Slaves*.

30. Savage, *Standing Soldiers, Kneeling Slaves*, 90–92.

31. "Half a Century of Freedom," *Outlook* 101, no. 7 (June 15, 1912): 321, American Periodicals, ProQuest; "Some Facts as to the Progress of the Race," *Outlook*, November 8, 1913, 534; J. C. H., "The Negro Has Accomplished Much since Emancipation," *New York Times*, September 22, 1912.

32. Dr. M. A. Majors, "Illinois National Half-Century Anniversary of Negro Freedom, 1865–1915," *Indianapolis Freeman*, December 20, 1913, 8.

33. J. C. H., "The Negro Has Accomplished Much," 6.

34. J. C. H., 6.

35. James Weldon Johnson, "Fifty Years: Written on the Fiftieth Anniversary of Lincoln's Emancipation Proclamation," *New York Age*, February 11, 1915, box 68, folder 343, James Weldon Johnson and Grace Nail Johnson Papers, Beinecke Library, Yale University.

36. Johnson.

37. Johnson.

38. "Fifty Years of Emancipation," *Independent*, September 19, 1912, 682.

39. "William H. Lewis Delivers a Masterly Address before the Massachusetts General Assembly," *Washington Bee*, February 15, 1913, 4.

40. "William H. Lewis Delivers a Masterly Address," 4.

41. Kautsky, *Karl Kautsky*, 35.

42. For a comprehensive analysis of African American military service during World War I, see Lentz-Smith, *Freedom Struggles*.

43. See Bonnell, *Iconography of Power*.

Bibliography

Primary Sources

ARCHIVAL COLLECTIONS

Atlanta, Georgia
   Stuart A. Rose Manuscript, Archives, and Rare Book Library, Emory University
      Joel Chandler Harris Papers
      Thomas Dixon Papers
Cambridge, Massachusetts
   Houghton Library, Harvard University
      Louisa May Alcott Papers
Durham, North Carolina
   David M. Rubenstein Rare Book and Manuscript Library, Duke University
      Advertising Ephemera Collection
      J. Walter Thompson Company, Domestic Advertisements Collection
         and Publications Collection
      North Carolina Mutual Life Insurance Company Archives
      Roy Lightner Collection of Antique Advertisements
      Thomas Nelson Page Papers
      Tobacco Collection
      W. Duke, Sons & Co. Advertising Materials
Fayetteville, North Carolina
   Charles W. Chesnutt Archive, Fayetteville State University
      Charles Chesnutt Papers
Moscow, Russia
   State Historical Museum
      Poster Collection
   State Tret'iakov Gallery Archives
      Abram Efimovich Arkhipov Papers, Fond 47
      Filipp Andreevich Maliavin Papers, Fond 41
      Grigorii Grigor'evich Miasoedov Papers, Fond 133
      Il'ia Efimovich Repin Papers, Fond 50
      Ivan Nikolaevich Kramskoi Papers, Fond 16
      Vasilii Maksimovich Maksimov Papers, Fond 81
New Haven, Connecticut
   Beinecke Rare Book and Manuscript Library, Yale University
      James Weldon Johnson and Grace Nail Johnson Papers
      Photographs of Prominent African Americans Collection

New York, New York
  Frick Art Reference Library Manuscript Collection
  Metropolitan Museum of Art, Watson Library
    Carl Gutherz Papers
    Eastman Johnson Papers
    Object Files for Thomas Anshutz's *The Way They Live*
    Object Files for Thomas Waterman Wood's *A Bit of War History*
    Object Files for Winslow Homer's *Dressing for Carnival*
    William Aiken Walker Papers
    William D. Washington Papers
  New-York Historical Society
    Caricature and Cartoon Collection
    Leslie Dorsey Collection
    Subject Files
St. Petersburg, Russia
  Russian National Library
    Ephemera Collection
    Poster Collection
  Russian State Archive of Literature and Art
    Aleksei Feofilaktovich Pisemskii Papers, Fond 375
    Il'ia Efimovich Repin Papers, Fond 842
    Nikolai Alekseevich Nekrasov Papers, Fond 338
Worcester, Massachusetts
  American Antiquarian Society
    Trade Cards and Pamphlets, Ephemera Collection

PERIODICALS AND NEWSPAPERS

American

The Advance

American Art Journal

American Citizen

American Monthly Review of Reviews

Appletons' Journal of Literature, Science and Art

Art Amateur

Book Buyer

The Bookman

Boston Courier

Cambridge (MA) Tribune

The Chautauquan

Chicago Defender

Christian Inquirer

Cincinnati Enquirer

Cleveland Press

Colored American Magazine

The Commonwealth

Congregationalist and Christian World

The Crisis

The Critic

Current Literature

Daily News

The Dial

Evening Transcript

Frank Leslie's Illustrated Newspaper

Frank Leslie's Weekly

The Galaxy

Greater Pittsburg Magazine

Harper's Weekly

Hearth and Home

The Independent

Indianapolis Freeman

Kansas Baptist Herald

The Liberator
Lippincott's Monthly Magazine
Macon Telegraph
McClure's Magazine
Methodist Review
National Anti-Slavery Standard
National Era
New Englander
New England Messenger
New York Evangelist
New York Evening Post
New York Herald
New York Monthly Magazine
New York Times

The Outlook
Philadelphia Daily Evening Telegraph
Richmond News-Leader
Savannah Tribune
Scribner's Magazine
Scribner's Monthly
Self Culture Magazine
Southern Cultivator
Southern Literary Messenger
St. Louis Globe-Democrat
St. Nicholas Magazine
Washington Bee
Worcester Evening Gazette

Russian

Delo (Business)
Gazeta-kopeika (St. Petersburg) (Kopek Gazette, St. Petersburg)
Golos Moskvy (Voice of Moscow)
Istoricheskii vestnik (Historical Journal)
Khudozhestvennye novosti (Art News)
Krasnaia niva (Red Grainfield)
Moskovskii listok (Moscow Sheet)
Nedelia (The Week)
Niva (The Grainfield)
Novoe slovo (New Word)
Novoe vremia (New Time)
Novyi put' (New Pathway)
Ogonek (Little Flame)

Otechestvennye zapiski (Notes from the Fatherland)
Pchela (The Bee)
Rabochaia gazeta (Workers' Gazette)
Russkaia beseda (Russian Conversation)
Russkaia mysl' (Russian Thought)
Russkie vedomosti (Russian News)
Russkii arkhiv (Russian Archive)
Sovremennik (The Contemporary)
Strekoza (The Dragonfly)
Vestnik finansov, promyshlennosti i torgovli (Journal of Finance, Industry, and Trade)
Vsemirnaia illiustratsiia (Worldwide Illustration)

FICTION, DRAMA, AND POETRY

Afanas'ev, N. "Za chuzhie den'gi." Supplement to *Moskovskii listok*, no. 2 (January 8, 1908): 12–14.

Alcott, Louisa May. "An Hour." In *Louisa May Alcott on Race, Sex, and Slavery*, edited by Sarah Elbert, 47–68. Boston: Northeastern University Press, 1997. Originally published in *The Commonwealth* 3, nos. 13 and 14 (1864).

———. "M.L." In *Louisa May Alcott on Race, Sex, and Slavery*, edited by Sarah Elbert, 3–28. Boston: Northeastern University Press, 1997. Originally published in *The Commonwealth* 1, nos. 21, 22, 23, 24, and 25 (1863).

———. "My Contraband." In *Louisa May Alcott on Race, Sex, and Slavery*, edited by Sarah Elbert, 69–86. Boston: Northeastern University Press, 1997. Originally published as "The Brothers," *Atlantic Monthly* 12, no. 73 (November 1863).

Browne, Martha Griffith. *Autobiography of a Female Slave*. New York: Redfield, 1857. http://docsouth.unc.edu/neh/browne/browne.html.

Bylov, M. "Razdum'e (iz narodnoi zhizni)." Supplement to *Moskovskii listok*, no. 1 (January 1, 1906): 12–16.

Chekhov, Anton. "Muzhiki." 1897. In *Polnoe sobranie sochinenii i pisem v tridtsati tomakh. Tom 9, 1894–1897*, xi–xvii. Moscow: Nauka, 1977. http://az.lib.ru/c/chehow_a_p/text_0090.shtml#10.

Chesnutt, Charles Waddell. *The Conjure Woman*. Boston: Houghton Mifflin, 1889.

———. "Her Virginia Mammy." In *Charles W. Chesnutt: Stories, Novels, and Essays*, 113–130. New York: Library Classics of the United States, 2002.

———. "The Sheriff's Children." In *Charles W. Chesnutt: Stories, Novels, and Essays*, 131–148. New York: Library Classics of the United States, 2002.

———. "The Wife of His Youth." In *Charles W. Chesnutt: Stories, Novels, and Essays*, 101–112. New York: Library Classics of the United States, 2002.

———. *The Wife of His Youth, and Other Stories of the Color Line*. 1899. Boston: Houghton Mifflin, 1901.

Chopin, Kate. *Bayou Folk*. Boston: Houghton Mifflin, 1894. http://docsouth.unc.edu/southlit/chopinbayou/bayou.html.

———. "Désirée's Baby." In *Bayou Folk*, 147–158. Boston: Houghton Mifflin, 1894. http://docsouth.unc.edu/southlit/chopinbayou/bayou.html.

———. "In and out of Old Natchitoches." In *Bayou Folk*, 51–77. Boston: Houghton Mifflin, 1894. http://docsouth.unc.edu/southlit/chopinbayou/bayou.html.

Danilevskii, Grigorii. *Kniazhna Tarakanova*. 1883. Kiev: Dnipro, 1987. http://az.lib.ru/d/danilewskij_g_p/text_0050.shtml.

Dixon, Thomas, Jr. *The Clansman: A Historical Romance of the Ku Klux Klan*. New York: Doubleday, Page, 1905.

———. *The Leopard's Spots: A Romance of the White Man's Burden, 1865–1900*. New York: Doubleday, Page, 1902.

———. *The Traitor: A Story of the Fall of the Invisible Empire*. New York: Doubleday, Page, 1907.

Elbert, Sarah, ed. *Louisa May Alcott on Race, Sex, and Slavery*. Boston: Northeastern University Press, 1997.

Gorskii, A. "Metel': Novogodnii rasskaz." Supplement to *Moskovskii listok*, no. 1 (January 2, 1894): 2–6.

Harris, Joel Chandler. *Balaam and His Master, and Other Sketches and Stories*. New York: Houghton Mifflin, 1891.

———. "Free Joe and the Rest of the World." In *Free Joe, and Other Georgian Sketches*, 1–20. New York: Charles Scribner's Sons, 1887. http://docsouth.unc.edu/southlit/harrisj/harris.html.

———. *On the Plantation*. New York: D. Appleton, 1909.

———. *Told by Uncle Remus: New Stories of the Old Plantation*. New York: Grosset and Dunlap, 1905.

———. *Uncle Remus, His Songs and His Sayings: The Folk-Lore of the Old Plantation*. New York: D. Appleton, 1881.

Kennedy, John Pendleton. *The Swallow Barn, or A Sojourn in the Old Dominion*. Philadelphia: Carey & Lea, 1832.

Leskov, Nikolai. *Sobranie sochinenii v piati tomakh*. Tom 3. 1881. Moscow: Pravda, 1981.

Nekrasov, Nikolai. "Na Volge." 1860. http://www.ilibrary.ru/text/1117/p.1/index.html.

———. *Sobranie stikhotvorenii*. Tom 1. 1854. http://az.lib.ru/n/nekrasow_n_a/text_0010 .shtml.

———. *Stikhotvoreniia*. Moscow: Sovetskii pisatel', 1950.

———. "Zabytaia derevnia." In *Polnoe sobranie stikhotvorenii*. Vol. 1. 1854. http://az.lib.ru /n/nekrasow_n_a/text_0010.shtml.

Opochinin, Evgenii. "Posledniaia 'dusha.'" Supplement to *Moskovskii listok*, no. 75 (October 9, 1905): 2–10.

P. B. "Soshnikov." Supplement to *Moskovskii listok*, no. 5 (January 27, 1908): 4–10.

Page, Thomas Nelson. "Bred in the Bone." In *Bred in the Bone*, 1–60. New York: Charles Scribner's Sons, 1904. Originally published in *Century Illustrated Magazine*, October 1901.

———. *In Ole Virginia, or Marse Chan, and Other Stories*. 1887. New York: Charles Scribner's Sons, 1895. http://docsouth.unc.edu/southlit/pageolevir/page.html.

———. "Marse Chan: A Tale of Old Virginia." In *In Ole Virginia, or Marse Chan, and Other Stories*, 1–30. 1887. New York: Charles Scribner's Sons, 1895. http://docsouth.unc.edu /southlit/pageolevir/page.html.

———. "Old Jabe's Marital Experiments." In *Bred in the Bone*, 169–182. New York: Charles Scribner's Sons, 1904.

———. "Unc' Edinburg's Drowndin': A Plantation Echo." In *In Ole Virginia, or Marse Chan, and Other Stories*, 39–77. 1887. New York: Charles Scribner's Sons, 1895. http: //docsouth.unc.edu/southlit/pageolevir/page.html.

Pisemskii, Aleksei. *Gor'kaia sud'bina*. 1859. In *Sobranie sochinenii v 9 tomakh*. Vol. 9. Moscow: Pravda, 1959. http://az.lib.ru/p/pisemskij_a/text_0410.shtml.

Salias, Evgenii Salias. *Arakcheevskii synok*. St. Petersburg: Pechatnyi dvor, 1993. 1888. http://az.lib.ru/s/salias_e_a/text_0100.shtml.

Solov'ev, Vsevolod. *Staryi dom*. 1883. In *Sobranie sochinenii v vos'mi tomakh*. Vol. 6. Moscow: Bastion, 1997. http://az.lib.ru/s/solowxew_w_s/text_1883_stary_dom.shtml.

Tolstoi, Lev. *Anna Karenina*. The Maude translation. New York: W. W. Norton, 1970.

———. *Plays*. Vol. 2. Evanston, IL: Northwestern University Press, 1996.

AUTOBIOGRAPHIES, CORRESPONDENCE, DIARIES, MEMOIRS, TRACTS

Addison, Daniel Dulany, ed. *Lucy Larcom: Life, Letters, and Diary*. Boston: Houghton Mifflin, 1894.

Brodhead, Richard H., ed. *The Journals of Charles W. Chesnutt*. Durham, NC: Duke University Press, 1993.

Bruce, Philip Alexander. *The Plantation Negro as a Freeman: Observations on His Character, Condition, and Prospects in Virginia*. New York: G. P. Putnam's Sons, 1889.

Cheney, Ednah D. *The Life of Louisa May Alcott: Life, Letters, and Journals*. Boston: Robert Brothers, 1889.

Douglass, Frederick. *Narrative of the Life of Frederick Douglass*. Boston: Anti-Slavery Office, 1845.

Gornyi, Sergei. *Al'bom pamiati*. St. Petersburg: Giperion, 2011.

Harris, Julia Collier. *The Life and Letters of Joel Chandler Harris*. Boston: Houghton Mifflin, 1918.

Klimenov, E. P. *Prazdnichnye vospominaniia dlia krest'ian, osvobozhdennykh ot krepostnoi zavisimosti Vsemilostiveishim Manifestom 19-go fevralia 1861 goda. Pisal byvshii krespostnoi.* St. Petersburg, 1863. Russian National Library.

Kropotkin, Petr. *Memoirs of a Revolutionist.* London: Smith, Elder, 1899.

Lowery, Irving E. *Life on the Old Plantation in Ante-Bellum Days, or A Story Based on Facts.* Columbia, SC: State Company Printers, 1911. http://docsouth.unc.edu/neh/lowery/lowery.html.

Merrill, Walter M., ed. *The Letters of William Lloyd Garrison: From Disunion to the Brink of War, 1850–1860.* Cambridge, MA: Harvard University Press, 1976.

Nikitenko, Aleksandr. *Diary of a Russian Censor.* Translated by Helen Saltz Jacobson. Amherst: University of Massachusetts Press, 1975.

Pickens, William. *The Heir of Slaves: An Autobiography.* Concord, NH: Rumford, 1911. http://docsouth.unc.edu/fpn/pickens/pickens.html.

Vrangel, Nikolai. *Vospominaniia: Ot krepostnogo prava do bol'shevikov.* Moscow: Novoe literaturnoe obozrenie, 2003. Originally published in Berlin, 1924. http://www.dk1868.ru/history/VRANG1.htm.

Wells, Ida B. *Southern Lynch Law in All Its Phases.* New York: New York Age Print, 1892.

Yarmolinsky, Avraham, ed. *Letters of Anton Chekhov.* New York: Viking, 1973.

MISCELLANEOUS

"Demon igry: Kartezhnaia igra ne prineset dobra." April 1881. *Lubok.* Museum of Wooden Architecture and Peasant Life, Suzdal, Russia.

Shchedrin, Rodion. *Levsha: Skaz o tul'skom kosom Levshe.* Playbill. Opera performed at the Mariinsky II theater, St. Petersburg, Russia, September 9, 2013.

Secondary Sources

BOOKS AND ARTICLES

Aguilar, Jessika. "Folklore and the Construction of National Identity in Nineteenth Century Russian Literature." PhD diss., Columbia University, 2016.

Alaniz, José. *Komiks: Comic Art in Russia.* Jackson: University Press of Mississippi, 2011.

Allen, William Francis, Charles Pickard Ware, and Lucy McKim Garrison. *Slave Songs of the United States.* New York: A. Simpson, 1867. http://docsouth.unc.edu/church/allen/allen.html.

Alston, Lee J. "Issues in Postbellum Southern Agriculture." In *Agriculture and National Development: Views on the Nineteenth Century,* edited by Louis Ferleger, 207–228. Ames: Iowa State University Press, 1990.

Andrews, William L. *The Literary Career of Charles W. Chesnutt.* Baton Rouge: Louisiana State University Press, 1980.

———. *To Tell a Free Story: The First Century of Afro-American Autobiography, 1760–1865.* Urbana: University of Illinois Press, 1986.

Anikst, Mikhail, Nina Baburina, and Elena Chernevich. *Russian Graphic Design, 1880–1917.* New York: Abbeville, 1990.

Apel, Dora. *Imagery of Lynching: Black Men, White Women, and the Mob.* New Brunswick, NJ: Rutgers University Press, 2004.

Apel, Dora, and Shawn Michelle Smith. *Lynching Photographs*. Berkeley: University of California Press, 2007.

Arnesen, Eric. *Waterfront Workers of New Orleans: Race, Class, and Politics, 1863–1923*. Urbana: University of Illinois Press, 1994.

Ascher, Abraham. *The Revolution of 1905: Russia in Disarray*. Stanford, CA: Stanford University Press, 1994.

Avdeev, Alexandre, Alain Blum, and Irina Troitskaia. "Peasant Marriage in Nineteenth-Century Russia." Translated by Heather Juby. *Population* 59, no. 6 (2004): 721–764.

Baptist, Edward. *The Half Has Never Been Told: Slavery and the Making of American Capitalism*. New York: Basic Books, 2014.

Barkhatova, Elena, Irina Alexeeva, Vladimir Alexeev, Nicolas Chkolnyi, and Thierry Devynck. *Le premier âge d'or de l'affiche russe, 1890–1917*. Paris: Bibliothèque Forney, 1997.

Barthes, Roland. "Myth Today." In *The Routledge Language and Cultural Theory Reader*, edited by Luce Burke, Tony Crowley, and Alan Girvin, 410–418. New York: Routledge, 2003.

Bartlett, Rosamund. *Tolstoy: A Russian Life*. New York: Houghton Mifflin Harcourt, 2011.

Basker, James G., ed. *American Antislavery Writings: Colonial Beginnings to Emancipation*. New York: Library of America, 2012.

Beaty, John Owen. *John Esten Cooke, Virginian*. New York: Columbia University Press, 1922.

Beckert, Sven. *Empire of Cotton: A Global History*. New York: Knopf, 2014.

Belasco, Susan, ed. *Stowe in Her Own Time: A Biographical Chronicle of Her Life, Drawn from Recollections, Interviews, and Memoirs by Family, Friends, and Associates*. Iowa City: University of Iowa Press, 2009.

Beliaev, Iurii, ed. *Evgenii Salias: Sochineniia v dvukh tomakh*. Moscow: Khudozhestvennaia literatura, 1991. http://az.lib.ru/s/salias_e_a/text_0020.shtml.

———. "Liubimets chitaiushchei Rossii." In *Evgenii Salias: Sochineniia v dvukh tomakh*, edited by Iurii Beliaev. Vol. 1. Moscow: Khudozhestvennaia literatura, 1991. http://az.lib.ru/s/salias_e_a/text_0020.shtml.

Benjamin, S. G. W. *Our American Artists*. Boston: D. Lothrop, 1879.

Bergad, Laird. *The Comparative Histories of Slavery in Brazil, Cuba, and the United States*. New York: Cambridge University Press, 2007.

Berger, John. *Ways of Seeing*. London: British Broadcasting Corporation; Harmondsworth: Penguin Books, 1972.

Birkenmayer, Sigmund S. "N. A. Nekrasov: A Glimpse of the Man and the Poet." *Études Slaves et Est-Européennes / Slavic and East-European Studies* 12, no. 4 (1967/68): 188–200.

———. "The Peasant Poems of Nikolaj Nekrasov." *Slavic and East European Journal* 11, no. 2 (1967): 159–167.

Blackmon, Douglas. *Slavery by Another Name: The Re-enslavement of Black Americans from the Civil War to World War II*. New York: Anchor Books, 2009.

Blight, David. *Race and Reunion: The Civil War in American Memory*. Cambridge, MA: Belknap Press of Harvard University Press, 2001.

Bloch, Marc. "Pour une histoire comparée des sociétés européennes." *Revue de synthèse historique*, no. 46 (1928): 15–50.

Bogdanov, Igor. *Dym otechestva, ili Kratkaia istoriia tabakokureniia.* Moscow: Novoe literaturnoe obozrenie, 2007.

Boime, Albert. *The Art of Exclusion: Representing Blacks in the Nineteenth Century.* Washington, DC: Smithsonian Institution Press, 1990.

Bonnell, Victoria E. *Iconography of Power: Soviet Political Posters under Lenin and Stalin.* Berkeley: University of California Press, 1997.

Bowman, Shearer Davis. *Masters and Lords: Mid-Nineteenth Century U.S. Planters and Prussian Junkers.* New York: Oxford University Press, 1993.

Boyd, Alexander F. *Aspects of the Russian Novel.* London: Chatto & Windus, 1972.

The Boy Lincoln: Eastman Johnson, 1824–1906. Boston: H. K. Turner, 1909.

Brooks, Jeffrey. "The Russian Nation Imagined: The Peoples of Russia as Seen in Popular Imagery, 1860s–1890s." *Journal of Social History* 43, no. 3 (2010): 535–557.

———. *When Russia Learned to Read: Literacy and Popular Literature, 1861–1917.* Evanston, IL: Northwestern University Press, 2003.

Browder, Laura. *Slippery Characters: Ethnic Impersonators and American Identities.* Chapel Hill: University of North Carolina Press, 2000.

Brown, Joshua. *Beyond the Lines: Pictorial Reporting, Everyday Life, and the Crisis of Gilded-Age America.* Berkeley: University of California Press, 2002.

Brown, Nikki L. M., and Barry M. Stentiford, eds. *The Jim Crow Encyclopedia: Greenwood Milestones in African American History.* Westport, CT: Greenwood, 2008.

Brown, Thomas J., ed. *Reconstructions: New Perspectives on the Postbellum United States.* New York: Oxford University Press, 2006.

Bruce, Henry Clay. *The New Man: Twenty-Nine Years a Slave, Twenty-Nine Years a Free Man.* New York: P. Anstadt & Sons, 1895. http://docsouth.unc.edu/fpn/bruce/bruce.html.

Brundage, W. Fitzhugh. *Civilizing Torture: An American Tradition.* Cambridge, MA: Harvard University Press, 2018.

———. *Lynching in the New South: Georgia and Virginia, 1880–1930.* Urbana: University of Illinois Press, 1993.

———. "Reconstruction in the South." *Journal of the Civil War Era* 7, no. 1 (2017). https://journalofthecivilwarera.org/forum-the-futureof-reconstruction-studies /reconstruction-in-the-south/.

———. *The Southern Past: A Clash of Race and Memory.* Cambridge, MA: Belknap Press of Harvard University Press, 2005.

Brunson, Molly. *Russian Realisms: Literature and Painting, 1840–1890.* DeKalb: Northern Illinois University Press, 2016.

Burbank, Jane. *Russian Peasants Go to Court: Legal Culture in the Countryside, 1905–1917.* Bloomington: Indiana University Press, 2004.

Burbank, Jane, and Frederick Cooper. *Empires in World History: Power and the Politics of Difference.* Princeton, NJ: Princeton University Press, 2010.

Burke, Peter. *Eyewitnessing: The Uses of Images as Historical Evidence.* Ithaca, NY: Cornell University Press, 2001.

Burns, Sarah. "Images of Slavery: George Fuller's Depictions of the Antebellum South." *American Art Journal* 15, no. 3 (1983): 35–60.

Bushnell, John. "Did Serf Owners Control Serf Marriage? Orlov Serfs and Their Neighbors, 1773–1861." *Slavic Review* 52, no. 3 (1993): 419–445.

Byron, Joseph. *New York Life at the Turn of the Century in Photographs*. Text by Albert K. Baragwanath. New York: Dover Publications and the Museum of the City of New York, 1985.

Callow, Philip. *Chekhov: The Hidden Ground*. Chicago: Ivan R. Dee, 2001.

Carey, Brycchan. "Arguing in Prose: Abolitionist Letters and Novels." In *British Abolitionism and the Rhetoric of Sensibility: Writing, Sentiment, and Slavery, 1760–1807*, 73–106. New York: Palgrave Macmillan, 2005.

Carlson, Leonard A. "The Dawes Act and the Decline of Indian Farming." *Journal of Economic History* 38, no. 1 (1978): 274–276.

Casper, Scott E., Jeffrey D. Groves, Stephen W. Nissenbaum, and Michael Winship, eds. *A History of the Book in America*. Vol. 3, *The Industrial Book, 1840–1880*, edited by David D. Hall. Chapel Hill: Published in association with the American Antiquarian Society by the University of North Carolina Press, 2009.

Cato, Mary Ann. "Winslow Homer's Visits to Virginia during Reconstruction." *American Art Journal* 12, no. 1 (1980): 4–27.

Chadwick, Bruce. *The Reel Civil War: Mythmaking in American Film*. New York: Vintage Books, 2001.

Chakraborty, Satyasikha. "Mammies, Ayahs, Baboes: Postcards of Racialized Nursemaids from the Early Twentieth Century." *Visual Culture and Gender* 13 (2018): 17–31.

Chernina, Eugenia, Paul Castañeda Dower, and Andrei Markevich. "Property Rights and Internal Migration: The Case of the Stolypin Agrarian Reform in the Russian Empire." Working Paper 147. Centre for Economic and Financial Research at New Economic School, Moscow, 2010.

Chernyshevskii, Nikolai. *The Aesthetic Relations of Art to Reality*. 1855. Reprinted in *Russian Philosophy*. Vol. 2, *The Nihilists, the Populists, Critics of Religion and Culture*, edited by James M. Edie, James P. Scanlan, and Mary-Barbara Zeldin. Chicago: Quadrangle Books, 1965. https://www.marxists.org/reference/archive/chernyshevsky/1853/aesthetics-reality.htm.

Chesnutt, Helen M. *Charles Waddell Chesnutt: Pioneer of the Color Line*. Chapel Hill: University of North Carolina Press, 1952.

Coates, Rodney D., Abby L. Ferber, and David L. Brunsma. *The Matrix of Race: Social Construction, Intersectionality, and Inequality*. Los Angeles: Sage, 2018.

Cobb, James C. *Away Down South: A History of Southern Identity*. New York: Oxford University Press, 2005.

Confino, Alon. "Collective Memory and Cultural History: Problems of Method." AHR Forum, *American Historical Review* 102, no. 5 (1997): 1386–1403.

Confino, Michael. *Russia before the "Radiant Future": Essays in Modern History, Culture, and Society*. New York: Berghahn Books, 2011.

Conn, Steven, and Andrew Walker. "The History in the Art: Painting the Civil War." In "Terrain of Freedom: American Art and the Civil War." *Art Institute of Chicago Museum Studies* 27, no. 1 (2001): 60–81, 102–103.

Cook, Robert. *Civil War Memories: Contesting the Past in the United States since 1865*. Baltimore: Johns Hopkins University Press, 2017.

Coope, John. *Doctor Chekhov: A Study in Literature and Medicine*. Chale, Isle of Wight: Cross Publishing, 1997.

Cooper, Frederick, Thomas C. Holt, and Rebecca J. Scott. *Beyond Slavery: Explorations of Race, Labor, and Citizenship in Postemancipation Societies*. Chapel Hill: University of North Carolina Press, 2000.

Cox, Karen L. *Dreaming of Dixie: How the South Was Created in American Popular Culture*. Chapel Hill: University of North Carolina Press, 2011.

Cruz, Bárbara C., and Michael J. Berson. "The American Melting Pot? Miscegenation Laws in the United States." *OAH Magazine of History* 15, no. 4 (2001): 80–84.

Culbertson, Tom. "Illustrated Essay: The Golden Age of American Political Cartoons." *Journal of the Gilded Age and Progressive Era* 7, no. 3 (2008): 276–295.

Culp, Daniel Wallace, ed. *Twentieth Century Negro Literature, or A Cyclopedia of Thought on the Vital Topics Relating to the American Negro*. Toronto: J. L. Nichols, 1902.

Dahn, Eurie, and Brian Sweeney. "A Brief History of the *Colored American Magazine*." *Colored American*. https://coloredamerican.org/?page_id=70. Accessed November 10, 2018.

Dal Lago, Enrico. *American Slavery, Atlantic Slavery, and Beyond: The U.S. "Peculiar Institution" in International Perspective*. London: Routledge, 2016.

Dal Lago, Enrico, and Constantina Katsari, eds. *Slave Systems: Ancient and Modern*. New York: Cambridge University Press, 2008.

Davidson, Cathy N. "Towards a History of Books and Readers." *American Quarterly* 40, no. 1 (1988): 7–17.

Davis, John. "Eastman Johnson's Negro Life at the South and Urban Slavery in Washington, D.C." *Art Bulletin* 80, no. 1 (1998): 67–92.

Degler, Carl N. *Neither Black nor White: Slavery and Race Relations in Brazil and the United States*. New York: Macmillan, 1971.

Dennison, Tracy. *The Institutional Framework of Russian Serfdom*. New York: Cambridge University Press, 2011.

Dennison, Tracy, and Steven Nafziger. "Micro-Perspectives on Living Standards in Nineteenth-Century Russia." Working paper. Williams College, Department of Economics, Williamstown, MA, 2011. https://web.williams.edu/Economics/wp /Nafziger_MicroLivingStandards.pdf.

Dianina, Katia. *When Art Makes News: Writing Culture and Identity in Imperial Russia*. DeKalb: Northern Illinois University Press, 2013.

Dmitriev-Mamonov, Vasilii Aleksandrovich. *Ukazatel' deistvuiushchikh v Imperii aktsionernykh predpriiatii i torgovykh domov*. Tom 2. St. Petersburg: E. Bern', 1905.

Downes, William Howe. *The Life and Works of Winslow Homer*. Vol. 3. Boston: Houghton Mifflin, 1911.

Doyle, Don H. *The Cause of All Nations: An International History of the American Civil War*. New York: Basic Books, 2015.

Dupuy, Ernest. *The Great Masters of Russian Literature in the Nineteenth Century*. Translated by Nathan Dole. New York: T. G. Cromwell, 1886.

Durant, Thomas J., Jr., and Joyce S. Louden. "The Black Middle Class in America: Historical and Contemporary Perspectives." *Phylon* 47, no. 4 (1986): 253–263.

Dzhivelegov, A., S. Mel'gunov, and V. Picheta, eds. *Velikaia reforma: Russkoe obshchestvo i krest'ianskii vopros v proshlom i nastoiashchem*. Tom 1. Moscow: I. D. Sytin, 1911.

Easley, Roxanne. *The Emancipation of the Serfs in Russia: Peace Arbitrators and the Development of Civil Society*. New York: Routledge, 2008.

Eklof, Ben. *Russian Peasant Schools: Officialdom, Village Culture, and Popular Pedagogy, 1861–1914*. Berkeley: University of California Press, 1986.

Eltis, David, ed. *Coerced and Free Migration: Global Perspectives*. Stanford, CA: Stanford University Press, 2002.

Engelsing, Rolf. *Der Bürger als Leser: Lesergeschichte in Deutschland, 1500–1800*. Stuttgart: Metzlersche, 1973.

Engelstein, Laura. *Slavophile Empire: Imperial Russia's Illiberal Path*. Ithaca, NY: Cornell University Press, 2009.

Fahs, Alice. *The Imagined Civil War: Popular Literature of the North and South, 1861–1865*. Chapel Hill: University of North Carolina Press, 2001.

Farah, Megan Dean. "Autocratic Abolitionists: Tsarist Anti-Slavery Campaigns." In *A Global History of Anti-Slavery Politics in the Nineteenth Century*, edited by William Mulligan and Maurice Bric, 97–116. New York: Palgrave Macmillan, 2013.

Farnsworth, Beatrice. *Russian Peasant Women*. New York: Oxford University Press, 1992.

Feyel, Gilles. "Presse et publicité en France (XVIIIe et XIXe siècles)." *Revue historique* 4, no. 628 (2003): 837–868.

Field, Daniel. *The End of Serfdom: Nobility and Bureaucracy in Russia, 1855–1861*. Cambridge, MA: Harvard University Press, 1976.

Figes, Orlando. *Natasha's Dance: A Cultural History of Russia*. New York: Henry Holt, 2002.

Finkelman, Paul. *Defending Slavery: Proslavery Thought in the Old South; A Brief History with Documents*. Boston: Bedford / St. Martin's, 2003.

Fitzgerald, Michael W. *Splendid Failure: Postwar Reconstruction in the American South*. Chicago: Ivan R. Dee, 2007.

Foner, Eric. *Forever Free: The Story of Emancipation and Reconstruction*. Illustrations edited and with commentary by Joshua Brown. New York: Knopf, 2005.

———. *Freedom's Lawmakers: A Directory of Black Officeholders during Reconstruction*. New York: Oxford University Press, 1993.

———. *A Short History of Reconstruction, 1863–1877*. New York: HarperCollins, 2010.

Foote, Shelby. Introduction to *Anton Chekhov: Later Short Stories: 1888–1903*, xi–xvii. Edited by Shelby Foote. Translated by Constance Garnett. New York: Random House, 1998.

Foster, Gaines. *Ghosts of the Confederacy: Defeat, the Lost Cause, and the Emergence of the New South, 1865 to 1913*. New York: Oxford University Press, 1987.

Françon, Marcel. "Poésie pure et art pour art." *French Review* 20, no. 1 (1946): 14–17.

Fredrickson, George M. *The Black Image in the White Mind: The Debate on Afro-American Character and Destiny, 1817–1914*. New York: Harper & Row, 1971.

———. "The Historical Construction of Race and Citizenship in the United States." Identities, Conflict, and Cohesion Programme Paper 1. United Nations Research Institute for Social Development, Geneva, 2003.

Freeborn, Richard. "The Nineteenth Century: The Age of Realism, 1855–80." In *The Cambridge History of Russian Literature*, edited by Charles A. Moser, 248–332. Cambridge: Cambridge University Press, 1989.

Freehling, William. *The Road to Disunion*. Vol. 1, *Secessionists at Bay, 1776–1854*. New York: Oxford University Press, 1991.

Frieden, Nancy Mandelker. *Russian Physicians in an Era of Reform and Revolution, 1856–1905*. Princeton, NJ: Princeton University Press, 2014.

Frierson, Cathy. *All Russia Is Burning! A Cultural History of Fire and Arson in Late Imperial Russia*. Seattle: University of Washington Press, 2002.

———. *Peasant Icons: Representations of Rural People in Late Nineteenth-Century Russia*. New York: Oxford University Press, 1993.

Frisken, Amanda K. "'A Song without Words': Anti-Lynching Imagery in the African American Press, 1889–1898." *Journal of African American History* 97, no. 3 (2012): 240–269.

Fuller, William C., Jr. *Civil-Military Conflict in Imperial Russia, 1881–1914*. Princeton, NJ: Princeton University Press, 1985.

Funke, V. V., ed. *Krepostnichestvo i volia*. Moscow: A. A. Levenson, 1911.

Furth, Leslie. "'The Modern Medea' and Race Matters: Thomas Satterwhite Noble's 'Margaret Garner.'" *American Art* 12, no. 2 (1998): 36–57.

Gallagher, Gary W. *The Union War*. Cambridge, MA: Harvard University Press, 2011.

Garrison Centenary Committee of the Suffrage League of Boston and Vicinity. *The Celebration of the One Hundredth Anniversary of the Birth of William Lloyd Garrison, by the Colored Citizens of Greater Boston*. Boston, 1906.

Gates, Henry Louis, Jr. *Life upon These Shores: Looking at African American History, 1513–2008*. New York: Knopf, 2011.

———. *Stony the Road: Reconstruction, White Supremacy, and the Rise of Jim Crow*. New York: Penguin, 2019.

Gavrilova, Liana. "K 150-letiiu so dnia rozhdeniia Evgeniia Opochinina—pisatelia, zhurnalista i kollektsionera." *Anfas-Profil'* 17, no. 171 (May 15, 2008). http://www.anfas -news.ru.postman.ru/news/index.php?ELEMENT_ID=1625.

Gheith, Jehanne. *Finding the Middle Ground: Krestovskii, Tur, and the Power of Ambivalence in Nineteenth-Century Russian Women's Prose*. Evanston, IL: Northwestern University Press, 2004.

Gleeson, David T., and Simon Lewis, eds. *The Civil War as Global Conflict: Transnational Meanings of the American Civil War*. Columbia: University of South Carolina Press, 2014.

Glinternik, Eleonora M. *Reklama v Rossii: XVIII–pervoi poloviny XX veka*. St. Petersburg: Aurora, 2007.

Goings, Kenneth. *Mammy and Uncle Mose: Black Collectibles and American Stereotyping*. Bloomington: Indiana University Press, 1994.

Goldsmith, Raymond W. "The Economic Growth of Tsarist Russia, 1860–1913." *Economic Development and Cultural Change* 9, no. 3 (1961): 441–475.

Golubev, A. E. *Nikolai Alekseevich Nekrasov: Biografiia, kriticheskii obzor poezii, sobranie stikhotvorenii, posviashchennykh pamiati poeta, svod statei o N. A. Nekrasove s 1840 goda*. St. Petersburg: M. Stasiulevicha, 1878.

Gorianskaia, S. F. "Pervye besplatnye gorodskie chital'ni v St. Peterburge (Organizatsiia ikh i itogi deiatel'nosti za 1888 god)." *Russkaia mysl'*, no. 10 (1889): 86–96.

Gorshkov, Boris B. *Peasants in Russia from Serfdom to Stalin: Accommodation, Survival, Resistance*. London: Bloomsbury, 2018.

Gossett, Thomas F. *"Uncle Tom's Cabin" and American Culture*. Dallas: Southern Methodist University Press, 1985.

Gregory, Paul. *Before Command: An Economic History of Russia from Emancipation to the First Five-Year Plan*. Princeton, NJ: Princeton University Press, 1994.

Griffin, Martin. *Ashes of the Mind: War and Memory in Northern Literature, 1865–1900.* Amherst: University of Massachusetts Press, 2009.

Griffin, Randall C. *Thomas Anshutz: Artist and Teacher.* Huntington, NY: Heckscher Museum, 1994.

Guelzo, Allen C. "Lincoln and the Abolitionists." *Wilson Quarterly* 24, no. 4 (2000): 58–70.

Hahn, Steven. "Class and State in Postemancipation Societies: Southern Planters in Comparative Perspective." *American Historical Review* 95, no. 1 (1990): 75–98.

———. *A Nation without Borders: The United States and Its World in an Age of Civil Wars, 1830–1910.* New York: Penguin, 2016.

Hale, Grace Elizabeth. *Making Whiteness: The Culture of Segregation in the South, 1890–1940.* New York: Vintage Books, 1999.

Hanne, Michael. *The Power of the Story: Fiction and Political Change.* Providence, RI: Berghahn Books, 1994.

Hapgood, Isabel Florence. *A Survey of Russian Literature, with Selections.* New York: Chautauqua Press, 1902.

Harris, M. Keith. *Across the Bloody Chasm: The Culture of Commemoration among Civil War Veterans.* Baton Rouge: Louisiana State University Press, 2014.

Harrisburg, Halley K., and Jonathan P. Binstock, eds. *African American Art: 200 Years.* New York: Michael Rosenfeld Gallery, 2008.

Harrold, Stanley. *The Rise of Aggressive Abolitionism: Addresses to the Slaves.* Lexington: University Press of Kentucky, 2004.

Harvey, Eleanor Jones. *The Civil War and American Art.* Washington, DC: Smithsonian American Art Museum in association with Yale University Press, 2012.

———. "Painting Freedom." *New York Times,* October 30, 2013.

Henze, Charlotte E. *Disease, Health Care and Government in Late Imperial Russia: Life and Death on the Volga, 1823–1914.* London: Routledge, 2010.

Hilton, Marjorie. *Selling to the Masses: Retailing in Russia, 1880–1930.* Pittsburgh: University of Pittsburgh Press, 2012.

Hochman, Barbara. *"Uncle Tom's Cabin" and the Reading Revolution: Race, Literacy, Childhood, and Fiction, 1851–1911.* Amherst: University of Massachusetts Press, 2011.

Hodes, Martha. *White Women, Black Men.* New Haven, CT: Yale University Press, 2014.

Holt, Thomas C. "'An Empire over the Mind': Emancipation, Race, and Ideology in the British West Indies and the American South." In *Region, Race, and Reconstruction: Essays in Honor of C. Vann Woodward,* edited by J. Morgan Kousser and James McPherson, 283–313. New York: Oxford University Press, 1982.

Iakubovich, P. F. *Nikolai Nekrasov: Ego zhizn' i literaturnaia deiatel'nost'.* Biograficheskaia biblioteka Florentiia Pavlenkova. 1907. http://az.lib.ru/j/jakubowich_p_f/text_0020.shtml.

Ignatiev, Noel. *How the Irish Became White.* New York: Routledge, 1995.

Izmailov, Aleksandr Alekseevich. *Sviatochnye rasskazy.* St. Petersburg: N. O. Merts, 1904. http://az.lib.ru/i/izmajlow_a_a/text_1904_v_s_soloviev_oldorfo.shtml.

Jackson, David. *The Wanderers and Critical Realism in Nineteenth-Century Russian Painting.* Manchester: Manchester University Press, 2006.

Janney, Caroline. *Remembering the Civil War: Reunion and the Limits of Reconciliation.* Chapel Hill: University of North Carolina Press, 2013.

JBHE Foundation. "Jonkonnu." *Journal of Blacks in Higher Education*, no. 17 (1997): 70.

Johns, Elizabeth. *American Genre Painting: The Politics of Everyday Life*. New Haven, CT: Yale University Press, 1991.

Johnson, Robert Eugene. "Peasant Migration and the Russian Working Class: Moscow at the End of the Nineteenth Century." *Slavic Review* 35, no. 4 (1976): 652–664.

Kachun, Mitch. *Festivals of Freedom: Meaning and Memory in African American Emancipation Celebrations, 1808–1915*. Amherst: University of Massachusetts Press, 2006.

Kaestle, Carl F. *Literacy in the United States: Readers and Reading since 1880*. New Haven, CT: Yale University Press, 1993.

Kaestle, Carl F., and Janice A. Radway, eds. *A History of the Book in America*. Vol. 4, *Print in Motion: The Expansion of Publishing and Reading in the United States, 1880–1940*, edited by David D. Hall. Chapel Hill: Published in association with the American Antiquarian Society by the University of North Carolina Press, 2009.

Kahan, Arcadius. *Russian Economic History: The Nineteenth Century*. Edited by Roger Weiss. Chicago: University of Chicago Press, 1989.

Kalashnikova, N. "Russia's First Ethnographic Exhibition." In *European Slavs and the Peoples of Russia: In Commemoration of the 140th Anniversary of the First Ethnographic Exhibition Held in 1867*, 11–37. St. Petersburg: Slavia, 2008.

Kantrowitz, Stephen. *More than Freedom: Fighting for Black Citizenship in a White Republic, 1829–1889*. New York: Penguin, 2012.

Kaplan, Max. *Leisure Time in America: A Social Inquiry*. New York: John Wiley and Sons, 1960.

Kappeler, Andreas. *The Russian Empire: A Multiethnic History*. Translated by Alfred Clayton. Essex, UK: Pearson Education, 2001.

Kautsky, John H. *Karl Kautsky: Marxism, Revolution, and Democracy*. New Brunswick, NJ: Transaction, 1994.

Kenez, Peter. *Cinema and Soviet Society, 1917–1953*. Cambridge: Cambridge University Press, 1992.

Kennedy-Nolle, Sharon D. *Writing Reconstruction: Race, Gender, and Citizenship in the Postwar South*. Chapel Hill: University of North Carolina Press, 2015.

Kerr-Ritchie, Jeffrey R. *Freedom's Seekers: Essays on Comparative Emancipation*. Baton Rouge: Louisiana State University Press, 2013.

Kingston-Mann, Esther, and Timothy Mixter, eds. *Peasant Economy, Culture, and Politics of European Russia, 1800–1921*. Princeton, NJ: Princeton University Press, 1991.

Kinney, James. "The Rhetoric of Racism: Thomas Dixon and the 'Damned Black Beast.'" *American Literary Realism* 15, no. 2 (1982): 145–154.

Klein, Herbert. *Slavery in the Americas: A Comparative Study of Virginia and Cuba*. Chicago: University of Chicago Press, 1967.

Knight, Nathaniel. *The Empire on Display: Ethnographic Exhibition and the Conceptualization of Human Diversity in Post-Emancipation Russia*. Washington, DC: National Council for Eurasian and East European Research, 2001.

Knowles, A. V. "Tolstoy's Literary Reputation before 'War and Peace.'" *Modern Language Review* 72, no. 3 (1977): 627–639.

Kokorev, A. "Salias-de-Tournemir." In *Literaturnaia entsiklopediia*, vol. 11, *[M.]*, *1929–1939*. T. 10, Stb. 500–501. Moscow, 1937. http://az.lib.ru/s/salias_e_a/text_0010.shtml.

Kolchin, Peter. "Comparative Perspectives on Emancipation in the U.S. South: Reconstruction, Radicalism, and Russia." *Journal of the Civil War Era* 2, no. 2 (2012): 203–232.

———. "Reexamining Southern Emancipation in Comparative Perspective." *Journal of Southern History* 81, no. 1 (2015): 7–40.

———. *A Sphinx on the American Land: The Nineteenth-Century South in Comparative Perspective*. Baton Rouge: Louisiana State University Press, 2003.

———. *Unfree Labor: American Slavery and Russian Serfdom*. Cambridge, MA: Belknap Press of Harvard University Press, 1987.

Kollmann, Nancy Shields. *The Russian Empire, 1450–1801*. New York: Oxford University Press, 2016.

Koonen, Alisa. *Stranitsy zhizni*. Moscow: Iskusstvo, 1985. http://teatr-lib.ru/Library /Koonen/Stranitsi_zhizni/#_Toc192914001.

Kousser, J. Morgan, and James McPherson, eds. *Region, Race, and Reconstruction: Essays in Honor of C. Vann Woodward*. New York: Oxford University Press, 1982.

Kruglov, Vladimir. "The Peasantry in Russian Painting." In *The World of the Peasantry in Russian Art: The State Russian Museum*. St. Petersburg: Palace Editions, 2005.

Leach, William R. *Land of Desire: Merchants, Power, and the Rise of a New American Culture*. New York: Pantheon Books, 1993.

Lears, T. J. Jackson. *Fables of Abundance: A Cultural History of Advertising in America*. New York: Basic Books, 1994.

———. *No Place of Grace: Antimodernism and the Transformation of American Culture, 1880–1920*. Chicago: University of Chicago Press, 1981.

Le Beau, Bryan. "African Americans in Currier and Ives's America: The Darktown Series." *Journal of American and Comparative Cultures* 23, no. 1 (2000): 71–84.

———. "'Colored Engravings for the People': The World according to Currier and Ives." *American Studies* 35, no. 1 (1994): 131–141.

Lee, Chulhee. "Socioeconomic Differences in the Health of Black Union Soldiers during the American Civil War." *Social Science History* 33, no. 4 (2009): 427–457.

Lentz-Smith, Adriane. *Freedom Struggles*. Cambridge, MA: Harvard University Press, 2010.

Lieven, Dominic. "The Elites." In *The Cambridge History of Russia*. Vol. 2, *Imperial Russia, 1689–1917*, edited by Dominic Lieven, 225–244. Cambridge: Cambridge University Press, 2006.

———. *Empire: The Russian Empire and Its Rivals*. New Haven, CT: Yale University Press, 2002.

Lovell, Stephen. *Russia in the Microphone Age: A History of Soviet Radio, 1919–1970*. New York: Oxford University Press, 2015.

Lubin, David M. *Picturing a Nation: Art and Social Change in Nineteenth-Century America*. New Haven, CT: Yale University Press, 1994.

Lykova, Tatiana, ed. *The State Tret'iakov Gallery*. Moscow: ScanRus Publishing House, 2012.

Lykova, Tatiana, Irina Volchenkova, and Kate Cook, eds. *Masterpieces of the State Tretyakov Gallery: Russian Art from the 12th to early 20th Century*. Moscow: Red Square Publishers, 2006.

MacKay, John. "'And Hold the Bondman Still': Biogeography and Utopia in Slave and Serf Narratives." *Biography* 25, no. 1 (2002): 110–129.

———, trans. and ed. *Four Russian Serf Narratives*. Madison: University of Wisconsin Press, 2009.

———. *True Songs of Freedom: "Uncle Tom's Cabin" in Russian Culture and Society*. Madison: University of Wisconsin Press, 2013.

Maiorova, Olga. *From the Shadow of Empire: Defining the Russian Nation through Cultural Mythology, 1855–1870*. Madison: University of Wisconsin Press, 2010.

Mankov, Lyubov. "Le Comte de Salhias-Tournemire (1840–1908), un Alexandre Dumas russe." *Sciences en Russie* 2 (1997). http://www.tournemire.net/salias.htm.

Manning, Chandra. *Troubled Refuge: Struggling for Freedom in the Civil War*. New York: Knopf, 2016.

Mazour, Anatole G. "Economic Decline of Landlordism in Russia." *The Historian* 8, no. 2 (1946): 156–162.

McElroy, Guy C. *Facing History: The Black Image in American Art, 1710–1940*. San Francisco: Bedford Arts, Publishers, in association with the Corcoran Gallery of Art, 1990.

McElya, Micki. *Clinging to Mammy: The Faithful Slave in Twentieth-Century America*. Cambridge, MA: Harvard University Press, 2007.

McPherson, James. *For Cause and Comrades: Why Men Fought in the Civil War*. New York: Oxford University Press, 1997.

McReynolds, Louise. *The News under Russia's Old Regime: The Development of a Mass-Circulation Press*. Princeton, NJ: Princeton University Press, 1991.

———. *Russia at Play: Leisure Activities at the End of the Tsarist Era*. Ithaca, NY: Cornell University Press, 2003.

McWhirter, David. "Introduction: Rethinking Southern Studies." In "'Southern Literature' / Southern Cultures: Rethinking Southern Literary Studies." Special issue, *South Central Review* 22, no. 1 (2005): 1–3.

Minchenkov, Ia. D. *Vospominaniia o peredvizhnikakh*. Leningrad: Khudozhnik RSFSR, 1965.

Mirsky, D. S. *A History of Russian Literature*. New York: Knopf, 1966.

Mizruchi, Susan L. *The Rise of Multicultural America: Economy and Print Culture, 1865–1915*. Chapel Hill: University of North Carolina Press, 2008.

Mogilner, Marina. "Beyond, against, and with Ethnography: Physical Anthropology as a Science of Russian Modernity." In *An Empire of Others: Creating Ethnographic Knowledge in Imperial Russia and the USSR*, edited by Roland Cvetkovski and Alexis Hofmeister, 81–119. Budapest: Central European University Press, 2014.

———. *Homo Imperii: A History of Physical Anthropology in Russia*. Lincoln: University of Nebraska Press, 2013.

Moon, David. *The Abolition of Serfdom in Russia, 1762–1907*. London: Pearson Education, 2001.

———. "Estimating the Peasant Population of Late Imperial Russia from the 1897 Census: A Research Note." *Europe-Asia Studies* 48, no. 1 (1996): 141–153.

———. "Peasant Migration, the Abolition of Serfdom, and the Internal Passport System in the Russian Empire, c. 1800–1914." In *Coerced and Free Migration: Global Perspectives*, edited by David Eltis, 324–357. Stanford, CA: Stanford University Press, 2002.

———. *The Russian Peasantry, 1600–1930: The World the Peasants Made.* New York: Addison Wesley Longman, 1999.

Moran, James. *Printing Presses: History and Development from the Fifteenth Century to Modern Times.* Berkeley: University of California Press, 1978.

Moser, Charles A., ed. *The Cambridge History of Russian Literature.* Cambridge: Cambridge University Press, 1989.

———. *Pisemsky: A Provincial Realist.* Cambridge, MA: Harvard University Press, 1969.

Nagel, James. *Race and Culture in New Orleans Stories: Kate Chopin, Grace King, Alice Dunbar-Nelson, and George Washington Cable.* Tuscaloosa: University of Alabama Press, 2014.

Nagler, Jörg, Don H. Doyle, and Marcus Gräser, eds. *The Transnational Significance of the American Civil War.* Cham, Switzerland: Springer Nature, 2016.

Nesterova, Yelena. *The Itinerants: The Masters of Russian Realism, Second Half of the 19th and Early 20th Centuries.* St. Petersburg: Aurora, 1996.

Neuberger, Joan. *Hooliganism: Crime, Culture, and Power in St. Petersburg, 1900–1914.* Berkeley: University of California Press, 1993.

———. "Stories of the Street: Hooliganism in the St. Petersburg Popular Press." *Slavic Review* 48, no. 2 (1989): 177–194.

Newman, Richard, *Go Down, Moses: A Celebration of the African-American Spiritual.* New York: Clarkson, 1998.

Nichols, Charles H. "Who Read the Slave Narratives?" *Phylon Quarterly* 20, no. 2 (1959): 149–162.

Nikolaev, P. A. *Russkie pisateli, 1800–1917.* 5 vols. Moscow: Bol'shaia rossiiskaia entsiklopediia, 1992–2007.

Nolan, Alan T. "The Anatomy of the Myth." In *The Myth of the Lost Cause and Civil War History,* edited by Gary W. Gallagher and Alan T. Nolan, 11–34. Bloomington: Indiana University Press, 2000.

Novak, Barbara. *American Painting of the Nineteenth Century: Realism, Idealism, and the American Experience.* New York: Praeger, 1969.

Okuda, Akiyo Ito. "'A Nation Is Born': Thomas Dixon's Vision of White Nationhood and His Northern Supporters." *Journal of American Culture* 32, no. 3 (2009): 214–231.

Ore, Tracey E. *The Social Construction of Difference and Inequality: Race, Class, Gender, and Sexuality.* New York: Oxford University Press, 2019.

Otterstrom, Samuel M., and Carville Earle. "The Settlement of the United States from 1790 to 1990: Divergent Rates of Growth and the End of the Frontier." *Journal of Interdisciplinary History* 33, no. 1 (2002): 59–85.

Oubre, Claude F. *Forty Acres and a Mule: The Freedmen's Bureau and Black Land Ownership.* Baton Rouge: Louisiana State University Press, 1978.

Ozerov, I. A. *Nevskii prospekt: Istoriia Sankt-Peterburga v fotografiiakh; Konets XIX–nachalo XX veka.* Moscow: Tsentrpoligraf, 2003.

Page, Thomas Nelson. "The Old-Time Negro." In *The Novels, Stories, Sketches, and Poems of Thomas Nelson Page,* vol. 12, 301–342. New York: Charles Scribner's Sons, 1908.

Painter, Nell. *Creating Black Americans: African American History and Its Meanings, 1619 to the Present.* New York: Oxford University Press, 2006.

Parkhurst, Jessie W. "The Role of the Black Mammy in the Plantation Household." *Journal of Negro History* 23, no. 3 (1938): 349–369.

Parmon, Fedor Maksimovich. *Russkii narodnyi kostium*. Moscow: V. Shevchuk, 2012.

Patterson, Orlando. *Slavery and Social Death: A Comparative Study*. Cambridge, MA: Harvard University Press, 1982.

Peppard, Murray B. *Nikolai Nekrasov*. New York: Twayne, 1967.

Perrie, Maureen. "The Russian Peasant Movement of 1905–1907: Its Social Composition and Revolutionary Significance." *Past and Present* 57 (1972): 123–155.

Phelps, Elizabeth Stuart. *Our Famous Women: An Authorized Record of the Lives and Deeds of Distinguished American Women of Our Times*. Hartford, CT: A. D. Worthington, 1884.

Pipes, Richard. *Russia under the Old Regime*. London: Penguin Books, 1995.

Potter, Richard H. "Negroes in the Fiction of Kate Chopin." *Louisiana History: The Journal of the Louisiana Historical Association* 12, no. 1 (1971): 41–58.

Prince, K. Stephen. *Stories of the South: Race and the Reconstruction of Southern Identity, 1865–1915*. Chapel Hill: University of North Carolina Press, 2014.

Prior, David, ed. *Reconstruction in a Globalizing World*. New York: Fordham University Press, 2018.

Prokhorov, Vadim. *Russian Folk Songs: Musical Genres and History*. Lanham, MD: Scarecrow, 2002.

Propp, V. Ia. *Narodnye liricheskie pesni*. Leningrad: Sovetskii pisatel', 1961.

Pryor, Elizabeth Brown. "An Anomalous Person: The Northern Tutor in Plantation Society, 1773–1860." *Journal of Southern History* 47, no. 3 (1981): 363–392.

Quirin, James. "W. E. B. Du Bois, Ethiopianism and Ethiopia, 1890–1955." *International Journal of Ethiopian Studies* 5, no. 2 (2010): 1–26.

Ravenscroft, Janet. "Invisible Friends: Questioning the Representation of the Court Dwarf in Hapsburg Spain." In *Histories of the Normal and the Abnormal: Social and Cultural Histories of Norms and Normativity*, edited by Waltraud Ernst, 26–52. New York: Routledge, 2004.

Reddick, Lawrence D. "Educational Programs for the Improvement of Race Relations: Motion Pictures Radio, the Press, and Libraries." *Journal of Negro Education* 13, no. 3 (1944): 367–389.

Reid, Brian Holden. *The Origins of the American Civil War*. London: Routledge, 2014.

Reitblat, A. I. *Ot Bovy k Bal'montu i drugie raboty po istoricheskoi sotsiologii russkoi literatury*. Moscow: Novoe literaturnoe obozrenie, 2009.

Reuter, Edward B. *The Mulatto in the United States*. New York: Haskell House, 1918.

Richardson, Heather Cox. *West from Appomattox: The Reconstruction of America after the Civil War*. New Haven, CT: Yale University Press, 2008.

Roark, James L. *Masters without Slaves: Southern Planters in the Civil War and Reconstruction*. New York: W. W. Norton, 1977.

Rohrbach, Augusta. "Profits of Protest: The Market Strategies of Sojourner Truth and Louisa May Alcott." In *Prophets of Protest: Reconsidering the History of American Abolitionism*, edited by John Stauffer, 235–255. London: New Press, 2012.

Roosevelt, Priscilla R. *Life on the Russian Country Estate: A Social and Cultural History*. New Haven, CT: Yale University Press, 1997.

Rose, Alan Henry. "The Image of the Negro in the Pre-Civil-War Novels of John Pendleton Kennedy and William Gilmore Simms." *Journal of American Studies* 4, no. 2 (1971): 217–226.

Rosen, Hannah. *Terror in the Heart of Freedom: Citizenship, Sexual Violence, and the Meaning of Race in the Postemancipation South.* Chapel Hill: University of North Carolina Press, 2009.

Rosenheim, Jeff, ed. *Photography and the American Civil War.* New York: Metropolitan Museum of Art, 2013.

Rosslyn, Wendy, and Alessandra Tosi, eds. *Women in Nineteenth-Century Russia: Lives and Culture.* Cambridge: Open Book Publishers, 2012.

Rothberg, Robert I., and Theodore K. Rabb, eds. *Art and History: Images and Their Meaning.* New York: Cambridge University Press, 1988.

Ruef, Martin. *Between Slavery and Capitalism: The Legacy of Emancipation in the American South.* Princeton, NJ: Princeton University Press, 2014.

———. "The Demise of an Organizational Form: Emancipation and Plantation Agriculture in the American South, 1860–1880." *American Journal of Sociology* 109, no. 6 (2004): 1365–1410.

Ruud, Charles A. *Russian Entrepreneur: Publisher Ivan Sytin of Moscow, 1851–1934.* Montreal: McGill-Queen's University Press, 1990.

Sands-O'Connor, Karen. "Anything to Suit Customers: Antislavery and *Little Women.*" *Children's Literature Association Quarterly* 26, no. 1 (2001): 33–38.

Savage, Kirk. *Standing Soldiers, Kneeling Slaves: Race, War, and Monument in Nineteenth-Century America.* Princeton, NJ: Princeton University Press, 1997.

Schermerhorn, Calvin. *The Business of Slavery and the Rise of American Capitalism, 1815–1860.* New Haven, CT: Yale University Press, 2015.

Seibels, Cynthia. *The Sunny South: The Life and Art of William Aiken Walker.* Spartanburg, SC: Saraland, 1995.

Selcer, Richard F., ed. *Civil War America, 1850–1875.* New York: Facts on File, 2006.

Senechal de la Roche, Roberta. "The Sociogenesis of Lynching." In *Under Sentence of Death: Lynching in the South,* edited by W. Fitzhugh Brundage, 48–76. Chapel Hill: University of North Carolina Press, 1997.

Seton-Watson, Hugh. "Preparation of the Reform." In *Emancipation of the Russian Serfs,* edited by Terence Emmons. New York: Holt, Rinehart and Winston, 1970.

Seyersted, Per. *Kate Chopin: A Critical Biography.* Baton Rouge: Louisiana State University Press, 1980.

Shafer, Boyd. *Faces of Nationalism: New Realities and Old Myths.* New York: Harcourt Brace Jovanovich, 1972.

Shera, Jesse. *Foundations of the Public Library: The Origins of the Public Library Movement in New England, 1629–1855.* Chicago: University of Chicago Press, 1949.

Silber, Nina. *The Romance of Reunion: Northerners and the South, 1865–1900.* Chapel Hill: University of North Carolina Press, 1993.

Sinha, Manisha. *The Slave's Cause: A History of Abolition.* New Haven, CT: Yale University Press, 2016.

Sivulka, Juliann. *Soap, Sex, and Cigarettes: A Cultural History of American Advertising.* Belmont, CA: Wadsworth, 1998.

Skocpol, Theda, and Margaret Somers. "The Uses of Comparative History in Macrosocial Inquiry." *Comparative Studies in History and Society* 22, no. 2 (1980): 174–197.

Smith, Adam I. P. *The Stormy Present: Conservatism and the Problem of Slavery in Northern Politics, 1846–1865.* Chapel Hill: University of North Carolina Press, 2017.

Smith, Jessie Carney, ed. *Encyclopedia of African American Popular Culture.* 4 vols. Santa Barbara, CA: ABC-CLIO, 2010–2011.

Smith, Mark M. *How Race Is Made: Slavery, Segregation, and the Senses.* Chapel Hill: University of North Carolina Press, 2006.

Smith, Shawn Michelle. "'Looking at One's Self through the Eyes of Others': W. E. B. Du Bois's Photographs for the 1900 Paris Exposition." *African American Review* 34, no. 4 (2000): 581–599.

Snopkov, Aleksandr E. *Reklama v plakate: Russkii torgovo-promyshlennyi plakat za 100 let.* Moscow: Kontakt-Kultura, 2007.

Sokolov, Ivan. "Rossiiskaia 'chainaia skazka': Ot istokov do kontsa XIX veka." *Kofe i chai v Rossii* 3 (2013): 20–23.

Soule, Sarah A. "Populism and Black Lynching in Georgia, 1890–1900." *Social Forces* 71, no. 2 (1992): 431–449.

Spulber, Nicolas. *Russia's Economic Transitions: From Late Tsarism to the New Millennium.* New York: Cambridge University Press, 2003.

Stampp, Kenneth M. "Rebels and Sambos: The Search for the Negro's Personality in Slavery." *Journal of Southern History* 37, no. 3 (1971): 367–392.

Stanton, William. *The Leopard's Spots: Scientific Attitudes toward Race in America, 1815–59.* Chicago: University of Chicago Press, 1960.

Starks, Tricia. *Smoking under the Tsars: A History of Tobacco in Imperial Russia.* Ithaca, NY: Cornell University Press, 2018.

Stauffer, John. *The Black Hearts of Men.* Cambridge, MA: Harvard University Press, 2004.

Steiner, Evgeny. "Pursuing Independence: Kramskoi and the Peredvizhniki vs. the Academy of Arts." *Russian Review* 70, no. 2 (2011): 252–271.

Stern, Madeleine B. "Louisa M. Alcott in Periodicals." *Studies in the American Renaissance,* 1977, 369–386.

———. *Louisa May Alcott: A Biography.* Boston: Northeastern University Press; Lebanon, NH: University Press of New England, 1996. Originally published 1950 by the University of Oklahoma Press.

Steussy, R. E. "The Bitter Fate of A. F. Pisemsky." *Russian Review* 25, no. 2 (1966): 170–183.

Stites, Richard. *Passion and Perception: Essays on Russian Culture.* Edited by David Goldfrank. Washington, DC: New Academia Publishing, 2010.

———. *Serfdom, Society, and the Arts in Imperial Russia: The Pleasure and the Power.* New Haven, CT: Yale University Press, 2005.

Summers, Mark Wahlgren. *The Ordeal of the Reunion: A New History of Reconstruction.* Chapel Hill: University of North Carolina Press, 2014.

Tannenbaum, Frank. *Slave and Citizen, the Negro in the Americas.* New York: Knopf, 1946.

Taylor, William R. *Cavalier and Yankee: The Old South and American National Character.* New York: Oxford University Press, 1993.

Terras, Victor, ed. *Handbook of Russian Literature.* New Haven, CT: Yale University Press, 1990.

Thomas, Brook. *The Literature of Reconstruction: Not in Plain Black and White*. Baltimore: Johns Hopkins University Press, 2016.

Thornbrough, Emma Lou. "American Negro Newspapers, 1880–1914." *Business History Review* 40, no. 4 (1966): 467–490.

Trovaioli, August P., and Roulhac B. Toledano. *William Aiken Walker: Southern Genre Painter*. Gretna, LA: Pelican, 2008.

Tucker, Amy. *The Illustration of the Master: Henry James and the Magazine Revolution*. Stanford, CA: Stanford University Press, 2010.

Ungurianu, Dan. *Plotting History: The Russian Historical Novel in the Imperial Age*. Madison: University of Wisconsin Press, 2007.

U.S. Census Bureau. "Table 1. United States—Race and Hispanic Origin: 1790–1990." http://www.census.gov/population/www/documentation/twps0056/twps0056.html (link now inactive). Accessed May 2014.

U.S. Centennial Commission. *International Exhibition, 1876*. Washington, DC: Government Printing Office, 1880.

U.S. Department of Commerce. *Historical Statistics of the United States, 1789–1945*. Washington, DC: Government Printing Office, 1949.

Valkenier, Elizabeth Kridl. *Ilya Repin and the World of Russian Art*. New York: Columbia University Press, 1990.

———. "The Peredvizhniki and the Spirit of the 1860s." *Russian Review* 34, no. 3 (1975): 247–265.

———. *Russian Realist Art: The State and Society; The Peredvizhniki and Their Tradition*. Ann Arbor, MI: Ardis, 1977.

Varon, Elizabeth. *Disunion! The Coming of the American Civil War, 1789–1859*. Chapel Hill: University of North Carolina Press, 2008.

Vasil'eva, S. A. *Belletristika Vs. S. Solov'eva*. Tver': Tverskoi gosudarstvennyi universitet, 2009.

Victor, Orville James. *The History, Civil, Political and Military, of the Southern Rebellion, from its Incipient Stages to Its Close*. New York: James D. Torrey, 1868.

Waldron, Peter. *Between Two Revolutions: Stolypin and the Politics of Renewal in Russia*. DeKalb: Northern Illinois University Press, 1998.

Wallace, Maurice O., and Shawn Michelle Smith. *Pictures and Progress: Early Photography and the Making of African American Identity*. Durham, NC: Duke University Press, 2012.

Wallenstein, Peter. "Reconstruction, Segregation, and Miscegenation: Interracial Marriage and the Law in the Lower South, 1865–1900." *American Nineteenth Century History* 6 (2005): 57–76.

Warkel, Harriet G. "Image and Identity: The Art of William E. Scott, John W. Hardrick, and Hale A. Woodruff." In *A Shared Heritage: Art by Four African Americans*, edited by William E. Taylor, Harriet G. Warkel, and Margaret T. Burroughs, 17–76. Indianapolis: Indianapolis Museum of Art, 1996.

Wartman, Michelle. "Contraband, Runaways, Freemen: New Definitions of Reconstruction Created by the Civil War." *International Social Science Review* 76, no. 3/4 (2001): 122–129.

Weissman, Neil B. "Rural Crime in Tsarist Russia: The Question of Hooliganism, 1905–1914." *Slavic Review* 37, no. 2 (1978): 228–240.

Wells, Jeremy. *Romances of the White Man's Burden: Race, Empire, and the Plantation in American Literature, 1880–1936*. Nashville: Vanderbilt University Press, 2011.

West, Sally. *I Shop in Moscow: Advertising and the Creation of Consumer Culture in Late Tsarist Russia*. DeKalb: Northern Illinois University Press, 2011.

White, Hayden. *The Content of the Form: Narrative Discourse and Historical Representation*. Baltimore: Johns Hopkins University Press, 1987.

White, Richard. *The Republic for Which It Stands: The United States during Reconstruction and the Gilded Age, 1865–1896*. New York: Oxford University Press, 2017.

White, Shane, and Graham White. "Slave Clothing and African-American Culture in the Eighteenth and Nineteenth Centuries." *Past and Present* 148 (1995): 146–184.

Wiethoff, William E. *The Insolent Slave*. Columbia: University of South Carolina Press, 2002.

Williams, Andreá N. "Cultivating Black Visuality: The Controversy over Cartoons in the Indianapolis *Freeman*." *American Periodicals: A Journal of History and Criticism* 25, no. 2 (2015): 124–138.

Williams, Heather. *Self-Taught: African American Education in Slavery and Freedom*. Chapel Hill: University of North Carolina Press, 2005.

Willis, Deborah, and Barbara Krauthamer. *Envisioning Emancipation: Black Americans and the End of Slavery*. Philadelphia: Temple University Press, 2013.

Wilson, Charles Reagan. *Baptized in Blood: The Religion of the Lost Cause, 1865–1920*. Athens: University of Georgia Press, 1980.

Wilson, Jackie Napoleon. *Hidden Witness: African American Images from the Birth of Photography to the Civil War*. New York: St. Martin's, 1999.

Wilson, Judith. "Lifting 'The Veil': Henry O. Tanner's *The Banjo Lesson* and *The Thankful Poor*." *Contributions in Black Studies* 9 (1992): 31–54.

Wirtschafter, Elise. *From Serf to Russian Soldier*. Princeton, NJ: Princeton University Press, 1990.

———. *Social Identity in Imperial Russia*. DeKalb: Northern Illinois University Press, 1997.

Wood, Peter H., and Karen C. C. Dalton. *Winslow Homer's Images of Blacks: The Civil War and Reconstruction Years*. Austin: University of Texas Press, 1988.

Woods, Naurice Frank. *Henry Ossawa Tanner: Art, Faith, Race, and Legacy*. New York: Routledge, 2018.

Work, Monroe N. *Negro Year Book: An Annual Encyclopedia of the Negro, 1921–1922*. Tuskegee, AL: Tuskegee Institute and the Negro Year Book Publishing Company, 1922.

The World of the Peasantry in Russian Art: The State Russian Museum. St. Petersburg: Palace Editions, 2005.

Wormser, Richard. *The Rise and Fall of Jim Crow*. New York: Macmillan, 2004.

Worobec, Christine. *Peasant Russia: Family and Community in the Postemancipation Period*. DeKalb: Northern Illinois University Press, 1991.

Yoder, Audra J. "Myth and Memory in Russian Tea Culture." In "Memory." Special issue, *Studies in Slavic Cultures* 13 (2009): 65–89.

Yukiko, Tatsumi. "Russian Illustrated Journals in the Late Nineteenth Century: The Dual Image of Readers." *Acta Slavica Iaponica* 26 (2009): 159–176.

Zboray, Ronald J. *A Fictive People: Antebellum Economic Development and the American Reading Public*. New York: Oxford University Press, 1993.

Zolotinkina, Irina, and Galina Polikarpova. *Reklamnyi plakat v Rossii, 1900–1920-e.* St. Petersburg: Palace Editions, 2010.

Zuckert, Michael P. "Completing the Constitution: The Fourteenth Amendment and Constitutional Rights." *Publius* 22, no. 2 (1992): 69–91.

DISSERTATIONS

Donskov, Andrew. "The Changing Image of the Peasant in Nineteenth Century Russian Drama." PhD diss., Suomalainen Tiedeakatemia, 1972.

Goldman, Hannah. "American Slavery and Russian Serfdom: A Study in Fictional Parallels." PhD diss., Columbia University, 1955.

Lystar, Kimberly. "Two Female Perspectives on the Slave Family as Described in Harriet Jacobs' *Incidents in the Life of a Slave Girl* and Mattie Griffith's *Autobiography of a Female Slave.*" Master's thesis, University of Ottawa, 1996.

Turner, Patricia A. "Tampered Truths: A Rhetorical Analysis of Antebellum Slave Narratives." PhD diss., University of California, Berkeley, 1985.

WEBSITES

African American Photographs Assembled for 1900 Paris Exposition. Library of Congress. http://www.loc.gov/pictures/collection/anedub/dubois.html.

Atlanta Rail Corridor Archive. http://atlrailcorridorarchive.org/.

Cartes-de-visite Collection. Schomburg Center for Research in Black Culture, Photographs and Prints Division, New York Public Library Digital Collections. https://digitalcollections.nypl.org/divisions/schomburg-center-for-research-in-black-culture-photographs-and-prints-division.

Charles Chesnutt Digital Archive. https://chesnuttarchive.org.

Documenting the American South. University of North Carolina at Chapel Hill. http://docsouth.unc.edu/.

From Blackface to Blaxploitation: Representations of African Americans in Film. Duke University Libraries. http://exhibits.library.duke.edu/exhibits/show/africanamericansinfilm.

Gail and Stephen Rudin Slavery Collection, 1728–1973. Cornell University Library Digital Collections. https://digital.library.cornell.edu/collections/rudin.

Internet Archive. https://archive.org/.

Internet-biblioteka Alekseia Komarova. http://ilibrary.ru/.

Jim Crow Museum of Racist Memorabilia, Ferris State University, https://ferris.edu/HTMLS/news/jimcrow/mammies/more/mammy-image-gallery-02.htm.

Kate Chopin International Society. http://www.katechopin.org/.

Klassika. Lib.ru. http://az.lib.ru/.

Le Comte de Salhias-Tournemire (1840–1908), un Alexandre Dumas russe. http://www.tournemire.net/salias.htm.

Lenin Internet Archive. https://www.marxists.org/archive/lenin/.

Literature and Life. http://dugward.ru/library/.

National Archives. http://www.archives.gov/.

National Center for Education Statistics. http://nces.ed.gov/naal/lit_history.asp.

Nebraska State Capitol. http://capitol.nebraska.gov/.

New Georgia Encyclopedia. http://www.georgiaencyclopedia.org/.

Runivers. https://runivers.ru/.

Russian Ethnographic Museum. http://eng.ethnomuseum.ru/.

Russian Museum of Ethnography. http://eng.ethnomuseum.ru/node/38.

Society of Traveling Art Exhibits. http://tphv.ru/ustav.php.

State Hermitage Volunteer Service. http://benevole.ru/.

Uncle Tom's Cabin. Harriet Beecher Stowe Center. https://www.harrietbeecherstowecenter
.org/.

Uncle Tom's Cabin and American Culture. Edited by Stephen Railton and the University
of Virginia. http://utc.iath.virginia.edu/sitemap.html.

Index

Printed in the USA
CPSIA information can be obtained
at www.ICGtesting.com
CBHW020648290624
10812CB00009B/515